Critical Issues
in Special Education

Critical Issues in Special Education

SECOND EDITION

James E. Ysseldyke
University of Minnesota

Bob Algozzine
University of North Carolina at Charlotte

Martha L. Thurlow
University of Minnesota

HOUGHTON MIFFLIN COMPANY   BOSTON   TORONTO
Dallas   Geneva, Illinois   Palo Alto   Princeton, New Jersey

Senior Sponsoring Editor: Loretta Wolozin
Senior Development Editor: Rosemary Winfield
Senior Project Editor: Rosemary Winfield
Assistant Design Manager and Cover Designer: Karen Rappaport
Production Coordinator: Frances Sharperson
Manufacturing Coordinator: Sharon Pearson
Marketing Manager: Diane McOscar

Cover art by Mary Heilmann: "Mode O'Day," 1991. Oil on canvas, 54″ × 54″.
Photograph by Tom Warren. Courtesy Pat Hearn Gallery, New York, New York.

Library of Congress Catalog Card number: 91-71949
ISBN: 0-395-59694-7
ABCDEFGHIJ-HA-954321

To our children: Amy, Heather, Kathryn, Mike, Lisa, and Rob

Contents

Preface

The state of the art in any area should be evaluated periodically. American public education received little systematic analysis in the first hundred years of its history, but in the past ten years numerous critical analyses have been issued. The field of special education, however, has received very little systematic critical analysis. This text is a comprehensive revision of the critical analysis we published in 1982 (Ysseldyke & Algozzine, 1982). *Critical Issues in Special Education*, Second Edition, presents a straightforward, objective analysis of the major conceptual and practical issues that face professionals involved in special education.

Critical Issues in Special Education is an original analysis written by the three of us. It is not a compilation of chapters and articles that are written by others. It represents our thinking and reflects perspectives derived from the results of much of our research on problems associated with providing special education to children and youth in America today.

In examining the development and status of special education and services to students with disabilities our purpose is to identify current issues in a thought-provoking fashion that will stimulate debate and discussion. The text does not offer solutions to the many problems confronting those who are attempting to serve America's public school children. Nonetheless, we believe we have at least identified the kinds of questions that need to be asked about special education. The kinds of questions professionals ask tell much about the development of their field.

The Second Edition

The second edition of this text is more extensive, current, and organized differently from the first edition. Because many of the major issues in general education—school restructuring and reform, the move to outcomes-based education, the push for accountability and national testing, public school choice, home-school collaboration—are having a significant impact on special education, and since in many instances the boundaries between special and general education are becoming more permeable, many of the issues addressed in this text are general education issues.

Each chapter comprehensively examines issues that need to be debated by individuals concerned with education. In part 1 of the text we lay the foundation for description and discussion of the issues. We describe competing perspectives on special education, because the views one holds about the purposes of special education shape positions on other matters. We describe the history of education and the place of special education in that history. And we describe the current condition of special education. Chapters 4 and 5 are discussions of two debates that cut across other issues in special education: debate about definitions of conditions and about the efficacy of alternative methods for classifying students.

Part 2 of the text is a discussion of critical issues in special education. We describe and discuss issues in school reform and the impact they are having on special education and students with disabilities. We consider issues in assessment, instruction, and transition. The second edition includes new coverage of early intervention, economics, legal issues, and interrelationships among homes, families, and community agencies. The chapters on definitional debate, school reform, early intervention, transition, economics, and homes, families and agencies are new to this edition.

Audience

This text is designed for use in many college and university courses. Because the issues discussed cut across specific courses and disciplines concerned with both special and general education, the text is appropriate for a variety of education-related courses, such as regular education for preservice and inservice teachers, special education, educational administration, school psychology, counseling, and school social work.

Acknowledgments

The initial impetus for the first edition of this book came while we were sitting in a diner in Dinkytown, Minnesota. Behind the counter was a new broom in a cellophane wrapper on which was written, "This broom sweeps four times better." We wondered, "Better than what?" and "Why not 3.5 times better?" The claim provoked a discussion about claims made for special education and its effectiveness. We thank the manufacturers of the broom.

We thank the many persons who helped us throughout the development of this text. Loretta Wolozin accepted the original idea, believed in the importance of doing a book like this, and consistently challenged us to do it better. Kathy Brown's friendship and editorial support added greatly to our writing and what has been written. Rosemary Winfield's editorial support made the challenges of a second edition "minor concerns for the authors." Michael Brady, University of Houston; Herbert J. Boyd, University of South Florida; Libby Cohen, University of Southern Maine; Robert J. Cross, Grand Valley State University; Larry Geffen, Eastern Michigan University; Jean Lokerson, Virginia Commonwealth University; Lillian D. McKethan, Eastern College; Calvin C. Nelson, California State University–Fullerton; and W. D. Stainback, San Diego State University, provided constructive criticism on early drafts of the manuscript. Sheila Hoover offered her professional assistance in preparation of the manuscript.

We also express thanks to the U.S. Department of Education for funding a number of research projects over the past 15 years that have enabled us to collaborate and critically analyze issues in special education and to learn about the many perspectives that drove contemporary practices. Specifically, we have been able to conduct extensive research on learning disabilities, assessment, pupil behavior, teacher interactions, classroom ecology, intervention, transition, preschool assessment and intervention, inservice training, dropout, personnel preparation, school organization and service delivery, public school choice, and assessment of educational outcomes.

This book is a collaborative effort in the fullest sense, and speaks for the three of us. We enjoyed writing it. We hope you enjoy reading it.

James E. Ysseldyke

Bob Algozzine

Martha L. Thurlow

**Critical Issues
in Special Education**

PART ONE

Conceptual Foundations for Understanding Issues in Special Education

CHAPTER 1

Competing Perspectives on Special Education

Conceptual Issues
 Right Versus Privilege
 Regular Education Component Versus Separate System
 Treatment Versus Prevention
 Mild Versus Severe Handicaps
 Dysfunction Versus Disadvantage

Practical Issues
 Administrative Arrangement Versus Instructional Method
 Service Versus Custodial Care
 Educational Service Versus Teacher Relief
 Core Curriculum Versus Special Curriculum
 Stay Put Placement Versus Pullout Program

Issues Reflected in Practice
 Full Versus Selective Exclusion
 Practices Versus People
 Special Versus General Responsibilities
 Profession Versus Practice

Education at the Margins

Toto, I've a feeling we're not in Kansas anymore.

—The Wizard of Oz

Special education is at a crossroads in its development. In the early years, simply standing up and being recognized were the primary goals of professionals concerned with students with special learning needs. As special education approaches adolescence, problems in the system related to gaining independence and growing too big to ignore are being addressed. Early concern for access to free appropriate education has been replaced by radical and mature perspectives that put people with special learning needs in regular classes to be educated with everybody else.

At the same time, people are beginning to question whether special education is appropriately placed as a subsystem of regular education.

Other questions are surfacing as well. Is special education a right or a privilege? What is the proper focus of special education intervention? Who should receive special education? Is special education a method, or is it just a vehicle for receiving services? How should special education services be delivered? Is special education an art or a science? Is it a profession or a practice? These and other conceptual as well as practical issues form the basis for the various, often competing perspectives that characterize and drive its practices. In discussing competing points of view with regard to these issues, we hope to stimulate change and continued improvement in special education. We also intend this discussion as a prologue to the broader, more detailed coverage of issues that makes up the book.

To present these competing perspectives, we use a variety of strategies. In some cases, we give both sides of the issue "equal time." When the preponderance of proof or support falls on one side of an issue, we present information that is biased by evidence. In rare cases, we simply frame the issue, ask the question, or state the problem. Sometimes, leaving an important and critical question unanswered or problem unresolved is the best way to stimulate an answer or a solution. Put another way, special education is different things to different people. Our goal is to evenhandedly set forth a broad set of issues that influence special education and the people who practice it. Some issues have more relevance than others for some groups of people.

To some parents who have children failing in school and needing special services, special education is a promise of renewed progress. The system becomes a problem when children "fall between the cracks" and present unusual cases that do not meet accepted eligibility standards or when placement in special education fails to produce desired benefits. Legal issues and issues related to assessment, intervention, choice, reform, and transition have considerable relevance to these parents.

To children, placement in special education is sometimes a symbol of difference that they want to avoid when they think placement means they have done poorly in school. (The dividends gathered by participating in this special system, however, often override the disappointment experienced by many of the children.) Categorical debate and placement controversies as well as issues in assessment, instruction, and transition create concerns for students with special needs.

To teachers working with students who receive special education, it means working closely with other professionals in ways that are not necessary for students who do not receive special education. This close collaboration creates problems in decision making, intervention, and home/school relations. Working with students with special needs, especially those who are very difficult to teach, is taxing, and as a result teachers of students in special education face professional concerns (e.g., attrition) that are less common than those faced by their colleagues in regular education.

For the administrator, with constituencies that are often at odds, special education classes are places for slow, disruptive, atypical learners, havens for the hard-to-teach. Seemingly endless hassles involved in arranging special transportation and class schedules, debating teacher responsibilities, and managing parent conferences cause headaches, too. When responsibility for special education is shared, the partnership may cause conflicts between administrators, who are affected by the same broad issues as parents, teachers, and students.

Conceptual Issues

The concerns about special education that affect parents, students, teachers, and administrators grow, in part, from conceptual issues. For instance, is special education a right or a privilege? Is it a component of regular education or a separate system? What is the appropriate focus of special education intervention: treatment or prevention? Who receives services? What drives interest in disabilities, deficits, dysfunctions, and disadvantages?

Right Versus Privilege

With the passage of the Education of All Handicapped Children Act (Public Law [PL] 94-142) in 1975, a free appropriate education became an expected, established right for people with handicaps and disabilities. The act established principles and guidelines for the delivery of special education services. Reauthorization (PL 101-476), revision, and renaming (Individuals with Disabilities Education Act) of the act on October 30, 1990, reaffirmed a national intent to support alternative education for students with special learning needs. Prior to passage of these laws, students with disabilities had no guarantee that they would be accepted in public school programs. Exclusionary clauses, refusal to provide services, special charges for services provided free to other students, and segregationist practices all occurred and were documented during hearings prior to enactment of the law (Lipsky & Gartner, 1989; Rothstein, 1990; Ysseldyke & Algozzine, 1990). The social and political action that led to the act grew out of parents' and professionals' dissatisfaction with the type and kind of services students with special learning needs were receiving (Bilken, 1989; Lipsky & Gartner, 1989; Ysseldyke & Algozzine, 1982).

Unfortunately, mandating changes in educational systems and practices does not always make them happen. In addressing the extent to which a "disabled student today [is] getting more than a student with a similar disability educated before 94-142," Adrienne Asch made the following comments:

> Running throughout my conversations with disabled students, parents, and professionals is the message that today's education is still largely separate and rarely equal. Separate means not only the segregated school or class but the *separate standards* used to measure the opportunities provided, or the progress

made, by the student with a disability who is physically integrated. Whether speaking of such "basics" as reading, writing, mathematics, science labs, organizing ideas and organizing time, or such "frills" as physical education, field trips, computer literacy, art, music, home economics, industrial arts, driver education, or enrichment programs, the nation's disabled students are deprived. In many instances, standards of attendance, discipline, participation, and performance are different and lower for disabled students than for nondisabled members of the same class, grade level, school district or state. (1989, pp. 183–184)

These inequities have a long-established history in education. A study of formal education prior to the development of public schools revealed that early schooling was directed toward a specific segment of the population (males, nobility, or the leisured, monied, privileged, upper class or trainees for high-status positions such as the priesthood), and it often included the teaching of ethics, moral conduct, or religion (Ysseldyke & Algozzine, 1982). When schools became public, these practices continued; emphasis was on educating a selective, limited population—the white, male children of upper-class families (Ramsey, Algozzine, & Henley, in press; Smith, Price, & Marsh, 1986). The select few are still the major beneficiaries of education, and it is still more a privilege than a right, federal laws to the contrary notwithstanding.

Regular Education Component Versus Separate System

Who is responsible for educating students with special learning needs? Who is responsible for students in special education? Where should special education services be delivered? Who should provide special education services? Answers to these questions depend on whether special education is a component of regular education or a separate education system.

Current organizational practices promote the separation of regular and special education students and programs. An elaborate system of assessment and classification has evolved to support the need and conduct of separate systems of education. From the moment children enter school, formal and informal assessments are carried out to order and explain individual differences that not so long ago passed as normal products of childhood. Lipsky and Gartner suggested that "the establishment of a separate system of education for the disabled is an outgrowth of attitudes toward disabled people" (1987, p. 72).

The history of providing care for people with handicaps and disabilities has only recently evolved to stages of progressive integration because not everyone supports the principle of a separate but equal special education system. In a report to the secretary of the U.S. Department of Education, Assistant Secretary Madeleine Will presented cogent arguments to support her belief that, although much has been accomplished in special education programs, "problems have emerged which create obstacles to effective education of students with learning problems" (1986, p. 4). She did not mean the term *obstacle* to "imply that special programs have failed dismally in their mission to educate children with learning

Sometimes School Is Not Fun

With very rare exceptions, today's adults with disabilities who recall segregated facilities, separate classes, or home instruction cannot say enough about how inadequate was their academic training. They compare their education with that of siblings or neighbors who were not disabled and speak only of the gaps. For example, they mention subjects, such as science, that they never studied, maps they never saw, field trips they never took, books that were never available, assignments that were often too easy, expectations of their capacity (by nearly all teachers) that were too low. Given the dismal descriptions of the previous era, one would expect that disabled students who received most of their elementary and secondary school education in the 1980s must be getting better opportunities. For those disabled people who have spent these years placed in separate schools or separate classes, many of the complaints are the same. Those in "regular" classes believe themselves better off than segregated disabled students, but they frequently feel disadvantaged compared to their nondisabled classmates (Asch, 1989, p. 183).

We were isolated. Symbolically—and appropriate to the prevailing attitudes—the "handicapped and retarded" classrooms were tucked away in the corner of the school basement. Our only activity with the other children was the weekly school assembly. We never participated in any school program. We watched. Although the school lunchroom was also in the basement, we ate lunch in our classrooms. During fire drills, we did not leave the building (were we expendable? . . .). We stood in the hallway outside of our classroom, watching the others file past . . . looking and being looked at.

Summing it up, the only contact we had with the "normal" children was visual. We stared at each other. On those occasions, I can report my own feelings: embarrassment. Given the loud, clear message that was daily being delivered to them, I feel quite confident that I can also report their feelings: YECH! We, the children in the "handicapped" class, were internalizing the "yech" message—plus a couple of others. We were in school because children go to school, but we were outcasts, with no future and no expectation of one. I, for one, certainly never contemplated my future. I could not even picture one, much less dream about it.

SOURCE: *The way out: Student exclusion practices in Boston middle schools.* Boston: Massachusetts Advocacy Center, 1986. Used with permission.

problems" or to suggest that the "existing general system of education for these children warrants radical reform and redesign" (Will, 1986, p. 4). She did use the term to "convey the idea that the creation of special programs has produced unintended effects, some of which make it unnecessarily cumbersome for educators to teach—as effectively as they desire—and children to learn—as much and as well as they can" (Will, 1986, p. 4).

Will identified several types of problems. The first is the result of a fragmented approach that has failed to provide services to many students who are "often not served adequately in the regular classroom and are not 'eligible' for special education or other special programs because they do not meet State or Federal eligibility requirements" (Will, 1986, p. 5). A second type of problem grows out of dual (perhaps dueling) administrative systems for special programs that "contribute to a lack of coordination, raise questions about leadership, cloud areas of responsibility, and obscure lines of accountability within schools" (Will, 1986, p. 6). A third type is created by segregating students from their peers and attaching labels to the segregated students, which sometimes result in lowered expectations for success that "have been fully described in the literature" (Will, 1986, p. 7). And a fourth type results from a decision-making process that sometimes turns a valuable partnership between parents and teachers into a series of "adversarial, hit-and-run encounters" (Will, 1986, p. 7) that leave everybody tallying points instead of considering students' unique learning needs and the most appropriate ways to meet them.

In describing "a solution to the problem," Will qualified her argument: "Although for some students the 'pullout approach' may be appropriate, it is driven by a conceptual fallacy: that poor performance in learning can be understood solely in terms of deficiencies in the student rather than deficiencies in the learning environment" (1986, p. 9). She believed that creating new educational environments as the primary way to improve student performance is a flawed approach; the alternative she advocated would "adapt the regular classroom to make it possible for the student to learn in that environment" (Will, 1986, p. 9). In closing, she challenged states "to renew their commitment to serve [children with learning problems] effectively," and she defined that commitment as a "search for ways to serve as many of these children as possible in the regular classroom by encouraging special education and other special programs to form a partnership with regular education" (Will, 1986, p. 19).

The principles embodied in Will's call for a partnership between regular education and special education in meeting the special learning needs of students have become known as the "regular education initiative." Called the "hottest debate in special education" (Viadero, 1988, p. 1), deciding whether and how to improve services provided to students with handicaps has sparked controversy throughout the field (Lipsky & Gartner, 1989; Stainback & Stainback, 1989). Conferences, professional presentations, and numerous articles and special journal issues have been devoted to praising or maligning professionals who believe that regular education should assume more responsibility for students with special learning needs (cf. Kauffman, Gerber, & Semmel, 1988; Kauffman, Lloyd, & McKinney, 1988; Keogh, 1988; Lloyd, Crowley, Kohler, & Strain, 1988; Wang & Walberg, 1988; Wang, Reynolds, & Walberg, 1987). Kauffman characterized the regular education initiative as a flawed policy lacking the support of critical constituencies. He called the movement a "trickle-down theory of education for the hard-to-teach" and suggested that "it rests on illogical premises, ignores the issue of specificity in proposed reforms, and reflects a cavalier attitude toward experimentation and research" (1989, p. 256). His position was reaffirmed and critically reviewed by other professionals (cf. Goetz & Sailor, 1990; Kauffman & Hallahan, 1990; McLeskey, Skiba, & Wilcox, 1990; Pugach, 1990). But after all the dialogue, the question of where best to educate special education students still remains.

Treatment Versus Prevention

The practice of special education is a three-stage process. Students are first declared eligible for special education services, then they are treated or taught differently, and finally their progress is evaluated (Ysseldyke & Algozzine, 1990). The terms *treatment* and *teaching* are used as synonyms by many professionals because in the early development of services for people with handicaps, medical perspectives dominated more than educational ones did. Treatment of students with special learning needs serves many purposes. Remediation and compensation are two of them.

Many students receive special education as a correction for their special learning needs and problems. The term *remediation* is derived from the word *remedy*, something that "corrects, counteracts, or removes" something that has gone wrong. Physicians treat people by using certain medications in an effort to correct, repair, or cure certain conditions. Regardless of whether the medicines work, they are often called remedies. In special education settings, this medical model obtains, and the focus of "treatment" is often on remediation. Specific skills, such as reading or math, are taught in an effort to overcome deficiencies in academic skill development. Or emphasis may be placed on remedying specific deficits in abilities, such as memory or perception of sounds. If students who are being asked to solve multiplication problems are shown to have deficits in the skill of adding numbers, they may be given training (or treatment) in adding numbers. Students with trouble reading may be provided perceptual-motor training because some professionals believe learning to visually track a target or discriminate visual images will overcome reading problems.

A second purpose of treatment is compensation. The term derives from the word *compensate*, which means "to make up for." If you do not own an automobile, you can make up for it by taking buses, riding bicycles, or getting rides from people who have cars. People who do not have the use of their legs compensate by getting around in wheelchairs, and those who lose the use of their voice may compensate by writing down what they want to say. Usually, compensatory treatments are employed when overcoming a problem seems impossible or when compensating for a condition seems easier than trying to correct it.

Many special education treatments are compensatory. Compensatory activities are usually most apparent in the treatment of sensory or physical disabilities, but they are often used with students with other disabilities and handicaps. The most obvious compensatory treatments are those in which students who do not see well are taught to communicate using braille, students who do not have the use of their arms are taught to write holding a pencil in their toes, or students who do not hear well are taught to communicate using sign language or finger spelling. Yet compensatory treatment is also used when students who have difficulty reading and/or writing are allowed to take oral, rather than written, examinations; when "talking books" (on audiotapes or records) are given to students who have visual disabilities; or when students who have difficulty taking notes are allowed to tape-record lectures.

Special education is also a preventive action when intervention is designed to prevent a disability from becoming a handicap or to control problem behaviors that sometimes result in classification of students as handicapped. For example, early interventions can result for students who are at risk for school failure, and specialized interventions can be used early in life with students who are blind or deaf to prevent serious problems later in school.

Deciding whether to use remedial/compensatory or preventive approaches can present challenges when the goals of treatment and prevention conflict with the goals of regular classroom instruction. For example, controversy periodically surfaces about whether people who are deaf should be taught to compensate for their limited verbal abilities with alternative communication systems or taught to correct faulty communication so they can be accepted in the hearing world. Similarly, questions about fairness and appropriateness of testing and instructional modifications for students with learning disabilities are regularly raised in school districts and other settings.

Mild Versus Severe Handicaps

More than 90 percent of students receiving special education in recent years are those placed in the special education categories "learning disabled," "speech impaired," "educable mentally retarded," or "emotionally disturbed" (U.S. Dept. of Education, 1988b, 1989b, 1990b). These students are sometimes referred to as "mildly handicapped." The term is not used to imply that these students do not have serious learning problems or that these problems are less important than those of any other students. We think the term has come to be used for this group of students because many of their characteristics overlap, they require less intensive treatment than some others, and many can be served in regular classroom environments or resource rooms with assistance from special education teachers

TABLE 1.1   Unique and common characteristics of students with handicaps referred to as mild

Characteristics	Condition		
	LD	MR	ED
Cognitive	Average IQ, memory problems, information deficits	Below average IQ, memory problems, information deficits	Varied IQ, memory problems, information deficits,
Achievement	Below average, reading problems, math deficits, writing problems	Below average, reading problems, math deficits, writing problems	Below average, reading problems, math deficits, writing problems
Language	Often delayed	Often delayed	Often delayed
Social	Hyperactivity, nonattention, interpersonal problems	Hyperactivity, nonattention, interpersonal problems	Hyperactivity, nonattention, interpersonal problems

SOURCE: Ramsey, R., Algozzine, B., & Henley, M. (in press). *Characteristics of students with mild handicaps*. Boston: Allyn and Bacon.

(U.S. Dept. of Education, Ysseldyke & Algozzine, 1990).

Students classified as learning disabled (LD), mentally retarded (MR), or emotionally disturbed (ED) account for more than two-thirds of all students with handicaps (U.S. Dept. of Education, 1990), and they share many characteristics (Hallahan & Kauffman, 1977). For example, students with learning disabilities often have problems with reading comprehension, language development, interpersonal relations, and classroom behavioral control (Lerner, 1985). These same characteristics are presented in descriptions of students called mentally retarded and emotionally disturbed (Coleman, 1986; Fessler, Rosenberg, & Rosenberg, 1991; Kauffman, 1985; Robinson & Robinson, 1976) and in descriptions of many students who are not handicapped (Ysseldyke & Algozzine, 1990). Because many of these characteristics are not severe and because they overlap in conditions with different names, students with learning disabilities, mental retardation, or emotional disturbance are sometimes grouped together and called "mildly handicapped." Some common and unique characteristics of these students are presented in Table 1.1.

In a widely accepted definition, people who are "severely handicapped" are described as constituting the lowest 1 percent of the population on any measure of intellectual functioning (Brown & York, 1974; Sailor, 1989). Clearly, this is a small group of people, but these students do not inspire optimism in administrators who feel forced to deal with them. For example, Sailor recounted an anecdote related to discussions of how to implement PL 94-142 in a number of midwestern states.

> Not all of these directors were certain, by any stretch of the imagination, that this law and its extensive regulatory language was such a good idea. The LRE [least restrictive environment] portion particularly rankled some participants. One vociferous administrator, in an oratorical denunciation of the process shouted, "the logical extension of this LRE stuff is that we are going to be forced to put vegetables in the regular classroom!" (1989, p. 53).

Less than 10 percent of all special education students are severely handicapped (Ysseldyke & Algozzine, 1990). But controversy and questions surrounding their education compete with those that drive education for other people with and without handicaps. Where should people with severe handicaps be educated? Who should be responsible for providing services to them? To what extent should schools be expected to bear all the costs of their education? What benefits can be expected? Are the benefits worth the costs when compared to those associated with meeting the needs of gifted and talented students or students with mild handicaps? How early and how long should services be available?

Dysfunction Versus Disadvantage

Oliver Sacks, the author of *The Man Who Mistook His Wife for a Hat and Other Clinical Tales* and *Awakenings*, noted in the former work that "neurology's favourite word is 'deficit,' denoting an impairment or incapacity of neurological function: loss of speech, loss of language, loss of memory, loss of vision, loss of dexterity, loss of identity, and myriad other lacks and losses of specific functions (or faculties)" (1985, p. 3). Special educators find plenty of room for deficits, disabilities, dysfunctions, and other disadvantages in their vocabulary as well.

Deficits such as an inability to process visually presented information or disabilities such as the loss of an arm can greatly influence performance in school activities. So can dysfunctions (the effects of these deficits and disabilities) and disadvantages (unfavorable situations or circumstances). When problems of people with special learning needs are being considered, differing opinions about deficits, disabilities, dysfunctions, and disadvantages affect perceptions and influence the behaviors of people who receive special education and those who interact with them (Ysseldyke & Algozzine, 1982, 1990).

These competing opinions often break down along nature versus nurture lines, and the perceived cause of special learning needs influences the actions and reactions that result from them. Nature theorists believe that special learning needs are the result of deficits, disabilities, and dysfunctions within people and that students are born with them. Nurture theorists believe that conditions outside people (i.e., disadvantages) cause special learning needs. According to this view, being unsuccessful in school is evidence of an unfavorable and/or unproductive environment for learning. McGill-Franzen (1987) noted that current explanations for school failure have changed over time, and she presented evidence that a shift from "disadvantagement" to "disability" characterized changes in explanations of reading failure.

A passage from an early report on the conditions of exceptional people in Massachusetts illustrates the perspective created when nature is blamed for disabilities:

> Idiocy is found in all civilized countries, but it is not an evil necessarily inherent in society; it is to an accident; and much less is it a special dispensation of Providence; to suppose it can be so, is an insult to the Majesty of Heaven. No! *It is merely the result of a violation of natural laws,* which are simple, clear and beautiful; which require only to be seen to be known, in order to be loved; and which, if strictly observed for two or three generations, would totally remove from any family, however strongly predisposed to *insanity or idiocy,* all possibility of its recurrence. (Howe, 1848, p. 2, emphasis added)

The tone of Howe's message and the presumed cause of insanity and idiocy probably reflected the actions and reactions of people during his times. Nevertheless, beliefs about natural causes of exceptionality are still prevalent today (cf. Hallahan & Kauffman, 1989; Kauffman, 1987; Rhodes & Tracy, 1972; Ysseldyke & Algozzine, 1990). The aim of those who treat persons with handicaps that are viewed as violations of nature is to rearrange biological and physical dysfunctions to produce improved behavior and learning.

"Insanity is inherited; you get it from your kids." This seemingly contradictory prophecy makes great copy for T-shirts and bumper stickers. We like it because it is a paradox, a statement with seemingly inconsistent content. We inherit characteristics from our parents, or we learn behaviors from our children. Professionals who support nurture theories believe that special learning needs are learned, not inherited. They argue that environmental events result in increases and decreases in behaviors and that the appropriateness or inappropriateness of these behaviors is the basis for special education needs. Nurture theories differ from nature theories in regard to four fundamental assumptions about behavior: what behavior is, what causes behavior, how to change behavior, and how to measure behavior (Alberto & Troutman, 1986; Criswell, 1981; Johnson & Pennypacker, 1980; Kauffman, 1989a).

The views people hold about the causes of behavior influence the opinions they hold about the people exhibiting the behaviors. Most of us can recall at least one time when our reactions to another person were influenced by knowledge of that person's condition. Most people are more tolerant of crabbiness or other minor, annoying behaviors in friends when the friends are "a little under the weather." That people's views about the cause of a problem influence outlooks about the problem is suggested in the results of at least one research project. Farina, Thaw, Felner, and Hust (1976) arranged an experiment in which undergraduate students gave mild electric shocks to labeled confederates. The shocks given to a confederate thought to be organically (i.e., naturally) retarded were shorter and less intense than those given to a subject thought to be normal or mentally (i.e., not organically) ill. When reactions to these categories were compared in other research, organic impairments (those believed to be caused by physical ailments) were considered more acceptable than functional impairments (those with unknown cause but obvious effects) (Ysseldyke & Algozzine, 1982).

Practical Issues

Practical issues in special education are no less fraught with controversy, and conceptual differences of opinion often spill over into the practical arena. For example, is special education a place to receive services, or is it the actual service being received? Is the focus custodial care or altered educational services? To what extent are services provided simply to offer relief for regular classroom teachers? What effects does special education have on core curriculum concerns? Where is the best place to provide special education? Continuing dialogue and attempts to resolve practical issues such as these form the foundation for many of the practices that characterize contemporary special education.

Administrative Arrangement Versus Instructional Method

When many teachers refer students for special education, their primary goal is placement in programs outside the regular classroom. These teachers believe that an alteration in instructional placement will be a sufficient basis for improving the educational opportunities of the student with special learning needs. Regular education teachers come to believe that there are others in the system who are better able to teach students with academic or learning problems. They assume that students should be sent to places where they can benefit from the services of these other people. As a result, many teachers see placement and altered instructional programs as synonymous. This view has been fostered by continuing inservice education presentations designed to inform and enlighten regular education teachers to the needs and benefits of special education. Professionals in special education perpetuate this perspective when they argue that process training, learning strategies, behavior modification, or any other instructional methods can and should be delivered only by special education teachers in special classes.

Some students do require specialized instruction to meet their special learning needs. Mobility training for students with visual limits, manual communication training for students with problems hearing, and communication boards for students with an inability to speak are a few examples of instructional needs and methods that make special education special (Ysseldyke & Algozzine, 1990). But there is no reason to believe that such altered instructional methods must be provided in special classes or segregated administrative classroom arrangements. Conversely, assignment to a special class does not guarantee receipt of an altered instructional program. For example, Allington and McGill-Franzen (1989) reviewed research on the quality of reading instruction provided in special programs and concluded that participation in special education programs, even when students were mainstreamed, mildly handicapped learners, did not ensure access to larger amounts of reading instruction. Algozzine, Morsink, and Algozzine (1989) found few differences in instructional behaviors of regular classroom teachers and teachers working with students classified as learning disabled, mentally retarded, or emotionally handicapped.

Service Versus Custodial Care

A history of the way society has cared for people with disabilities can be captured in four words: ignorance, isolation, insulation, and integration. Earliest records reveal ignorant, inhumane treatment of people with disabilities. Boring holes in the head to let out evil spirits, burning at the stake as a test of witchcraft, and imprisonment without consideration for civil rights gave rise to a countermovement for moral treatment. Brookover noted that "moral treatment was never clearly defined, possibly because its meaning was self-evident during the era in which it was used; it meant compassionate and understanding treatment of innocent sufferers" (1963, p. 12). Ullman and Krasner pointed out that moral treatment represented "the first effort to provide systematic and responsible care for large numbers of deviant people" (1969, p. 126). And certainly Dorothea Dix's (1843) plea to the Massachusetts legislature for "insane" people, whom she described as "in cages, closets, cellars, stalls, pens, chained, naked, beaten with rods, and lashed into obedience" can be viewed as evidence of movement into a new era of treatment for people with disabilities and handicaps. Unfortunately, as Brookover also noted, interest in providing facilities for treatment may have been responsible for the false notion that "institutional treatment is better treatment" (1963, p. 17).

The limited perspective on care created by isolation in large public institutions is evident in this quote:

> These early institutions were in a sense a branch of the public school system, boarding schools having for their purpose the education of the mentally defective. . . . When these early education methods proved less fruitful than had been anticipated in the intellectual rehabilitation of the mentally defective, the institutions . . . were forced to face reality in the demands made upon them for the custodial care of many relatively unimprovable cases, and they entered upon that second and familiar stage in which custodial care and segregation were most prominent. (Davies, 1925, p. 210)

Davies added that isolation as custodial care arose because of a fear in society about what people with disabilities might do if left to their own devices.

As attitudes toward people with disabilities improved and concern for their care became more a social issue, perspectives changed from protecting members of society to protecting people with disabilities from society. Practices akin to sheltering, nurturing, and shielding were part of the movement to provide insulation from the ills of society. Special classes with related special curricula and specially trained teachers were hallmarks of this historical phase (Hendrick & Macmillan, 1989; Ysseldyke & Algozzine, 1982).

Recently, special education entered a period when custodial care and service were viewed either as separate and independent activities or as related aspects of treatment in special education. The perspective that care should provide service caused parents, teachers, and other professionals to critically assess the developments created by providing services that were not much like those received by normal students. This led to the birth of PL 94-142 and the requirement of an appropriate placement in the least restrictive environment (Lipsky & Gartner, 1989). A 1983 Sixth Circuit Court of Appeals decision helps illuminate the LRE concept: "Where a segregated facility is considered superior, the court should determine whether services which make the placement superior could feasibly be provided in a nonsegregated setting. If they can, the placement in the segregated school should be inappropriate under the Act [PL 94-142]" (*Ronicker* v. *Walker*, 700 F. 2d, 1058, cert. denied, 104 S. Ct. 196). Concepts of normalization (life as much like other people as possible), mainstreaming (education as much like other people as possible), least restrictive environments (service in places as much like those provided for other people), and integration (life experiences with people who are not disabled or handicapped) remain the goals and objectives of improved special education systems during the integration phase that continues today (Asch, 1984; Lipsky & Gartner, 1989; Ysseldyke & Algozzine, 1990).

Educational Service Versus Teacher Relief

What purpose is served by special education? Some argue that it is a service provided to students with special learning needs to help them acquire more fully the benefits of education and schooling (Hallahan & Kauffman, 1989; Heward & Orlansky, 1989; Kirk & Gallagher, 1986, 1989; Ysseldyke & Algozzine, 1990). From this perspective, special education is delivered in a variety of settings by specially trained professionals, and the provision of special education services is a benefit of an improved educational system trying to accommodate people with special learning needs. But special education was not always seen this way, and not everyone sees it this way today.

To some people, special education is a means of providing relief for regular classroom teachers and students; it is a reprieve from the rigors of working and learning with students who are difficult to teach. This perspective has its origins in the early history of special education (Hendrick & Macmillan, 1989). For example, in evaluating the outcomes of early alternative education programs, Lincoln (1903) pointed out that by removing many trying pupils from the regular classes, the special education movement accomplished precisely what it set out to accomplish. The implications of comments made by Elizabeth Daniels Nash at the turn of the century remain as challenges today: "Of all the schools that have recently sprung up in this country for the instruction of various classes of unfortunate children, perhaps none have met with so hearty a welcome from the public school teacher as the special class for the mentally deficient" (1901, p. 42).

Indeed, many regular education teachers are opposed to having students with handicaps in their classrooms (Hudson, Graham, & Warner, 1979; Jones, Gottlieb, Guskin, & Yoshida, 1978; Miles & Simpson, 1989; Williams & Algozzine, 1979). In some cases, however, their opinions become more positive when they have some say in decision making (Miles & Simpson, 1989). Placement of students with handicaps in regular education classrooms for all or part of the school day (i.e., mainstreaming) faces obstacles because segregationist thinking is still prevalent (Fuchs & Fuchs, in press). Efforts to encourage regular and special education teachers to work together (i.e., consultation) to meet the special learning needs of students with handicaps and disabilities (Morsink, Thomas, & Correa, 1990) and other efforts to "merge" special and regular education systems (cf. Stainback & Stainback, 1984) share the burden of this type of thinking as well. If efforts to educate students with disabilities and handicaps are to be successful in regular classrooms, shared responsibilities and mutual respect for individual differences among parents, teachers, and students are essential.

Core Curriculum Versus Special Curriculum

Special education exists to provide educational opportunities to people with special learning needs. In the early days, the curriculum in special education was based on educational principles established in Europe. It centered on physical (motor and sensory), intellectual (speech and academic), and moral (socialization) training (Talbot, 1964; Ysseldyke & Algozzine, 1982). Although this looks similar to the curriculum being provided in regular classrooms, closer inspection reveals important differences. For example, Fort described the "course of instruction" in special classes this way:

> The elementary training must of necessity be specially adapted to the child and, so far as my own experience goes, I would limit the primary work to reading and writing with special work in arithmetic that could simply be supplementary to what I am a firm believer in as the proper sphere of such children, viz. manual training. . . .
> The choice of instruction when we come to manual training is large and continually growing. For the younger children, all the occupations of the kindergarten; for the older boys, woodwork, basket-weaving, machine sewing, cane-seating, brush and broom making; the girls, needle-work, cooking, and laundry work with some of the lighter handicrafts usually taught the boys. (1900, pp. 33–34)

This perspective on curriculum was prevalent because a common view held that the future for students with special learning needs was very limited: "Learn to expect little from your deficient child" (Nash, 1901, p 47).

Today the views of most professionals in special education are radically different and clearly more optimistic. For example, in his opening address to the First International Conference on Special Education, in Beijing, China, the president of the China Welfare Fund for the Disabled presented the purpose of special education as preparing people with disabilities to fulfill social obligations (Lipsky

& Gartner, 1989). Earlier, Lipsky and Gartner argued for seeing people with handicaps in new ways—as "capable of achievement and worthy of respect" (1987, p. 69). Partly as a result of concern for the efficacy of special education and partly as a result of the changing population of students eligible for special education, concepts such as normalization and mainstreaming are uppermost in the views held by many contemporary special educators (Bilken, 1989; Stainback & Stainback, 1989; Ysseldyke & Algozzine, 1990).

This shift in outlook brings with it a concern for curriculum. The idea that people with handicaps and disabilities ought to be allowed to live as normal a life as possible (i.e., normalization) and the implementation of this principle in schools through education of students with handicaps in regular environments whenever possible have greatly influenced what is and should be taught in special education programs.

Students with handicaps and disabilities are entitled to special education; it is a right provided to them by federal laws. As Abeson and Zettel indicated, "On the opening day of school . . . [it became] a violation of federal law for any public education agency to deny to a handicapped child in need of a special program an appropriate program" (1977, p. 115). The mechanism used to ensure that students with handicaps and disabilities receive a free appropriate public education is the individualized education program (IEP). Students who receive special education have IEPs that delimit what teachers and other professionals will do to meet their special learning needs (Kirk & Gallagher, 1989; Lipsky & Gartner, 1989). The IEP is one factor that differentiates special education from regular education (Ysseldyke & Algozzine, 1990). It is "in some ways the most important step in the [special education] process, for it has the potential to make or break the child's educational future" (Rothstein, 1990, p. 201). An IEP, however, is not a guarantee that acceptable levels of performance will be achieved after a specified period of time (Rothstein, 1990; Ysseldyke & Algozzine, 1990). It is a statement of goals and related services that will be used to meet them and a reflection of the curriculum that a student in special education will receive—a "blueprint for appropriate instruction and delivery of service" (Smith, 1990, p. 85).

Unfortunately, research has demonstrated that the IEP process and the documents that accompany it are inadequate, ineffective, and incomplete (Comptroller General, 1981; McBride & Forgnone, 1985; Pyecha et al., 1980; Schenck, 1980; Smith & Simpson, 1989). Often, key objectives in IEPs show little correspondence between the core curriculum in regular education and the alternative curriculum in special education (Bilken, 1989). The following quote illustrates the curricular dilemmas created by IEPs:

> In educating a student with a hearing impairment, for example, a major focus is on communication. Curricula are likely to include instruction in sign language or oral communication [such as] techniques, auditory training instruction from a specialist; amplification systems; . . . special seating; . . . captioned films, good acoustics, and someone to take notes in class; and modified curricula. . . . The IEP will specify each of these items. But the IEP will leave many unanswered questions, all related to the student's place in school. How does the student's

curriculum fit with the curriculum of the other students, the curricular goals of the school, and the educational atmosphere of the school? What are the attitudes of teachers and peers about disability and other perceived differences? How obtrusively or unobtrusively are special services presented? (Bilken, 1989, p. 15).

Stay Put Placement Versus Pullout Program

In attempts to "assure that all handicapped children have available to them . . . a free appropriate public education which emphasizes special education and related services designed to meet their unique needs" (U.S. Dept. of Education, *Annual Report to Congress*, 1988, p. 2), federal government programs provide supplementary funds for states to use in educating children and youth with handicaps. The federal government provides support for children and youth aged three to twenty-one under provisions of Part B of the Education of the Handicapped Act (EHA-B). Support is also provided to children and youth from birth through age twenty in programs operated by state agencies through Chapter 1 of the Education Consolidation and Improvement Act—State-Operated Programs (ECIA-SOP) authorization. These two initiatives "share the common feature of primarily serving children who have not been successful in regular classrooms through specialist teachers who remove children from the regular classroom for some part of the school day" (Allington & McGill-Franzen, 1989, p. 75). In recent years, more students in every category except speech impaired, visually handicapped, other health impaired, and orthopedically impaired were educated in resource rooms or separate special education classes than in regular classrooms (U.S. Dept. of Education, 1989).

Not everyone is satisfied with the existence and perpetuation of separate, and sometimes unequal, special education programs and facilities (Heller, Holtzman, & Messick, 1982). Educators are being challenged to work together in identifying and implementing alternatives for meeting the special learning needs of children and youths in regular classrooms (Wang, 1989; Wang, Reynolds, & Walberg, 1986; Will, 1986; Ysseldyke & Algozzine, 1990). Efforts to meet the challenge are evident in federal funding initiatives and recent literature, both of which illustrate a growing movement to adapt instruction so that the services traditionally provided in separate programs can be incorporated into regular education (cf. Fuchs & Fuchs, in press; Gartner & Lipsky, 1987; Stainback, Stainback, & Forest, 1989; U.S. Dept. of Education, 1989, 1990; Wang, 1989).

Adaptive instruction means increasing the capabilities of schools so they can better accommodate diverse students' characteristics and provide instructional interventions that improve every student's ability to choose from the menu of experiences provided in America's schools (Wang, 1989). Effective adaptive instruction includes the following features:

1. Assessed capabilities of students are the basis for instruction. Teachers provide varied amounts and types of instruction in meeting needs identified by individualized assessments.

2. Instructional methods and materials provide opportunities for students to master content being presented at their own pace.

3. Continual systematic assessment is the basis for feedback on mastery of content and student progress.

4. Students take increasing responsibility for their educational experiences.

5. Alternative activities and materials are available.

6. Students have opportunities to make choices about goals, learning activities, and learning outcomes.

7. Students cooperate in achieving group educational goals. (Wang & Lindvall, 1984)

Clearly, the intent that students "stay put" in regular education programs, rather than be placed in "pullout" special education environments, is evident in efforts to adapt instruction to meet individual learner needs and in efforts to enhance the education of difficult-to-teach students in the mainstream (Fuchs & Fuchs, in press; Kaufman, Kameenui, Birman, & Danielson, 1990; Wang, 1980, 1981; Wang & Birch, 1984; Wang & Walberg, 1988). This is true despite equivocal support for mainstreaming and related practices:

> Assuming we have not missed reports of successful implementations of the [adaptive learning environments model], we believe currently there is insufficient cause to view it as a successful, large-scale, full-time mainstreaming program. (Fuchs & Fuchs, 1988, p. 126)

> Perhaps the "hardest" evidence of the [model's] feasibility and effectiveness is its successful implementation by hundreds of teachers in a variety of school settings for more than a decade. (Wang & Walberg, 1988, p. 132)

Issues Reflected in Practice

The adage that the more things change, the more they stay the same has continuing relevance in special education. When mainstreaming, individualized education programs, resource rooms, and other "innovations" were introduced, they were promoted as significant educational reform for the ills that characterized special education. And, indeed, much has been accomplished. Special education is no longer seen as an evil or as a distant relative of regular education. People with special learning needs are participating more actively in experiences that are as much as possible like those of their peers without disabilities or handicaps. They are being viewed as "full-fledged human beings, capable of achievement and worthy of respect" (Lipsky & Gartner, 1987, p. 73). And professionals are calling for more and more changes. But despite movement in a favorable direction, competing perspectives on important issues continue to be reflected in the practice of special education. People still argue about who should receive special education. There is continuing concern for the character of special education (e.g., is it a practice applied to people or the people themselves?) And who is responsible for it?

Full Versus Selective Exclusion

The competing ideals of inclusion and exclusion have been evident throughout the history of education in America. The earliest schools were exclusionary, developed to serve a selective group in society (i.e., white male children of upper-class families). With progressive inclusion of broader ranges of students (e.g., girls, children of color, children of noncitizens, children of slaves and nonproperty owners), states began to prohibit exclusion of ordinary students by passing compulsory attendance laws (Ysseldyke & Algozzine, 1982). The stage for the development of special education was set by the requirement that all children attend school and by the recognition that schools (as currently or historically conceived) were not for everybody.

Around the turn of the century, James Van Sickle, superintendent of schools in Baltimore, noted that "before the attendance laws were effectively enforced, there were as many of these special cases in the community as there are now; few of them, however, remained long enough in school to attract attention or to hinder the instruction of the more tractable and capable" (1908–1909, p. 102). Students with special learning needs were always (and always will be) part of the national education system. Social policies forced them to go to school, and once there, efforts to provide benefits segregated them from their regular class peers (Lipsky & Gartner, 1989; Stainback, Stainback, & Forest, 1989; Ysseldyke & Algozzine, 1982). Mainstreaming, the process whereby students with special learning needs receive all or part of their education in regular classes, does not mean that all children with handicaps will be retained in or returned to regular classes. But it does reflect the view that the experiences of these students should be as much as possible like those of their peers who are not handicapped.

With the enactment of the Education for All Handicapped Children Act of 1975, each state was directed to establish

> procedures to insure that, to the maximum extent appropriate, handicapped children, including children in public and private institutions or other care facilities, are educated with children who are not handicapped and that special classes, separate schooling, or the removal of handicapped children from the regular education environment occurs only when the nature or severity of the handicaps is such that education in regular classes with the use of supplementary aids and services cannot be achieved satisfactorily (PL 94-142, 1975, sec. 612, 5, B, p. 125).

These principles remained unchanged in the Individuals with Disabilities Education Act (PL 101-476), which reauthorized discretionary programs established by PL 94-142 (NASDSE, 1990). Not only is free education of students with handicaps compulsory; the law mandated that it must be as similar as possible to the education provided students who are not handicapped. As is true with any law, principles embodied in legislation to provide assistance to people with disabilities and handicaps are subject to interpretation.

As Stainback and Stainback pointed out, the pendulum is swinging back once again:

> We appear to be at a point in history wherein we are no longer satisfied with just discussing the mainstreaming or integration of some students into regular education. Rather, we have begun to analyze how we might go about integrating or merging special and regular education personnel, programs, and resources to design a unified, comprehensive regular education system capable of meeting the unique needs of all students in the mainstream of regular education. (1989, p. 41)

This radical mainstreaming perspective is different from the view that mainstreaming means moving students with mild handicaps into the regular classes for some of their educational experiences. Again, as Stainback and Stainback warned, the situation is simply more complex.

> A growing number of researchers, parents, and educators are beginning to advocate that *all* students be integrated into the mainstream of regular education, including those who have traditionally been labeled severely and profoundly handicapped (Sailor, 1989; Forest, 1987; Gartner & Lipsky, 1987; Jacobs, 1986; Ruttiman & Forest, 1986; Stainback & Stainback, 1987; Strully, 1986). They essentially believe that it is time to stop developing criteria for who does or does not belong in the mainstream, and turn the spotlight instead toward increasing the capabilities of the regular school environment, the mainstream, to meet the unique needs of *all* students. (1989, pp. 41–42)

Despite support for radical mainstreaming, however, the belief that adaptive instruction in regular education is not for everybody is still prevalent, and the opinions of some professionals reflect this perspective. For example, Braaten, Kaufman, Braaten, Polsgrove, and Nelson (1988) recently argued that "(a) some students *require* special education, (b) these students can be identified in many cases on the basis of their problem behavior(s), (c) these students require different educational technology, (d) teachers of these students need different skills than most teachers, and (e) the efforts to develop partnerships with regular education to provide services to students with special learning needs jeopardizes the meager services already available and probably would cause many of them to be shunted out of education altogether."

Practices Versus People

Special education is an alternative means of meeting the educational demands of students with special learning needs. For most children, school begins as fun and games—something like the life they led before entering the hallowed halls of learning. And for these children, "satisfactory" progress is the outcome of these early school experiences. But for some children, report cards carry unsatisfactory ratings, and school becomes a difficult place to demonstrate competence and gain self-esteem. Special education was developed to meet the needs of these students.

And if it were possible to deliver special educational services without assigning names to students and without seeing the special education system as distinctly different from regular education, the world would probably be a better place (Bilken, 1989; Bilken, Ferguson, & Ford, 1989a, 1989b; Ferguson, 1989; Ferguson & Asch, 1989; Stainback & Stainback, 1989). Unfortunately, special education is not simply a set of practices applied to students to make them do better in school. Special education is also a complex system of names and labels assigned to students before they can receive special services. The practice of assigning names has caused significant problems for adolescents with special learning needs and for the professionals who serve them.

Students who are labeled learning disabled, emotionally disturbed, or mentally retarded do share some characteristics. For example, they often experience academic difficulties and similar behavior problems. Of the characteristics used to describe and classify these students, performance on intelligence tests seems to be the main differentiating characteristic. But even this is of little value because any two children with different scores on an intelligence test may be similar in their abilities. The commonly reported overlap in other characteristics of ED, LD, and MR students also influences the extent to which actions and reactions to those conditions vary (cf. Hallahan & Kauffman, 1977; Neisworth & Greer, 1975; Ysseldyke & Algozzine, 1982).

Katz investigated people's attitudes toward and reactions to specific kinds of disabilities. He concluded that

> attitudes toward persons with physical disorders tend to be ambivalent. On the friendly, compassionate side, there appears to be concern for those who suffer, respect for persons who cope with adversity, and acceptance of a norm of kindness toward the sick and injured; on the critical, rejectant side are apparent tendencies to dislike anyone who arouses fear or guilt and to perceive [people with handicaps] as inferior, as perhaps responsible for their fate, as marginal people who should know their place and refrain from testing the limits of acceptance. (1981, p. 21)

Balancing the benefits of special education practices with the difficulties people assigned to special education encounter is not easy. Consider the following:

• As much as 80 percent of the students in some schools can be classified as learning disabled by one or more sets of criteria presently in use across the country.

• Many of the characteristics associated with some conditions of special education are evident in large numbers of students who never require special services to be successful in school.

• People with varying degrees of disabilities are successful in all walks of life.

• Being declared eligible for special education in no way guarantees that the services provided will be qualitatively different from those received by regular education students in some classrooms.

• People with disabilities consistently report that their biggest problem is overcoming negative attitudes held by other members of society.

Differentiating people from practices in special education is difficult for several reasons. Special services are not available to all students. To receive special education a student must be assigned a label and declared eligible for services. This act often separates the person from the practice. People are referred to by their disability names (e.g., the mentally retarded, the learning disabled), and the focus of concern shifts to what people cannot do, rather than what they can do.

Special Versus General Responsibilities

During the 1980s, more than 4 million students each year received special education services. In some states, groups of these students (e.g., with learning disabilities) more than doubled during this same period (U.S. Dept. of Education, 1988b, 1989b, 1990b). At the same time, professionals argued that significant portions of some categories of students (e.g., seriously emotionally disturbed) were radically underserved (Braaten et al., 1988), and data indicated that some groups (i.e., Hispanic students with special needs) were radically underserved (Fradd & Correa, 1989). Each year, more and more people seem to need special education. The "medically fragile," those with attention deficit–hyperactive disorder (ADHD), the gifted and learning disabled, "crack babies," children born with acquired immune deficiency syndrome (AIDS), children who transfer between schools, Hispanic students with special needs, and adults with learning disabilities are among the latest people at risk for special education to have their collective pasts and futures exposed and debated in the professional literature (Barnes, 1986; Byers, 1989; Cantwell & Baker, 1991; Centers for Disease Control, 1987a, 1987b; Fradd & Correa, 1989; Interagency Committee on Learning Disabilities, 1987; Jason et al., 1990; Shaywitz & Shaywitz, 1991; Stevens & Price, 1991).

Justified concern for burgeoning masses of people at risk for significant school failure is complicated by the broad issues currently affecting special education (Figueroa, Fradd, & Correa, 1989; Fradd & Correa, 1989; Rueda, 1989). For example, Rueda pointed out that issues affecting Hispanic students with special learning needs "cannot be considered outside the larger institutional context of special education as a whole" (1989, p. 121). Concerns identified by Figueroa, Fradd, and Correa as evidence that "miseducation of many bilingual children with disabilities may well be the norm" (1989, p. 175) are broadly representative of issues in special education in general (see Table 1.2).

All these concerns are also complicated by issues that beg questions of responsibilities for meeting the needs of students who fail to profit in regular classes. Who should pay for special education? How do fiscal and budget concerns influence special education services? Why do not all students receive some form of special education? To what extent do biased assessment practices, untrained psychologists, limited access to related services, the absence of model programs,

TABLE 1.2   Findings from handicapped minority research institutes

Assessment Concerns	Instruction Concerns
1. Language proficiency is not seriously taken into account in special education assessment.	1. The behaviors that trigger teacher referral suggest that English-language-acquisition stages and their interaction with English-only programs are being confused for handicapping conditions.
2. Testing is done primarily in English, thereby increasing the likelihood that achievement or intelligence discrepancy will be found.	2. Few children receive primary language support before special education; even fewer, during special education.
3. English-language problems that are typical of second-language learners (poor comprehension, limited vocabulary, grammar and syntax errors, and problems with English articulation) are misinterpreted as handicaps.	3. The second and third grades are critical for bilingual children in terms of potential referral.
4. Learning disability and communication handicapped placements have replaced the misplacement of students as educable mentally retarded during the 1960s and 1970s.	4. Prereferral modifications of the regular programs are rare and show little indication of primary language support.
5. Psychometric test scores from Spanish or English tests are capricious in their outcomes, though, paradoxically, internally sound.	5. Special education produces little academic development.
6. Special education placement leads to decreased test scores (IQ and achievement).	6. Individual education plans had few, if any, accommodations for bilingual children.
7. Home data are not used in assessment.	7. The few special education classes that work for bilinguals are more like good regular bilingual education classes (whole-language emphasis, comprehensible input, cooperative learning, and student empowerment) than traditional behavioristic, task-analysis driven, worksheet-oriented special education classes.
8. The same few tests are used with most children.	
9. Having parents who were born outside the United States increases the likelihood a student will be found eligible for special education.	
10. Reevaluations usually lead to more special education.	

SOURCE: From Findings from handicapped minority research institutes by Figueroa, R. A., Fradd, S. H., & Correa, V. I. *Exceptional Children*, 56, 1989; p. 176. Copyright © by The Council for Exceptional Children. Reprinted with permission.

the inability to hire competent aides, and administratively fragmented programs force some students into special education that they do not need? Will there ever come a time when all students receive special education? Who will control the growth? Who should teach students in need of special education? Who is responsible for students receiving special education? Who should be accountable when they fail to meet IEP objectives or when they are not employable after school? Whose students are they anyway?

Profession Versus Practice

In professional conversations, it is not uncommon to hear debate about whether the profession of teaching is an art or a science, a profession or a practice (Dunkin, 1987). It has been said that the character of a profession can be measured by the nature of training required to do it. For example, learning about Impressionism, Cubism, and Realism probably has very little to do with whether an artist becomes an Impressionist, a Cubist, or a Realist. Art, or becoming an artist, has probably less to do with what a student studies in school and more to do with what that student can do without it; people become artists in spite of schooling. Scientific professions, in contrast, are characterized by recognizable bodies of knowledge that are essential for acceptance and competence. Principles of mechanics, motion, and stress are taught to young people as a basis for assimilation into a society of professional engineers. Of course, practicing the principles in real-life situations helps an engineer to mature and profit, but as in most sciences, fundamental knowledge is required before practice is expected or permitted.

Arguments in support of the art or science of teaching usually lead to discussions of the purposes and functions of teacher training programs and the relevance of improving teaching without considering its origin and base. For example, Gallagher (1970) argued that teaching is an art but that it should become more of a science. He also believed that improvement of teaching would be more likely if some of the mystery typically associated with art was removed by identification of the scientific aspects of teaching. Gage (1978) believed the real issue in understanding and improving teaching is to identify its scientific basis. He was concerned with the extent to which scientific methods could be employed in studying teaching. The nature of the scientific basis, according to Gage, will be "established relationships between variables in teaching and learning" (1978, p. 22), and the stronger these relationships are, the more likely teaching will be improved.

If the nature of a profession is evident in the character of the training provided novice practitioners, teaching is more an art than a science. Significant certification requirements reflect the belief that coursework and experience are important but that coursework is essential. But teachers consistently complain about the irrelevance of undergraduate and graduate education training (if there is a scientific basis for teaching, it is not being presented or perceived as such by people learning to teach). Large portions of coursework have little to do with a science of teaching; there are few principles taught that apply directly and uniformly to solution of problems in classrooms, and much professional literature contains "almost nothing in the way of specific, practical help for teachers" (Swart, 1990, p. 317). People who enter teaching from other professions, without formal pedagogical training, often turn out to be exemplary teachers. People who stay in teaching for many years often report that few changes occur during their tenure in classrooms (Swart, 1990).

A brother of one of the authors is a clinical pharmacist in a large hospital. He is an active agent in providing medical assistance to patients. He is responsible for monitoring the effects of remedies prescribed by physicians. His knowledge needs and his levels of knowledge attainments have grown significantly during his tenure in his profession. As is true for most hospital pharmacists, he "had to keep pace with the development of new products, assimilate new findings about old ones, and learn to use new tools within new systems" (Swart, 1990, p. 315). Similar levels of professional growth are not necessary or common in the teaching profession.

Teaching is the systematic presentation of content assumed necessary for mastery of the subject matter being taught. A practice is a set of principles that can be applied in the solution of problems. If we use these definitions, we can conclude that teaching in special education is a practice that requires general professional training. Preservice training in special education is a mixture of courses similar to those taken by regular education students and some "professional" courses within a specialized program of training. For example, prospective elementary school teachers take foundations and general methods courses (e.g., introduction to education, social and/or psychological foundations of education, elementary school curriculum) and specific methods courses (e.g., teaching reading, mathematics, social studies); they also spend some time student teaching. Prospective special education teachers take background courses in the foundations of education (e.g., introduction to education, social and/or psychological foundations of education, elementary school curriculum) and then specialize in foundations and methods of exceptional student education; they also spend some time student teaching (Ysseldyke & Algozzine, 1982). Marston (1987) found that the focus of a special education teacher's certification (e.g., mental retardation versus learning disabilities) had little to do with the nature of the instruction provided to students. Interestingly, training programs for school psychologists offer courses in the same general areas (Brown, 1979), and some evidence suggests that their practices are not categorically different either (Ysseldyke & Algozzine, 1982). In recent years, inservice training in special education has focused on procedures for compliance with federal laws (e.g., writing acceptable IEPs), rather than on innovative ways to organize and present content. New products do not enter special education at a pace that makes inservice training essential or practicing teachers' knowledge deficient to an extent that matters.

Paralleling development in other professions, several hundred organizations have formed to support the development and maintenance of services to people with handicaps or disabilities. Groups consist of teachers who serve special students, related services personnel, administrators, parents with children who have handicaps, and people who have disabilities and handicaps themselves (Ysseldyke & Algozzine, 1990). Often several organizations serve the same category of special education students, but their members may work in slight opposition to one another. For example, members of the Association for Children and Adults with Learning Disabilities, the Council for Learning Disabilities, the Division for Learning Disabilities of the Council for Exceptional Children, the Society for Learning Disabilities and Remedial Education, and the Orton Society are all concerned with people with learning disabilities. State departments and any or all of these professional organizations may hold different perspectives on eligibility criteria for learning disability services and the kinds of treatment students should receive in special education.

Similarly, disagreements among members of organizations occur because different types of people join for different reasons. Parents may be charter members of one group and advocate quite different things than university professors who are the founders of another similarly named group. This does not mean that one organization is better than another. It simply is a final illustration of the variety of perspectives that drive a profession and practice as diverse as special education.

Whether viewed as a profession or a practice, information about competing perspectives and issues is valuable for people interested in special education. From a professional point of view, information about issues that affect special education practices serves as foundation knowledge for organizing the development of professionals. From a practical point of view, information about issues that affect special education professionals serves as foundation knowledge for improving practices.

Education at the Margins

Special education and regular education share common goals. As more and more students are served by people in special education, the boundaries between the two systems become less distinct, and the unique characteristics of special education become harder to specify. When more and more students are considered at risk, the concept of specialized instruction to meet individual learning needs becomes moot. As more students are identified with special learning needs, multiple, even competing perspectives all begin to make sense.

Special education is a subsystem of education that exists to enhance experiences of people with special learning needs. Because it is not available to everyone, special education is a controversial practice. The controversy takes up issues of access, availability, and accountability. Concerns about access ask who should receive special education. Concerns about availability center on where special education should be provided and what should be provided. Concerns about accountability address the extent to which special education makes a difference. The rest of this book looks at the evolution of special education services, the condition of special education today, and the issues and concerns that professionals who practice special education face each day.

Discussion Questions

1. Special education is a subsystem of education organized to provide alternative experiences for students with special learning needs. What views held by regular education teachers support this practice? Why do some professionals argue for less use of pullout programs in special education?

2. In the beginning, the curriculum in special education classes was different from that provided in regular classrooms. Today, people who have spent consid-

---

Being Special Isn't Easy

WENDY: When I took one of my first mainstream courses in ninth grade, I was absent because of bladder infections and missed a lot of book reports. I was not marked down when other students would have failed. I spoke with the teacher and said that I didn't need extra help, that I wanted to earn my grade. Then she treated me the same. (Asch, 1989, p. 184)

ZACH: Looking back on it now, I think my teachers couldn't do enough to let me out of things. I didn't care enough to challenge them. (Asch, 1989, p. 185)

CYNTHIA: You begin to question yourself. Are you smart, or are they making exceptions? It confuses you. (Asch, 1989, p. 184)

SUN: When I first came to the States, it took two years before I could speak English fluently. By the time I started middle school, I realized that most of my fellow students had never met many kids like me before. They had this idea, probably from TV and movies, that all Asians are nerds and all Asians are smart. It's true that some are. I know many smart people. But what about those Asians who aren't smart? Having a reputation for brains is nice, I guess, but it can also be a pain. For instance, sometimes when my classmates do not know something, they come to me for the answer. Often I can help them. But when I can't, they get these weird expressions on their faces. If I were a genius, I would not mind being treated like one. But since I am not, I do.

   The problem isn't just limited to the classroom. My mother and father expect an awful lot from me, too. (Park, 1990, p. 62)

---

erable time in special education programs complain that their education is inferior to that of their regular class peers. Should the curriculum in special education be the same as that provided in regular education?

3. How do people at your school view special education? Do students in other programs think teaching is an art or a science? Do they see teaching as a profession or a practice? What do faculty members in other departments think about faculty in special education and other education programs?

CHAPTER 2

Foundations of Education and Effects on Special Education Practice

The Evolution of Education's Mission
Educational Foundations

School and Society
Ideals of Education
Social and Economic Characteristics of Society
School as a Social Institution
Effective Schools
Characteristics of Families

Goals and Objectives of Education

The Changing and Unchanging Face of Education
Student Progress and Outcomes
Content and Context of Schooling
Educational Resources

Legal Basis for Special Education
Fundamental Court Action
Public Law 101-476
Recent Court Action

Special Education: Why Now and What For?
Capable of Achievement and Worthy of Respect

The foundation of every state is the education of its youth.

—*Diogenes*

In this chapter, we examine the mission of schooling in America and the extent to which the mission differs according to the type of student. We review the social, political, and legal bases for both general and special education. Inasmuch as the current mission of schooling has evolved over the decades, a brief history of important educational events offers a beginning perspective on the basis for special education.

Because large numbers of students are failing to accomplish the goals and objectives of America's schools, this chapter also examines the objectives of American education and the failure to achieve them. We provide some current evidence on the progress of education and some information on those students who are failing to accomplish the objectives set for them by parents, teachers, and other members of society. We also describe the legal precedents that have evolved in support of society's willingness to help failing students.

The Evolution of Education's Mission

Many of the issues that emerged when schools (or society through its schools) were perceived as failing in their obligations to the nation's children and youths have their origins in the evolution of the school's mission and purposes in American education. Because the provision of special services emerged as one way to improve educational opportunities for students who were difficult to teach, special education's history can perform the same function of clarifying how special education has come to its current crossroads.

According to Hendrick and Macmillan, the first special education classes were justified politically on two grounds:

> First, the larger social and political force of progressivism in American life called for humane treatment of poor and disadvantaged children. Second, even if politicians were unmoved by the humanitarian motive, probably they would be persuaded that it was in society's best interest to provide educational opportunities to children who otherwise might grow up with antisocial tendencies. (1989, p. 395)

Humanitarian reform and social control were not the only reasons for expanding the mission of the public schools at the turn of the century to include students with special needs. Practical problems played a part as well: "Although the age-graded plan of pupil organization and promotion was well in place in 1900, large, urban school systems were groping for ways to cope with an increasingly large and diverse student population" (Hendrick & Macmillan, 1989, p. 399).

As the need for special classes was increasingly met, the need for definitions, criteria, and curriculum for students who would be served there intensified as well. The development and use of intelligence testing helped early educators to address questions about definitions and criteria (Sarason & Doris, 1979; Ysseldyke & Algozzine, 1990). Curriculum took the form of more physical engagement than was the case within regular classrooms: "Instead of books, copy books, and written questions to answer," students with special learning needs "[made] toys, play[ed] games, and work[ed] with things" (Hendrick & Macmillan, 1989, p. 401). Even though the content of special education was different, early pioneers believed the methods that worked with normally achieving students would work for students needing special education (Farrell, 1908).

Early educators did consider students with special learning needs different from their peers:

> In all its work the ungraded class emphasizes, for the purpose of preserving and enhancing his self-respect and his personal esteem, those things which the [special student] has in common with his more fortunate brothers and sisters, it believes his differences are already too apparent; it preaches as well as practices its belief and knowledge that his mental power is like theirs only of less degree. By having one such class in an elementary school it is possible to get the moral support of the whole body of pupils in developing and molding the child who is "different." (Quoted in Hendrick & Macmillan, 1989, p. 397)

Today, however, it is not "politically correct" to speak of differences as primary characteristics of people with disabilities and handicaps. A central concern within special education is to make the curriculum provided to students with special needs as much like that received by their peers as possible (Lipsky & Gartner, 1989; Ysseldyke & Algozzine, 1990). Yet despite significant and continuing efforts to reform education, the signs of failing schools are still evident everywhere (Sarason, 1990). Dropout rates continue to increase despite massive federal, state, and local expenditures supporting programs to keep students in school (Seligmann, 1990). In many urban areas and for some groups of students with handicaps, the rate exceeds 50 percent of the student body that should graduate (Macchiarola, 1989; U.S. Dept. of Education, 1990b). Because the failures cut across all education, let us start by scrutinizing the original purposes of schooling and the extent to which schools do what they purport to do.

Educational Foundations

The first schools in this country were secondary schools established in Massachusetts in the early seventeenth century. Called Latin grammar schools, largely because of their curricula, the first one was established in Boston, Massachusetts, in 1635. The sole purpose of the Latin grammar schools was to prepare students to enter Harvard College, America's first institution of higher education, which was established in 1636. The pattern of schooling followed that established in Europe, where higher education in general was reserved for the top two classes in society—the landed nobility and the landed gentry. When John Adams attended Harvard, students were ranked according to social standing, not academic achievement. He was near the bottom. The curricula of the Latin grammar chools consisted almost entirely of the study of Latin and Greek, an emphasis that had its historical roots in the early religious basis of education to train youths to read the Old and New Testaments.

Between 1634 and 1638, the first laws were enacted for the public support of education; they enabled the Commonwealth of Massachusetts to tax its populace

and assume responsibility for schooling. The Commonwealth took on the responsibility of public education because parents were allegedly doing an inadequate
job of educating their children at home. The first laws establishing public support
of education had a religious basis, as evidenced in the Massachusetts law of 1647,
often called "the old deluder, Satan, Act." This law read, in part, as follows:

> It being one chiefe project of that old deluder, Satan, to keepe men from the
> knowledge of the Scriptures, as in former times by keeping them in an unknown
> tongue, so in these latter times by persuading from the use of tongues, that so at
> least the true sence and meaning of the originall might be clouded by false glosses
> of saint seeming deceivers, that learning may not be buried in the grave of our
> fathers in church and commonwealth, the Lord assisting our endeavors.—
>
> It is therefore ordered that every township in this jurisdiction, after the Lord
> hath increased their number to 50 householders, shall then forthwith appoint
> one within their towne to teach all such children as shall resort to him to write
> and reade, whose wages shall be paid either by the parents or masters of such
> children, or by the inhabitants in general, . . . and it is further ordered that
> where any towne shall increase to the number of 100 families or householders
> they shall set up a grammar schoole, the Master thereof being able to instruct
> youth so farr as they shall be fitted for the University, provided that if any town
> neglect the performance hereof above one year, that every such town shall pay
> five pounds to the next school till they shall perform this order. (Cubberley, 1934,
> pp. 18–19)

Virtually the only kind of public secondary school in America until the middle
of the eighteenth century was the Latin grammar school. But a significant change
occurred in 1750 when Benjamin Franklin opened his academy (later the University of Pennsylvania). Franklin believed that students should be educated in
modern languages, especially English, and in practical subject matter such as
navigating, surveying, and kite flying. Franklin's school also included instruction
in history, geography, rhetoric, logic, astronomy, geometry, and algebra.

School and Society

To study education and the ideals that motivate it and contribute to its sense of
mission and purpose is to study society and culture (Silberman, 1970). Inasmuch
as schools reflect culture, it is not surprising to find educational ideals reflecting
societal ideals. Three ideals have guided the development of education in America
and are evident in all aspects of schooling (although, of course, as with any
generalization, exceptions can readily be found).

Ideals of Education

One of the primary characteristics of American society is that it is democratic.
Countless books have been written on the meaning of democracy, but it can be
described quite simply as a system in which the individual is perceived as central

and in which all political, social, and economic institutions serve the individual's well-being. Many people readily repeat Abraham Lincoln's words in the Gettysburg Address—"government of the people, by the people, and for the people"— to define democracy. Corollaries of the democratic ideal include beliefs in the individual's worth, equality of opportunity, freedom of thought, and faith in reason. Based on this societal ideal, "we are committed to the democratic proposition that each child—genius or moron, black or white, rich or poor—should be educated to bring out the best that is in him [or her]" (Callahan, 1961, p. 145). As you will see in this chapter as well as in others, the democratic ideal that *all* should be appropriately educated has directed much educational thinking, especially that related to the schooling of minority students and students with handicaps.

A second ideal, one that characterizes American society and through it American education, is nationalism. Americans regard this nation as the center of the universe, and this strong loyalty is symbolized by the American flag and the national anthem, heroes, myths, and legends. Nationalism is developed and nurtured through the process of education, both in and out of schools. When children learn to read English, they encounter national symbols in their earliest readers, and teachers tell them the stories of George Washington and the cherry tree, Paul Bunyan and his blue ox, and Thanksgiving. Children learn the pledge of allegiance and the national anthem, and they study the lives of American presidents. Yet American education is often caught between fostering nationalism and promoting respect for and concern with other nations, understanding their rights, and recognizing their contributions, especially when numbers of immigrants from particular countries become concentrated political forces in cities and towns across the country.

The third characteristic of American society is individualism. The schools' emphasis on individualism has led to an emphasis on achievement or success. Because individual success is a dominant value in American society, it is nurtured in the schools and forms the basis for evaluations of schools and their students.

Social and Economic Characteristics of Society

Just as the American ideals of democracy, nationalism, and individiualism shape the nature of American education, the specific social and economic characteristics of American society direct and constrain the purposes of schooling (Callahan, 1964). American society is scientific and technical, and the curricula of its schools reflect the role of science and technology in the development of modern America. Although in principle this is a classless society and America is called a "land of equal opportunity," vocation, income and source of income, family background, and type of house or residential area do indeed establish class membership and the boundaries between classes. Class membership often determines the amount of schooling a person receives, and membership in a particular class is in turn influenced by the amount of a person's schooling.

America is also segregated by race, despite the belief in equality and equal opportunity. In most sections of the country, cities are divided into neighborhoods on the basis of ethnicity and race. Although segregation in schools has been declared unconstitutional, it still exists to a considerable extent.

American society is also industrial. Industrialization has encouraged increases in population because there are more resources to feed and clothe people, has created high-density population centers around industries with large work forces, and has led to the organization of labor unions. Schools are patterned after industry and often adopt such industrial goals as operational efficiency, increased productivity, and inservice training.

American society is further characterized by mass education. Conformity and uniform standards for education are emphasized, and only recently have individual differences and efforts to devise IEPs been recognized.

Finally, American society is characterized by capitalism. Competition is basic to this society, and commercialism flourishes. Schools no longer exist solely to prepare students for the next level of education; they are also expected to prepare students for different roles in the world of work. In most secondary schools the offerings include business, commercial, and vocational curricula.

School as a Social Institution

The establishment of schools presumes that human beings lack the general knowledge, morals, and intellect necessary to culture; that people are capable of learning and attending to the presentation of knowledge; that they wish to learn; and that "there is a body of knowledge and skill to be taught" (Broudy, 1978, p. 25). Wallace defined school as follows:

> School is an institution which deliberately and systematically, by the presentation of symbols in reading matter, lectures, or ritual, attempts to transform from a condition of ignorance to one of enlightenment of the intellect, the morality, and the technical knowledge and skills of an attentive group of persons in a definite place at a definite time. (1973, p. 231)

A number of implications follow from the preceding definition of school. As a social institution, school is charged with instilling in children society's beliefs and knowledge base. This charge presupposes that school instruction is both systematic and deliberate.

As a social reflection, school has a class system, segregation, and competition, and the administrative model parallels that of industry. School conforms to standards set by local, state, and federal governments to ensure uniformity, productivity, and efficiency, and school models the social values it is designed to instill and cultivate.

As a social organization, a public school is an instrument for the public good. It is a place where societal ideals can be inculcated and to which society has entrusted a valued resource—its youths. School is a first-line defense against poverty, ignorance, and other ills. Because of this, a school is a tough place for people to live. To achieve the "greater good," a school must operate within parameters that sometimes compete with individual educational needs and ideals. For example, classroom rules are necessary and prominent components of any school program. But the order achieved by having rules often competes with and sometimes cancels out individual goals of independence and freedom of expression.

The American school is a graded organization. Rights of passage between grades are controlled by scores obtained on performance indicators presumed to be important (e.g., tests). Achievement of rights of passage (promotion) is valued by members of society. Success and promotion serve as important sources of competition within American schools, much as they do within American business (Glasser, 1990; Sarason, 1990). Often, important interpersonal skills (e.g., cooperation) are devalued as a result (Deming, 1982).

Effective Schools

Much has been written about the characteristics of effective schools (cf. Edmonds, 1982; Lezotte, 1989; Purkey & Smith, 1985; Robinson, 1983). Most professionals agree that effective schools share five common characteristics:

1. They have an effective leader (generally the principal) or leaders.

2. They have a well-articulated instructional focus.

3. They offer safe, orderly climates for teaching and learning.

4. People in them have high expectations for student success.

5. Student achievement is monitored regularly.

In recent years, this taxonomy has offered the promise of educational reform to many professionals.

But despite the progress that has been made in articulating the characteristics of effective schools and in improving what goes on in them, concern for the future of education remains. For example, Sarason argued that schools are intractable to change and that efforts at educational reform will fail as they have in the past.

> There are two basic issues. The first is the assumption that schools exist primarily for the growth and development of children. That assumption is invalid because teachers cannot create and sustain the conditions for the productive development of children if those conditions do not exist for teachers. The second issue is that there is now an almost unbridgeable gulf that students perceive between the world of the school and the world outside of it. Schools are uninteresting places in which the interests and questions of children have no relevance to what they are required to learn in the classroom. Teachers continue to teach subject matter, not children. Any reform effort that does not confront these two issues and the changes they suggest is doomed. (1990, p. xiv)

There are no simple answers in education. Recognizing that special education is a subsystem of education helps to illustrate why there are no simple answers in special education either. Issues created by the social, political, and economic characteristics of schools influence special education in complex ways. For example, English is the primary language of American society, and transmission of the proper grammatic rules of English is an important curricular goal in America's schools. When large numbers of students enter school from homes in which English is a second language, special education becomes a dominant alternative in the search for ways to meet the special learning needs created by diversity among students. Similarly, achievement and school performance are sometimes considered reflections of the educational health of a nation. Evidence the interest generated when the College Entrance Examination Board periodically makes public the distribution of Scholastic Aptitude Test (SAT) scores for high school students.

Every fall, state education officials wait impatiently for the College Board to release the latest figures on high school students' performance on the SAT. Much like the arrival of the first report card of the year (SAT reports typically appear in September), these proclamations from the College Board sometimes bring misery and fear to even the most optimistic educators. For example, when his state moved from fiftieth to forty-ninth in the national rankings provided by the College Board, a spokesperson for the South Carolina Department of Education said, "We've lived in this misery for all these years. Now it's somebody else's turn" (Morell, 1989, p. 1A). At the same time, officials in North Carolina (bumped to the bottom in 1989 by South Carolina's two-point gain) said the state superintendent would outline a plan for improvement immediately. Next year, when scores of students climbed from last place to forty-ninth, the North Carolina superintendent of public instruction, Bob Etheridge, was quick to take credit: "I'm pleased that North Carolina is no longer at the bottom of the heap. . . . We promised progress and we delivered some measure of progress and, in the next few weeks, I plan to issue a report to keep the heat on so we can continue to make progress" (*Charlotte Observer*, August 28, 1990, p. 1A). South Carolina schools superintendent Charlie Williams partly blamed private schools and said "Hurricane Hugo could have played a role" in scores in his state falling from 838 to 834 (*Charlotte Observer*, August 29, 1990, p. 5A). Because SAT scores are treated as indicators of the quality of education in America as well as reflections of intelligence and objects of devotion for individual students, they have accrued a power completely out of proportion to what they actually reflect.

Concern for achievement and the relationship between achievement and perceptions of effectiveness are powerful forces in education. Their effects on the development and progress of special education are illustrated in opinions about "how the raising of reading standards, coupled with social expectations that schools help America's cold war effort and also sort students for future work roles in a stratified economy" led to the creation of the category of learning disabilities (Sleeter, 1986, p. 48).

A significant escalation of standards for academic achievement followed the launching of *Sputnik I* in 1957 and the related "race for space" that captured the intellectual interests of technicians, practitioners, and the public. According to Sleeter, recommendations during this time for

> reforming American education included (a) toughening elementary reading instruction . . . ; (b) introducing uniform standards for promotion and graduation and testing students' mastery of those standards through a regular, nationwide examination system . . . ; (c) grouping students by ability so the bright students can move more quickly through school and then go on to college and professional careers, while slower students move into unskilled or semiskilled labor . . . ; and, (d) assigning the most intellectually capable teachers to the top group of students. (1986, p. 48)

When students failed to keep up, few blamed the raising of standards. Instead, the students were blamed for their failure (Sarason & Doris, 1979; Ysseldyke & Algozzine, 1982). Once traditional and existing categories of special education (e.g., mental retardation, emotional disturbance) became suspect as inappropriate classifications for many of these students, the way was paved for the emergence of learning disabilities as a category, which became increasingly popular. Using underlying process disorders as the reason for discrepancies between ability and achievement as well as other deficits, dysfunctions, and academic disadvantages made infinitely good sense to many people (especially parents frustrated by the search for reasons for their children's lack of achievement in school), and education was changed forever.

Characteristics of Families

Because the family is the fundamental social unit in this society, the larger social changes that have affected education have also affected the family. And the opposite is also true: the evolving nature of the family is modifying, sometimes profoundly, educational practice and philosophy. A recent report of the House of Representatives Select Committee on Children, Youth, and Families provided clear evidence of the extent and ways families are changing.

- Of the 63 million children 0 to 17 years of age in 1985, 19 percent were nonwhite and 10 percent of Spanish-origin. By the year 2000, these percentages are estimated to be 21 percent and 13 percent respectively.

- In 1970, 45 percent of household had one or more children 0 to 17 years of age, by 1986 the figure dropped to 36 percent. And in those same years, the percentage of single parent household grew from 5 percent of family households to 8 percent, with an increasing proportion of them male-headed.

- The percentage of families with children that are female-headed grew from 7 to 19 percent between 1960 and 1986. Among blacks, the growth was from 21 to 48 percent.

- The percentage of children under 18 living with two parents dropped from 84 percent in 1970 to 73 percent in 1986. Among blacks, the figures for the two years were 58 and 40 percent, respectively.

TABLE 2.1   Demographic profile of students in America's schools

Characteristic	Percent
Children from families in poverty	25
Children of teenaged mothers	14
Children from immigrant families that speak a language other than English	15
Children of unmarried parents	14
Children from broken homes	40
Latchkey children	25–33

SOURCE: Hodgkinson, H. L. (1985). *All one system*. Washington, D.C.: Institute for Educational Leadership. Used with permission.

• The number of children per family has dropped. Between 1960 and 1986, families with no children grew from 43 to 50 percent, those with three children dropped from 11 to 7, while those with four or more children dropped from 10 to 3 percent.

• The participation of mothers in the labor force has increased substantially. For all children under 18 years of age, it grew from 39 percent in 1970 to 58 percent in 1986; from 29 to 50 percent of children 0 to 5 years of age, and from 43 to 62 for those 6 to 17 years of age.

• The median income of families with children dropped (in constant dollars) between 1975 and 1985 for all types of families and especially for mother-only families.

• The percentage of children under 18 years of age living in poverty grew between 1970 and 1985, from 14 to 20 percent; this growth was true for all racial and ethnic groups. (Lipsky & Gartner, 1989, p. 163)

Hodgkinson (1985) has written extensively on the changing nature of families and their impact on the schools. More students from minority cultures with a greater diversity of languages are present in today's classrooms, as are more children from families in stress. Many students come to school with limited educational support. Others are sophisticated, "streetwise," and skeptical; most are less willing to be directed without acceptable reasons. A demographic profile of children attending school at the height of the school reform movement is presented in Table 2.1. Because students have diverse backgrounds and attitudes, making a difference in their lives is hard work. Teachers need high levels of creativity, energy, and effort to make classrooms full of these students work. Given the current nature of schools, many children and youths go there and fail. And at a time when students are requiring more varied and comprehensive programs to be successful, political support for schools is undergoing detrimental changes. Today only about 20 percent of the nation's taxpayers have children in school, and many of these parents are taking advantage of opportunities to place their children in schools of choice (Goens & Clover, 1990). Coupled with the diverse characteristics students are bringing to school, this potential lack of funding support makes finding productive ways to meet special learning needs an increasingly critical concern in America's schools.

Goals and Objectives of Education

The ideals of American society and the nation's social and economic characteristics have interacted to shape and influence the nature of American education. What, then, are the goals or objectives of American education?

Stated broadly and in nonoperational terms (as most statements about school philosophy or objectives are), schools in America exist to educate all children; inculcate in them an appreciation of democratic principles, a sense of nationalism, and a belief in the worth of the individual; and educate them to their utmost capacity. There is little disagreement over these general goals. But because objectives are statements of preferences, choices, or values, they change over time, and they vary from one social group to another. Thus, the public, according to Broudy, is not a singular entity: "It is no longer possible to speak meaningfully of a public school serving a public good. For there are as many publics as there are constituencies vocal enough to make their expectations—often conflicting—known to local, state, and federal educational agencies" (1978, p. 24).

Because there may be considerable debate over the specific objectives of schooling and considerable variance in objectives among states and among local education agencies, let us look at the educational goals of representative national groups. In the past, the first formally stated educational goals or objectives were the seven cardinal principles of education identified in 1918 by the Commission on Reorganization of Secondary Education of the National Education Association: (1) health, (2) command of the fundamental processes, (3) worthy home membership, (4) vocation, (5) citizenship, (6) worthy leisure, and (7) ethical character.

In 1938, the Educational Policies Commission of the National Education Association proposed a new classification of educational objectives. These were based on four domains: (1) development of the individual; (2) development of home, family, and community life; (3) response to economic demands; and (4) development of civic and social duties. Four groups of objectives with related subdivisions were formulated (see Table 2.2). For example, the objectives of "self-realization" indicate that the "educated person has an appetite for learning" and "can speak the mother tongue clearly." The objectives of "human relationships" indicated that the "educated person can work and play with others" and "is skilled in homemaking." More recent purposes, goals, objectives, and educational priorities for all students have included the "ability to think," the "development of rational powers," and the ability to learn how to learn, attack problems, and acquire new knowledge."

News reports throughout the country in 1990 featured stories about the national goals agreed to by "the education president" and chief state officials. For the first time in two hundred years of education history, the public was provided

TABLE 2.2   National Education Association classification of educational objectives

The Objectives of Self-Realization

The inquiring mind. The educated person has an appetite for learning.
Speech. The educated person can speak the mother tongue clearly.
Reading. The educated person reads the mother tongue efficiently.
Writing. The educated person writes the mother tongue effectively.
Number. The educated person solves his problems of counting and calculating.
Sight and hearing. The educated person is skilled in listening and observing.
Health knowledge. The educated person understands the basic facts concerning health and disease.
Health habits. The educated person protects his own health and that of his dependents.
Public health. The educated person works to improve the health of the community.
Recreation. The educated person is a participant and spectator in many sports and other pastimes.
Intellectual interests. The educated person has mental resources for the use of leisure.
Esthetic interests. The educated person appreciates beauty.
Character. The educated person gives responsible direction to his own life.

The Objectives of Human Relationships

Respect for humanity. The educated person puts human relationships first.
Friendships. The educated person enjoys a rich, sincere, and varied social life.
Cooperation. The educated person can work and play with others.
Courtesy. The educated person observes the amenities of social behavior.
Appreciation of the home. The educated person appreciates the family as a social institution.
Conservation of the home. The educated person conserves family ideals.
Homemaking. The educated person is skilled in homemaking.
Democracy in the home. The educated person maintains democratic family relationships.

The Objectives of Economic Efficiency

Work. The educated producer knows the satisfaction of good workmanship.
Occupational information. The educated producer understands the requirements and opportunities for various jobs.
Occupational choice. The educated producer has selected his occupation.
Occupational efficiency. The educated producer succeeds in his chosen vocation.
Occupational adjustment. The educated producer maintains and improves his efficiency.
Occupational appreciation. The educated producer appreciates the social value of his work.
Personal economics. The educated consumer plans the economics of his own life.
Consumer judgment. The educated consumer develops standards for guiding his expenditures.
Efficiency in buying. The educated consumer is an informed and skillful buyer.
Consumer protection. The educated consumer takes appropriate measures to safeguard his interests.

The Objectives of Civic Responsibility

Social justice. The educated citizen is sensitive to the disparities of human circumstance.
Social activity. The educated citizen acts to correct unsatisfactory conditions.
Social understanding. The educated citizen seeks to understand social structures and social processes.
Critical judgment. The educated citizen has defenses against propaganda.
Tolerance. The educated citizen respects honest differences of opinion.
Conservation. The educated citizen has a regard for the nation's resources.
Social applications of science. The educated citizen measures scientific advance by its contribution to the general welfare.
World citizenship. The educated citizen is a cooperating member of the world community.
Law observance. The educated citizen respects the law.
Economic literacy. The educated citizen is economically literate.
Political citizenship. The educated citizen accepts his civic duties.
Devotion to democracy. The educated citizen acts upon an unswerving loyalty to democratic ideas.

SOURCE: Educational Policies Commission. (1938). *The purposes of education in American democracy.* Washington, D.C.: National Education Association and the American Association of School Administrators, pp. 50, 72, 90, 108. Used with permission.

The Six Goals of America's Latest Educational Crusade

• All children in America will start school ready to learn.

• The percentage of students graduating from high school will increase to at least 90 percent.

• Students will leave grades four, eight, and twelve having demonstrated competency in challenging subject matter, including English, mathematics, science, history, or geography; and every school in America will ensure that all students learn to use their minds well so they may be prepared for responsible citizenship, further learning, and productive employment in our modern economy.

• U.S. students will be first in the world in science and mathematics achievement.

• Every adult American will be literate and will possess the knowledge and skills necessary to compete in a global economy and exercise the rights and responsibilities of citizenship.

• Every school in America will be free of drugs and violence and offer a disciplined environment conducive to learning.

---

with an educational mission of national prominence. The six broad goals dealt with inculcating school readiness, improving student achievement, making the United States first in the world in math and science achievement, improving school completion rates, increasing adult literacy, and making schools safe and drug free (see box). When the nation's governors prepared a list of twenty-one objectives to supplement the goals, the commitment represented by their action was heralded as evidence of a "national crusade" ("With goals in place," 1990). This effort "put American education on the front burner for the 1990s" and set challenges for achievement of the goals as components of a national reform agenda: "Making substantial progress toward achieving our national goals for education will require a *national* commitment: from business and industry, social agencies, all levels of government, parents, the general public, educators—*everybody*" (Gough, 1990, p. 259).

The six goals articulated by the president are a source of concern for professionals in varied fields of general education. Kagan (1990), for instance, identified questions related to assessment and effectiveness in ongoing programs for young children as central to practical issues in meeting the "readiness" goal. Racial and cultural differences in the economic and social effects of dropping out of school continued to justify interest in improving graduation rates (Gage, 1990). Concerns that reduced the likelihood of American students leaving grades four, eight, and twelve having demonstrated competency in challenging subject matter were evident in issues identified by Darling-Hammond (1990). Rotberg (1990) criticized the representativeness of samples used to compare math and science achievement across national groups, and Mikulecky (1990) presented a pessimistic view of the likelihood of success for the literacy goal based on the dismal success of past programs. Finally, Hawley (1990) presented competing perspectives on the extent of the "drug" problem as evidence of concern for achievement of the drug-free schools goal. Issues in special education reflected in the national goals are illustrated in Table 2.3.

In addition to general educational objectives, such as those outlined by President Bush and the nation's governors, schools take on other objectives, many of which are more than simple compliance with ideals of intellectual growth, development, and responsibilities. Goodlad observed that

> our school system, a huge enterprise, operates as though its social purpose is exclusively educational; it sets goals that are educational, and it is evaluated as though what it does is educational. Meanwhile, it serves purposes appearing to be other than educational, performs functions other than educational, but it is generally not evaluated by criteria that are other than educational. (1979b, *What Schools Are For*, p. 8)

Although objectives and resources for doing so are seldom provided, members of society call on schools to solve such problems as racism, unemployment, divorce, poverty, drug abuse, and war. And assessments of what schools have done are not always complimentary:

> Some who would rewrite American educational history say that they also have served to select winners and losers on the basis of circumstances of birth; to increase the gap between the haves and have-nots in our economic system; to turn off certain kinds of talent while fostering others; and to lower the self-concept of those who do not adjust easily to the expectations and regimens of schooling. What schools have done is not necessarily what they should have done. (Goodlad, 1979b, p. 2)

A fundamental goal of American schools is the education of students regardless of race, religion, sex, national origin, creed, or handicapping condition. But on almost any standard at almost any time in history, schools have failed to educate significant numbers of students, or significant numbers of students have failed to profit satisfactorily from schooling. The double-edged nature of the preceding sentence indicates the multidimensional nature of the problem.

The Changing and Unchanging Face of Education

During the 1980s, members of society became more fully aware of the range of critical issues facing education. As noted in *A Nation at Risk*, "The educational

TABLE 2.3 Issues in special education reflected In national goals

Goal	Perspective	Concerns	Special Education Issues
Readiness	Kagan (1990)	Assessment practices to determine readiness have been challenged.	Assessment Instruction Early intervention
		School entry is individualized, and school services are homogenized.	
Graduation	Gage (1990)	Effects of dropping out are not singular.	Identification Classification Diversity
		Definitions for dropouts are varied.	School outcomes Transition
		Causes for dropping out are varied.	
Competencies	Darling-Hammond (1990)	Curricula in American schools are not challenging.	School outcomes Instruction Assessment Transition
		Testing is overused and misused in decision making.	
Math and science achievement	Rotberg (1990)	Representativeness of samples is used in comparisons.	Assessment School outcomes Instruction School reform
		Test scores are not an accurate reflection of productivity.	
		Narrow definitions lead to trivial solutions.	
Literacy	Mikulecky (1990)	Success of past programs is dismal.	Transition School outcomes
Drug-free schools	Hawley (1990)	Competing perspectives exist on the extent of the problem.	Instruction Homes, families, community agencies School reform

foundations of our Society are presently being eroded by a rising tide of mediocrity that threatens our very future as a Nation and a people" (U.S. Dept. of Education, 1983, p. 5). Not unlike other times throughout history, criticism stimulated rhetoric, research, and reform regarding effective schools. Descriptions of effective schools cropped up everywhere, and "school reform" became the catch phrase of the decade. But despite all this activity the issue of how well schools are really doing remains.

Student Progress and Outcomes

Consistent progress through school is a characteristic of academic success. One indicator of academic progress is the modal grade, which is the grade in which most students of a certain age are enrolled. According to the National Center for Education Statistics (1990), since 1980, all groups have experienced substantial increases in the number of students below modal grade; more male students are below modal grade than are female students. Since 1970, black thirteen-year-old males have had the highest average percentage of students below modal grade (an average of 44.2 percent for 1985).

A failure to make satisfactory progress in school sometimes manifests in dropping out. Recently, concern about dropouts has increased considerably at all levels of education. The National Center for Education Statistics (1990) revealed that:

• Black male dropout rates fell from 11 percent in 1969 to about 6 percent in 1987.

• Hispanic dropout rates have not declined and are much higher than black or white rates (e.g., 9.5 percent in 1987).

• Even though the 1980 dropout rate for sophomores was 17 percent, almost 50 percent had returned to receive a high school diploma or an equivalency certificate by 1986.

• The overall high school completion rate for twenty-five- to twenty-nine-year-olds increased from 70 to 85 percent between 1965 and 1977. From 1977 through 1987 the completion rate remained about 85 percent. Figure 2.1 breaks this rate down according to white, black, and Hispanic populations.

Progress and success in school are also based on development of reading and writing skills. In 1988, these academic skills were assessed as part of the National Assessment of Educational Progress (NAEP). Overall, American students demonstrated continued low levels of performance in these important basic skill areas. For example, no group at any age level achieved an average score in either the "adept" (can find, understand, summarize, and explain relatively complicated information) or "advanced" (can synthesize and learn from specialized reading materials) level. About 42 percent of seventeen-year-olds were "adept" readers;

FIGURE 2.1 Percent of 25- to 29-year-olds completing school

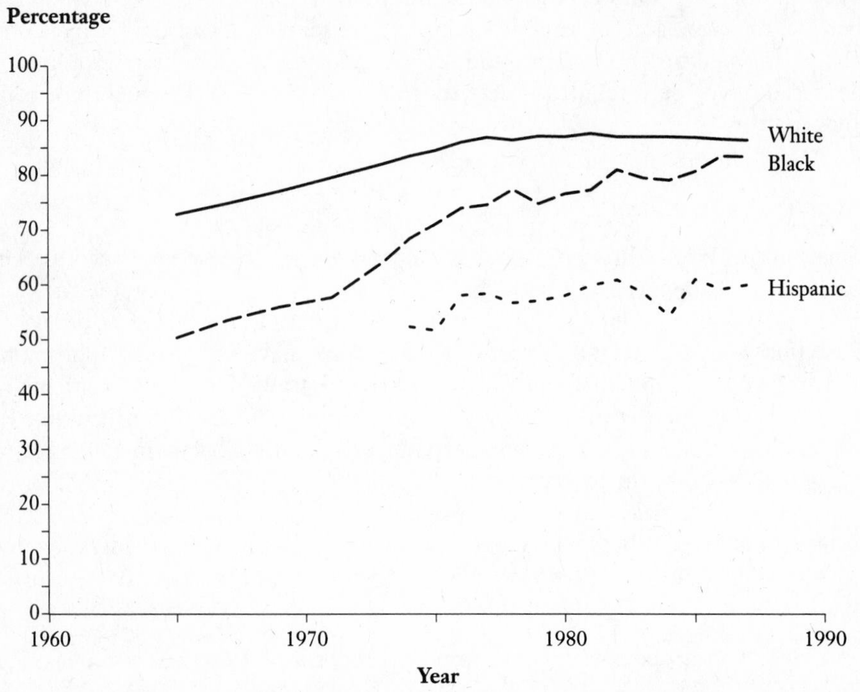

SOURCE: National Center for Education Statistics. (1990). *The condition of education*. Washington, D.C.: United States Department of Education, Office of Educational Research and Improvement.

scores of both blacks and Hispanics were well below those of their white class-mates. Results for writing were similar; few students demonstrated performance at the highest levels of the scale (National Center for Education Statistics, 1990).

Relative to critical math and science skills, results from recent NAEP assessments were similar to those from reading and writing assessments. Mathematics proficiency was about the same as it was in 1973, and science proficiency for thirteen- to seventeen-year-olds was lower in 1986 than it was in 1970. Overall, levels of mathematics and science performance remained low; most students even at age seventeen were unable to perform at the upper levels of proficiency (National Center for Education Statistics, 1990).

Content and Context of Schooling

Who attends school and what goes on there are changing. In recent years, pre-school enrollment doubled for white children three to four years old. About 5 percent of the total population of three- to five-year-olds were attending prepri-mary programs on a full-day basis in 1969; by 1987, the figure had more than

FIGURE 2.2   Special and regular education enrollment trends

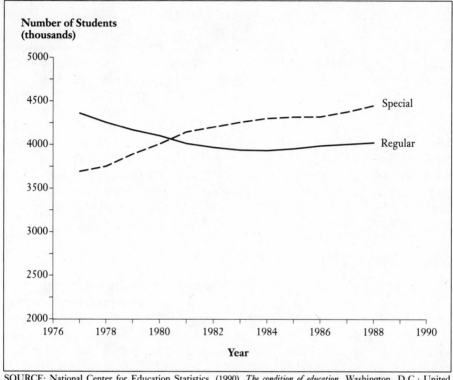

SOURCE: National Center for Education Statistics. (1990). *The condition of education*. Washington, D.C.: United States Department of Education, Office of Education, Office of Educational Research and Improvement.

tripled. Average kindergarten enrollment rates for white children increased from 74.1 percent in 1972 to 80.4 percent in 1986; rates for black children increased from 67.1 to 82.1 percent during the same time period. Total public school enrollments fell by about 8 percent from 1977 to 1988; largely as a result of increases in numbers of students classified as learning disabled (U.S. Dept. of Education, 1989b), special education enrollments rose by about 20 percent during the same period (see Figure 2.2).

Total minority enrollment in elementary and secondary schools rose from 24 percent in 1977 to almost 30 percent in 1986. Hispanic student enrollments increased from 6.4 percent to 9.9 percent during this time period, and Asian/ Pacific Islander student enrollments rose from 1.2 percent to 2.8 percent of the public school enrollment. The percentage of black and Hispanic children attending school and living below poverty levels was about three times higher than that of their white classmates.

In terms of behavior and attitudes, recent reports indicated that 18 percent of black students and about 16 percent of Hispanic students did not feel safe in their schools; but only about 10 percent of white students felt unsafe in their schools. Students from private schools expressed generally more positive attitudes toward school, and 88 percent of them believed teachers were interested in the students at the school (less than 74 percent of students in public school shared this view). Eighty percent of eighth graders believed the teaching they were receiving was "good." More than 40 percent of students surveyed in public schools indicated that disruptions were interfering with their abilities to learn, and the numbers reportedly using drugs and alcohol remained high (National Center for Education Statistics, 1990).

Problems that affect public schools have been well documented. Teen pregnancy, drug abuse, vandalism, and student disruptions are among the problems identified by professional and lay analyses (cf. Kantrowitz, 1990; National Center for Education Statistics, 1990). Teachers believe that lack of parental support or interest is the biggest problem in the schools. The general public disagrees; it believes drug use is the most serious problem facing the schools. Teachers believe students' lack of interest is a serious problem, but a small percentage of the general public agrees (National Center for Education Statistics, 1990).

Educational Resources

Support for public education is provided by a combination of federal, state, and local revenues. The share provided by different sources is determined by factors such as public perception of the role of governmental bodies, taxes, tax bases, and competing demands for revenues. Funding of education is accomplished through formulas and equations that vary from state to state and even within school districts. In recent years, state funds have accounted for larger percentages of the costs of education, and federal funds have consistently remained below 10 percent of total costs (see Figure 2.3). This pattern of funding is largely due to expanding federal efforts to improve education without supporting the costs these efforts entail. As federal requirements for mandated programs alter the costs of education, funding patterns change. For example, when free lunch programs are supported as part of a national initiative to control the effects of poverty, states and local agencies bear the burden unless federal financial support follows a mandated function. If a national initiative to meet the needs of more students with special learning needs is not coupled with increased levels of federal financial support, state and local education agencies bear the burden of compliance with national directives.

Per pupil expenditures are higher today than ever before in history (e.g., $4,719 in 1989 compared to $1,127 in 1950), and even though the number of teachers as a percent of the total staff has been declining, many more teachers will be needed in coming years (National Center for Education Statistics, 1990). And even though teachers' salaries are rising, fewer people are becoming teachers. The shortage of professionals in special education and related services has reached the level of a "national emergency" according to information presented in News and Notes of the American Association on Mental Retardation (Ludlow, 1989, p. 1).

FIGURE 2.3   Trends in revenue sources for education

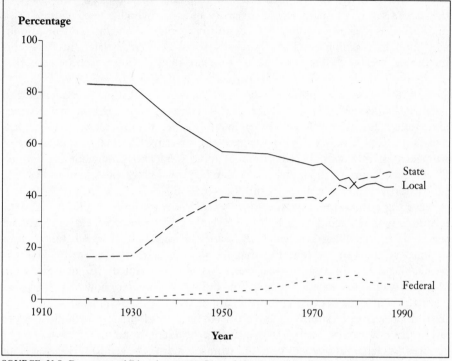

SOURCE: U.S. Department of Education. (1989). *Digest of education statistics.* Washington, D.C.: National Center for Education Statistics.

Education goals are in place. More than ever before in history, efforts to improve educational achievement are among those being addressed by federal, state, and local policymakers and practitioners. How will students with special learning needs fare in a restructured system of education? There is reason to believe that they may fall further behind when standards for achievement are raised, unless sufficient resources are redistributed in attempts to reform education. Most special educators are concerned that students with handicaps and disabilities will not fare well in a restructured education system, and they want assurances that a free, appropriate education will remain a central part of special education's services. This concern and desire for assurances is grounded in the history and legal base of special education.

Legal Basis for Special Education

The first piece of legislation containing specific provisions related to people with handicaps was an 1827 act setting aside land for location of the deaf and dumb asylum of Kentucky. The first substantive law establishing a government hospital for the insane was not passed until 1857. The facility, located in Washington, D.C., and later named St. Elizabeth's Hospital, was designed primarily for delivery of services to members of the army and navy who became "insane." Also in 1857, Congress passed an act to establish an institution for the deaf, dumb, and blind in Washington, D.C. Almost one hundred years later, in 1954, this institution became Gallaudet College, a school that continues to provide higher education to students who are deaf or hearing impaired (LaVor, 1979).

In 1858, Congress provided the first funds for education of students with handicaps when $3,000 per year for five years was appropriated for maintenance and student tuition at the Columbia Institution for the Instruction of the Deaf and Dumb and Blind. In 1879, Congress appropriated $250,000 for purchase of supplies and materials for education of blind students throughout the United States. Such supplies and materials were to be provided by the American Printing House for the Blind, another organization that still exists.

For the next forty years, there was very little legislation specifically relevant to people who had handicaps. Following World War I, however, Congress passed the Soldiers' Rehabilitation Act (1918), which enabled vocational rehabilitation of disabled veterans of the war. But that act was restricted to services for veterans because Congress maintained that rehabilitation of disabled citizens other than veterans was not a federal responsibility. Two years later, however, Congress passed the Citizens Vocational Rehabilitation Act providing counseling, job training, job placement, supplying of artificial limbs and other prosthetic devices (LaVor, 1979). World War II furnished a different impetus for provision of services. As large numbers of men and women entered the armed services, a labor shortage developed in industry. In response, Congress passed legislation providing job training and rehabilitation for people with handicaps to enable them to fill positions in industry.

During the late 1950s and early 1960s, a significant increase occurred in federal legislation for exceptional persons. Some of the laws were enacted after advocacy groups put pressure on Congress to meet their needs. Yet much of the legislation was initiated by President John F. Kennedy and Vice President Hubert H. Humphrey. As LaVor noted:

> Possibly the biggest assist that the handicapped received in terms of public acceptability, the stimulus for further legislation, was the fact that President Kennedy had a retarded sister and Vice President Humphrey had a retarded grandchild. As a result of personal commitments on the part of both men, in 1961 the President appointed the "President's Panel on Mental Retardation" with a mandate to develop a national plan to combat mental retardation. Two years later legislation was passed that implemented several of the panel's recommendations.
>
> In the years that followed, legislation was passed providing funds for states to develop state and community programs and to construct facilities to serve the mentally retarded. Funding was also made available to establish community mental health centers and research, to provide demonstration centers for the education of the handicapped, and to train personnel to work with the handicapped. (1979, p. 99)

In 1958, following the Soviet launching of *Sputnik I*, Congress passed the National Defense Education Act, a defense-oriented legislation designed to increase education of mathematicians and scientists. The law implied that gifted students should receive extra educational services. In 1961, Congress passed legislation to support the training of teachers of the deaf and in 1963 amended the legislation to provide for training of teachers of the hard of hearing, speech impaired, visually handicapped, emotionally disturbed, crippled, and other health impaired.

Beginning in 1963, there was a significant increase in legislation relevant to the education of students with handicaps. At that time, funds were provided to states to enable provision of vocational education, and in 1965 Congress passed the Elementary and Secondary Education Act (ESEA). Title I of ESEA was amended to establish grants to state agencies to enable them to provide a free appropriate public education to students who had handicaps. In 1967, ESEA was amended again to provide even more services for these students. Regional resource centers for testing students with handicaps and deaf/blind service centers were established. Funds were authorized to facilitate both personnel recruitment and information dissemination of special education services. In 1968, the Handicapped Children's Early Education Act was passed, funding model demonstration programs for preschool students with handicaps. On April 13, 1970, provisions related to gifted and talented children were included as amendments to ESEA.

In 1972, the Vocational Rehabilitation Act was extended, and state rehabilitation agencies were required to give first service priorities to those who were most severely handicapped. During the late 1960s and early 1970s, there was a dramatic increase in court cases regarding the education of students with handicaps. This litigation led eventually to passage in November 1975 of the Education for All Handicapped Children Act. Legislation and legal action addressing special education concerns have increased significantly (Rothstein, 1990). Major practices today (ranging from the inclusion of children with severe handicaps in educational programs to barrier-free architecture) might not have occurred without legislative action.

Fundamental Court Action

Changes in laws and specific court cases have brought about modification of special education services. Prior to 1950, legislation focused on the provision of institutional care or rehabilitative services to people with handicaps. For example, in the nineteenth century, legislation was enacted to provide financial support to asylums, hospitals, and institutions for people with physical and mental handicaps. In the first half of this century, acts were passed to support vocational rehabilitation of disabled war veterans and counseling and job placement for citizens with physical handicaps. The late 1950s and early 1960s saw legislation to provide funds to develop state and community programs and facilities to serve people with mental retardation and to establish research and training in that area.

Legislation soon followed that increased funds to states for vocational education, assessment, teacher training, and special education services.

The landmark case of *Brown* v. *Board of Education* (1954) forcefully established a philosophy of integration in America's schools based on constitutional principles established by the Fourteenth Amendment, which provided that people could not be denied "equal protection of the laws" or deprived of "life, liberty, or property, without due process of law." The *Brown* decision "recognized that educating black children separately, even if done so in 'equal' facilities, was inherently unequal because of the stigma attached to being educated separately and because of the deprivation of interaction with children from other backgrounds" (Rothstein, 1990, p. 2). The view that separate education was wrong for people with handicaps followed the movement away from racial segregation in the schools.

In 1975, it was estimated that more than half of the children and youths with handicaps were receiving either inappropriate or no educational services (Lynn, 1984). Common practices that characterized special education and led to the passage of PL 94-142 were summarized by Rothstein: identification and placement of children with handicaps were haphazard, inconsistent, and generally inappropriate; blacks, Hispanics, and some other groups were often stereotyped and disproportionately placed in special education programs; parental involvement was generally discouraged; special education placements were often made with the goal of avoiding disruption in the regular classroom; both special educators and regular educators were competitors for resources, and consequently the two groups did not work in a spirit of cooperation (1990, p. 2).

Court action addressed these problems and focused on a person's right to a free appropriate education by establishing guidelines for states' rights to educate students (Gilhool, 1989). In *Hanson* v. *Hobson* (1967), the court ruled that educational placements based on pupil performance on standardized tests was unconstitutional. In *Mills* v. *Board of Education* (1972), the court asserted the right of students with handicaps to due process before they could be excluded from a school; their right to an appropriate education was upheld in *Mills* as well as in *PARC* v. *Commonwealth of Pennsylvania* (1972). Misclassification of students from minority and non-English-language backgrounds was the issue in *Diana* v. *State Board of Education* (1970). As a result of this case, schools in California agreed to test all children in their primary language and to reevaluate those minority students and children from non-English-language backgrounds who had been enrolled in special classes based on their performance on standardized intelligence tests.

There is no federal constitutional provision establishing a national education system or rights to education. When state rules and regulations provide education, the Fourteenth Amendment comes into play. This means that education must be provided to all citizens on an equal basis, and it cannot be denied without due process of the law. The Education for All Handicapped Children Act of 1975 established principles for how these rights and responsibilities were to be exercised for people with handicaps.

PL 94-142 required that a free appropriate education be made available to all students with handicaps between the ages of three and twenty-one by September 1980. It prohibited exclusion of these students from school and mandated that federal funds be made available only to those school districts that complied with these provisions. This law provided assurances protecting students with handicaps and their parents or guardians through due process, protection in evaluation procedures (PEP), least restrictive environment (LRE), and individualized education program (IEP). The right to due process and the PEP provisions were attempts to deal with problems in eligibility for and classification in special education. The LRE and IEP provisions focused on decisions concerning placement of classified students and on how learning would differ from that of the regular curriculum. All provisions of PL 94-142 affected aspects of decisions made about progress in special education programs.

Pubic Law 101-476

On October 30, 1990, President Bush signed into law the Education of the Handicapped Act Amendments of 1990 (PL 101-476). This action reauthorized the discretionary programs under Parts C through G of the Education for All Handicapped Children Act; made certain changes in Parts A, B, and H of the act; and renamed the EHA as the Individuals with Disabilities Education Act (IDEA) (Lewis, 1990). In addition to changing the title of the law, the reauthorization modified the general provisions of the act to reflect contemporary perspectives. For example, all references to "handicapped children" were replaced with "children with disabilities." Two new categories (autism and traumatic brain injury) were added to the definition of "children with disabilities," and the following comprehensive definition of "transition services" was added to Section 602(a)(19):

> A coordinated set of activities for a student, designed within an outcome-oriented process, which promotes movement from school to post-school activities, including post-secondary education, vocational training, integrated employment (including supported employment), continuing and adult education, adult services, independent living, or community participation. The coordinated set of activities shall be based upon the individual student's needs, taking into account the student's preferences and interest, and shall include instruction, community experiences, the development of employment and other post-school adult living objectives, and when appropriate, acquisition of daily living skills and functional vocational evaluation.

A summary of other changes in PL 101-476 is presented in Table 2.4.

PL 101-476 came about because parents, advocacy groups, and professionals observed certain conditions and brought these to the attention of legislators. Among other findings, Congress reported that (1) there were more than eight million handicapped children in the United States, and more than half were not

TABLE 2.4   Selected changes authorized in the IDEA

Provision	Change
Part A General provisions	
Title of the law	Changed title to Individuals with Disabilities Education Act and made the same change in other laws that currently make reference to the Education of the Handicapped Act
Definition of related services	Added "rehabilitation counseling" and social work services
Definition of individualized education program	Added requirements that IEP include: "(D) a statement of the needed transition services for students beginning no later than age 16 and annually thereafter (and, when determined appropriate for the individual, beginning at age 14 or younger), including when appropriate, a statement of the interagency responsibilities or linkages (or both) before the student leaves the school setting," and "(F) in the case where a participating agency, other than the educational agency, fails to provide agreed upon services, the educational agency shall reconvene the IEP team to identify alternative strategies to meet the transition objectives."
Part B Assistance for education of all handicapped people	
Evaluation and program information	Changed the title of this section and authorized new/revised activities to increase knowledge as well as access to and use of this knowledge to improve programs and foster systems change
State data requirements	Required that data on children ages 0–2 be reported by the Part H agency Required that data on children with autism and traumatic brain injury be reported starting in FY 1993 Replaced requirement for annual data reporting on the anticipated needs of students exiting the educational system with requirement that such data (on students in age groups 12–17 and 18–21 who have exited) be obtained by the secretary every three years using a method determined by secretary to be appropriate Deleted requirement for data on personnel needed but required, starting in FY 1993, that states report data specified in Sec. 613(a) (3) on current and projected personnel employed on emergency/provisional basis Deleted requirement for annual data on federal, state, and local expenditures for special education and related services Deleted requirement for annual data describing special education and related services needed to fully implement the act Required the secretary to provide technical assistance to state agencies to achieve accurate and comparable data required under Sec. 618(b)

TABLE 2.4   Selected changes (cont.)

Provision	Change

Part C   Centers and services to meet needs of handicapped people

Early education for handicapped children	Under the demonstration and outreach program, added several new priority areas for funding, which enables projects to Facilitate and improve early identification of children with disabilities or at risk of developmental delay Facilitate the transition of infants from medical care to early intervention services and from early intervention to preschool special education or regular education services Promote the use of assistive technology devices and services to enhance the development of infants and toddlers with disabilities Increase the understanding of and address the needs of young children exposed prenatally to maternal substance abuse Directed the national technical assistance development system to provide assistance to parents of and advocates for young children with disabilities as well as to direct service and administrative personnel involved with such children; information from the system to be disseminated through existing information networks and assistance provided by the system to include assistance to Part H lead agencies on procedures for use by primary referral sources in referring a child to appropriate agencies for evaluation or service
Programs for children with severe disabilities	Revised certain of the provisions under this program to emphasize the funding of projects that address the needs of children with severe disabilities in integrated settings Statewide projects authorized to improve the quality of special education and related service and "to change the delivery of those services from segregated to integrated environments" Secretary directed to include a priority on programs that increase the likelihood that children and youths with severe disabilities will be educated with their nondisabled peers Projects authorized for the development and operation of extended school year demonstrations for infants, toddlers, children, and youths with severe disabilities; authorization level for this program increased to permit appropriations sufficient to cover the system change grants no longer authorized under the Deaf-Blind Program
Programs for children and youths with serious emotional disturbance	Established a new program of support for projects to improve special education and related services to children and youths with serious emotional disturbance (eligible applicants: IHEs, SEAs, LEAs, and other appropriate public and private nonprofit institutions or agencies); projects such as studies of services provided; development of methods and curricula; development and demonstrations of strategies to reduce the use of out-of-community residential programs and increase the use of school district-based programs; development of effective collaboration among educators, related services personnel, and others; and development/demonstration of innovative approaches to prevent children with emotional and behavioral problems from developing serious emotional disturbance Authorized grants to LEAs in collaboration with mental health entities that Increase the availability, access, and quality of community services Improve working relations among education, community mental health and other personnel, families, and their advocates Target resources to school settings (e.g., providing access to school and/or community mental health and other resources to students who are in community school settings) Address the needs of minority children

TABLE 2.4   Selected changes (cont.)

Provision	Change
Part D Training personnel for the education of handicapped people	
Grants for personnel training	Added authority to fund preservice training in instructional and assistive technology and placed priority on the preparation of personnel from minority groups:
Training for careers	Applicants to describe strategies they will employ to recruit and train members of minority groups and persons with disabilities
	IHEs using grants to support fellowships or traineeships to give priority in the selection of qualified recipients to persons from disadvantaged backgrounds, including minorities and persons with disabilities who are underrepresented in the profession or specialization in which they are being trained
	Secretary to make grants to historically black colleges and universities and other IHEs with minority enrollments of at least 25 percent ($19.25 million authorized for FY 1991, increasing to $25.6 million in FY 1994)
	Grant recipients to conduct interdisciplinary training to assist special educators in coordinating service provision with related services personnel and to require practica to demonstrate the delivery of related services in various education and community settings
Special projects	Revised the special projects authority to provide support for projects to develop and demonstrate effective approaches in such areas as inservice and preservice training for early intervention, assistive and instructional technology, personnel to work with minorities, and recruitment and retention of personnel

receiving an appropriate education; (2) more than one million children with handicaps were excluded entirely from the educational system, and many other such children were enrolled in regular education classes where, because their handicaps were undetected, they were not profiting as much as could be expected; and (3) families were being forced to find services outside the school because of inadequate educational services within the school. When evidence that postschool adjustment of young adults with disabilities was less than outstanding, concern for transition services grew and prospered by elaboration in the IDEA. And when large-scale public interest was evident in the inclusion of another category (attention deficit disorder), the IDEA required the secretary of education to publish a notice of inquiry in the *Federal Register* soliciting comments on an appropriate operational definition for the term.

Congress set forth a number of mandates in the EHA and the IDEA to be enforced by withholding federal funds from states that did not meet them. Specifically, laws required that each state assure the federal government that its policies ensured all students with handicaps the right to a free appropriate education. Furthermore, each state had to have a plan describing in detail the policies

TABLE 2.4   Selected changes (cont.)

Provision	Change
Part E Research in education of people with disabilities	
Research and demonstration of the education of children with disabilities	Revised the purpose of the research authority to emphasize advancing and improving the knowledge base and practice of professionals, parents, and others providing early intervention, special education, and related services to contribute to improvements in the instruction and learning of children
Research and related activities	Specified likely activities to improve the provision of instruction: Organization, synthesis, and interpretation of current knowledge and identification of knowledge gaps Identification of knowledge and skill competencies needed by personnel Improvement of knowledge regarding the developmental and learning characteristics of children to improve the design and effectiveness of interventions and instruction Evaluation of approaches and interventions Development of instructional strategies, techniques, and activities Improvement of curricula and instructional tools Development of assessment techniques, instruments, and strategies for the identification, location, and evaluation of eligible students and for measurement of their progress Testing of research findings in practice settings Improvement of knowledge regarding families, minorities, LEP, and disabling conditions Identification of environmental, organizational, resource, and other conditions necessary for effective professional practice Specified likely activities to advance the use of such knowledge by personnel providing services: Improvement of knowledge regarding how such people learn new knowledge and skills and strategies for effectively facilitating such learning Organization, integration, and presentation of knowledge so it can be incorporated into training programs Expansion and improvement of networks that exchange knowledge and practice information
Center on attention deficit disorder	Directed the secretary to fund one or more centers designed "to organize, synthesize, and disseminate current knowledge relating to children with attention deficit disorder"; information such as assessment techniques, instruments, and strategies for identification, location, evaluation, and measurement of progress; competencies needed by professionals providing special education and related services; conditions needed for effective professional practice; developmental and learning characteristics; instructional techniques, strategies, and activities
Model demonstration program for ombudsman services	Added a new program of support to demonstrate models for providing services of an ombudsman to assist in resolving problems that are barriers to appropriate educational, related services, or other services for children and youth with disabilities; ombudsman services provided by social workers, parent advocates, psychologists, and persons with similar qualifications

TABLE 2.4   Selected changes (cont.)

Provision	Change
Part G Technology, educational media, and materials for people with disabilities	
Technology, media, and materials	Removed all reference to the phrase *technology*, replacing it with the term *technology, media, and materials*
	Authorized new activities under this program and placed new restrictions on fund recipients:
	Funds to be used to increase access to and use of assistive technology devices and assistive technology services in the education of infants, toddlers, children, and youths with disabilities and other activities authorized under the Technology Related Assistance for Individuals with Disabilities Act (PL 100-407) as such act relates to the education of students with disabilities
	Funds to be used to examine how program purposes can address the problem of illiteracy among people with disabilities
	With respect to new technology, media, and materials utilized with funds under this section, secretary directed to make efforts to ensure that such instructional materials were closed captioned
	No funds to be awarded under Sec. 661(a) (1)–(4) unless the applicant agrees that activities carried out with the assistance will be coordinated, as appropriate, with the state entity receiving funds under the Title I State Grant Program of PL 100-407
Part H Early intervention services for infants and toddlers	
Early intervention services for infants and toddlers	Two amendments adopted to emphasize congressional intent that primary referral sources, such as hospitals and physicians, provide parents of infants and toddlers with disabilities with information about the availability of early intervention services:
	Under the public awareness component of the statewide system, lead agency to prepare and disseminate to all primary referral sources information materials for parents on the availability of early intervention services and procedures for determining the extent to which primary referral sources disseminate information on the availability of early intervention services to parents
	Under the CSPD component, system to include training of primary referral sources regarding the basic components of early intervention services available in the state

SOURCE: Lewis, L., director, governmental relations, National Association of State Directors of Special Education. (1990). *Education of the Handicapped Act Amendments of 1990 (P.L. 101-476): Summary of major changes in Parts A through H of the act.* Washington, D.C.: National Association of State Directors of Special Education Liaison Bulletin.

and procedures that would be used to ensure that a free appropriate education would be available to all students with handicaps between the ages of three and eighteen by September 1978 and all these students between the ages of three and twenty-one no later than September 1980. States had to assure the federal government they had procedures in place for identifying these students. In mandating a free appropriate education, Congress said that a state's first priority should be to those students who were not at that time in school, with the most severely handicapped in each disability area at the top of the list.

Recent Court Action

Current practice in special education is driven in part by laws that have established provision of services to students with special needs. Because of the abusive conditions that have existed in special education, the intent of the most recent legislation was massive educational reform for students with handicaps. The major provisions of PL 94-142 (retained in the IDEA) targeted different steps in a three-step process: declaring students eligible for special education services, providing special treatment for them, and periodically evaluating the extent to which they are making progress. Due process provisions protected individual rights and together with the PEP provisions addressed concerns at the eligibility/classification decision-making step. These provisions attempted to reduce the problems inherent in trying to decide who should receive special education. The LRE and IEP provisions targeted treatment practices, and all the provisions addressed aspects of the progress evaluation phase of the special education process.

Of course, passing a law in no way guarantees that changes will occur in the ways the law directs. Interpretation of the law influences what effect the law has on practice. Indeed, Bersoff observed that "legislation itself may serve as a springboard to future litigation, as parties seek to define, implement, and enforce its provisions. Federal and state statutes may evoke what may be called 'second generation' issues" (1979, p. 103). Legal cases that followed the enactment of PL 94-142 challenged the procedures by which schools assessed and made placement decisions and the practices that were used to educate students with handicaps (Gilhool, 1989; Rothstein, 1990; Ysseldyke & Algozzine, 1990).

The best known of these court decisions, *Larry P. v. Riles*, was rendered in 1979 in response to a California case that began in 1971. Plaintiffs in that case represented the class of black children in California who had been or in the future might be wrongfully placed and maintained in special classes for the educable mentally retarded. The plaintiffs challenged the placement process, particularly the use of standardized intelligence tests in the decision-making process. The plaintiffs contended that the IQ tests were biased and discriminated against black children. Plaintiffs cited as evidence the disproportionate placement of black students in these classes. The defendant in the case was Wilson Riles, California superintendent of public instruction.

In January 1975, the California State Department of Education voluntarily imposed a moratorium on IQ testing for *all* children regardless of race. In January 1977, the plaintiffs filed an amended complaint reflecting recent legislative concerns, and in August 1977 the U.S. Department of Justice entered the case as *amicus curia* (friend of the court), contending that provisions of PL 94-142 and Section 504 of the Rehabilitation Act of 1973 had been violated. The Justice Department maintained that intelligence tests had not been validated for the purpose of diagnosing mental retardation and that the use of such tests had a disproportionate impact on black children. Judge Peckham concluded his opinion by stating:

Whatever the future, it is essential that California's educators confront the problem of the widespread failure to provide an adequate education to underprivileged minorities such as the black children who brought this lawsuit. Educators have too often been able to rationalize inaction by blaming educational failure on an assumed intellectual inferiority of disproportionate numbers of black children. That assumption without validation is unacceptable, and it is made all the more invidious when "legitimized" by ostensibly neutral, scientific I.Q. scores. (*Larry P.*, pp. 109–110)

The issue of bias in assessment clearly was not settled by the *Larry P.* case because the issue continues to be debated in the nation's courtrooms. A case of significant note, *PASE* v. *Hannon* (1980), was a class-action suit brought by Parents in Action on Special Education on behalf of "all black children who have been or will be placed in special classes for the educable mentally handicapped in the Chicago school system." Plaintiffs observed that while 62 percent of the enrollment of the Chicago public schools was black, black students made up 82 percent of the enrollment in EMH classes. The plaintiffs claimed that the misassessment of children was caused by racial bias in the standardized intelligence tests they were given.

At issue in *PASE* as in the *Larry P.* case, was the detrimental effect on students of placement in classes for students believed to be retarded: "an erroneous assessment of mental retardation, leading to an inappropriate placement of a child in an EMH class, is nearly an educational tragedy. However beneficial such classes may be for those who truly need them, they are likely to be almost totally harmful to those who do not" (*PASE*, p. 4).

Judge Grady, who presided in this case, took a unique approach to the issues. He systematically examined every item on the Stanford-Binet and the Wechsler Intelligence Scale for Children—Revised (WISC-R). He read every item into the court record and rendered his own opinion on the extent to which each item was biased against blacks. Judge Grady said:

It is obvious to me that I must examine the tests themselves in order to know what the witnesses are talking about. I do not see how an informed decision on the question of bias could be reached in any other way. For me to say that the tests are either biased or unbiased without analyzing the test items in detail would reveal nothing about the tests but only something about my opinion of the tests. (*PASE*, p. 8)

The judge ruled in favor of the defendants, stating that he could find little evidence that the tests were biased. He further stated that poor performance on these items alone was not sufficient to result in the misclassification of black students as educable mentally handicapped.

The other post–PL 94-142 court cases addressed legal issues of critical importance to special education. *Frederick L.* v. *Thomas* (1976, 1977) was a class-action suit in which the Philadelphia school district was charged with the failure to provide students with learning disabilities with appropriate education. Using a 3 percent incidence of learning disabilities as a criterion, the plaintiffs charged

TABLE 2.5   Recent legal developments related to special education

Case	Precedent
Battle v. *Commonwealth* (629 F. 2d 269, 3rd Cir. 1980)	Established that educational policies would violate the Education for All Handicapped Children Act if they denied handicapped students a free appropriate public education
Board of Education v. *Rowley* (458 U.S. 176, 1982)	Established that an "appropriate" education is found when a program of special education and related services is provided such that the individual benefits and due process procedures have been followed in developing it
Irving Independent School District v. *Tatro* (468 U.S. 883, 1984)	Established that catheterization and similar health-type services are "related services" when they are relatively simple to provide and medical assistance is not needed in providing them
School Board of Nassau County v. *Arline* (107 S. Ct. 1123, 1987)	Established that contagious diseases are a handicap under Section 504 of the Rehabilitation Act and that people with them are protected from discrimination, if otherwise qualified (actual risk to health and safety of others may deem persons unqualified)
Honig v. *Doe* (108 S. Ct. 592, 1988)	Established that expulsion from school program for more than ten days constitutes a change in placement for which all due process provisions must be met; temporary removals permitted in emergencies

SOURCE: From *Special education law* by Laura F. Rothstein. Copyright © 1990 by Longman Publishing Group. Reprinted with permission from Longman Publishing Group.

that the schools were serving too few such children. They said that 7,900 students (3 percent) should be identified as learning disabled, yet only 1,300 students were being served in special programs for the learning disabled. The schools argued that other students who had not been referred were being served appropriately in regular classrooms. The court ordered the school district to engage in "massive screening and follow-up individual psychological evaluations" designed to identify students with learning disabilities.

Lora v. *New York City Board of Education* (1978) was a class-action suit brought by black and Hispanic students. The plaintiffs asserted that their statutory rights were violated by the procedures and facilities used by New York for the education of children whose emotional problems led to severe acting out and aggression in school. In his opinion, Judge Weinstein held that (1) the process of evaluating students to determine if they should enter "special day schools" violated students' right to treatment and due process; (2) to the extent that students were referred to largely racially segregated schools, there was a denial of equal educational opportunity in violation of Title VI; and (3) New York City's monetary problems did not excuse violation of the students' rights. In both *Lora* and *Frederick L.*, the schools were mandated to engage in more extensive assessment and evaluation. Thus, the two cases forced school systems to spend more money and change current practices. A summary of additional legal developments subsequent to the passage of PL 94-142 is presented in Table 2.5.

Special Education: Why Now and What For?

As the review of the history of education in America reveals, there was a time when people with handicaps and disabilities were treated poorly by other members of society, and children were excluded from school solely on the basis of a handicapping condition. Today, education is a guaranteed right for students with handicaps and disabilities. According to Gilhool (1989, p. 244), the linchpin of recent disability enactments was the "integration imperative expressly articulated in P.L. 94-142," which required that all states establish procedures to ensure

> that to the maximum extent appropriate, handicapped children, including those children in public or private institutions or other care facilities, are educated with children who are not handicapped, and that special classes, separate schooling, or other removal of handicapped children from the regular educational environment occurs only when the nature or severity of the handicap is such that education in regular classes with the use of supplementary aids and services cannot be achieved satisfactorily.

Recent federal legislation has also taken the civil rights of people with handicaps to unprecedented levels. The Americans with Disabilities Act (ADA), which was signed into law in July 1990, gave protections to people with disabilities that were the same as those provided to people on the basis of race, sex, national origin, and religion. The ADA guaranteed equal opportunity in employment, public accommodations, transportation, government services, and telecommunications (U.S. Department of Justice, 1990). Requirements established by the ADA are presented in Table 2.6.

But despite legal guarantees of rights that have belonged for some time to people without disabilities, life is still not rosy for many people with disabilities (Asch, 1984; Brightman, 1984; Fine & Asch, 1988). The negative beliefs held by some members of society about people with disabilities contribute to this state of affairs. As Lipsky and Gartner (1989) pointed out:

> The assumptions underlying such beliefs can be tersely summarized: "(1) disability is a condition that individuals have, (2) disabled/typical is a useful and objective distinction, and (3) special education is a rationally conceived and co-ordinated system of services that help children labeled disabled. . . . This view of students labeled as handicapped adversely affects expectations regarding their academic achievement. It causes them to be separated from other students, to be exposed to a watered-down curriculum, to be excused from standards and tests routinely applied to other students, to be allowed grades that they have not earned, and, in some states, to be awarded special diplomas. (1989, p. 259).

Capable of Achievement and Worthy of Respect

As Justice Brennan noted in *School Board of Nassau County* v. *Arline (1987),* "Society's accumulated myths and fears about disability and disease are as handicapping as are the physical limitations that flow from actual impairment" ("On cases

TABLE 2.6   Requirements established by Americans with Disabilities Act

Employment

- Employers may not discriminate against a person with a disability in hiring or promotion if the person is otherwise qualified for the job.
- Employers can ask about a person's ability to perform a job but cannot inquire if someone has a disability or subject a person to tests that tend to screen out people with disabilities.
- Employers have to provide "reasonable accommodation" to people with disabilities. This includes steps such as job restructuring and modification of equipment.
- Employers do not need to provide accommodations that impose an "undue hardship" on business operations.
- All employers with 25 or more employees must comply, effective July 26, 1992.
- All employers with 15–24 employees must comply, effective July 26, 1994.

Transportation

- New public transit buses ordered after August 26, 1990, must be accessible to people with disabilities.
- Transit authorities must provide comparable paratransit or other special transportation services to people with disabilities who cannot use fixed route bus services unless an undue burden would result.
- Existing rail systems must have one accessible car per train by July 26, 1995.
- New rail cars ordered after August 26, 1990, must be accessible.
- New bus and train stations must be accessible.
- Key stations in rapid, light, and commuter rail systems must be made accessible by July 26, 1993, with extensions up to 20 years for commuter rail (30 years for rapid and light rail).
- All existing Amtrak stations must be accessible by July 26, 2010.

Public Accommodations

- Private entities such as restaurants, hotels, and retail stores may not discriminate against people with disabilities, effective January 26, 1992.
- Auxiliary aids and services must be provided to people with vision and hearing impairments or other people with disabilities unless an undue burden would result.
- Physical barriers in existing facilities must be removed if removal is readily achievable. If not, alternative methods of providing services must be offered if they are readily achievable.
- All new construction and alterations of facilities must be accessible.

State and Local Government

- State and local governments may not discriminate against qualified people with disabilities.
- All government facilities, services, and communications must be accessible consistent with the requirements of Section 504 of the Rehabilitation Act of 1973.

Telecommunications

- Companies offering telephone service to the general public must offer telephone relay services to people who use telecommunications devices for the deaf or similar devices.

SOURCE: U.S. Department of Justice, Civil Rights Division, Coordination and Review Section. (1990). *Americans with Disabilities Act Requirement: Fact Sheet*. Washington, D.C.: Author.

of contagion," 1987, p. A21). If the situation is going to change, positive alternative views of people with disabilities must gain the upper hand. Beliefs that disabilities cause impairments and limitations must be replaced by views that disabilities cause challenges that many people overcome. Negative social attitudes toward people with disabilities must be replaced by opinions, perspectives, and points of view that reflect acceptance, agreement, and approval of differences as character- istics of all people. The human service practices that cause providers to believe that clients (students) have inadequacies, shortcomings, failures, or faults that must be corrected or controlled by specially trained professionals must be replaced by conceptions that people with disabilities are capable of setting their own goals and achieving or not. Watered-down curricula, alternative grading practices, spe- cial competency standards, and other "treat them differently" practices used with "special" students must be replaced with school experiences exactly like those used with "regular" students. Conceptions of teaching as control and coercion must be modified to reflect cooperative, collaborative, and common perspectives. The direction for significant reform in educational practices is relatively clear. The only nagging question that remains is why the process labors so tediously and takes so long.

Discussion Questions

1. Special education has just recently become a prominent topic in regular edu- cation. Why has it taken so long for special education to gain this attention? What factors account for this increase in interest among professionals in regular education?

2. What problems will special educators face in meeting the six goals for education suggested by President Bush?

3. What differences characterized legal actions that preceded PL 94-142? What legal actions are likely as PL 101-476 is implemented?

CHAPTER 3

The Condition of Special Education

Current Definitions in Special Education
Visual Handicaps
Hearing Handicaps
Physical and Health Impairments
Mental Retardation
Emotional Disturbance
Speech and Language Problems
Gifted and Talented
Learning Disabilities
Categories of the Future

Current Conditions of Special Education
Who Receives Special Education?
What Services Are Provided?
Where Are Services Provided?
Who Provides Services?
Who Fails in Special Education?

Questions About the Condition of Special Education
Special Education Funding
A Perspective on Reports to Congress

I can complain because rose bushes have thorns or rejoice because thorn bushes have roses. It's all how you look at it.

—*J. Kenfield Morley*

During the 1980s, the country became increasingly aware of a broad range of issues facing educational professionals. Low achievement, teacher qualifications, school violence, drugs and alcohol, teenage pregnancy, dropping out, and teacher effectiveness were among the problems identified as critical for solution if education was to improve in the next century. Special education was not exempt from critical review, nor should it be. The state of the art in special education has

TABLE 3.1   Categories of exceptionality used in the United States

State or Territory

Categories	Alabama	Alaska	Arizona	Arkansas	California	Colorado	Connecticut	Delaware	District of Columbia	Florida	Georgia	Hawaii	Idaho	Illinois	Indiana	Iowa	Kansas	Kentucky	Louisiana
Autistic[a]		X						X	X		X								X
Deaf[b]		X		X			X		X		X			X					X
Deaf-blind[b]	X			X			X	X	X	X	X			X			X	X	X
Early childhood special education[c]		X		X								d		X		X			d
Gifted/talented[a]	X	X		X			X		X					X				X	X
Hard of hearing[b]		X		X			X		X		X								X
Hearing impaired/disordered/handicapped[a]	X		X	X		X		X		X	X		X	X	X	X	X	X	
Homebound/hospitalized[a]		X									X								X
Mentally retarded[b]		X		X												X			
Mentally impaired/disabled/handicapped[a]			X						X	X				X			X	X	
Educable (mild)[a]	X	X			X				X	X	X			X				X	X
Trainable (moderate)[a]	X	X			X				X	X	X			X				X	X
Severe/profound[a]	X	X				d			X	X	X			X				X	X
Multihandicapped[b]	X				X														X
Multiply impaired/handicapped[a]		X	X	X		X			X					X	X		X		
Severely/profoundly (multiply) impaired/handicapped[a]												X				X	X		
Orthopedically impaired[b]	X	X		d	X		X		X		d	X							d
Physically impaired/disabled/handicapped[a]						d	X		X		X		X	X	X	X		X	
Other health impaired[b]	X	X		X	X		X	X	X		X	X	d	X			X	X	X
Seriously emotionally disturbed[b]	d	X	X	X	X	X	d	d		d	X	d	d		X			X	X
Behaviorally impaired/disordered[a]								d			X			X			X	X	X
Emotionally disturbed/handicapped[a]	d							d		X		X	d						
Specific learning disabilities[b]	X			X	X				X	X	X	X					X		
Learning disabled/impaired/handicapped[a]		X	X				X	X					X	X	X	X		X	X
Speech-language impaired[b]	X	X	X	X	X		d	X	X	X		X	X	X			X	X	
Speech-language Disabled/disordered/handicapped[a]					X						X								d
Communication disorder/handicap[a]					X											X			
Visually handicapped[b]			X		X	X	X				d		d	X			X	X	d
Visually impaired[a]	X	X		X					X	X	X	X		X	X		X	X	

(a) Nonfederal category
(b) PL 94–142 category
(c) PL 99–457 category
(d) Category reported but not the same as PL 142 category, PL 99–457 category, or nonfederal category

SOURCE: Adapted from Garrett, J. E. & Brazil, N. M. (1989). Categories of exceptionality: A ten-year follow up. Unpublished manuscript. Used with permission.

TABLE 3.1 Continued

State or Territory

	Maine	Maryland	Massachusetts	Michigan	Minnesota	Mississippi	Missouri	Montana	Nebraska	Nevada	New Hampshire	New Jersey	New Mexico	New York	North Carolina	North Dakota	Ohio	Oklahoma	Oregon	Pennsylvania	Rhode Island	South Carolina	South Dakota	Tennessee	Texas	Utah	Vermont	Virginia	Washington	West Virginia	Wisconsin	Wyoming	Off. of Indian Progs.	American Samoa	Guam	Palau	Puerto Rico	Saipan	Virgin Islands
			X	X		X						X	X					X							X	X	X		X										
	X	X					X			X			X		X		X	X							X			X	X						X	X	X	X	X
	X	X		X	X	X	X	X		X				X	X							X	X		X	X			X	X			X					X	X	X
			d	X				d				d	d	d			d	d						X					d	d	d				X				X	X
					X					X				X		X	X		X	X	X				X				X					X					
	X	X						X			d	X	d		X				X						d	X		X	X			X	X			X	X	X	X
			X	X	X	X			X					X				X	X	X			X	X	X	X		X			X	X	X						X
																										X										X			
	X				X					X			X			X	X		d	X							d					X						X	X
		X					X	X				X			X			X							X	X	X			X	X	X	X				X	X	X
				X		X			X			X							X					X	X	X			d		X	X							
				X		X			X			X							X					X	X	X			d		X	X							
				X		X			X			4							X					X	X	X			d		X	X							
	X	X		X	X	X	X			X						X						X			X		X		X	X			X						
										X		X	X	X	X			X							X					X									
			X																X						X			X											
	X	X					X	X			X	X		X	X		X	X	X	X	X			X	X			X	X	X	X			X	X	X	X	X	X
	X	X		X	X	X	X			X			X				X	X	X	X	X	X	X		X	X	X				X	X					X	X	X
	X	X				X	X				X		X	d			X			X			X		X			X	X	X	d		X					X	X	X
	X				X			X				X				d		d				X			X			X			X	X							
			d	d	X		X					X	X		X							d		X							X	X		X	X				
		X		X	X				X			X	d			X	X	X				X			X			X	X	X	X	X			X	X	X		
	X					X	X	X			X			X	X					X			X		X			X			X				X					
	X	X		X	X			X	X			X			X				X	X	X			X	X	X			X	X			X				X	X	X	X
					X	X				X												X	X		X					X	X								
													X	X												X			X	X									
		X			X			X	X	X	X							X							X	X			X	X		d				X	X		
	X			X		X	X							X	X	X	X			X	X	X	X			X	X		X			X	X	X		X	X		X

to be periodically reviewed if progress is going to be made. Toward this goal, we review the current conditions of special education in this chapter. These conditions represent the primary building blocks for the field and act as a benchmark for progress and future analyses of it. Before looking at these conditions, we review the definitions on which these conditions are based.

Current Definitions in Special Education

School personnel use the term *exceptional* to refer to students with special learning needs. In most states, exceptional students are classified or categorized and grouped for instructional purposes. Prior to 1991, the U.S. Department of Education recognized eleven categories of special students and provided federal financial support for educational services to these students. Garrett and Brazil (1989) reported the categories of exceptionality used in each of the fifty states for delivery of special educational services. Only two states, Massachusetts and South Dakota, used no categories. Categories used by other states are listed in Table 3.1.

Visual Handicaps

By law, students who are blind or who show significant visual impairments are eligible for special education services. Definitions of blindness or visual impairment rely on *visual acuity*, or the ability to see things at specified distances. Visual acuity is usually measured by having the person read letters or discriminate objects at a distance of twenty feet. A person who is able to read the letters correctly is said to have normal vision. Visual acuity is usually expressed as a ratio, such as 20/90, which tells us how well the person sees. The ratio 20/90 means that the person can read letters or discriminate objects at twenty feet that a person with normal vision can read or discriminate at ninety feet. The expression "20/20 vision," which is familiar to most people, is used to describe normal, or perfect, vision; it means that the person can see at twenty feet what people with normal vision see at twenty feet.

A legal definition of blindness was established in 1935 by the Social Security Act, and the definition continues to be used today in decisions about who is blind. The act specifies that *blindness* "is visual acuity for distant vision of 20/200 or less in the better eye, with best correction; or visual acuity of more than 20/200 if the widest diameter of field of vision subtends an angle no greater than 20 degrees" (National Society for the Prevention of Blindness, 1966, p. 10). A person who can see, with correction, at twenty feet what a person with normal vision can see at two hundred feet or more is considered blind. The second part of the definition includes people with restricted visual fields; such people are said to have *tunnel vision*.

People who are *visually impaired*, yet not blind, are also eligible for special education services. These are persons with visual acuity greater than 20/200 but not greater than 20/70 in the better eye with correction. For all practical purposes, any student who has visual acuity with correction of less than 20/70 is eligible for special services for the visually handicapped. All cases employ the standard "with correction." This simply means that if the condition can be corrected with glasses or contact lenses, the student is not eligible for special services.

Hearing Handicaps

Students who are deaf, which means they are unable to understand speech even with the assistance of a hearing aid, or who have significant hearing impairments are eligible for special education services. Hearing impairment falls on the continuum between normal hearing and deafness, and it is the degree of hearing loss that defines the extent to which people are handicapped and eligible for special services.

As with visual acuity, *hearing acuity* is measured in reference to an objective standard. People hear sounds at certain levels of loudness, or intensity, which is measured by an audiometer. Loudness is expressed in *decibels (dB);* larger dB numbers refer to increasingly louder sounds. In addition to differing degrees of loudness, sounds also occur at different frequencies, or pitch. Frequency is measured in *hertz (Hz)*, or cycles per second. In educational settings, the extent to which a person can hear sounds within the frequency range for conversational speech, a range of from five hundred to two thousand hertz, is the generally accepted standard.

Moores offered the following definitions of hearing handicaps:

> A "deaf person" is one whose hearing is disabled to an extent (usually 70 dB or greater) that precludes the understanding of speech through the ear alone, without or with the use of a hearing aid.
> A "hard of hearing person" is one whose hearing is disabled to an extent (usually 35 to 69 dB) that makes difficult, but does not preclude, the understanding of speech through the ear alone, without or with a hearing aid. (1982, p. 5)

For practical purposes, *deafness* means the absence of hearing in both ears, whereas *hard of hearing* means significant difficulties in hearing.

Physical and Health Impairments

Reynolds and Birch (1982) indicated that a number of terms have been used to refer to students with physical and other health-impairing conditions. The terms generally indicate little about the needs of the students, but they do reflect conditions grounded in differences among people that can be objectively identified. For example, *arthritis* is a measurable inflammation of a joint that makes movement difficult, painful, and limited in scope. *Cerebral palsy* is paralysis resulting from brain damage. *Epilepsy* is also a brain disorder, which results in measurable convulsive episodes and periods of unconsciousness.

During the 1979–1980 school year, approximately two hundred thousand students identified as orthopedically handicapped or other health impaired were served in special and remedial education programs (U.S. Dept. of Education, 1988b). These students represented about 4 percent of those classified as handicapped. In federal law, *other health impairments* include severe orthopedic impairments that adversely affect educational performance and limit strength, vitality, or alertness because of chronic or acute health problems. Impairments caused by congenital anomalies (for example, clubfoot, spina bifida, absence of a body member) or other physical causes (for example, cerebral palsy, amputation, infections) as well as other general health problems (for example, heart disease, asthma, diabetes) are included in this group of disorders.

Mental Retardation

The Manual on Terminology and Classification in Mental Retardation provides a succinct definition of *mental retardation*: "Mental retardation refers to significantly subaverage general intellectual functioning existing concurrently with deficits in adaptive behavior, and manifested during the developmental period" (Grossman, 1973, p. 11). The manual also defines the key elements of mental retardation. They are *intellectual functioning*, which "may be assessed by one or more of the standardized tests," and *significantly subaverage* scores, which reflect "performance which is more than two standard deviations from the mean or average of the tests" (Grossman, 1973, p. 11).

To be considered mentally retarded, a person must perform very poorly on an intelligence test. The person must also demonstrate deficits in adaptive behavior. Because the term *adaptive behavior* refers to the way in which a person functions in his or her social environment, many different tests of adaptive behavior have been developed. The judgment that a person is deficient in adaptive behavior is subjective. You may view the behavior of a given person as adaptive, whereas several classmates may view the same behavior as maladaptive. Trying to define adaptive behavior is like trying to define normal behavior. The requirement that people demonstrate a deficit in adaptive behavior is included in the definition of mental retardation so that people who perform poorly on intelligence tests but manage to adapt or adjust to their environment, thus functioning adequately outside of school, will not be considered mentally retarded.

Emotional Disturbance

In the current federal definition, *seriously emotionally disturbed* is defined as follows:

> (i) The term means a condition exhibiting one or more of the following characteristics over a long period of time and to a marked degree, which adversely affects educational performance: (a) an inability to learn which cannot be explained by intellectual, sensory, or health factors; (b) an inability to build or maintain satisfactory interpersonal relationships with peers and teachers; (c) inappropriate

types of behavior or feelings under normal circumstances; (d) a general pervasive mood of unhappiness or depression; or (e) a tendency to develop physical symptoms or fears associated with personal or school problems. (ii) The term includes children who are schizophrenic or autistic. The term does not include children who are socially maladjusted, unless it is determined that they are seriously emotionally disturbed.

Interestingly, this definition is similar to that used in the early 1960s and to a more recent description of less severely emotionally handicapped or behavior problem children (cf. Bower, 1982; Kauffman, 1980). Professionals make up the definitions based on research and implications drawn from it; professionals also decide if the definitions represent serious or ordinary versions of the disorders.

The Individuals with Disabilities Education Act (PL 101-476) placed increased emphasis on meeting the needs of students with emotional handicaps. Specifically, recent amendments to PL 94-142 established a new program of support for projects to improve special education and related services to children and youths with serious emotional disturbance. It is expected that the new projects will study services provided; develop methods, curricula, and strategies to reduce the use of out-of-community residential programs; and increase the use of school district–based programs. At the time of the reauthorization, there was a need for effective collaboration among educators, related services personnel, and others charged with meeting the special learning needs of students with severe emotional problems. The federal initiatives were also proposed to develop innovative approaches to prevent children with mild emotional and behavioral problems from developing serious emotional disturbance. Whereas learning disabilities was the category of growth in the 1970s and 1980s, emotional disturbance will hold that position in the 1990s.

Speech and Language Problems

Current federal regulations indicate that students with *speech impairments* are those who have "a communication disorder, such as stuttering, impaired articulation, a language impairment, or voice impairment, *which adversely affects* . . . educational performance." Many students are classified as speech impaired, and according to data provided by the comptroller general, many receive therapy for problems such as "lisping, stuttering, and word pronunciation problems (e.g., they said 'wabit' instead of 'rabbit,' 'pasketti' instead of 'spaghetti,' or 'bud' for 'bird')," or they had voice tones that were "low, high, nasal, harsh, or hoarse" (U.S. GAO, 1981, p. 29). There are no standards for determining when a person's speech is "too" nasal or "too" harsh or when it will adversely affect educational performance. Some teachers are better than others at understanding the language produced by their students. Similarly, the context in which speech occurs influences the judgments made about it. As Reynolds and Birch noted, "If speech cannot be readily understood, if it is upsetting to the person speaking, or if it causes distraction or negative reactions from the audience, it is a . . . problem" (1982, p. 336). The subjectivity inherent in this description should be obvious. Approximately 30 percent of the students with handicaps served during recent school years were classified as speech impaired (U.S. Dept. of Education, 1989b). There were more students in this category than in any other, except learning disabilities, which is probably not surprising for a category based on such subjective judgments as speech clarity or tone.

Gifted and Talented

Children who do more than expected have always been a part of the educational system. Whenever a standard for achievement is set, some performers will miss the mark and others will excel. Horn, in the first textbook about exceptional children, pointed out why highly endowed students were often overlooked: "The special education of [these children] is in a far less advanced state than that of the dull and feeble, partly because [they] do not force themselves as a problem on the consciousness of the teacher and the school administrator" (1924, p. 24). Cubberly, however, suggested they should not be overlooked.

> We know that the number of children of superior ability is approximately as large as the number of the feeble in mind, and also that the future of democratic governments hinges largely upon the proper education and utilization of these superior children. One child of superior intellectual capacity, educated so as to utilize his talents, may confer greater benefits upon mankind, and be educationally far more important, than a thousand of the feeble-minded children upon whom we have recently come to put so much educational effort and expense. (1922, p. 451)

In the Gifted and Talented Children's Act of 1978, *gifted and talented* students were defined as those

> who are identified at the preschool, elementary, or secondary level as possessing demonstrated or potential abilities that give evidence of high performance capabilities in areas such as intellectual, creative, specific academic, or leadership ability, or in the performing and visual arts, and who by reason thereof, require services or activities not ordinarily provided by school.

According to Newland (1980), the definition of gifted (and talented) students has gone through a number of variations. Early definitions were based on scores on intelligence tests alone. Later criteria included evidence of superior performance in areas other than solely intellectual ones (Renzulli, 1987).

Official federal policy toward gifted and talented students recommends but does not mandate (that is, legally require) the provision of special educational services for these students. The government encourages a cooperative venture between private and public sectors in the establishment and funding of programs for gifted and talented students. Nevertheless, the primary responsibility for developing and implementing services lies with the states and school districts; the national role is one of technical assistance and support (cf. Reynolds & Birch,

1982; Gallagher, 1988). Recently, interest has been shown in gifted students who show evidence of other exceptionalities and in gifted members of minority groups (Patton, Prillaman, & VanTassel-Baska, 1990; Richert, 1987; VanTassel-Baska, Patton, & Prillaman, 1989).

Learning Disabilities

Learning disabilities is the most recent addition to the categories of special education. Since the category's inclusion as a specific handicap, it has grown to include the largest groups of students receiving special services. In some states, more than half the students enrolled in special education are classified as learning disabled. The most commonly accepted definition of *specific learning disabilities* is that they comprise

> a disorder in one or more of the basic psychological processes involved in under-standing or in using language, spoken or written, which may manifest itself in an imperfect ability to listen, think, read, write, spell, or do mathematical cal-culations. The term includes such conditions as perceptual handicaps, brain injury, minimal brain dysfunction, dyslexia, and developmental aphasia. The term does not include children who have learning problems which are primarily the result of visual, hearing, or motor handicaps, of mental retardation, or emo-tional disturbance, or of environmental, cultural, or economic disadvantage. (U.S. Office of Education, 1977, p. 65083).

For the most part, students with learning disabilities have average or above-average scores on intelligence tests and below-average scores on at least one achievement test. When the differences between ability and achievement are large, classification is likely.

Recent years have witnessed significant efforts to identify subgroups of students with learning disabilities. For example, Kirk and Gallagher (1986) distinguished developmental from academic learning disabilities: attention, memory, perceptual, perceptual-motor, thinking, and language disorders are primary characteristics of developmental learning disabilities, and disorders in reading, spelling, written expression, handwriting, and arithmetic characterize academic learning disabilities. Others differentiated among types of academic and developmental behavior problems of students classified as learning disabled (Lyon, 1983, 1985; McKinney, 1984, 1988; McKinney & Speece, 1986; Rourke, 1985; Short, Feagans, McKinney, & Appelbaum, 1986; Speece, McKinney, & Appelbaum, 1985). McKinney, for instance, "discovered that children with LD could be classified into more specific subgroups according to their patterns of behavioral strength and weakness, and that those patterns were prognostic of developmental trends in academic progress" (1989, p. 148). We believe fractionating categories of special education is largely an academic exercise of little practical consequence. We mention it here as evidence of the pursuits that engage professionals who believe the names assigned to students are indications of real characteristics, rather than words accepted as indications of presumed differences between people.

Categories of the Future

Although a disorder currently known as Attention-Deficit–Hyperactivity Disorder has been part of clinical practice since the 1930s, interest in ADHD within educational practice has only recently peaked (Silver, 1990). Indeed, the most controversial issue addressed during debate leading to the passage of the Education for the Handicapped Act Amendments of 1990 was the proposal to add attention deficit disorder (ADD) as a separate category or subcategory included in "handicapping conditions" under the law (Johns, 1991). At the final passage of the amendments, ADD was not added as a new category, however; input from professional organizations, parents, and others concerned with this group of students was solicited, and the secretary of education was directed to fund one or more centers designed to organize, synthesize, and disseminate current knowledge relating to children and youths with ADD. Information to be disseminated includes: assessment techniques, instruments, and strategies for identification, location, evaluation and measurement of progress; competencies needed by professionals providing special education and related services; conditions needed for effective professional practice; developmental and learning characteristics; and instructional techniques, strategies and activities.

Recently other factors have been associated with serious learning problems in infants, children, and youths. According to Greer, children exposed to cocaine and other drugs

> will be prominent among the next generation of special ed students and each of them may be a neurochemical time-bomb, likely to experience the same dysphoria and thought and mood disorders as a recovering addict, which is what the child is. We do not have anywhere near the knowledge base or the educational technology to even begin to create the appropriate support structure for dealing with these children. (1990, p. 383)

Children with AIDS and fetal alcohol syndrome as well as those suffering because of homelessness, child abuse, continuing need of medical treatment, and other traumatic and difficult life events are among the constituencies likely to need special education in this decade (Stevens & Price, 1991).

Growing numbers and types of children with medical, social, and educational problems will tax special education's resources as never before in history. Greer (1990) identified the following six ways to "get ourselves ready" for the future and the increasingly complex group of students who will likely need special education:

• First, no single human service agency, including the schools, has the human and fiscal resources to meet the needs of these children and their families. A full scale coordination effort must begin now to integrate the institutions and agencies providing policy/rulemaking/legislative leadership at community, state/province, and national levels.

• Second, because we don't even know the full extent of the problem, we have to begin immediately to collect data on these children to serve as the foundation for programming and personnel training. Every educator must be involved in information gathering and sharing. Fortunately, mechanisms such as the ERIC Clearinghouse and ECER (Exceptional Children Education Resources) already exist to support this task. They must be fully utilized.

• Third, every special education degree-granting institution has to get a grip on this problem now. Our profession's academic leadership will need all of its imagination and skill to train a new generation of teachers to deal with a whole new category of disability.

• Fourth, school district administrators, teachers, principals, parents, and others must begin to rethink the meaning of a "free, appropriate public education" in this new context. We need to ensure that assessment teams are prepared for the mounting wave of referrals and prepared to set up IEPs and programs.

• Fifth, the drug babies are going to reintensify the need for vigorous and successful "child find" activity to make sure that the spectrum of agencies with which they are likely to come in contact closes up the holes in the safety nets.

• Sixth, at a time when "excellence is king" as a result of the preoccupations of the 1980s school reform movement, there will be resistance to curriculum additions. That resistance must be met and overcome. There will also be added impetus for using these children collectively as an excuse for backing away from many special education initiatives such as mainstreaming and plug-in programs. But we cannot afford to lose ground now. (1990, pp. 383–384)

Current Conditions of Special Education

In attempts to "assure that all handicapped children have available to them . . . a free appropriate public education which emphasizes special education and related services designed to meet their unique needs" (U.S. Dept. of Education, 1988b, p. 1), federal government programs provide supplementary funds for states to use in educating children and youths with handicaps. The federal government provides support for children and youths aged three to twenty-one under provisions of EHA-B. Support is also provided to children and youths from birth through age twenty in programs operated by state agencies through Chapter 1 of the ECIA-SOP. The Office of Special Education Programs (OSEP) uses many sources to evaluate the extent to which funding is used to achieve its purpose. Each year, personnel in the U.S. Department of Education assess progress in providing services to children and youths with handicaps and prepare a report of their findings for dissemination. These annual reports to Congress include data provided by states in compliance with requirements associated with accepting monies under these federal funding programs.

When the *Tenth Annual Report to Congress on the Implementation of the Education of the Handicapped Act* was published, it marked the end of a decade of "extraordinary change" (U.S. Dept. of Education, 1988b, p. i). The *Tenth Annual Report* provided a "detailed description of the activities undertaken to implement the EHA and an assessment of the impact and effectiveness of its requirements" (U.S. Dept. of Education, 1989b, p. xiii). Chapter 1 presented national statistics reported to OSEP by the states. Chapter 2 presented data on circumstances in which students with handicaps left school and on their anticipated needs. Services provided to infants, toddlers, and preschool children with handicaps were discussed in Chapter 3, and federal monitoring and ongoing efforts were described in Chapter 4. We review this report because of its historical significance and because of the representativeness of its content relative to the condition of special education.

Who Receives Special Education?

Special education is provided to students who meet eligibility criteria established by state education department personnel. These criteria are based on the definitions that the states have adopted for each of the special education categories. In recent years, more than four million students with handicaps between the ages of zero and twenty-one have received special education services supported in part by EHA-B and by Chapter 1 of ECIA-SOP (U.S. Dept. of Education, 1988b). The number served in 1986–1987 represented an increase of 1.2 percent over the number served during the previous year and an increase of 19.2 percent over the number served ten years earlier.

The numbers and percentages of students under ECIA-SOP and EHA-B are presented in Table 3.2. The most frequent handicapping conditions of these students were learning disabilities (43.6 percent), speech impairments (25.8 percent), mental retardation (15.0 percent), and emotional disturbance (8.7 percent); these four groups accounted for 93 percent of the students with handicaps. Of students served under EHA-B, 94 percent were classified as students with learning disabilities (45.6 percent), speech impairments (26.7 percent), mental retardation (13.9 percent), or emotional disturbance (8.2 percent). These same groups accounted for 71 percent of the students served under Chapter 1 of ECIA-SOP. While two to three times more students with mental retardation and emotional disturbance were served under ECIA-SOP, three to four times more students with learning disabilities and speech impairments were served under EHA-B. At least 10 percent of the students were served under ECIA-SOP in all categories except learning disabilities and speech impairments.

Growth in selected special education categories is illustrated in Figure 3.1. The number of students classified as learning disabled has risen consistently in recent years; the increase from 1977 to 1987 was approximately 142 percent, and it was greatest (i.e., 12 percent per year) between 1977 and 1983 (U.S. Dept. of Education, 1988b). The desire not to stigmatize students with other labels, the need to reclassify students previously called mentally retarded, and the desire to obtain funds for students failing in school were among reasons provided for the

TABLE 3.2 Students served under Chapter 1 of ECIA-SOP and EHA-B

Category	ECIA-SOP		EHA-B		Total	
	Number	%	Number	%	Number	%
Learning disability	25,358	9.9[a] 1.3[b]	1,900,739	45.6[a] 98.7[b]	1,926,097	43.6[a]
Speech impairment	26,012	10.2[a] 2.3[b]	1,114,410	26.7[a] 97.7[b]	1,140,422	25.8[a]
Mental retardation	86,675	34.0[a] 13.1[b]	577,749	13.9[a] 86.9[b]	664,424	15.0[a]
Emotional disturbance	43,386	17.0[a] 11.3[b]	342,294	8.2[a] 88.7[b]	384,680	8.7[a]
Multiple handicaps	23,686	9.3[a] 23.8[b]	75,730	1.8[a] 76.2[b]	99,416	2.2[a]
Deaf/hard of hearing	21,701	8.5[a] 32.6[b]	45,060	1.1[a] 67.4[b]	66,761	1.5[a]
Orthopedic impairment	11,636	4.6[a] 19.9[b]	46,692	1.1[a] 80.1[b]	58,328	1.3[a]
Other health impairments	7,692	3.0[a] 14.5[b]	44,966	1.1[a] 85.4[b]	52,658	1.2[a]
Visual handicaps	7,848	3.1[a] 29.1[b]	19,201	0.4[a] 70.9[b]	27,049	0.6[a]
Deaf/blind	915	0.4[a] 51.8[b]	851	0.1[a] 48.2[b]	1,766	0.1[a]

Note: Percentages are within a column ([a]) or within a row ([b]).
SOURCE: U.S. Department of Education. (1988b). *Tenth annual report to Congress on the implementation of the Education of the Handicapped Act.* Washington, D.C.: Author, Table 3, p. 9.

FIGURE 3.1   Trends in services provided under EHA-B and ECIA-SOP

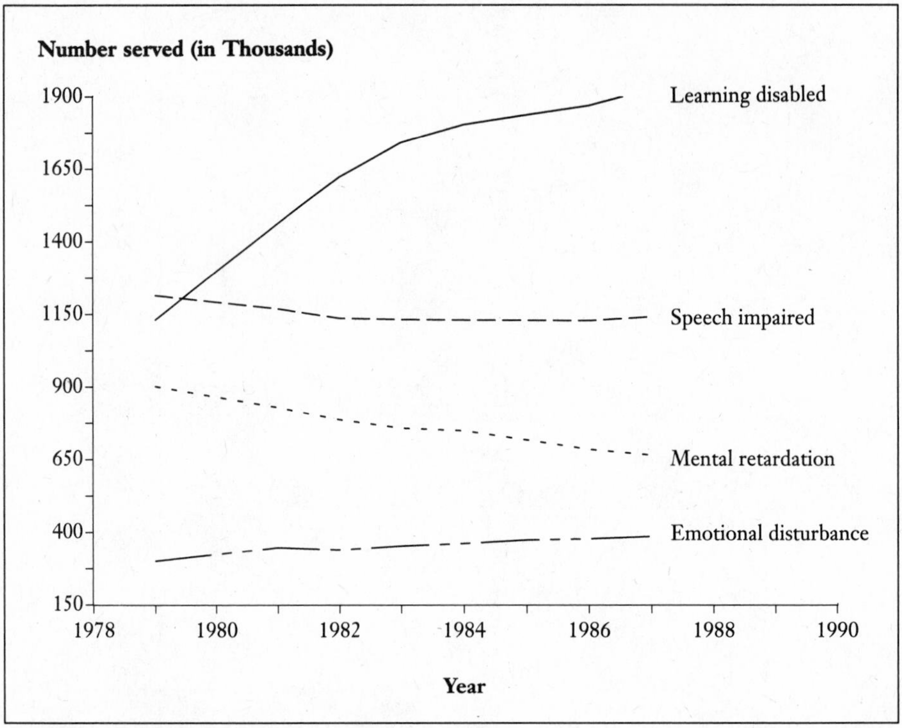

Number served (in Thousands)

SOURCE: U.S. Department of Education. (1988). *Tenth annual report to Congress on the implementation of the Education of the Handicapped Act.* Washington, D.C.: USDOE.

large increases in numbers of students classified as learning disabled (Singer & Butler, 1987; Ysseldyke & Algozzine, 1990).

The changes in the number of students served in other categories was much less dramatic for the same time period than those for students classified as learning disabled. The next largest increase was in the category of emotional disturbance, with 35.9 percent more students. There were 63 percent fewer students with other health impairments, 33 percent fewer with orthopedic impairments, and 32 percent fewer students classified as mentally retarded in 1987 than ten years earlier; change in numbers of students classified with orthopedic impairments was probably due to the introduction of the category of multiple handicaps in 1981 (U.S. Dept. of Education, 1988b).

The number of students classified as handicapped varies considerably at different ages. As indicated in the *Tenth Annual Report,* "More 9-year-olds were served under EHA than any other age," and the "number of handicapped children counted declines substantially at age 16 and decreases rapidly for the older children" (U.S. Dept. of Education, 1988b, pp. 12, 15). During the 1986–1987 school year, about 48 percent of the students with handicaps were between the ages of

FIGURE 3.1   Trends in services (cont.)

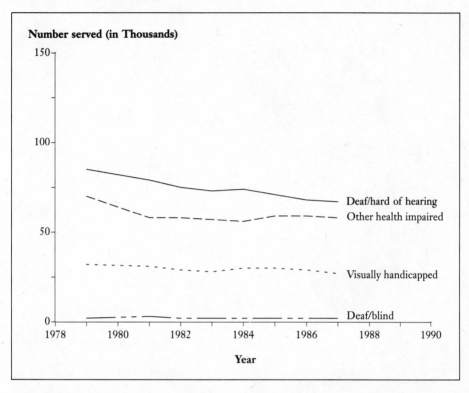

six and eleven (see Figure 3.2). Very small percentages were younger than six or older than seventeen (6 percent and 5 percent, respectively).

Typically, the largest group is between the ages of six and eleven; this, of course, is the time when demands for independent academic and basic skill competencies are highest and when performance discrepancies are most likely to be first recognized. Note that the two major groups making up the six- to-eleven-year-olds are students classified as learning disabled and speech impaired. Students classified as learning disabled are also the largest group in the twelve- to seventeen-year-old age group, and students classified as mentally retarded or learning disabled are largest for the oldest age group (U.S. Dept. of Education, 1988b).

What Services Are Provided?

In accordance with provisions of EHA-B, states are required to report the number of students receiving related services during the school year. The total number of students receiving various types of related services during the 1986–1987 school year is reported in Table 3.3. Testing services (i.e., diagnostic services, counseling services, psychological services) represented a large portion (42 percent) of the

FIGURE 3.2 Students served under EHA-B by age group

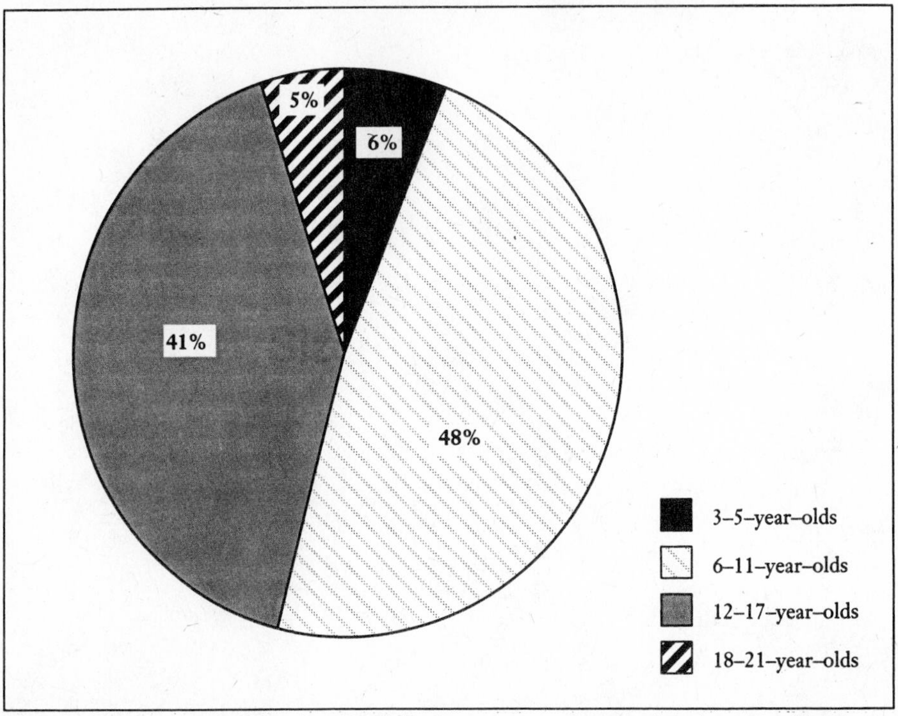

5%

6%

41%

48%

■ 3–5–year–olds

☐ 6–11–year–olds

▨ 12–17–year–olds

▨ 18–21–year–olds

SOURCE: U.S. Department of Education. (1988b). *Tenth annual report to Congress on the implementation of the Education of the Handicapped Act*. Washington, D.C.: USDOE.

related services provided to students with handicaps. Transportation and related special assistance (e.g., school social work and speech/language pathology) were also among the most frequently received related services. Occupational therapy and physical therapy were not received by many special education students.

Where Are Services Provided?

People in special education believe that exceptional students are more like normal students than different from them. This leads to the belief that students should be provided ample opportunities to receive all or part of their education in the same settings as their nondisabled neighbors and peers. The principle used in deciding where a student should receive special education is called the *least restrictive environment* (LRE). Special education students are expected to be educated in environments that are as much like normal, or as least restrictive, as possible. The assumption is that settings (places) and programs (what goes on in settings) are synonymous; of course, this is not always true (cf. Tucker, 1989).

TABLE 3.3   Numbers of students receiving related services

Related Service	Number of Students	Percent of Services
Diagnostic services	777,436	17
Counseling services	620,262	13
Transportation services	569,673	12
Psychological services	557,119	12
School social work services	472,785	10
Speech/language pathology	432,157	9
School health services	419,237	9
Recreational services	215,435	5
Other-related services	186,849	4
Audiological services	184,817	4
Occupational therapy	106,710	3
Physical therapy	87,888	2

SOURCE: U.S. Department of Education. (1988b.) *Tenth annual report to Congress on the implementation of the Education of the Handicapped Act*. Washington, D.C.: Author, Table 6, p. 23.

LRE does not mean that all special needs students must be placed in regular classrooms, even though many are enrolled full time in regular classes. Other students are enrolled primarily in regular classes but leave these rooms part of the time to go to other locations where they receive direct services from special education teachers or related-services personnel such as social workers, occupational therapists, or psychologists. Still others are enrolled primarily in special education classes, but to the maximum extent possible they attend regular classes for part of the school day for certain instructional activities. Some students are enrolled full time in special education settings and receive all their instruction in those settings. Some exceptional students are educated in hospitals or at home when they cannot attend their regular classes because of illness or other medical problems. Still others receive their instruction in a residential (institutional) setting in classes run and staffed by personnel from local school districts. The most restrictive setting for students with handicaps is one in which they live in a residential school or institution and receive education services from a staff employed by that school or institution.

The percent of students with different handicapping conditions served in different educational environments is presented in Table 3.4. For about 26 percent of these students, special education was provided primarily in regular classroom settings. An "additional 41 percent received special education and related services primarily in resource rooms, while another 24 percent received special education and related services in separate classes within a regular building," and "most

TABLE 3.4   Percent of students with handicaps served in different educational environments

Condition	Environment								
	Regular Class	Resource Room	Separate Class	Separate Public School Facility	Separate Private School Facility	Public Residential Facility	Private Residential Facility	Correctional Facility	Home-bound
Learning disabled	15.29	61.80	21.05	0.93	0.54	0.04	0.04	0.23	0.09
Speech impaired	66.26	25.55	5.54	0.87	1.46	0.06	0.02	0.04	0.19
Mentally retarded	3.06	25.29	55.81	10.12	1.90	2.78	0.35	0.27	0.41
Emotionally disturbed	8.85	33.78	35.88	8.81	4.51	1.81	2.36	1.68	2.33
Deaf/hard of hearing	18.72	21.02	34.62	9.47	3.84	10.53	1.06	0.12	0.59
Multihandicapped	4.06	15.25	43.23	19.26	9.26	2.96	2.04	0.33	3.58
Orthopedically impaired	25.62	16.14	32.03	13.06	4.12	0.61	0.44	0.09	7.90
Other health impaired	25.88	18.79	25.77	5.26	2.54	3.06	0.77	0.19	17.74
Visually handicapped	31.48	24.00	19.44	10.32	2.05	10.27	0.95	0.11	1.37
Deaf/blind	6.55	17.68	23.30	11.99	3.11	27.56	8.41	0.04	1.36
All	26.26	41.39	24.49	3.79	1.64	0.97	0.37	0.31	0.79

SOURCE: U.S. Department of Education. (1988b). *Tenth annual report to Congress on the implementation of the Education of the Handicapped Act.* Washington, D.C.: Author, Table 10, p. 30.

handicapped students were being educated in a building with nonhandicapped peers" (U.S. Dept. of Education, 1988b, p. 29). Most (greater than 25 percent) of the students receiving special education in regular classes were classified as speech impaired (66 percent), visually handicapped (31 percent), orthopedically impaired (26 percent), or other health impaired (26 percent). Few (less than 10 percent) of the students classified as emotionally disturbed (9 percent), deaf/blind (7 percent), multihandicapped (4 percent), or mentally retarded (3 percent) received special education services in regular classes. Most of the students classified as learning disabled, speech impaired, mentally retarded, or emotionally disturbed received special education at least 21 percent of the school day but not more than 60 percent of it in resource rooms. Students in all categories except speech impaired received special education for more than 60 percent of the school day in separate classes.

Who Provides Services?

The average rate of increase in the number of students receiving special education services during recent years has been almost 2 percent a year (U.S. Dept. of Education, 1988b). The increase in the number of students enrolled in special education classes occurred at the same time that enrollment in general education decreased. This growth meant that plenty of new teaching positions were created in special education. For example, using a conservative average of fifteen students per class, approximately forty-five hundred new teachers were needed each year from 1977 to 1987.

States reported that the number of teachers employed in special education increased approximately 6 percent from 1984–1985 to 1985–1986. The number of teachers employed increased for students with learning disabilities, emotional disturbance, speech impairments, who are hard of hearing and deaf, with multi-handicaps, orthopedic impairments, and visual handicaps. The number of teachers employed to teach students classified as having mental retardation, other health impairments, and deafness/blindness decreased (U.S. Dept. of Education, 1988b). As would be expected based on number of students, states reported the greatest need to fill positions for teachers of students with learning disabilities, emotional disturbance, speech impairments, and mental retardation (see Table 3.5).

Personnel other than teachers also provide services to students with special learning needs. In 1985–1986, the number of people employed other than special education teachers was 229,872; more than half of these people worked as teacher aides (see Table 3.5). Occupational therapists, physical therapists, and audiologists were the most-needed personnel (U.S. Dept. of Education, 1988b).

Who Fails in Special Education?

The number of students with handicaps leaving school during the 1985–1986 school year is presented in Table 3.6. In recent years, about 43 percent of students

TABLE 3.5   Personnel needs in special education

Handicapping Condition	Teachers			
	Employed	Needed	Percent[a]	Percent[b]
Learning disabled	111,427	10,785	9.7	39.3
Mentally retarded	61,411	5,014	8.2	18.3
Emotionally disturbed	32,774	4,701	14.3	17.1
Speech impaired	39,747	3,504	8.8	12.8
Deaf/hard of hearing	8,200	679	8.3	2.5
Multihandicapped	9,078	868	9.6	3.2
Orthopedically impaired	4,681	446	9.5	1.6
Other health impaired	3,376	230	6.8	0.8
Visually handicapped	3,261	342	10.5	1.3
Deaf/blind	298	46	15.4	0.2

Type of Personnel	Other Personnel			
	1984–1985	1985–1986	Percent[c]	Percent[d]
Teacher aides	112,330	122,504	9.0	54.2
Noninstructional staff	39,593	31,164	−2.1	13.8
Psychologists	16,249	16,313	0.0	7.2
Administrators	13,841	14,957	8.0	5.3
School social workers	8,027	7,833	−2.4	3.5
Diagnostic staff	6,790	8,624	2.7	3.8
Counselors	6,284	6,808	8.3	3.0
Voc education teachers	5,339	5,782	8.3	2.5
Phys education teachers	3,377	5,931	7.6	2.6
Occupational therapists	2,886	3,120	8.1	1.4
Physical therapists	2,234	2,534	13.4	1.1
Work-study coordinators	1,515	1,989	31.3	0.9
Audiologists	966	961	0.0	0.4
SEA administrators	925	829	−10.4	0.3
Recreational therapists	616	367	−40.4	0.2

[a]Percent needed as percent of employed
[b]Percent of total needed
[c]Percent change in number employed
[d]Percent of total employed, 1985–1986.
SOURCE: U.S. Department of Education. (1988b). *Tenth annual report to Congress on the implementation of the Education of the Handicapped Act.* Washington, D.C.: Author, Table 13, p. 35 and Table 14, p. 37.

TABLE 3.6   Numbers of students exiting special education

Category	Graduated with Diploma		Graduated with Certificate		Reached Maximum Age		Dropped Out		Other Reasons for Exit	
	Number	%	Number	%	Number	%	Number	%	Number	%
Visually handicapped	865	59.7	174	12.0	48	3.31	180	12.4	181	12.5
Deaf/hard of hearing	2,066	55.8	711	19.2	74	2.0	486	13.1	366	9.9
Orthopedically impaired	1,426	53.9	492	18.6	104	3.93	384	14.5	241	9.1
Learning disabled	51,628	49.7	13,150	12.7	590	0.6	26,644	25.6	11,955	11.5
Speech impaired	5,032	37.4	3,399	25.3	103	0.8	2,381	17.7	2,530	18.8
Other health impaired	1,094	35.9	456	15.0	132	4.3	941	30.9	426	14.0
Mentally retarded	18,447	34.4	15,136	28.3	3,018	5.6	12,858	24.0	4,122	7.7
Emotionally disturbed	9,691	33.5	2,534	8.8	657	2.3	11,803	40.7	4,283	14.8
Multihandicapped	640	24.3	749	28.4	399	15.2	466	17.7	380	14.4
Deaf/blind	32	17.7	70	38.7	57	31.5	13	7.2	9	5.0
All	90,921	42.6	36,871	17.3	5,182	2.4	56,156	26.3	24,493	11.5

SOURCE: U.S. Department of Education. (1988b). *Tenth annual report to Congress on the implementation of the Education of the Handicapped Act.* Washington, D.C.: Author, Table 17, p. 42.

with handicaps have graduated from high school. Approximately 60 percent of students with visual handicaps have graduated, as have 56 percent of those classified as hard of hearing or deaf and 54 percent of those with orthopedic handicaps. About 50 percent of the students with learning disabilities have graduated. An average of 312 students with handicaps dropped out of high school each day (U.S. Dept. of Education, 1988b). Interestingly, more students with mild handicaps have dropped out of school than have students with other handicaps.

Questions About the Condition of Special Education

Publication of the annual reports typically stimulates interest and dialogue among professionals (cf. Algozzine, 1991; Gerber, 1984; Greenburg, 1984; Ysseldyke, 1989) and provides a unique basis for examining what is going on in special education across the country (Blackman, 1989; Danielson & Bellamy, 1989; Tucker, 1989). To stimulate thinking about previous and future progress in meeting the needs of students who are handicapped, the executive summary of the *Tenth Annual Report* and three reactions to it were published in *Exceptional Children* (Gerber & Levine-Donnerstein, 1989; Greenburg, 1989; U.S. Department of Education, 1988b; Wyche, 1989).

Greenburg's perspective on the *Tenth Annual Report* reflected disappointment and dissatisfaction:

> The current report again seems overly dependent on congregated numbers and on reports of federally supported projects awarded to a limited number of selected agencies with little or no practitioner contact. Though there may be gross understaffing in the office responsible for the report, both Congress and special education practitioners are justified in anticipating a quality characterization of the implementation of EHA and the *Tenth Annual Report* seems to fall short of this expectation. (1989, p. 10)

In reference to related services, least restrictive environment, and personnel sections, his opinions varied. For example, he found references to average numbers of related services "totally meaningless" and information on students exiting school programs limited but helpful; relative to information presented about special education personnel, he identified several questions worthy of further consideration (e.g., Are state education agencies better at enforcing class size and caseload regulations? Do emerging service delivery options require more, rather than fewer, personnel?) (Greenburg, 1989, p. 11). But despite the shortcomings, he believed "the annual reports are essential reading for those interested in the perspective of the Department of Education on the field and the practice of special education" and that the report was "filled with potential areas for further questions and research" (Greenburg, 1989, p. 12). He did not identify a research agenda related to these questions.

Information about handicapped youths who dropped out of school was the primary focus of Wyche's analysis of the *Tenth Annual Report*. After reviewing figures related to minority dropout rates from several resources, he made a plea for continued research and development to address dropout problems:

> Systematic strides must be taken to devise a diagnostic assessment battery that will identify potential dropouts in elementary grades, before they choose to leave school. Psychological and educational tests have an accepted tradition of being used to predict future behavior. An assessment battery that could identify specific cutoff scores and predict the possibility of dropping out with at least 80% accuracy would give educators a valuable tool. (1989, p. 15)

Although limited in its analysis of the overall report, Wyche's review illustrated the interest generated by annual reporting of figures related to special education.

Gerber and Levine-Donnerstein's plan was "to update some earlier observations, identify some newer issues, and make some recommendations about treatment of data such as those provided by the annual reports" (1989, p. 17). They reviewed the main sections of the *Tenth Annual Report*, discussed issues debated in the literature as reflected in information in the report, and concluded that the "power of our historical experience with special education, culminating in the *Tenth Annual Report*, lies not in the answers special education provides, but rather in the questions it makes us ask" (Gerber & Levine-Donnerstein, 1989, p. 26).

Algozzine (1991) identified a number of unanswered questions and interesting areas of inquiry in the *Tenth Annual Report*. He wondered whether the steady increase (19.2 percent since 1976–1977) in number of students served was a reflection of better, more consistent reporting or of real increases in students becoming handicapped and what the implications of this answer might be. He asked what was happening in regular education while the number of students in special education increased. And he speculated on what significance the differences in numbers of students might have in terms of services provided to children with different handicapping conditions.

As Greenburg indicated the sections describing numbers of related services and least restrictive environment "seem the least useful" and perhaps most misleading to lay readers (1989, p. 11). Reporting the "total number of related services provided" as an average of 1.21 services per student did seem ineffective and unenlightening; but, interesting information was nonetheless contained in these sections of the report. Algozzine (1991) offered suggestions for improving reporting information about related services. Groupings would go a long way in simplifying, and clarifying for practitioners, the overall presentation related to related services. For example, diagnostic-related services might include psychological services, speech/language pathology, diagnostic services, and audiological services. Treatment-related services might include occupational therapy, physical therapy, and counseling, and general-related services might include school social work services, recreational services, transportation services, school health services, and other related services. Groupings such as this (and analyses related to them) would make discussion and interpretation more straightforward. For example, 42 percent of the related services received by students with handicaps during the 1985–1986 school year could be categorized as diagnostic-related services, 17 percent as treatment-related services, and 41 percent as general-related services. Students classified as learning disabled received more diagnostic-related services (46 percent) than treatment or general-related services.

Greenburg (1989) and Algozzine (1991) identified questions that should be of interest to professionals addressing teacher training needs. Is there evidence of district attempts to reduce special education class sizes or caseloads? Do emerging service delivery options require more, rather than fewer, personnel? What is the overall teacher/pupil ratio in special education? What are teacher/pupil ratios by category? How much do teacher/pupil ratios vary across states? How much do other personnel/pupil ratios vary across states? How do teacher/pupil ratios in special education compare to the same ratios in regular education?

Special Education Funding

The costs of educating exceptional students are tremendous. Figures provided in the *Tenth Annual Report* indicated that approximately 9 percent of these costs were supported by federal government expenditures; state (56 percent) and local (35 percent) governments were primary sources of funding special education. Under the EHA-B State Grant Program from 1977 to 1987, federal funding increased fivefold from $251,769,927 to $1,338,000,000. Accordingly, the per pupil allocation to each state increased from $72 to $315, a 435 percent increase (see Figure 3.3 and Table 3.7). Similar relations were evident in federal spending related to ECIA-SOP (see Figure 3.4). Analysis of relations between expenditures, per child allocations, and student populations coupled with the fact that federal expenditures represented a small portion of the total funding in special education revealed the incentives associated with classifying students as handicapped. These figures, and analyses of them, did not address the cost associated with classifying students and providing services to them.

Information about how federal monies are being spent in exemplary ways is interesting and serves one of the purposes of reporting to Congress (i.e., that the money is being well spent). From a policy perspective, however, more critical analyses of these figures are revealing. Recall that "data on percentage of population served . . . show a more or less steady increase between 1977 and 1987" (U.S. Dept. of Education, 1988b, p. 3) and that the number of learning disabled students increased by more than 140 percent during this time. These increases in student population statistics have social, political, and economic implications. For example, the steady increase in ECIA-SOP State Formula Grant Funding from 1966 to 1979 resulted in corresponding increases in per pupil allocations; put another way, the growth in the exceptional student population did not adversely affect the federal funding balance over those years. But from 1980 to 1987, relatively stable funding was coupled with consistent decreases (i.e., $620 to $588) in per pupil allocations.

FIGURE 3.3   Relation between federal funding and per pupil expenditures under EHA-B

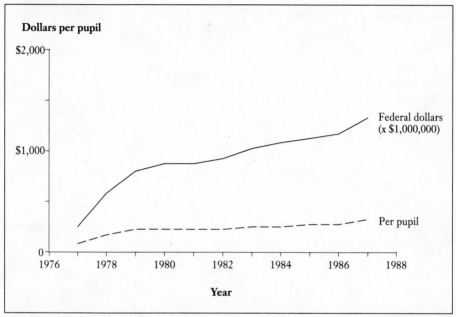

SOURCE: U.S. Department of Education. (1988b). *Tenth annual report to Congress on the implementation of the Education of the Handicapped Act.* Washington, D.C.: USDOE.

Proponents of categorical perspectives in special education often cite funding as an advantage of labeling students (Hallahan & Kauffman, 1988; Heward & Orlansky, 1989; Kirk & Gallagher, 1989). For example, among the "possible benefits of labeling," Heward and Orlansky noted that "funding of special education is often based on specific categories of exceptionality" (1989, p. 11). Clearly, federal documents do support the perceived importance of categories. Nevertheless, the logic of basing funding on categories is not established, and evidence exists suggesting that categorical funding is not necessary. For example, federal funds allocated under Part H of EHA to expand and improve the provision of early intervention programs for infants and toddlers are not distributed by category; in fact, a high relation ($r = 0.963$) exists between total numbers of students and federal dollars allocated. States with large student populations (e.g., California, Florida) receive larger allocations, and states with less students receive smaller allocations (with no state receiving less than $244,444). Federal, state, and local funds can be allocated without classifying students. Therefore, why is it necessary to continue classifying them when evidence suggests it is scientifically and practically difficult to do so?

TABLE 3.7   Federal spending patterns under EHA-B

Fiscal Year	State Grants Expenditures	Per Child Allocation	Student Population
1976–1977	$251,769,927	$72	3,485,088
1977–1978	566,030,074	159	3,554,554
1978–1979	804,000,000	217	3,693,593
1979–1980	874,500,000	230	3,802,475
1980–1981	874,500,000	222	3,933,981
1981–1982	931,008,000	233	3,990,346
1982–1983	1,017,900,000	251	4,052,595
1983–1984	1,068,875,000	261	4,094,108
1984–1985	1,135,145,000	276	4,113,312
1985–1986	1,163,282,000	282	4,121,104
1986–1987	1,338,000,000	315	4,166,692

SOURCE: U.S. Department of Education. (1988b). *Tenth annual report to Congress on the implementation of the Education of the Handicapped Act.* Washington, D.C.: Author, Table 1, p. 4 and Table 28, p. 75.

FIGURE 3.4   Relation between federal funding and per pupil expenditures under ECIA-SOP

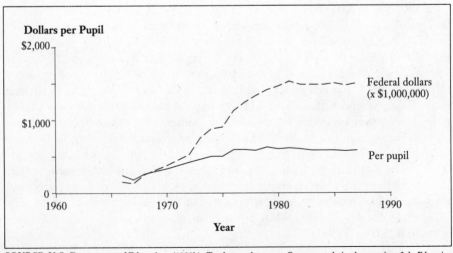

SOURCE: U.S. Department of Education. (1988b). *Tenth annual report to Congress on the implementation of the Education of the Handicapped Act.* Washington, D.C.: USDOE.

A Perspective on Reports to Congress

Section 618(f) (1) of EHA-B requires the secretary of education to transmit to Congress an annual report that describes the *progress* being made in implementing the act. These reports have become a rich source of information about numbers of students being served and a grand repository of other special education facts. Their value clearly lies in the definitions readers assign to the progress associated with providing education for students with handicaps.

If readers define progress as more students being classified, more money being allocated, and more questions being answered, then the *Tenth Annual Report* is evidence of progress. If readers define progress as student improvement in special education, special educators' willing assumption of new roles, and a dearth of unanswered questions, then the *Tenth Annual Report* is more a measure of reality and less a measure of improvement than it probably should be.

Clearly, annual reporting about efforts to meet the special learning needs of students who are handicapped is a rich source of power for those willing to wade through evidence of progress and treat it as evidence of need. As Greenburg suggested:

> Many practitioners face the conflict of feeling both a part of and far removed from federal policies, practices, and priorities. The reality of day-to-day service delivery may or may not be reflected in the concerns of federal officials. Nevertheless, we all have personal responsibility to continue communicating front-line issues and concerns to those in positions to effect public policy. (1989, p. 13)

Continued analysis of special education practices and discussions related to them will go a long way in improving services if professionals make the receipt of facts about special education the basis for action.

Discussion Questions

1. Students in some categories represent large numbers of the people who receive special education, while students in other categories require more intensive services than others. What effects do these facts have on social, political, economic, and educational attitudes, perspectives, and practices?

2. Special education is a subsystem of regular education. How does the condition of special education influence the condition of regular education?

3. What information should be used to judge the condition of special education? Who should be responsible for collecting, compiling, and reporting it?

4. What effect does growth in numbers of students classified as emotionally disturbed have on the condition of special education?

Definitional Debate in Special Education

"When I use a word," Humpty Dumpty said, in a rather scornful tone, "it means just what I choose it to mean—neither more nor less."

—*Lewis Carroll*
Through the Looking Glass
and What Alice Found There

Categories of special education do not exist in and of themselves. They are constructs given meaning and life through comparison of performance to criteria. Blindness is a name assigned to visual performance judged different from that called average or normal. Giftedness and mental retardation are names assigned to intellectual performance judged different from that called average or normal. Criteria accepted as evidence for a condition form the cornerstones of a definition. Definition is the cornerstone for the existence of the condition. For all practical purposes, without definitions there are no categories. Myers and Hammill put it well with regard to learning disabilities:

Before 1965, local, state, and federal education agencies did not officially recognize learning disabled as a category of handicapped individuals, that is, as a *defined* group of individuals whose special education or other treatment needs could be paid for with public money. As a result, there were few classes for learning disabled children, fewer remedial or habilitation facilities for youths and adults, and almost no college preparation programs in the learning disabilities area. (1990, p. 3; emphasis added)

They also remarked that with formal definition, learning disabilities has become "a legally constituted category of handicapped students, the use of the term has become pervasive in American education, and the number of students said to have learning disabilities is larger than any other group of handicapped students" (p. 3). (How things change with official definition and sanction!)

Interestingly, too, no area of special education has generated more controversy and debate than that of defining learning disabilities (Myers & Hammill, 1990; Ysseldyke & Algozzine, 1982, 1984, 1990). Fueled by burgeoning masses of students being identified as eligible for special education services, concern has centered on finding the "right" definition for this condition. Right has come to mean the definition that produces the right number of students—a goal shadowed by searches for the "real" students with learning disabilities. Clearly, definitions drive conditions; without definitions there are no conditions in ways that are important to a profession (e.g., funding, teacher preparation programs, facilities).

Creating conditions and categories generates problems. For example, in his seminal work on classification and labels, Hobbs noted that "only when one looks beyond definitions, beyond categories, beyond labels, and examines the needs of individual children can he break away from the familiar but inadequate solutions manifested in current arrangements for exceptional children" (1975, pp. 181–182). In that same work, Goldstein, Arkell, Ashcroft, Hurley, and Lilly (1975) identified the following disadvantages of then-current classification systems:

• Classification systems reinforced the belief that school failure was primarily the responsibility of the student.

• Classification systems (and related lists of characteristics) reinforced simplistic generalizations about what people could do.

• Classification systems (and related labels) served as explanations for, rather than simple descriptions of, behavior.

• Classification systems downplayed the importance of teacher-pupil interactions as central to success in school.

Classifying students and assigning labels to them are not benign activities. They affect the people who do the labeling and the people who receive the labels; they also affect the people who live and work with people who receive the labels. Blackman referred to children who receive special education because they have or *have been assigned a disability* as "children with negative school labels" (1989, p. 459).

This situation raises several questions: What criteria are the basis for assigning these labels? What concerns and debates consistently surface when definitions are developed and evaluated? Have all categories of children with negative school labels been similarly affected by labeling? Clearly, debate about defining and classifying students according to the definitions has not produced negative effects in terms of growth or interest. But such debate has consistently been a source of task force formulations and professional flagellation in some areas of special education more than in others.

Hardware Versus Software

The function of definitions in special and remedial education is to provide a conceptual model for understanding the condition(s) created by the act of defining. In addition, definitions provide the bases from which identification practices evolve. When we know what we are looking for, we have some indication of how to find it. Note, however, that the categories or names assigned to the observed differences in other people do not represent real "things." The meanings of the terms used to refer to these categories (for example, idiocy, mental retardation, learning disability, blindness) depend on purposes the people who use the terms have for assigning them to students. Bogdan and Taylor offered the following examples:

> Some have argued [that] mental retardation is a social construction or a concept which exists in the minds of the "judges" rather than in the minds of the "judged." . . . A mentally retarded person is one who has been labeled as such according to rather arbitrarily created and applied criteria.
>
> *Retardation*, and other such clinical labels, suggests generalizations about the nature of men and women to whom the term has been applied. . . . We assume that the mentally retarded possess common characteristics that allow them to be unambiguously distinguished from all others. We explain their behavior by special theories. It is as though humanity can be divided into two groups, the "normal" and the "retarded." (1976, p. 47)

Sarason and Doris put it this way: "Mental retardation is not a thing you can see or touch or define in terms of shape and substance. It is a *concept* serving two major purposes: to separate a group of people; and to justify social action in regard to those who set apart" (1979, p. 11; emphasis added).

The position we take is that learning disability, emotional disturbance or handicap, underachievement, blindness, deafness, and other special education categories are simply terms people use to refer to concepts that they have constructed to confirm a belief that people in this society differ from one another. These categories are also used to explain people's behavior.

The definitions created to describe people with special learning needs fall into two groups: those definitions that have a sensory basis and functional disability or handicap (that is, blindness, deafness) associated with them and those that have a psychometric basis and assigned disability or handicap (that is, learning disabilities, mental retardation) associated with them. Conditions in special education have different origins or bases. Some conditions are grounded in performances measured primarily by hardware (i.e., machines or instruments) that provides objective scores. For example, visual functioning is evaluated by machines such as the Keystone Telebinocular and the Lomb Orthorater. When screening instruments such as a Snellen Wall Chart are used, decision making becomes more subjective.

In decision making for categories such as blindness and deafness, multiple measures of the same type of performance do not generally provide different results. For example, a person typically does not have 20/60 vision on a vision screening based on the Snellen Wall Chart and 20/80 based on another instrument. Similarly, it is not the case that a person is blind with one instrument and normally sighted with another or that normally sighted people are consistently misidentified using certain vision tests. In sensory based conditions, there is a widely accepted standard for measuring performance, and criteria for identification using it are more likely to be universally accepted. The procedures for identifying some of these conditions are so transparent and universally accepted that professionals have endorsed home versions (see box) for distribution in popular magazines (Yeager, 1990).

In contrast, virtually any published test, observation, or interview can be used in making decisions about conditions (e.g., mental retardation, emotional disturbance) that have a psychometric basis, and considerable controversy surrounds special education categories that are based primarily on scores on commercially available pencil and paper tests or on classroom observations and interpersonal interviews. To illustrate, consider that a student can be classified as emotionally disturbed in a school district that uses one behavioral checklist and not classified as emotionally disturbed in a neighboring district that uses a different checklist or screening procedure. And even though this could happen to students with visual handicaps, it seldom does. Similarly, students are identified as learning disabled if differences between scores on tests of intelligence and academic achievement are significant. Virtually any test of intelligence and any test of academic achievement can be used in making this decision, and the magnitude of the difference can be determined by any number of commonly used practices.

The flux created when such educational software is the basis for special education identification is evident in decision-making practices with unacceptable validity and reliability. Instruments that produce scores that are open to large degrees of interpretation produce soft signs of disability and create problems for professionals concerned with the integrity of the identification system. Such use permits criteria that vary with the whims of society. "Both the label and definition can lead to different conceptualizations of what constitutes a disorder depending upon how one understands and uses them" (Center, 1990, p. 141). An analysis

The Reader's Digest Home Eye Test

By Robert C. Yeager

Technical associates:
Weylin G. Eng, O.D., and George W. Weinstein, M.D.

TEST NO. 1: ADULT "E" TEST

GOAL: To measure your visual acuity.
1. Fasten the "E" chart to the wall at eye level.
2. Stand ten feet from the chart. Wear any lenses you normally use.
3. Cover your left eye.
4. Begin with the largest E's. Can you tell which direction their "legs" are pointing? Continue to the lowest line on which you can clearly see at least half the E's.
5. Repeat with the other eye.

If you can read line 4 or lower, you've passed. If you can't read line 4, or can't make out the same line with each eye, schedule an appointment with your eye doctor.

TEST NO. 3: CHILD'S "E" TEST

GOAL: To help determine if your child needs glasses or has amblyopia—lazy eye.
1. Have the child stand ten feet from the "E" chart, wearing any lenses he normally uses.
2. Gently cover his left eye. (Watch out for peeking.)
3. Tell the child to pretend the E's are tables and to point in the same direction as the table legs. Begin with the largest E. (You may need to point to each letter.)
4. Stop when the child reaches the lowest line on which he can clearly identify at least half the E's.
5. Repeat with the left eye. To guard against memorizing, have the child read the rows backward.

Scoring for visual acuity is the same as in the adult "E" test. If the pinhole test improves the child's vision, he may simply need glasses. If, however, one eye scores more than two lines poorer than the other, your child may have amblyopia or another eye problem, and should see a vision specialist at once.

The Reader's Digest Home Eye Test (cont.)

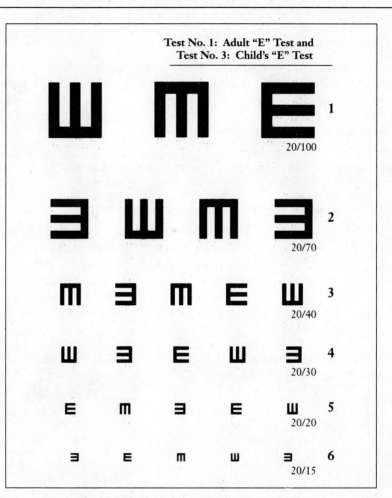

Test No. 1: Adult "E" Test and
Test No. 3: Child's "E" Test

1   20/100

2   20/70

3   20/40

4   20/30

5   20/20

6   20/15

SOURCE: Excerpted with permission from "The Reader's Digest Home Eye Test" by Robert C. Yeager, *Reader's Digest*, September 1990, pp. 93–100.

of current special education conditions illustrates the basis for identification and provides information about the historical dilemmas associated with definitions for these categories.

Blindness

Blindness was first legally defined in 1935 by the Social Security Act (Hatlin, Hall, & Tuttle, 1980). Students in this category represent less than 1 percent of those receiving special education (U.S. Dept. of Education, 1990; Ysseldyke & Algozzine, 1990). The National Society for the Prevention of Blindness offered the following definitions of blindness and partial sight:

> Blindness is generally defined in the United States as visual acuity for distance vision of 20/200 or less in the better eye, with acuity of more than 20/200 if the widest diameter of field of vision subtends an angle no greater than 20 degrees.
> The partially seeing are defined as persons with a visual acuity greater than 20/200 but not greater than 20/70 in the better eye with correction. (1966, p. 10)

The exact criterion (20/200 rather than 20/100) for blindness or partial sight is subjective but is founded on objective standards that reflect similar functional difficulties among people who are similarly defined. Application of these criteria has not resulted in excessive numbers of students being classified, and little controversy has surfaced with regard to the appropriateness of using them.

Deafness

Moores gave two definitions of people with sensory problems related to hearing. Each differs from the other on the extent of hearing loss:

> A "deaf person" is one whose hearing is disabled to an extent (usually 70 dB ISO or greater) that precludes the understanding of speech through the ear alone, without or with the use of a hearing aid.
> A "hard of hearing" person is one whose hearing is disabled to an extent (usually 35 to 69 dB ISO) that makes difficult, but does not preclude, the understanding of speech through the ear alone, without or with a hearing aid. (1978, p. 5)

The definitions of blindness/deafness and associated functioning have changed little over time. Students in each of these categories represent less than 1 percent of those receiving special education (U.S. Dept. of Education, 1990b; Ysseldyke & Algozzine, 1990). Defining conditions of special education through the use of hardware has produced conditions characterized by little definitional controversy and relatively low prevalence rates.

Physical and Health Impairments

In recent years, about 2 percent of students receiving special education have been classified as orthopedically or other health impaired (Ysseldyke & Algozzine,

1990). Definitions for these conditions illustrate the functional impairments associated with some special education categories. For example, federal rules and regulations define orthopedic handicap as an "impairment which adversely affects a child's educational performance. The term includes impairments caused by congenital anomaly (e.g., clubfoot, absence of some member, etc.), impairments caused by disease (e.g., poliomyelitis, bone tuberculosis, etc.), and impairments from other causes (e.g., cerebral palsy, amputations, and fractures or burns which cause contracture)."

Because of the obvious nature of some of their problems, people with physical disabilities have been mistrusted and mistreated in the past. As a result of the medical, measurable nature of some of their problems, however, people with orthopedic and health impairments are less often misidentified than people with disabilities whose assignation is based on psychometric performances. Because range of motion and other bodily functions are measured using clinical hardware, definitions for specific conditions fluctuate little, and specific types of orthopedic and health impairments are seldom confused. And even though controversy surrounding these conditions has arisen (e.g., autism currently considered a health impairment was formerly considered part of emotional disturbance and more generally part of developmental disabilities), it has been minimal.

Changing Definition of Mental Retardation

The *Manual on Terminology and Classification in Mental Retardation* defined mental retardation as "significantly subaverage general intellectual functioning existing concurrently with deficits in adaptive behavior, and manifested during the developmental period" (Grossman, 1973, p. 11). This definition is similar to others that have been devised since the development of intelligence tests: mental retardation is a condition characterized by abnormal intellectual functioning. The basis for this conception was the work of Binet and Simon, who recognized the need for a *"precise basis for differential diagnosis. . . .* We do not think that we are going too far in saying that at the present time very few physicians would be able to cite with absolute precision the objective and invariable sign, or signs, by which they distinguish the degrees of inferior mentality" (1916, p. 335). What would probably come as a surprise to Binet and Simon is that there is no absolute, objective, and invariable sign of mental retardation; indeed, intelligence, the sign that comes the closest and is the most frequently used, is also a construct that has defied definition and remains the center of controversy (cf. Gardner, 1983; Sarason & Doris, 1979; Sternberg, 1985; Thorndike & Lohman, 1990).

When Binet discovered a way to measure a construct that was thought to reflect an important social concern, his work became the basis for subsequent conceptualizations of mental retardation. Over time, professionals have struggled with defining levels of intelligence and identifying cutoff scores for establishing a category. As Robinson and Robinson noted:

> The most significant change in 1973 as compared with the 1959 definition [of mental retardation] is a return to a *more traditional cut-off score,* two standard deviations below the mean. The 1959 definition had defined "borderline retardation" as intelligence only one standard deviation below the mean and thereby had tended to shift the emphasis from the severely retarded to the much larger group with mild and borderline retardation. (1976, p. 31)

From 1959 to 1973, a student with subaverage general intellectual functioning that was one standard deviation below the mean was likely to be classified as retarded; after 1973, that same student was not considered retarded. The label then applied only to students whose intellectual functioning was at least two standard deviations below the mean. Thus, many students ceased to be retarded simply by a pen stroke of the American Association on Mental Deficiency. And even though reasons for changing criteria make sense (e.g., too many minority students placed in programs; federal, state, and local litigation; excessive demand relative to teacher supply), the ease and acceptability with which change occurs illustrate problems inherent in using purely psychometric criteria in decision making.

LD or Not LD

According to the most recent definition by the U.S. Department of Education, the term *specific learning disability*

> means a disorder in one or more of the basic psychological processes involved in understanding or in using language, spoken or written, which may manifest itself in an imperfect ability to listen, think, read, write, spell, or to do mathematical calculations. The term includes such conditions as perceptual handicaps, brain injury, minimal brain dysfunction, dyslexia, and developmental aphasia. The term does not include children who have learning problems which are primarily the result of visual, hearing, or motor handicaps, or mental retardation, or emotional disturbance, or environmental, cultural, or economic disadvantage.

Although the primary manifestation of specific learning disability is imperfect ability in important school-related areas, the definition itself offers no basis for differentiating a child with learning disabilities from a school underachiever. The criteria for determining the condition of learning disability, which are outlined in the same *Federal Register,* add very little to the specifics necessary to identify imperfect abilities and/or to quantify achievement that is not commensurate with assumed ability. Although these guidelines for applying the federal definition of learning disability suggest that the discrepancy between ability and achievement should be severe, no standards for determining when a discrepancy is "severe" are given; thus local or state education agencies must flesh out the skeletal structure offered by the federal agency. So, like early educators faced with carrying out decisions relating to the nation's "simpletons," contemporary educators dealing with other, more subjective, highly prevalent, and popular notions of disability or deviance must also rely on a standard that can be "adapted to different localities and conditions of society" (see Howe, 1848, p. 13).

In work at the Institute for Research on Learning Disabilities, Ysseldyke and his colleagues examined overlap among categorical groups in performance on psychometric measures and the extent to which diagnostic personnel could differentiate clinically among special education groups. In one such investigation, more than forty tests were administered to forty-nine students called learning disabled by their schools and to fifty low-achieving students who scored below the twenty-fifth percentile on a group-administered achievement test. Performances on intellectual, achievement, and perceptual-motor tests; on measures of classroom behavior; and on self-concept tests showed an average of 96 percent overlap between groups, thereby making it difficult psychometrically to differentiate between low-achieving students and those labeled learning disabled (Ysseldyke, Algozzine, Shinn, & McGue, 1982). In a follow-up study (Ysseldyke & Algozzine, 1983), professionals were asked to review the scores of students called learning disabled and low-achieving students and to use clinical judgment to identify those students who were learning disabled. Using both school placement and the federal definition as criteria, professionals consistently were right about half the time. Both investigations provided evidence that professionals had difficulty trying to differentiate, either psychometrically or clinically, between low-achieving students and those called learning disabled by school personnel.

In an article in the *Journal of Learning Disabilities* addressing screening and diagnosis in the "future of the LD field," Algozzine and Ysseldyke summarized their research related to classification:

> While many school identified learning disabled students do meet commonly applied criteria (e.g., 15 point difference between ability and achievement, subtest scatter), some do not. . . . Many low-achieving students, never classified as LD, also meet these same criteria . . . and many normal students are classifiable using these criteria. . . . In fact, the overlap in scores for many of these students is so great . . . that it is difficult for them not to be classified when commonly used criteria are applied to performance estimates on commonly used assessment devices. (1986, p. 396)

Recent attempts to redefine LD have done little to create a condition with diagnostic purity greater than that created by operationalizing the commonly used federal definition.

Variance in Gifted and Talented Identification

There is much disagreement about concepts underlying the definition of gifted and talented and in procedures applied to identify students who are gifted and talented (Algozzine & Algozzine, 1990; Gallagher, 1988; Hagen, 1980). According to Algozzine and Ysseldyke:

> The history of classification is replete with examples of definitional changes and dilemmas provoked by dissatisfaction with the current practice; those who champion the cause of gifted students argue over the appropriateness of intellectual cutoff scores and how much creativity, task, commitment, and other variables should be considered in diagnostic efforts. (1987, p. 55)

Cohn, Cohn, and Kanevsky in their discussion of giftedness pointed out that the variety of definitions, strategies, and instruments that can be used to identify or select students is infinite; "this diversity contributes to the confusion one meets in attempting to estimate the number of truly gifted individuals" (1988, p. 460).

The extent to which the category of gifted and talented varies from state to state and in relation to the major special education classifications was investigated by Shriner, Ysseldyke, Franklin, and Gorney (1990). They studied the variability among states in their definitions of gifted and talented students and the subjective use of these definitions as evidenced by state criteria and guidelines for classification. They found that a majority of states followed the current federal definition, which included "children who give evidence of high performance capability in areas such as intellectual, creative, artistic, leadership capacity, or specific academic fields and who require services or activities not ordinarily provided by the school in order to fully develop such capabilities." Some states still followed the 1978 federal definition, which included psychomotor ability as a qualifying area, and other states developed their own definitions using the federal definition as a point of reference. States actively sought subjective data and subjective evaluations in identification procedures for the gifted; at least eight states (Hawaii, Minnesota, Tennessee, New Jersey, Idaho, Iowa, Maryland, and Virginia) identified "subjective data" or "expert opinion" as necessary in determining eligibility, and one state included the phrase "inclusion of 5–10 % 'gut instinct' in the rating, selection, and placement sections of their guidelines" (p. 5). Shriner et al. also found that definitional variability and subjectivity had been highlighted as key issues in gifted identification practices, and they demonstrated that depending on the statistic of choice, the category of gifted was as variable as, if not more than, the categories of learning disabled, educable mentally retarded, and emotionally disturbed. This is hardly a surprise given the "soft" base that characterizes definitions of gifted and talented and identification practices that necessarily derive from them.

EBD, ED, EH, BD, SM, SED, SLBP, EI, or EIEIO

Verbal subjectivity and word play that may be fine for fairy tales and children's stories present significant problems when evident in definitional practices in special education. For instance, current government regulations define seriously emotionally disturbed as follows:

> (i) The term means a condition exhibiting one or more of the following characteristics over a long period of time and to a marked degree, which adversely affects educational performance: (a) an inability to learn which cannot be explained by intellectual, sensory, or health factors; (b) an inability to build or maintain satisfactory interpersonal relationships with peers and teachers; (c) inappropriate

types of behavior or feelings under normal circumstances; (d) a general pervasive mood of unhappiness or depression; or (e) a tendency to develop physical symptoms or fears associated with personal or school problems. (ii) The term includes children who are schizophrenic or autistic. The term does not include children who are socially maladjusted, unless it is determined that they are seriously emotionally disturbed.

Interestingly, this definition is similar to that used in the early 1960s and to a more recent description of children who have less severe emotional handicaps or behavior problems (cf. Bower, 1969, 1982; Kauffman, 1980, 1989a; Nelson & Rutherford, 1990; Reinert, 1967; Shea, 1978). Bower (1982) noted that the first section of the federal definition was an exact restatement of his earlier work. He also indicated that section (ii) did not appear in the original definition and appeared to him to be a "codicil to reassure traditional psychopathologists and budget personnel that schizophrenia and autism are indeed serious emotional disturbance on the one hand, and that just plain bad boys and girls, predelinquents, and sociopaths will not skyrocket costs on the other hand" (p. 56). Unquestionably, especially with moderate and high-prevalence conditions, social, political, and economic motives may drive practice more than do sound pedagogical policies or profound principles (Ysseldyke & Algozzine, 1990). Because people make up the definitions, they can decide who is included and excluded by the words they write and the categories they imply.

The exclusion of social maladjustment from the category of serious emotional disturbance has created significant concern among professionals engaged in special education of students with behavioral disorders (cf. Bower, 1982; CCBD, 1990a; Center, 1990; Cline, 1990; Nelson & Rutherford, 1990; Weinberg & Weinberg, 1990; Wood, 1990). As Nelson and Rutherford pointed out, "One of the factors affecting the abilities of policy makers and researchers to clarify this issue is the lack of a generally accepted definition of social maladjustment" (1990, p. 38). The problem is clear-cut: the definition of serious emotional disturbance excludes a group of students without defining them. It is as if professionals had defined mental retardation as significantly subaverage intelligence without having an accepted standard for intelligence. And the problem is further complicated by the absence of any valid evidence or thought justifying the separation of social maladjustment and emotional disturbance (Grosenick & Huntze, 1980).

The consequences of definitional confusion are professional debate and practical absurdity. For example, "vast differences exist among the states regarding the percentage of special education students served as seriously emotionally disturbed" (Weinberg & Weinberg, 1990, p. 149). Estimates vary from less than 1 percent to more than 25 percent of the student population in some states (U.S. Dept. of Education, 1988b), and "varying interpretations" of the federal definition have been blamed for these disparities (Weinberg & Weinberg, 1990, p. 149). It is not difficult to see that different numbers of students will be identified based on how the social maladjustment exclusionary clause is interpreted; there is evidence that it is completely ignored in many state definitions (Center, 1990; Mack, 1985).

Likewise, educators regularly debate alternative explanations for observed differences. Hallahan, Keller, and Ball compared prevalence rates for categories of exceptional students. They reported that the category of learning disabilities was less variable than other categories and concluded that "definition and identification criteria for learning disabilities are at least as well articulated, and perhaps more so, than those for other categories in special education" (1986, p. 13). Algozzine and Ysseldyke took issue with the Hallahan et al. analysis and argued that high-prevalence categories (learning disabled, speech/language impaired, mentally retarded, emotional/behavioral disorders) had more variable prevalence rates because they were more subjectively defined than were low-prevalence categories (physical and other health impaired, hearing impaired). Algozzine and Ysseldyke stated that "the conclusions one makes about variance in prevalence are a function of the methods one uses to examine differences among prevalence rates" (1987, p. 32).

The consequences of using software-based decisions is clearly evident in efforts to identify and classify students as behaviorally disordered, emotionally disturbed, seriously emotionally disturbed, emotionally handicapped, emotionally/behaviorally disordered, or other psychometrically based conditions. Professionals argue about the terms to be applied to the condition, and typically there is no universal acceptance of a term across service delivery systems (i.e., states and agencies within them). This softness spills over to produce wide variation in numbers of students served in different locations (see Table 4.1) and to create considerable disagreement among professionals as to what exactly is a (insert a category name of your choice in appropriate form) student. For example, in addition to continued debate over similarities and differences between students with learning disabilities and other low-achieving students, professionals identify subtypes of students as more or as less evidence of "real" students with learning disabilities. And arguments about the importance of creativity, motivation, task commitment, and intellectual ability continue to motivate and frustrate people concerned with educating students who are gifted. And the answer to the question "Who are the *real* (insert label) students" is, "Nobody knows."

Categorical Drift

Definitions used to create categories in special education are based on prevailing professional opinions about the nature and characteristics of students who fail to profit from the educational experiences provided in regular education programs. Because these opinions are constantly changing, special education's categories should be considered ephemeral representations for people with special learning needs that leave the field susceptible to categorical drift. This situation is evident when professionals name and rename groups of students to meet socially accepted value systems and thereby please important constituencies. Categorical drift is also evident when students move easily among supposedly distinct groups and

TABLE 4.1   Variation in numbers of students served

State	Learning Disabled	SI	Mentally Retarded	ED
		Condition		
Hawaii (6.64%)	[92%] 3.81	1.24	0.62	0.45
Nevada (7.86%)	[95%] 4.77	1.70	0.51	0.48
Idaho (7.88%)	[95%] 4.71	1.46	1.13	0.21
Texas (8.53%)	[93%] 4.82	1.78	0.62	0.69
Tennessee (10.94%)	[93%] 5.69	2.77	1.42	0.29
Alabama (11.56%)	[96%] 3.90	3.06	3.39	0.77
Connecticut (11.75%)	[96%] 6.35	1.94	0.68	2.30
Rhode Island (12.92%)	[96%] 8.66	2.17	0.61	1.00
New Jersey (13.93%)	[95%] 7.03	4.55	0.42	1.18
Massachusetts (15.55%)	[93%] 5.46	3.55	3.28	2.13
All states, District of Columbia, and Puerto Rico (9.83%)	[94%] 4.71	2.39	1.25	0.89

NOTE: Numbers are percentages based on estimates of enrollment. Numbers in parentheses are totals for all conditions; numbers in brackets are percentages of total represented by the four conditions.

SOURCE: U.S. Department of Education. (1990b). *Twelfth annual report to Congress on the implementation of the Education of the Handicapped Act*. Washington, D.C.: Author, Table AA25.

thereby begin to look like a psychometric Dow Jones average rather than clinical cases (e.g., special education increased substantially for the fourth year in a row; fueled in large part by continuing and large increases in learning disabilities, coupled with corresponding but smaller decreases in mental retardation, special education remains the growth profession of the 1990s). Categorical drift surfaces when similarities between groups blend to the extent that larger, less specific names (e.g., varying exceptionalities, mildly handicapped, educationally handicapped) serve as generic titles for classrooms and students. Categorical drift can also be found regarding some conditions of special education more than others.

Definitions based on hardware are founded, at least, on measurable phenomena; that is, the distance a person can see or the level at which a person can hear can surely be measured more objectively than the information a person knows or the intelligence level a person demonstrates. The former conditions are much less susceptible to categorical drift. Even so, it is still difficult to define them. For example, what is the appropriate definition for a person whose measured hearing is 68 dB ISO (within the hard-of-hearing range of 35–69 dB ISO) but whose ability to hear is disabled to the extent that it precludes understanding speech through the ear alone? More pervasive problems relative to mashing of categories are evident in the use of definitions based on software such as those for learning disabilities, emotional disturbance, and mental retardation.

Numbers Tell a Story

One important reason for defining categories of disabilities is that people are then able to evaluate the extent or pervasiveness of the problem. For example, having defined blindness, researchers can count the number of people who fall within that definition and are therefore "blind" and then can determine the course and direction of the social policies for these disabled persons. Similarly, having defined mental retardation, professionals can estimate the extent of the problem and construct programs to remedy it. The number of students served as mentally retarded has declined steadily since 1976; the decrease has averaged 3 percent a year (U.S. Dept. of Education, 1990b). Reasons proposed for this and other variations in numbers of students served clearly illustrate that categorical drift is a product of contemporary special education practice.

> Some professionals and parents seek to classify educationally handicapped children as learning disabled, developmentally delayed, or developmental disabled, rather than mentally retarded. Also, criteria for identification of mental retardation have gradually become more exclusive. For example, in 1973 the American Association on Mental Deficiency lowered the IQ ceiling for mental retardation to 70 IQ points. (Previously, a person with an IQ up to 85 could be classified as mentally retarded). In 1983, the association added, as a co-requisite element in the definition, deficits in adaptive behavior. In addition, litigation which stipulated that placement of many minority group children in special classes had been based on discriminatory assessment and classification procedures . . . has had a major impact on State and local placement practices. (p. 16)

Broader strokes are used to explain interstate variation in percentages of students served in special education.

> It may be that State-to-State variation in the percentage of students served is related to State classification procedures, resulting in greater or lesser numbers of students identified as requiring special education services. Use of pre-referral interventions in some States may reduce the number of students assessed or identified for special education service needs. Other causes of State-to-State variation may include: data reporting practices; State funding formulas; and differences in student populations. (p. 2)

When people admit that definitions are at best arbitrary attempts to objectify social, political, and moral constructs, they will have a better basis for understanding the problems created by such a system. Until that time, considerable effort will likely be expended in a search for the "right" students to place in special education classes; we predict that such effort will be largely unproductive.

Make Mine Mild

All the ambiguity created by efforts to come up with a precise basis for differential diagnosis generates controversies in special education that cause professionals to redefine and question practice. Evidence the consistent use of the term *mildly handicapped* without a widely accepted definition for it (Ramsey, Algozzine, & Henley, in press) and without a justifiable basis for using it (i.e., there is nothing mild about a student three to five years behind in school, or functioning socially at levels significantly below those of peers, or suffering serious childhood depression). As boundaries between categories meld, questions of instructional effectiveness and appropriateness become relevant, and at the highest levels distinctions between special and regular education become questionable (Lipsky & Gartner, 1989; Stainback, Stainback, & Forest, 1989; Will, 1986; Ysseldyke & Algozzine, 1990). The implications of categorical drift, whether from blending similarities to generic classes (e.g., varying exceptionalities), moving students between and within categories, or creating new, more acceptable names present serious questions for the continued existence of special education as an educational subsystem that supports categorical differentiation of students with special learning needs. The problems associated with classifying mild learning problems are evident in analyses of relations between classification and intervention practices.

Recently, increasing interest has been focused on students with attention deficit disorders (Abidoff, 1991; American Psychiatric Association, 1987; Anastopoulos, DuPaul, & Barkley, 1991; Atkins & Pelham, 1991; Atkins, Pelham & White, 1990; Silver, 1990). An analysis of the characteristics of these students suggests that common school problems are associated with this condition. For example, according to criteria in the *Diagnostic and Statistical Manual (DSM III)* of the American Psychiatric Association,

> to diagnose a child as having [ADHD] s/he must display for six months or more at least eight of the following characteristics before the age of seven:
>
> 1. Fidgets, squirms or seems restless
> 2. Has difficulty remaining seated
> 3. Is easily distracted
> 4. Has difficulty awaiting turn
> 5. Blurts out answers
> 6. Has difficulty following instructions
> 7. Has difficulty sustaining attention
> 8. Shifts from one uncompleted task to another
> 9. Has difficulty playing quietly
> 10. Talks excessively
> 11. Interrupts or intrudes on others
> 12. Does not seem to listen

13. Often loses things necessary for tasks

14. Frequently engages in dangerous actions. (in CHADD, 1988, unnumbered p. 1)

Clearly, large numbers of students will be eligible for services when a definition built on these software-based characteristics undergirds the condition. To some extent, one could argue that professionals should be concerned when a child *does not* demonstrate these characteristics before the age of seven. Observations of characteristics such as "talks excessively," "is easily distracted," and "does not seem to listen" can be made, but standards for inappropriate levels of such behaviors are nonexistent. More importantly, levels of these characteristics are most often derived from interviews with people living and working with the child, rather than from the child. The futility of separately classifying students with such broad, generic psychometric characteristics is further illustrated by analyzing "interventions" recommended for teaching students with conditions like ADHD (see p. 112). Virtually any student can profit from these recommendations, and there is only a marginal link between the condition and the teaching strategies. The absence of a meaningful link between diagnosis and category-specific interventions characterizes all conditions based on soft decision-making processes (Ysseldyke & Algozzine, 1990).

In Search of Students with Real Disabilities

The history of special education is replete with controversy over *the* definition of mental retardation, *the* definition of learning disabilities, and *the* definition of all other types and kinds of special children and youths. As soon as someone comes out with *a* definition, it stimulates other persons to criticize, convene, propose a new definition, and take their turn on the defensive. The main implication of this continuing discussion among professionals is that these definitions do not exist in a vacuum: each change in definition directly or indirectly affects the identification and treatment of children and youths with learning problems. At a round-table conference on the assessment of students with learning disabilities, Lovitt captured the dilemma of professionals when he said:

> I believe that if we continue trying to define learning disabilities by using ill-defined concepts, we will forever be frustrated, for it is an illusive concept. We are being bamboozled. It is as though someone started a great hoax by inventing the term then tempting others to define it. And lo and behold scores of task forces and others have taken the bait. (1978, p. 3)

Similar problems surface with regard to emotional disturbance: "Definition provides the basis for prevalence" (Kauffman, 1980, p. 524). We add that definition is the basis for the existence of the conditions and for the interest in them; without definition, for all practical purposes, there is no category or problem! Lambert recounted an example of the way in which labeling a condition creates interest in it. She stated that during the early 1960s, she and Bower were writing a summary of research in California on students with emotional handicaps in preparation for legislation to be introduced in the state legislature in the winter of 1961. They described different levels of intervention for students based on the degree of handicap:

> Inasmuch as the children we had studied who needed the small group instruction most, and benefited most from it, were those who were significantly behind in their academic subjects, we called them "learning disability groups." When this name appeared in California special education parlance, the search was on to find the deficit responsible for the failure rather than the method to teach the child. It was only a matter of time before the discovery would be made that explanations for significant discrepancies between ability and achievement were many, chief among them failure of the instructional program to provide an appropriate level of tasks for the child as well as appropriately modified regular class learning situations. (1981, p. 200)

Once defined, the importance of the category becomes a function of the number of children assigned to it. For years, the U.S. government estimated that 2 percent of the school population was "disturbed," but recent "child counts" indicated that the figure was actually 0.8 percent (U.S. Dept. of Education, 1988b). Kauffman argued that the reported difference in prevalence stemmed from the differences in identification practices brought about by federal rule making:

> If federal law has had and will continue to have a suppressing effect on identification of most disturbed children, then it is obvious that legal precedent is supplanting, or at least is being used to define, clinical judgment in our society's view of deviance. Bureaucratic-legal domination of our thinking about disordered behavior and the tacit assumption that extralegal considerations are the least pressing issues in special education today may represent advancement or regression, depending on one's view of what forces should move the field forward. To the extent that extralegal judgment is trusted, one could argue that the bureaucratic-legal approach will result in the unfortunate denial of services to many mildly and moderately disturbed children who would benefit from identification and intervention. To the extent that legislation, bureaucratic control, and litigation are trusted as the best means for defining children's deviance, one could rejoice in the fact that social institutions such as schools will be required to tolerate behavioral difference unless it violates standards of conduct that are unassailable in court. (1980, p. 526)

Thus, for instance, if the federal government or any other group of professionals for whatever reason decides that it is time to serve individuals with severe handicaps and either through outright changes in definitions or through financial grants and contract bargaining establishes an interest in children and youths with severe handicaps, interest in identifying and serving youngsters with more moderate or mild handicaps will diminish.

In an editorial entitled "What Happened to Mild and Moderate Mental Retardation?" in the *American Journal of Mental Deficiency*, Haywood noted that despite the plans and good intentions that must have been the basis for the shift in the emphasis of research and service from mild to severe retardation, the outcome has been unfavorable:

It is practically certain that the individuals who pleaded for increased attention to severely and profoundly retarded persons hoped that the increased attention would represent a total increase in scholarly interest, public funds, and services for the entire field of mental retardation, i. e., that additional funds, research, and services directed toward severely and profoundly retarded persons would be "added on" to the existing levels of support for the entire field. What has happened instead has been a shift of resources away from mildly and moderately retarded persons, to such a marked degree that it is frequently quite impossible to obtain public funds to support both research and services in this important area unless one promises to give primary emphasis to those individuals who are severely or profoundly handicapped. (1979, p. 429)

Students receiving special education sometimes exhibit behaviors that interfere with progress in school, and this fact seldom creates controversy within the field. Problems do arise when professionals try to assign names to clusters of behaviors or characteristics and thereby create categories that can be subjected to initial analysis and review. The problems are compounded when names assigned to students serve as signals for lowered expectations for parents or teachers. These problems are not easily resolved.

Creating Categories for the Future

The dilemma that psychologists and educators face is one of their own making: should they provide special services for more students by expanding the definitions of disabilities and court the risks of labeling, or should they provide fewer formal special services by narrowing the definitions of disabilities and hazard denying some students the special supports they need? Obviously, plenty of students are failing in school (see Chapter 3), and professionals can create definitions that characterize many of these students. The problem is that the definitions are conceptual models whose effects cannot be specified. Professionals can say what mental retardation is (for example, subaverage intellectual functioning), but they cannot say what effect will be produced when the definition is applied (for example, special classes enrolling 80 percent boys or disproportionate numbers of minority students). The current definition of mental retardation is a product of the social, political, and moral history of a particular country, state, or other locality, and in this regard we agree with Sarason and Doris, who said:

We are not opposed to definitions in principle, but we are opposed to the lack of recognition that definitions tell us what to exclude as well as what to include. The thrust of this discussion is that by virtue of what definitions of intelligence and mental retardation have excluded, they have contributed to confusion and fruitless controversy. One can live with confusion and fruitless controversy were it not for the fact that these definitions give rise to techniques for measurement which in turn are used to determine policies that will affect the lives of people. In the areas with which we are concerned definitions have not been empty exercises. The quest for clear and rigorous definition was a consequence of society's need to act and deal with what it had come to see as a problem. And if

> the definitions changed over time, it was less because of new knowledge and more because societal attitudes toward the problem had changed. (1979, p. 29)

Historically, there has been considerable interest in the similarities and differences among children who are classified as learning disabled, mentally retarded, and/or emotionally disturbed. Hallahan and Kauffman (1977) discussed the difficulty of identifying differences among students with mild handicaps. Neisworth and Greer pointed out that there was much overlap among the characteristics of some students with mental retardation, learning disabilities, and/or emotional disturbance and indicated that the "degree and nature of such overlap depends, in part, upon the measures employed to describe performance" (1975, p. 19). In this sense, differences among children and youths may be psychometric contrivances, rather than characteristics that have diagnostic or practical importance.

Psychological diagnosis has always been regarded with some suspicion; and as far back as 1924 one observer described the situation as follows:

> Clinical psychology today is more an art than it is a science. In spite of the very marked improvement in clinical technique, one cannot escape the conclusion that mental diagnosis is more subjective than it is objective, and that accuracy of diagnosis is largely a matter of expertness and skill rather than of exact measurement. One of the most important needs of clinical psychology, in view of its wide-spread application and the great social importance of its findings, is greater objectivity. (Doll, 1924, p. 26)

This need for objectivity was also expressed by Rutter in regard to the diagnosis of autism:

> By suggesting autism constituted a syndrome, Kanner meant two things: first, that there were certain behaviors which tended to group together, and second, that these behaviors differed from those found in other psychiatric conditions. Accordingly, the first step was to determine by comparative studies how far this was true in order to clarify the diagnostic criteria. There was a need to find out which symptoms were both universal and specific—that is, those which were present in all or nearly all autistic children and also which were relatively infrequent in children who did not have the syndrome. A differentiation had to be made between behaviors which could occur in autism (but which also occurred in other conditions) and those behaviors which were specifically characteristic of autism. (1978, p. 4)

The search for both universal and specific characteristics of the conditions (for example, mental retardation, learning disability, or any education disability) has been largely fruitless: features that overlap the least (for example, intelligence scores) are themselves constructions; those that overlap the most (for example, overt behaviors) have the least diagnostic or practical value. The search for universal and specific features of various conditions is dependent on the nature of measurement instruments used to identify them and society's need to deal with what it sees as problems. If the definitions are not adequate, they are changed, or new ones are created; and the defining of, searching for, and treating of problems continue with renewed interest.

The most recent evidence of professionals' willingness to be seduced by categories and individual differences is provided by concern for where to place students with attention deficit disorders (ADD). Prior to the 1940s, students having difficulty in school were considered emotionally disturbed, mentally retarded, or physically disabled (e.g., blind, deaf). Research during that time illustrated the relationship between a person's performance on a variety of measures and "soft signs" of abnormal brain functioning (Strauss & Lehtinen, 1947; Werner & Strauss, 1941). The term *minimal brain dysfunction* was coined to refer to the syndrome evidenced by children exhibiting soft signs of neurological dysfunctioning. As Silver indicated, "Using current concepts, the term minimal brain dysfunction referred to children with (a) learning disabilities; (b) difficulties with hyperactivity, distractibility, and impulsivity; and (c) emotional and social problems" (1990, p. 395). The term *attention deficit disorder* was used in *DSM III* to refer to this same group of people, and two subtypes were used to differentiate disorders with and without hyperactivity (American Psychiatric Association, 1982).

According to the education committee of Children with Attention Deficit Disorders (CHADD, 1988), ADD is characterized by serious and persistent difficulties in attention span, impulse control, and hyperactivity (sometimes). A chronic disorder, ADD can begin in infancy and extend through adulthood, having negative effects on life at home, in school, and within the community. The term *attention deficit–hyperactive disorder* appeared in the revised *DSM III* to reflect recent research indicating that hyperactivity was an important factor in this disorder (American Psychiatric Association, 1987). Questions related to the nature, characteristics, and treatment of ADD continue to surface (Silver, 1990).

The passage of the IDEA Amendments of 1990 was delayed by serious debate as to whether ADD should be made a separate category of eligibility for special education services (Reynolds, 1991). Proponents argued that creation of a new (within IDEA) category would serve a growing number of students who needed specialized instruction and who were currently inappropriately labeled as emotionally disturbed or learning disabled. Opponents argued that the category ADD faced serious questions with regard to definition and identification practices. The Council for Exceptional Children's response to inquiry (cf. *Federal Register*, November 29, 1990, p. 49598) regarding issues related to ADD clearly delimited concerns of professionals in opposition to creating a new category. This organization maintained that adding ADD to the list of handicapping conditions under part B of IDEA was unnecessary because students diagnosed with ADD who manifested symptoms severe enough to impair educational performance were currently being served with existing categories. The organization also contended that strategies recommended for teaching students with ADD (see Table 4.2) could easily be implemented in regular classrooms and probably would benefit any students receiving education there. At this writing, the controversy was not resolved.

TABLE 4.2   Teaching strategies for students with ADD

Recommendations for the proper learning environment

1. Seat ADD student near teacher's desk but include as part of regular class seating.
2. Place ADD student up front with his or her back to the rest of the class to keep other students out of view.
3. Surround ADD student with "good role models," preferably students that the ADD child views as "significant others." Encourage peer tutoring and cooperative collaborative learning.
4. Avoid distracting stimuli. Try not to place the ADD student near air conditioning, high traffic areas, heater, or doors or windows.
5. The ADD student does not handle change well, so avoid transitions, physical relocation, changes in schedule, or disruptions; also monitor closely on field trips.
6. Be creative! Produce "stimuli-reduced study area." Let all students have access to this area so the ADD student will not feel different.
7. Encourage parents to set up appropriate study space at home with routines established as far as set times for study, parental review of completed homework, and periodic notebook and/or book bag organized.

Recommendations for giving instructions to students

1. Maintain eye contact with the ADD student during verbal instruction.
2. Make directions clear and concise. Be consistent with daily instructions.
3. Simplify complex directions; avoid multiple commands.
4. Make sure ADD student comprehends before beginning the task.
5. Repeat in a calm, positive manner, if needed.
6. Help ADD student to feel comfortable with seeking assistance (most ADD students will not ask).
7. The ADD student will need more help for a longer period of time than the average student will. Gradually reduce assistance.
8. Require a daily assignment notebook if necessary.
    a. Make sure student correctly writes down all assignments each day. If the student is not capable of this, then help the student.
    b. Parents and teacher sign notebook daily to signify completion of homework assignments.
    c. Parents and teachers may use notebook for daily communication with each other.

Recommendations for students performing assignments

1. Give out only one task at a time.
2. Monitor frequently. Use a supportive attitude.
3. Modify assignments as needed. Consult with special education personnel to determine specific strengths and weaknesses of the student. Develop an IEP.
4. Make sure you are testing knowledge, not attention span.
5. Give extra time for certain tasks. The ADD student may work more slowly. Do not penalize for needed extra time.
6. Keep in mind that the ADD student is easily frustrated. Stress, pressure, and fatigue can break down the ADD student's self-control and lead to poor behavior.

(Continued)

TABLE 4.2　Teaching strategies (cont.)

Recommendations for behavior modifications and self-esteem enhancement

Providing Supervision and Discipline
1. Remain calm, state infraction of rule, and do not debate or argue with student.
2. Have preestablished consequences for misbehavior.
3. Administer consequences immediately, and monitor proper behavior frequently.
4. Enforce rules of the classroom consistently.
5. Discipline should "fit the crime" but be without harshness.
6. Avoid ridicule and criticism. Remember, the ADD student has difficulty staying in control.
7. Avoid publicly reminding students on medication to "take their medicine."

Providing Encouragement
1. Reward more than punish to build self-esteem.
2. Praise immediately any and all good behavior and performance.
3. Change rewards if not effective in motivating behavioral change.
4. Find ways to encourage the student.
5. Teach the student to reward himself or herself. Encourage positive self-talk (i.e. "You did very well remaining in your seat today. How do you feel about that?"); This encourages the student to think positively about himself or herself.

Other educational recommendations

1. Some ADD students may benefit from educational, psychological, and/or neurological testing to determine their learning style and cognitive ability and to rule out any learning disabilities (common in about 30 percent of ADD students).
2. Provide a private tutor and/or peer tutoring at school.
3. Place the ADD student in a class that has a low student-teacher ratio.
4. Give social skills training and organizational skills training.
5. Give training in cognitive restructuring (positive "self-talk").
6. Enable the ADD student to use a word processor or computer for schoolwork.
7. Encourage individualized activities that are mildly competitive or noncompetitive, such as bowling, walking, swimming, jogging, biking, and karate. (The ADD student may do less well in team sports.)
8. Involve the ADD child in social activities such as scouting, church groups, or other youth organizations that help develop social skills and self-esteem.
9. Allow the ADD student to play with younger students if that is where he or she "fits in." The student can still develop valuable social skills from interaction with younger students.

SOURCE: CHADD. (1988). *Attention deficit disorders: A guide for teachers.* Plantation, Fla.: Author, pp. 3–5. Used with permission.

Interest in the effects definitions have on who needs and receives special education has been a topic of interest in special education for some time. The idea that "public schools should be the institution with primary advocacy responsibility for providing or obtaining educational and related services for all children in need of special assistance" would not be rejected by many educators (Hobbs, 1975, p. 250), but the problems created by doing so cannot be ignored. Edgar and Hayden put it this way:

> Definitions of handicapping conditions, whether they are included in legislation or whether they are derived from other sources, must be reviewed periodically. We must continue to impose upon ourselves a system of checks and balances—a system that does not allow a compounding of errors. We must look at

the impact and benefits of our procedures for those children we do and do not serve in special education. Those of us in special education need to carefully reflect on our mandate from Congress (PL 94–142) in terms of what special education can now do, and how best to provide services to all children. This is certainly not to abandon the ideals of Hobbs, nor to turn our backs on children in need. Rather, it is to clarify our mission (special education's mission) and regular education's mission before others, particularly politicians, dictate the extent and the content of special education. (1984–1985, p. 525)

We cannot predict the future. We cannot tell you what categories will grow, develop, or demise, although we seriously doubt there will ever be a recognized category for the "severely and profoundly good." We are reasonably sure, after many years of frustration with professional practice, that special education will continue to be organized along categorical lines and that some people will continue to find the practice unacceptable. We are also reasonably sure that concern for including new groups of students among those currently receiving special services will remain prominent among issues driving us into the next century. Unquestionably, the legacy of confusion, controversy, and debate that surrounds definitions in special education will remain.

Discussion Questions

1. The category of learning disabilities grew more than any other category of special education during the ten years following the implementation of PL 94–142. How do you explain this growth? Why did other categories decrease or stay about the same during the same time period?

2. Why are some professionals opposed to including social maladjustment in definitions of emotional disturbance? What effect does including or excluding subgroups have on a category? What evidence exists to illustrate that exclusionary practices permeate other definitions with psychometric bases?

3. Passage of the IDEA Amendments was delayed by debate that focused on including a new category. Why would members of a professional group oppose development of a new category? Why was similar opposition not evident when the learning disabilities category was created and added to federal special education practices?

4. What dangers are there in using subjective criteria to define a category of special education students?

CHAPTER 5

Categorical Debate and Placement Controversy

Comparisons do ofttime great grievance.

—*John Lydgate*

It is not a benign activity to label a person as emotionally disturbed, learning disabled, mentally retarded, blind, deaf, silly, or dumb. Quite simply, assigning names to people creates conditions that foster not always beneficial comparisons. Most often doing so in schools is justified by promises of needed and improved educational services. Despite good intentions, "with rare exceptions, today's adults with disabilities who recall segregated facilities, separate classes, or home instruction cannot say enough about how inadequate was their academic training" (Asch, 1989, p. 183). Clearly there is a dilemma here: people who see, hear, walk, talk, and manage tasks in school differently from their neighbors and peers may need special assistance, but sometimes it comes at a great personal cost, if it comes at all. Creating categories for people also makes problems when professionals argue about the best place to provide special education.

Names Still Mean Places for Students with Special Needs

> When I first started teaching I was called the "retarded teacher." When I taught
> boys who couldn't read I was called the "disabled reading teacher," students with
> emotional problems, the "emotionally disturbed teacher," incarcerated young
> adults, the "prison teacher." Never had the good fortune of being known as the
> "gifted teacher."

There was a time when very few people with unique abilities received special
education. In the old days, segregated treatment was reserved for "special cases"
that attracted attention because it was believed they hindered the instruction of
their "more tractable and capable" peers (Van Sickle, 1908–1909, p. 102). As
education became more formalized and people were required to attend school,
the need for special education became greater. As Sarason and Doris noted, "These
two educational developments that called for a lock-step progression of pupils
through class-graded schools, and forced attendance of all children within a given
age range, immediately confronted the educator with the problem that not all
children were capable of maintaining the necessary rate of progress required by
the lockstep instructional system (1979, p. 137). And what began as a noble effort
to bring order to public education has become a massive alternative educational
system with elaborate diagnostic classification systems, powerful professional advocacy groups, and significant numbers of students being served each year. Today,
more students receive special education than receive undergraduate education in
America's two-year colleges and universities (National Center for Education Statistics, 1990).

Special education exists to serve people with special learning needs. Access
to this alternative education system is controlled by identification and classification
practices. A procedure similar to that in medicine has emerged: catalogues of
symptoms of various conditions are accepted, and diagnostic information is collected to determine the extent to which a person has characteristics similar to
those of the known conditions. The picture that emerges during a diagnostic
evaluation serves as a basis for classification and subsequent treatment. Simply
put, students classified as mentally retarded are treated in programs for the
mentally retarded; students classified as seriously emotionally disturbed receive
all or part of the education in programs for the seriously emotionally disturbed;
and so it goes for students with other handicaps and disabilities.

But there is a difference from medicine. When a person receives a medical
diagnosis, treatment for the condition is provided in an appropriate setting. But
the setting is not the treatment, which is much more specific than a setting or a
program. The effects of the problem are often more short-lived, and the outcomes
are often much more obvious. For example, a diagnosis of diabetes does not render
life all that different from life before the diagnosis. In medicine, classification
directly links to treatment.

Children and youths receive special education because parents and other
professionals believe it is important for them to do so. Students are entitled to

special education because federal laws guarantee them a free appropriate individualized education program based on their needs. These beliefs and mandates have created difficulties within the educational system. Concerns have emerged relative to the appropriateness of large numbers of students (especially those called learning disabled) receiving special education, the effects the whole practice has on the people involved in it, the best place to provide special education services, and how long they should be provided.

Perspectives on Classification

Each year, personnel in the U.S. Department of Education assess progress in providing services to children and youths with handicaps and prepare a report of findings for dissemination. Annual reports provide a "detailed description of the activities undertaken to implement the [EHA] and an assessment of the impact and effectiveness of its requirements" (U.S. Dept. of Education, 1989b, p. xiii). National statistics reported to the OSEP by the states are usually provided in the first chapter. Special concerns (e.g., circumstances in which students with handicaps leave school and their anticipated needs) and other evidence of federal initiatives and support (e.g., services provided to infants, toddlers, and preschool children with handicaps, federal monitoring activities) are described in other chapters. Publication of the annual reports provides a basis for examining what is going on in special education across the country (Blackman, 1989; Danielson & Bellamy, 1989).

In attempts to "assure that all handicapped children have available to them . . . a free appropriate public education which emphasizes special education and related services designed to meet their unique needs" (U.S. Dept. of Education, 1988b), federal government programs provide supplementary funds for states to use in the education of children and youths with handicaps. The federal government provides support for children and youths aged three to twenty-one under provisions of Part B of the EHA. Support is also provided to children and youths from birth through age twenty in programs operated by state agencies through Chapter 1 of the ECIA-SOP. The OSEP uses many sources to evaluate the extent to which funding provided is used to achieve its purpose. The number of students served in special education categories is one source used in making these judgments. The annual reports to Congress include data provided by states (grouped by category) in compliance with requirements associated with accepting federal funds under these two programs. Even states that do not have categorical programs (e.g., Massachusetts) provide data in categorical form.

In recent years, more than four million students have received special education in programs developed and maintained in part by principles embodied in PL 94–142. When the *Tenth Annual Report to Congress on the Implementation of the Education of the Handicapped Act* was published, it marked the end of a decade of "extraordinary change." During 1986 to 1987, the school year ten years after passage of PL 94–142, 4,421,601 children and youths with handicaps from birth to twenty-one were served under Chapter 1 of ECIA-SOP and EHA-B. Almost all (94.2 percent) of these children and youths were served under EHA-B, with the remainder served under ECIA-SOP. This represented a steady increase (19.2 percent since 1976–1977) in the number of students being served and was viewed as a measure of progress. Analysis of numbers of children reported under EHA-B and ECIA-SOP revealed that "the largest number of handicapped children were classified as learning disabled (43.6 percent), followed by speech impaired (25.8 percent)" and that "the four most frequent handicapping conditions (learning disability, speech impairment, mental retardation, and emotional disturbance) accounted for the great majority of the children served under the two acts" (U.S. Dept. of Education, 1988b, p. 7). The "great majority" was actually 93 percent, 94 percent of the students served under EHA-B and 71 percent of those served under ECIA-SOP were from the "four most frequent handicapping conditions," 94 percent of all students were served under EHA-B, and while more (two to three times) students with mental retardation and/or emotional disturbance were served under ECIA-SOP, more (three to four times) students with learning disabilities and/or speech impairment were served under EHA-B. But questions remain. Are steady increases in numbers of students served a reflection of better, more consistent reporting or real increases in students becoming handicapped? If the figures represent incidence, what is causing the pandemic growth? If the figures represent artifacts of reporting, where were these students before and why the sudden interest in identifying them? What difference do differences in where students are served make in terms of services provided to children with different handicapping conditions?

Identifying students by category permits official agencies to allocate assistance and provide progress reports. It also provides incentives for school personnel to identify and label certain students more than others. If funds are linked to numbers of students and no checks and balances are attached to classification systems, the temptation of more money for more students is very real. Similarly, if special funding is provided for special groups of students (e.g., preschool students with handicaps, students with learning disabilities), the additional pressure can be compelling.

The basis for providing services (and receiving financial support for doing it) is categorical identification. Diagnostic decisions are made on the basis of performance on tests, observations, and interviews. Few tests, observations, or interviews adequately provide diagnostic information suitable for making decisions about individual students. There is just too much flotsam in the system. This is evident in classification research conducted in learning disabilities.

Since the first student was classified as learning disabled, the condition has been characterized by process disorders producing problems in reading, mathematics, writing, and other academic content areas. The search for critical links between process disorders and academic performance has been unproductive (Samuels & Miller, 1985; Sleeter, 1986), and research has consistently demonstrated that only severity of academic underachievement consistently differentiates students with learning disabilities from those without them (Furlong & Yanagida, 1985; Ysseldyke & Algozzine, 1990). After five years of research, Ysseldyke and Algozzine (1983) concluded there was no defensible system for classifying students with learning disabilities. Problems evident in this area within special education are evident in other areas as well.

Perspectives on Categorical Treatment and Labeling

Scholars predict that Lenny Ng will become America's best mathematician. There is nothing very remarkable about such a prediction, except that it was made when Lenny was in elementary school. He took the Scholastic Aptitude Test at age ten; his score on the quantitatitve items was 800. Lenny's talents are not limited to numbers. He plays tennis, writes stories, and composes music. He seldom watches television or goes to movies. "I'm just not that kind of person," he says. His perspective on being gifted and labeled is revealing. "It's fun to do this stuff. . . . There are no ill effects as long as people don't call me a nerd" (*Parade Magazine*, December 2, 1990, p. 5).

Classifying and labeling students are fundamental activities in contemporary special education. Each year more than 250 million standardized tests are administered to the forty-four million public school students in America's schools. The purpose of much of this testing is identification of students performing below expectations. Every category of special education, except gifted and talented, has poor performance in school as a central or peripheral part. And concern would be minimal if being labeled had only positive effects, but as Ysseldyke and Algozzine (1982) indicated, perspectives on categorical treatment center on the extent to which the negative effects of being labeled outweigh the positive ones.

The effects of labeling must be studied from two perspectives: the impact of the label on the perceptions and behavior of the person being labeled and the impact of the label on the perceptions and behavior of those who interact with the person being labeled. This perspective on labels and their effects is illustrated in Figure 5.1. Labels serve as sources of perceptions and behaviors for the person being labeled, which in turn serve as the basis for personal expectancies and performance. Labels also serve as sources of perceptions and behaviors for others about the person being labeled, which in turn serve as the basis for altered expectancies and performance. Perceptions, behavior, expectations, and performance represent personal and interpersonal aspects of the effects labels have on the people who are labeled. Labeling is justified by its presumed advantages and challenged by its presumed disadvantages.

Presumed Advantages

Labeling is justified on the basis of its presumed advantages. Foremost among them is that labels serve as admission tickets to alternative educational services.

FIGURE 5.1   Model for examining the effects of labeling

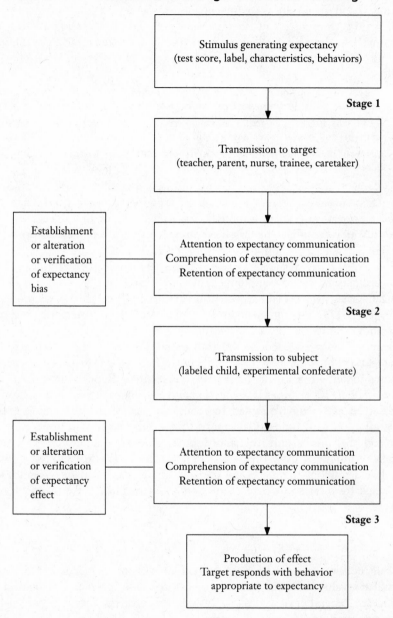

According to Gorham, Des Jardins, Page, Pettis, and Scherber, "Practically speaking, 'good' labels are those marshalling resources on [the student's] behalf" (1976, p. 155). Supporters of labeling believe the labels that serve as "passports" to improved educational services are ideal. Gallagher pointed out that labels serve other purposes as well; in his discussion, he suggested the "sacred" uses of labeling as follows:

1. A means for beginning a classification, diagnosis, and treatment sequence peculiarly designed to counteract certain identifiable negative conditions.

2. The basis for further research which will give more insight into etiology, prevention, and possible treatment applications of such conditions in the future.

3. A means of calling attention to a specific problem in order to obtain additional resources through special legislation and funding. (1976, p. 3)

Gallagher's first use parallels the use of labels in medicine. When a physician labels a patient as diabetic, the classification and diagnostic process sets a prescribed treatment sequence in motion. The logic follows that once a student is labeled learning disabled, the classification and diagnostic process sets prescribed treatment sequences in motion as well.

The second use also has a base in medical practice. Once the profession accepted a specific set of symptoms as acquired immune deficiency syndrome, a significant basis was available for continued research into the causes, cures, and courses of AIDS. Giving symptoms a name facilitates systematic research to better understand what the name means.

Annual reports to Congress illustrating the number of students being served by categories function as a basis for continuing efforts to provide additional resources to some (or all) of the groups represented. Reports that more than 4 million students receive special education and that more than 1.5 million of them are classified as learning disabled serve as evidence of the continuing need for special allocations of funds, Gallagher's third use. The problem is seen as very large, and this means only that more must be done. Unquestionably, there is strength in numbers, especially when they are large. It is difficult to argue that more than 1 million students really are not handicapped, and so systems become entrenched by indications that large numbers of members of categorical groups exist.

Presumed Disadvantages

There is nothing inherently good or bad in labeling a student. The practice accumulates value with the effects it generates. The problems associated with labeling are generally viewed along two dimensions: the extent to which labels lead to expected and desired outcomes (e.g., improved educational services) and the extent to which labels are actually harmful (i.e., result in undesired effects).

Many professionals have argued that labeling does not necessarily lead to improved education treatment. Hallahan and Kauffman noted widespread disenchantment with labeling and commented that "there is no rational basis, in terms of instructional efficacy, for grouping children in accordance with some of the categorical labels now in use" (1977, p. 139). At best, labels appear to serve as passports that in no way guarantee differential or improved educational treatment.

And there is evidence that labels may be harmful. According to Gorham, Des Jardins, Page, Pettis, and Scherber, "Labels have damaged many children, particularly minority group children whose cultures and lifestyles differ sufficiently from the "norm" to make any measurement of their abilities and aptitudes by norm-biased scales a certain disaster for them" (1976, p. 155). In addition to the harm done to students, Gallagher noted other "profane" uses of labeling:

> 1. A means for tranquilizing professionals by applying labels (i.e., autism or minimal brain dysfunction) to children without following with subsequent differentiated programs of treatment, merely filling a need for closure on a difficult diagnostic issue.

> 2. As a means to preserve a social hierarchy by using labels to keep minority group children from opportunities and to force them to remain at the bottom of the social ladder.

> 3. To delay needed social reform by focusing the problem on the individual, rather than on complex social and ecological conditions needing specific change and repair. (1976, p. 3)

Labeling students is not a benign activity. Names assigned to characteristics have profound effects on individuals being categorized by them. Labels affect parents, teachers, and other professionals who live and work with people who are labeled. Few professionals deny these facts. Most justify continuing to label students by arguing that the advantages (e.g., special education placements) outweigh the disadvantages for most students.

Perspectives on Environments and Prevalence

Danielson & Bellamy (1989) presented data showing national stability but considerable variance among states in the number of students placed in separate facilities. Tucker (1989) and Blackman (1989) proposed alternative explanations for the reported findings. Tucker argued that the variance among states in out-of-school placements reflected current understanding of what LRE meant more than variability in applying a well-defined concept. Blackman argued that the data reflected a failure on the part of many states to live up to the intent of PL 94–142, which "clearly sets for the states a presumption in favor of regular class placement in regular school buildings for children with disabilities" (1989, p. 459). Thus, there are two alternative explanations for observed variance in prevalence: either the variance is due to differing understandings of the LRE concept, or it is due to diversity in applying clearly understood concepts.

For years, the field of learning disabilities has been plagued by definitional debates (Hallahan, Keller, & Ball, 1986; Ysseldyke & Algozzine, 1990). Arguments have focused on the lack of a universally accepted definition and the multiple operational criteria that are applied to the definitions that do exist (Algozzine & Ysseldyke, 1983; Kavale & Forness, 1985; Keogh, Major-Kingsley, Omori-Gordon, & Reid, 1982; Shepard & Smith, 1983; Ysseldyke, Algozzine, Shinn, & McGue, 1982; Ysseldyke, Thurlow, Graden, Wesson, Algozzine, & Deno, 1983). Hallahan, Keller, and Ball pointed out that "other areas of special education have definitional problems too" (1986, p. 9). For example, the category of emotional disturbance has experienced definitional problems for years (cf. Kauffman, 1985), and considerable disagreement has periodically surfaced relative to levels of intelligence and operational criteria for adaptive behavior used in definitions of mental retardation (MacMillan, 1982). Hallahan, Keller, and Ball also observed that "although learning disabilities, in particular, has received more criticism pertaining to its identification procedures than have other areas, no data exist to indicate it is more or less culpable than other areas of special education in this regard" (1986, p. 9). To fill this void, they compared the variability of prevalence rates from state to state for each of the categories of special education.

Using the coefficient of variation (Friedman, 1971) as an index of variation in prevalence rates within a special education category, they found that "higher prevalence categories (i.e., learning disabilities, speech and language impairment, mental retardation, and emotional disturbance) are as a group no more variable than lower prevalence categories (i.e., hearing impairment, orthopedic impairment, visual impairment, health impairment, multiple handicaps, and deaf/blind)" (p. 10). They pointed out that other researchers had reported conflicting conclusions with regard to variability in categories and suggested that none of those "investigators has made a direct, data based comparison of the variability of the prevalence rates for all the categories" (p. 9). The implication of their work is that their conclusions are better because they are based on statistics other than those used (or reported) by other investigators (Keller, Ball, & Hallahan, 1987).

Algozzine and Ysseldyke argued, however, that there was more than one way to look at variability in prevalence rates for categories of exceptionality. Using other criteria, they found that

> the variance for the learning disabilities prevalence rate was greater than that for emotional disturbance, but differences among other rates were nonsignificant. Prevalence rates for speech and language impairments, learning disabilities, and mental retardation were similar. Emotional disturbance was not most variable and learning disabilities was not least variable among the high prevalence rates. (1987, p. 54)

Once again, the importance of definitions and operational criteria is obvious in analyses of what is going on in special education. Concepts such as least restrictive environment, learning disabilities, statistical significance, and intelligence or adaptive behavior are given meaning by the definitions and operational criteria used to study them. The alternative perspectives professionals take in doing this have important implications. For example, Algozzine and Ysseldyke believed that "learning disabilities prevalence rates are alarmingly high and that much of the variability in them is due to the manner in which professionals in the states are permitted to operationalize the category" (1987, p. 56). Blackman argued that "too many children with [negative school labels] are being segregated in separate facilities and separate classrooms" (1989, p. 459), and Tucker argued that conclusions about conditions of implementing LRE in the states "represent more the state of current understanding of what LRE means rather than the state of the art in applying a well-defined concept" (1989, p. 457).

Perspectives on the Regular Education Initiative

Opinions about research and identification practices; about the effects of labeling; about teachers' attitudes, skills, and priorities; and about the effects of the excellence in education movement have stimulated some professionals to seriously question the appropriateness of classifying and placing students in special education classrooms. A summary of the concerns and alternative courses of actions were presented in a position paper by Will (1986). (See Chapter 1 for a more in-depth analysis of this report.) The following points were noteworthy:

1. The term *learning problem* was used broadly, but the intent was to limit the universe of students being discussed.

2. Will's statement was not designed to pull services away from people in need; there was no failure to recognize the unserved.

3. Although much had been accomplished in special education programs, they had also produced unintended effects, among them a fragmented approach that failed to provide services for many children, lowered expectations for "labeled" students, and an adversarial relationship between parents and teachers.

4. The pullout approach, although appropriate for some students, was conceptually fallacious: it understood poor performance as a function of the student, not as a function of the learning environment.

5. She advocated that the regular classroom be adapted so that the student could learn. "We need to visualize a system that will bring the program to the child rather than one that brings the child to the program." (p. 21)

Will's position on developing partnerships to meet the special learning needs of students was not particularly radical, but it generated considerable professional debate. Some of the arguments against sharing responsibilities for educating students with handicaps in regular classrooms center on issues related to integration and right to treatment. The *integration arguments* are based on concerns that some students with handicaps are not overidentified groups in special education. Advocates of these positions believe that regular classrooms may be the most appropriate places for many students with handicaps to receive their education but that research clearly does not support the assertion that all students can be managed and taught effectively in regular classes. These advocates also believe that expecting general education teachers to welcome, successfully teach and manage, and tolerate the most disruptive students is extremely naive and illogical, both from the viewpoint of common sense and from the perspective of available research.

The *right to treatment arguments* are based on opinions about eligibility for services, rights to privacy, and appropriate interventions. Some opponents of the principles embodied in the regular education initiative believe that students with handicaps are underidentified and that under alternative educational initiatives even more will be denied appropriate help. These opponents also believe that being served in special class settings affords some students privacy that they welcome in dealing with their problems (segregation is better than integration argument). And these advocates of right to treatment believe that research does not support the contention that the long list of complex interventions that are appropriate for use with some students with handicaps can be effectively used in general education settings.

The principles embodied in the regular education initiative involve four fundamental changes in how special education is provided (Davis & Maheady, 1990).

1. Students with learning problems would receive more instruction in regular, as opposed to special education, settings.

2. General, compensatory, and special education teachers would work collaboratively to provide "special" education in integrated settings.

3. All instructional resources (i.e., financial, educational, and personnel) would be "pooled" under a single administrator.

4. Administrative policies and procedures would be developed to encourage placement of students with special learning needs in regular classes.

Unfortunately, empirical study of problems associated with these principles has been sparse, and what has been done has been criticized for ignoring important constituencies (e.g., teachers, students, administrators). For example, McKinney and Hocutt pointed out that "regular educators, who constitute the largest single group to be affected by these proposals, have not had significant input" (1988, p. 15), and Kauffman, Gerber, and Semmel added that "data reflecting attitudes of regular classroom teachers toward proposed changes in the structure of general and regular education" have been "conspicuously absent" from literature supporting the regular education initiative (1988, p. 9).

Fuchs and Fuchs framed the controversies surrounding the integration movement as a debate between abolitionists (those who argue for elimination or reduction of special education alternatives) and conservationists (those who wish to preserve special education's current structure). According to Fuchs and Fuchs, these contrasting perspectives are based on differing levels and types of experiences with regular education and differing opinions about the ways and means of achieving important educational goals. For example, the conservationists' skepticism is based on "observation of many educators' unwillingness or inability to work with [mildly handicapped] children"; on "blatant intolerance, and sometime visceral dislike expressed by many teachers toward them"; and, on "arbitrary and adamant refusals to permit the return of these pupils, even parttime, to their classrooms" (in press, p. 20). Relative to goals, the social and attitudinal interests expressed by abolitionists clash with the academic concerns of conservationists.

As we see it, there is much to recommend efforts to restructure special education so that more students receive effective instruction in regular education classrooms. We believe the regular education initiative suffered because of a lack of definition and the significant misunderstandings that resulted from it. Simply put, the regular education initiative is a movement to educate as many students as possible in regular class learning environments. If this were to happen, education of students with special learning needs might look different (Davis, 1989).

We see nothing wrong with the ideals expressed in the initiative. Clearly, such an alternative educational system is not hard to imagine and would not be difficult to take, but the misconceptions that surround it severely limit the likelihood it will be successful or that it will even come to pass.

• The regular education initiative is not an evil, or an innocent, plot to place all special education students in regular classrooms. Therefore, it is not sufficiently radical to motivate the concern that "school reform" does.

• The regular education initiative is not a *regular education* initiative. This limits the extent to which it will be successful because there are no clamoring masses anxious to teach students with unique abilities and special learning needs, especially those with serious behavior problems.

• The regular education initiative is not an instructional intervention. This limits the extent to which it can be successful because it cannot be evaluated as a teaching method or instructional program is. The parameters are simply too varied.

To the optimist, a proposal for adopting shared responsibility in teaching students with unique abilities offers a virtual, empirical "gold mine" of opportunities for improving practice. But in the context of previous efforts at school reform, the same proposal may be perceived as simply another opportunity for widespread disappointment and failure. To professionals engaged with students with handicaps, a number of interesting practical questions emerge as driving concerns at the student, classroom, and system levels of practice (Maheady & Algozzine, 1991).

Perhaps the first question that can be asked is whether a heterogeneous group of students, some with serious problems, can be taught effectively in general education classrooms given existing instructional resources. Related issues concern the conditions in which such populations can be taught and the limits of accommodation, both with and without additional instructional resources or more powerful interventions. On a social level, issues remain as to the effect that abled and disabled populations have on each other in the same classroom. Indeed, whether students with handicaps prefer integrated or segregated placements remains a fundamental, yet unanswered, question.

For years, teachers have been told that homogeneous grouping (by age, ability, or behavior) was a preferred practice, and most of them have desired classes with as few problem students as possible. In light of this, which teachers really welcome students with learning and behavior problems into their classrooms, and does anybody really want to teach them? Even though resources for teaching students with problems are readily available (Algozzine, 1992), many questions still remain regarding how often "effective" strategies are actually used by classroom teachers, how acceptable these procedures are, and whether they can be generalized to other students with problems and to regular classrooms.

Presently, very little is known about how school systems operate, particularly with regard to the adoption and support of innovative instructional and classroom management practices. It is quite clear, however, that many teachers do not want to serve "hard-to-teach" students or implement specific management approaches if district level professionals do not support them for doing so. Even though the instructional capability to serve many more students with problems in general education classrooms is available, this capability will not be actualized until the complex administrative processes that support teachers in carrying out this agenda are harnessed and controlled. Again, a number of interesting practical questions emerge about the conditions, both pedagogical and administrative, that facilitate adoption of innovative or effective classroom management practices; the "rewards" that can be offered to districts for selecting effective interventions; the money and resources needed to sustain implementation; and the role(s) the community will play in the adoption and maintenance of these new programs.

Deciding where to provide special services will remain an important issue in special education for some time. There simply is no easy way to meld what have become separate educational systems. Restructuring education to better meet the needs of students with special needs will not be among the priorities of regular educators for some time (e.g., few current goals of education even address special education's needs).

Perspectives on Categorical Relevance

When pushed for the reasons that students continue to be labeled despite concern that the practice further handicaps them, school officials often respond that labels are a necessary evil. Without being labeled, students in need of services cannot receive them. Without labeling students, state departments are not eligible for federal assistance. Without labels, research on categorical interventions cannot be conducted. But despite presumed and justified needs, labels are an unfortunate by-product of a system that attaches money to acts resulting in classifications and categories. The problems go beyond simple effects.

Labels are often irrelevant to the instructional needs of students. Put another way, students classified as mentally retarded, emotionally handicapped, learning disabled, visually handicapped, or gifted have diverse educational needs. The whole student is more than any one part, especially if the part is as ill-gotten as most labels.

Labels, often arbitrarily defined and assigned, become real attributes that prevent meaningful understanding of actual individual learning needs. By causing some to believe that students labeled mentally retarded cannot do certain things, the act of classifying condemns these students to a life of lesser expectations and performance.

Labels require official sanction. Resources diverted to the process of identifying and classifying students are extensive. Time and money spent on labeling are time and money not spent on teaching. Time spent being labeled is time not spent being taught or learning.

Labels provide excuses for not meeting the special learning needs of individual students. At times, the decreased willingness of teachers to work with students borders on total abdication of responsibility to modify instruction to meet any individual needs.

Troubled by continuing concerns with categorical perspectives, labeling, and classification, the National Coalition of Advocates for Students and the National Association of School Psychologists proposed "the development and piloting of alternatives to the current categorical system." The "rights without labels" (Lipsky & Gartner, 1989, p. 276) movement that resulted was grounded in important beliefs:

- All children can learn. Schools have a responsibility to teach them, and school personnel and parents should work together to assure every child a free and appropriate education in a positive social environment.

- Instructional options, based on the individual psychoeducational needs of each child, must be maximized within the general education system. Necessary support services should be provided within general education, eliminating the need to classify children as handicapped in order to receive these services.

- Psychoeducational needs of children should be determined through a multi-dimensional, nonbiased assessment process. This must evaluate the match between the learner and his or her educational environment, assessing the compatibility of curriculum and system as they interact with the child. Referral to the assessment and placement process must always relate directly to services designed to meet psychoeducational needs.

- In addition to maintaining current protection for handicapped children, protections and safeguards must be developed to assure the rights of children who are at risk for school failure and require services while remaining in general education without classification as handicapped. (National Coalition of Advocates for Students & the National Association of School Psychologists, 1989, 235–236)

Toward the goal of generating effective solutions to the problems plaguing special education because of its categorical perspective, national efforts were required:

We will actively work toward the collaboration of a wide variety of individuals and organizations, joining together to develop a strong base of knowledge, research, and experience in order to establish new frameworks and conceptualizations on which to base decisions, design feasible service delivery options, advocate for policy and funding changes needed to implement these alternatives, and coordinate efforts and share information for positive change. (p. 236)

Perspectives on Out-of-School Placements

The LRE provision of PL 94-142 is a key concept driving efforts to provide special education to children and youths with handicaps and disabilities (Ysseldyke & Algozzine, 1990). The enabling legislation and implementing regulations require that

first, educational services appropriate for each child be defined annually in an Individualized Education Program (IEP); and, then, an educational placement be selected from a continuum of alternatives so that the individually appropriate education can be delivered in the setting that is least removed from the regular education environment and that offers the greatest interaction with children who are not handicapped. (Danielson & Bellamy, 1989, p. 448)

The concept reflects the belief that segregating students with disabilities and handicaps is unsound social, political, economic, and educational practice (Ysseldyke & Algozzine, 1982, 1984, 1990). The concept brings ideals of normalization and mainstreaming convincingly to life by establishing assistance to states in the form of monitoring, discretionary grants, and technical assistance from the federal government.

Even though significant professional debate abounds regarding the merits of least restrictive placements, there has been little published research revealing the extent to which alternative placements (e.g., resource rooms, separate classes, separate school facilities) are used to operationalize the ideals inherent in LRE provisions (Blackman, 1989; Danielson & Bellamy, 1989; Tucker, 1989; Ysseldyke & Algozzine, 1990). An exception to this generalization is evident in data presented in the U.S. Department of Education's annual reports to Congress on the implementation of the Education of the Handicapped Act (cf. U.S. Dept. of Education, 1988b, 1989b, 1990b). Percentages of students with handicaps served in regular schools and segregated facilities over the ten-year period following implementation of PL 94-142 are illustrated in Figure 5.2. Little change occurred in the use of separate facilities, and the use of regular class placements increased.

The federal government uses time spent in regular and special settings in definitions of alternative placements (see Table 5.1). What appear to be clear-cut statements of differences between environments used to provide special education have created problems (U.S. Dept. of Education, 1990b). Analyses of data on the use of these alternative placements revealed great variability in estimates provided by individual states (cf. Danielson & Bellamy, 1989). According to Tucker (1989,

FIGURE 5.2   Percentage of children with handicaps, aged six through seventeen, served from 1976–1977 to 1985–1986

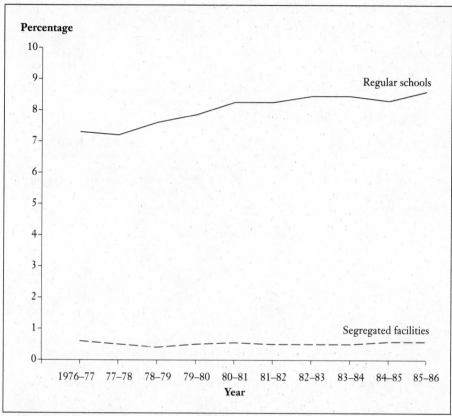

NOTE: Regular schools include regular rooms, resource rooms, and separate classes; segregated facilities include public and private separate schools and residential facilities and homebound/hospital environments.

Percentage of children served is based on estimated resident population counts for July 1986; resident populations are estimated by the U.S. Bureau of the Census.

SOURCE: L. C. Danielson & G. T. Bellamy. (1989). State variation in placement of children with handicaps in segregated environments. *Exceptional Children, 55,* 448–455. Figure 1.

TABLE 5.1 Definitions of placement categories used by federal government

Placement	Definition
Regular class	Includes students who receive a majority of their education in a regular class and receive special education and related services for less than 21 percent of the school day (approximately 72 minutes of a 6-hour day). It includes students placed in a regular class and receiving special education within the regular class as well as students placed in a regular class and receiving special education outside the regular class.
Resource room	Includes students who receive special education and related services for 60 percent or less of the school day and at least 21 percent of the school day (from 76 minutes to about 3½ hours of a 6-hour day). This may include resource rooms with part-time instruction in the regular class.
Separate class	Includes students who receive special education and related services for more than 60 percent of the school day (more than 220 minutes of a 6-hour day) and are placed in self-contained special classrooms with part-time instruction in regular class or placed in self-contained classes full-time on a regular school campus.
Separate school	Includes students who receive special education and related services in separate day schools for the handicapped for more than 50 percent of the school day (more than 3 hours of a typical school day).
Residential facility	Includes students who receive education in a public or private residential facility at public expense for more than 50 percent of the school day (more than 3 hours of an average day).
Homebound/hospital	Includes students placed in and receiving education in hospital or homebound programs.

SOURCE: Adapted from U.S. Department of Education. (1990b). *Twelfth annual report to Congress on the implementation of the Education of the Handicapped Act*. Washington, D.C.: Author.

p. 456), the variability was due more to definitions of LRE than to actual conditions existing within the states. A similar argument was used to explain variation in prevalence of students with learning disabilities (Algozzine & Ysseldyke, 1989).

Interest in analyzing variation in placement was justified by its policy implications: if state-to-state variability did exist, this would demonstrate potential for improvement in the national effort to educate children with handicaps in less restrictive environments (Danielson & Bellamy, 1989, p. 449). Two assumptions drove this interest. First, data reflective of placements were assumed to be accurate representations of the state of practice (i.e., students in one setting really spent less time in special education than students in another setting did, and the numbers reflected realistic pictures of where students were served). Second, placement and program were used synonymously; therefore arguing that one place was less restrictive than another ignored the possibility that what went on in that place may have been more restrictive regardless of what it was called. The issue at the base of concern generated by such analyses was whether restrictive definitions were creating inappropriate pictures of the benefits accrued by students with handicaps and disabilities.

The accuracy of the data used to compare variation in placement of students with handicaps was questioned by Danielson and Bellamy: "Of course, some of the variability across states may be the result of measurement error" (1989, p. 453), and "states need to strengthen efforts to improve the accuracy and state-to-state comparability of data" (p. 455). Tucker argued that narrow interpretations of the LRE concept had created conditions calling for *less required energy* in implementation. He used the following example to illustrate that placement should not always be equated with program and that to assume otherwise "sets up a false premise which can serve as the foundation for any number of more restrictive alternatives (e.g., emotionally disturbed students need a separate facility)" (1989, p. 457):

> A deaf person needs a program which accommodates his or her loss of hearing. If a hearing aid is all that is *needed* (as defined by the nature and severity of the handicap), then the LRE is any location whatsoever that is normal for a child of that age and other presenting characteristics, *so long as a hearing aid is provided and working.*
>
> If a hearing aid is not sufficient, and one or more alternative forms of communication, such as signing, are needed, then again, the physical location of the person does not determine the least restrictive environment, but rather the conditions surrounding the person. To educate a deaf person with other deaf persons because it is easier to assemble the needed services in one place may be a practical solution to a financial problem, but it does not make the separate facility the least restrictive environment for deaf students. Again, it is the path of least resistance. (p. 457)

Clearly, deciding what is the best environment for providing special education is difficult, especially in light of the opinion that *any* environment may be appropriate. Complex social, political, economic, and educational factors enter the decision-making process, and few standards exist for making objective decisions about who should receive special education and where it should be provided (Ysseldyke & Algozzine, 1982, 1984, 1990). The "softness" of definitions continues to create problems for professionals who practice and students who receive special education (U.S. Dept. of Education, 1990b).

Names Still Mean Problems for People with Special Needs

Research on the effects of labeling was very prevalent about ten years ago. There were studies of the effects of different types of labels on teachers, students, and other professionals (e.g., school psychologists). But recent literature has not reflected these same issues and concerns.

The problem is that labeling was popular when access to special education was an issue (even though a label has always been a necessary passport to special education). Questions arose when professionals questioned the benefits of providing service against the negative effects labeling might have on its recipients. Not so long ago, the question was, "To provide service at what price?" Now access is expected, guaranteed, and assured, so labels are assigned, and research into effects (despite evidence that they still present problems) is perfunctory. Now professionals are concerned about the appropriateness of placement, not the effects of labels. In a sense, the labels have become so ingrained that systematic questioning no longer exists as a topic of educational research.

Before his success with the Simpsons, Groenig wrote a book entitled *School Is Hell*, in which he chronicled his perceptions of the trials and tribulations that faced people forced to be there. Make no mistake, school is not fun for the vast majority of people who attend (Sarason, 1990). Students with handicaps and their families find schools particularly trying places:

> The stigmatizing circumstance under which many deaf persons learned and began using sign language has had its impact on the language and on the level of linguistic sophistication of many sign language users. The signs themselves often tell a story about the frustrations of ineffective education. For example, one composite sign stands for "Too many big words." There are signs that indicate negative self-image, such as "dummy" and "pea-brain," and deaf people often apologize to hearing persons or to more educated deaf persons with comments such as "Me dummy—know nothing." . . . Pat, who emigrated to this country from South America at age 9, said that most of her elementary and junior high school years were spent in special education courses that were far too easy. Comparing special education with mainstream classes, she said: "In ninth grade I had four special education classes. They were very, very easy. I told my mother I wanted out. Now that I'm in all mainstreamed classes, even homeroom, I don't think I'm favored because I'm disabled. I have to work for my grades. Some other disabled kids are passed along." (Asch, 1989, p. 188)

The life experiences of a group of people released from a large institution were analyzed and presented in *The Cloak of Competence* (Edgerton, 1967) more than twenty years ago. We think the comments of many of these people still have relevance. For example, the book presented evidence of the kind of "passing" that was, and still is, part of the social behaviors of many exceptional people:

- "I don't like to read. It hurts my eyes. I'd rather watch TV" (p. 131).

- "When I try to get a job they always ask me where I'm from. I don't tell nobody I'm from there [the hospital]—I say I'm just an outsider like anybody, but I've been working in the East" (p. 151).

- "You know old ___ (another ex-patient). He's always putting on. He went and got these books at the junk shop for ten cents a piece, and now he's got 'em all over his place like he was some kind of millionaire. Well, I went and got me some books too, real classy ones, I paid a dollar for some of 'em. Got all kinds, I think they look real nice" (p. 159).

The powerful impact of being exceptional was also illustrated in the words of a middle-aged mother of four children:

> I never had an interpreter when I went to the hospital for my children's births. The first time I was really scared. . . . I didn't know what was happening. No one told me what to expect. Later on, when the kids were getting older, I struggled with writing notes back and forth to the kids' doctors and school counselors. It was a waste of time. I never understood what people were trying to tell me. . . . When a child was sick, I never knew just how serious it was, or what I could do if one of them was having trouble in school. I get angry just thinking about it. (Becker & Jauregui, 1985, p. 29)

Degan and Brooks presented an analysis of the life experiences of exceptional people who had to deal with the double handicap of being women who were disabled. The following passage from the introduction to that book illustrates the less positive aspects of being exceptional:

> During the 1970s a social movement arose to address the concerns of people with disabilities. Action groups pressed for reforms in architectural barriers, educational and employment opportunities, deinstitutionalization, and legal protection of civil rights. Although accurate demographic information is lacking, estimates indicate that approximately one in ten Americans has a disability or chronic disease and would be directly affected by the disability movement. These people experience serious limitations in major activities such as housework, employment, or education. Although physical restrictions pose significant problems, social restrictions generated by negative attitudes impose greater handicaps, because socially created barriers effectively prevent full community participation. The primary purpose of the disability movement therefore has been to combat both environmental and social handicaps through public education and legal advances. (p. 1)

Evidence of negative feelings about being exceptional and the lowered expectations experienced by exceptional people is also easily documented (Asch, 1984, 1989). And although negative views may not represent the perspective of all people called handicapped, testimonials proclaiming the joys of being labeled and receiving special education are harder to find, especially in books focused on issues. What joys do accrue are often more from the social than from the academic aspects of schooling.

> Annee, a senior from a small rural district in Washington State, was proud of the opportunities she had received. Her blindness did not stop her from conducting lab work in chemistry or from being selected to participate in a 2-month exchange student program in Latin America through the American Field Service. April, a high school senior from a city in South Carolina, who is blind, participated in her school's physical education program. Her itinerant teacher demonstrated the physical skills she needed in order to participate in activities, and her classmates took over from there by guiding her when she ran and by warning her of balls she couldn't see during volleyball games. (Asch, 1989, p. 185)

It is not easy being exceptional. Actual or perceived difference is the source of a number of specific beliefs and actions on the part of the exceptional person. Stigmatized people may choose to avoid social contacts or may use defensive covering to reduce the likelihood of having to deal with other people socially. Some put forth an unnatural, hostile bravado that is designed to make others think differently of them. Research findings on the social interactions, self-concept, peer acceptance, and general social communication skills of children and youths called learning disabled shed some light on the difficulties these students experience in interpersonal relationships. For example, the conversational skills of students with learning disabilities have been found to be more hostile and less cooperative than those of normal children. Students who have learning disabilities are less skilled than nondisabled children in starting and maintaining a conversation with a peer, and they are less able to sustain a dominant speaker role than are nondisabled children. Of course, such students are not the only exceptional students who exhibit such characteristics. Regardless of the actual behaviors demonstrated, the perceptions and interactions of exceptional people are affected by the names they receive and by the effects those names have on others.

Discussion Questions

1. According to many professionals, the positive effects of being classified as hearing impaired outweigh the negative effects of labeling. According to many people classified as hearing impaired, the negative effects outweigh the positive effects of being labeled. How can this discrepancy be, and who is right?

2. What are the benefits and liabilities of being classified as gifted? How do they compare with the benefits and liabilities of being classified as learning disabled, mentally retarded, or visually handicapped?

3. Placement is not synonymous with program. How would you support or refute this statement?

PART TWO

Issues in Special Education

CHAPTER 6

School Reform and Special Education

School Reform, Restructuring, and Excellence in Education
  The Reform Movement in General Education
  Parallel Play in School Reform

Six New National Goals for Education
  Readiness for School
  High School Completion
  School Achievement and Citizenship
  Science and Mathematics
  Adult Literacy and Lifelong Learning
  Safe, Disciplined, and Drug-Free Schools
  Programs to Meet the National Education Goals

Reform, Restructuring, and Excellence in Special Education?

General Education Reforms and Their Effects
  Choice in Education
  Comprehensive Restructuring of Education

Change in Education

Our dilemma is that we hate change and love it at the same time; what we really want is for things to remain the same but get better.

—Sydney J. Harris

As the 1980s came to a close, educators wrote, heard, and spoke a language that had taken on new meaning—"reform," "restructuring," and "excellence" were among the terms more frequently used. The push for educational reform reflected in these new terms arose from a series of reports and public opinion polls that pointed to the presence of significant problems in current educational practice. Many of these reports also suggested novel approaches to the solution of the identified problems. These reforms reflected a belief that educators had to deliver more than ever before as they strove, along with businesses and families, toward excellence in education.

School reform has been primarily a general education initiative, even though the potential effects on special education are great. Yet in a summary of the "education reform decade" (ETS Policy Information Center, 1990), there was not a single mention of students with disabilities or even special education. The closest the report came to recognizing the possible relationship was in the introduction, which noted that there was "some concern as to whether higher standards would result in lower-achieving populations leaving the schools" (p. 2). This document and others written about educational reform implied that special education was a separate system, uninfluenced by what happened in regular education.

In this chapter, we examine what is meant by school reform, restructuring, and the notion of excellence in education, and we look at the relevance of all three to special education. The six national goals articulated by President Bush and the nation's governors are discussed in relation to issues and educational goals for students with disabilities particularly the extent to which the goal and objectives reflect any cognizance at all of students served in special education and the implications for students in special education of attempts to meet each goal and its associated objectives. We examine the issues that arise for students in special education programs from two large-scale reforms of the 1990s (statewide "choice" in education and statewide educational restructuring). Finally, we address some general issues of change in education and the complicating factors that serve as barriers to change in special education.

School Reform, Restructuring, and Excellence in Education

Many different initiatives designed to change education for the better, to improve education, have been called school reform. These initiatives include lengthening the school day or setting higher expectations for all students. Restructuring, however, is considered a different approach to reform: "It is a systematic approach that acknowledges the complexity of fundamentally changing the way schools are organized in order to significantly increase student learning. It shifts the focus of reform from mandating what educators do to looking at the results their actions produce" (National Governors' Association, 1990, p. 1). Examples of restructuring include site-based management (decision making carried out at a school site, rather than at a central office), the changing of staff roles (special education teachers serve special education students after school, rather than pulling them out of mainstream classes), the implementation of a higher-order thinking curriculum (emphasis on strategies for learning, for example, rather than on basic skills), and the adoption of an accountability system (student assessment to measure outcomes of learning). Excellence, the desired outcome of reform and restructuring, is the condition in which schools are successful in ultimately preparing students for adulthood.

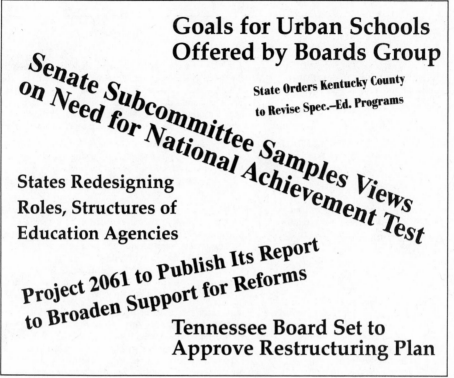

Goals for Urban Schools Offered by Boards Group

Senate Subcommittee Samples Views on Need for National Achievement Test

State Orders Kentucky County to Revise Spec.–Ed. Programs

States Redesigning Roles, Structures of Education Agencies

Project 2061 to Publish Its Report to Broaden Support for Reforms

Tennessee Board Set to Approve Restructuring Plan

SOURCE: *Education Week* (various issues).

The Reform Movement in General Education

How did the nation get to the point where it believed there was a critical need to reform or restructure education? The evolving attitude that America's educational system is in trouble has come from many different reports identifying those qualities in which America's schools are lacking or those areas in which outcomes for American youths are below those for youths from other countries. The reports identifying problems/needs and possible avenues for change have been part of what has been referred to as the "three waves of educational reform."

In 1983, the nation was shocked when the National Commission on Excellence in Education produced its report, *A Nation at Risk: The Imperative for Educational Reform*, which was one of many to appear in this first wave of educational reform. The first wave reports, some of which are summarized in Table 6.1, focused on the dangers of mediocre education to the nation's growth and strength. Most reports emphasized the importance of commitment to excellence by advocating higher standards and "more"—more courses, more homework, more time, and more state and local responsibility. In 1984, President Ronald Reagan presented four national education goals to be reached by the target year 1990:

TABLE 6.1   Selected first-wave educational reform reports

Report	Focus/Major Points
A Nation At Risk: The Imperative for Educational Reform (National Commission on Excellence in Education, 1983)	This report argues that the nation is at risk because "mediocrity," not excellence, is the norm in education. Recommendations include more time for learning, better textbooks and other materials, more homework, higher expectations, stricter attendance policies, and improved standards, salaries, rewards, and incentives for teachers.
A Place Called School: Prospects for the Future (Goodlad, 1983)	This report presents recommendations derived from a study of schooling. Included are changes such as establishing smaller schools, ending the tracking system, and requiring a core curriculum of general courses in high school.
Making the Grade (Twentieth Century Fund Task Force on Federal Elementary and Secondary Education Policy, 1983)	This report argues that schools have been forced to play so many roles that they are in danger of forgetting their purpose and that federal government should support local and state efforts because the problems with education are "national and acute in intensity." Recommendations are made for curriculum change, rewards for teachers, and collection of information about education and academic performance of students.
Action for Excellence—A Comprehensive Plan to Improve Our Nation's Schools (Education Commission of the States & Task Force on Education for Economic Growth, 1983)	This report stresses the need for greater intensity and increased productivity throughout the educational system, arguing that technological change and increases in demand for knowledge within the workplace make the current definition of basic skills inadequate. The report argues that a new and higher regard for teachers is essential.
High School: A Report on American Secondary Education (Boyer, 1983)	This Carnegie Report focuses on establishing a core of common learning both to facilitate instruction and to foster connections among schools and workplaces. The need to identify and reward excellence in teaching is also emphasized.
Academic Preparation for College: What Students Need to Know and Be Able to Do (College Board, Educational Equality Project, 1983)	This report identifies what it takes to do competent and worthwhile college work, with a description of learning outcomes that exceed those in most secondary schools. Better preparation for the collegebound is predicted to spill over and improve the schooling of those who are not collegebound and also to lower the number of high school dropouts.

- To raise high school graduation rates to more than 90 percent

- To raise scores on college admissions tests above the 1985 average

- To make teachers' salaries competitive with entry-level business and engineering graduates' salaries

- To stiffen high school graduation requirements

TABLE 6.2   Selected second-wave educational reform reports

Report	Focus/Major Points
Children in Need: Investment Strategies for the Educationally Disadvantaged (Committee for Economic Development, 1987)	This report focuses on needs specific to children who are disadvantaged, noting that most reform efforts have bypassed this group. Business leaders, educators, and policy makers are urged to look beyond the classroom to establish new partnerships that bolster not only education but also the health and well-being of the whole child.
Educational Achievement: Explanations and Implications of Recent Trends (Congressional Budget Office, 1987)	This report appraises trends in achievement test scores and their causes. Implications drawn from findings focus on overreliance on test scores for assessing effects of educational initiatives, the importance of improving higher-order skills, and the need to focus on traditionally low-scoring groups such as minorities.
Time for Results: The Governors' 1991 Report (National Governors' Association, 1986)	This report identifies key educational issues for five-year period: teacher pay, educational recruitment, parental choice of schools, strategies for the poor, school year, technology, college education, and clear, measurable educational goals.
What Works (U.S. Department of Education, 1986)	This report presents research findings and comments on them in areas of home, classroom, and school. It provides a highly readable translation of technical information, with citations for further reference.

These goals, while admirable, seemed to ignore the growing population of students considered to be in need of special education services. More of the same hardly seemed the answer to their needs. These goals were feasible only if special education students were considered to be separate from general education students. Only by excluding students with mental retardation, significant emotional and behavioral disorders, or learning disabilities was it possible to think about goals such as a 90 percent graduation rate and higher scores on college entrance exams.

A second wave of educational reform began with the 1986 *Time for Results* report from the National Governors' Association. This and the other reports of the second wave, which are summarized in Table 6.2, emphasized the need to improve school organization and policy as well as the quality of teachers. The governors' report did not argue for more of the same; it argued for changes in the form of improvements. And the need for early educational experiences for children at risk was recognized. This was perhaps the first recognition that children with special needs did exist and that they would require extraordinary procedures and approaches to reach the level required to progress through school successfully and to ultimately attain national goals of excellence. This still was not the same as recognizing the population of children and youths being served in special education, but it did reveal the tip of the iceberg!

TABLE 6.3   Selected third-wave educational reform reports

Report	Focus/Major Points
Turning Points: Preparing American Youth for the 21st Century (Carnegie Council on Adolescent Development, 1989)	This report identifies the early adolescence period as one in which key decisions are made that affect a person's entire future and provides many recommendations to improve the educational experiences of all middle school students, especially those at risk of being left behind.
America's Shame, America's Hope: Twelve Million Youth at Risk (Smith & Lincoln, 1988)	This report presents itself as an inquiry into the education reform movement of the 1980s, with at-risk youth as the frame of reference. The argument is that despite reform reports, the numbers of at-risk youth have increased. Recommendations are primarily policy related, focusing on legislatures, governors, and commissioners of education.
The Forgotten Half: Non-College Youth in America (William T. Grant Foundation, 1988)	This report calls attention to the needs of youths not planning to go to college to help them to move from school to careers, identifies the problem as being in the economy and the paths for youths to enter it, and indicates that education can help but is not the sole solution.
Results in Education: 1988 (National Governors' Association, 1988)	This report describes state efforts to track the results of earlier education reforms, provides information on a state-by-state basis, and summarizes results.
Youth Indicators, 1988: Trends in the Well-Being of American Youth (Office of Educational Research and Improvement, 1988)	This report provides a broad view of the welfare of youths through presentation of statistical information; goes beyond educational indicators to include family structure, economic well-being, drug use, suicide, employment prospects, and so on; and provides a longitudinal perspective.

The third wave of school reform emphasized more than ever before the needs of children and youths who were at risk or disadvantaged, who had dropped out of school, or whose needs were not being met by the educational system (see Table 6.3). It was argued that to be effective in helping prepare students for the twenty-first century, the educational system would have to be reconstructed. There was a call to reach consensus about national educational goals and strategies to reach them. These calls led eventually to the 1989 education summit of President Bush and the nation's governors and the development of a new set of national education goals.

Parallel Play in School Reform

As young children develop, their social interactions with other children begin as "parallel play." In this type of play, two children may sit side by side without ever having any interchange between them. Yet when asked, they will say that they were playing with each other. It is in this way that school reform began in special education.

During the time when general education was thinking deeply about educational reform, the regular education initiative was proposed. Despite its name, this was a call from special education for reform in the way services were provided to students with disabilities. It called for a sharing of responsibility by regular educators and special educators for students considered handicapped (Will, 1986). For the most part, debate about the initiative caused great furor among special educators and parents. Some special educators worried about the need for their services if regular educators really were to assume responsibility for students with disabilities. Others wondered whether they had the consultation skills required for the shared responsibility espoused by backers of the initiative. Parents expressed concerns about due process rights and about whether their children would be appropriately educated. Personnel in the general education system knew relatively little about the debate until years after it began. The regular education initiative was not viewed as an educational reform in the way that other recommendations were. In Chapter 5, we discussed the regular education initiative more fully in the context within which it had its greatest impact—debates about appropriate placement of students with disabilities. For educational reform in general, it had limited impact.

Six New National Goals for Education

In September 1989, President Bush and the governors from the fifty states met in Charlottesville, Virginia, for a "historic education summit" that for the first time produced goals that all governors supported. The six goals for education and their associated objectives were stated in the final report from the summit (January 31, 1990) and reiterated in a press release from the White House (February 26, 1990) as well as in numerous other publications. The goals focused on school readiness, school completion, student achievement and citizenship, science and mathematics, adult literacy and lifelong learning, and the school environment (safe, disciplined, and drug free).

Readiness for School

The focus of the first educational goal is readiness for school and three associated objectives:

• *Goal 1:* By the year 2000, all children in America will start school ready to learn.

• All disadvantaged and disabled children will have access to high-quality and developmentally appropriate preschool programs that help prepare children for school.

• Every parent in America will be a child's first teacher and devote time each
day helping his or her preschool child learn; parents will have access to training
and support they need.

• Children will receive the nutrition and health care needed to arrive at school
with healthy minds and bodies, and the number of low birthweight babies will
be significantly reduced through enhanced prenatal health systems. (White House,
1990, p. 3)

This goal is the one that most directly recognizes the child with a disability
and is the only one to use the term *disabled*. In discussing this goal, the press
release from the White House demonstrated a recognition of the importance of
early childhood experiences, early preventive measures, and parent involvement.
This recognition reflected findings in much of the research on early childhood
programs for children with disabilities (e.g., Casto & Mastropieri, 1986; White &
Casto, 1989). The press release noted the great strides that had been made
nationally in maternal and child health care, in effective delivery systems for
prenatal and postnatal care, and in successful preschool programs. It did not,
however, even begin to hint at the difficulties inherent in deciding who should
receive early childhood services, particularly services for children designated as
having disabilities. (These and other issues related to early identification and
intervention are discussed in Chapter 10.)

The press release argued that "we still need more prevention, testing, and
screening, and early identification and treatment of learning disorders and disabilities" (1990, p. 6). It assumed, however, that implementation of the recommended measures would result in all children being ready for school. The definition of "ready for school" was not provided. Does it mean ready to learn with
a group of children? Does it mean ready to learn the names of colors? Does it
mean ready to learn the alphabet? Or does it mean ready to read? Whatever the
definition, it may have to be broadened before it can apply to all children. Even
if this is done, however, the remaining education goals raise many additional
issues with regard to children and youths with disabilities.

High School Completion

The completion of high school is the focus of the second national education goal
and its two objectives.

• *Goal 2:* By the year 2000, the high school graduation rate will increase to at
least 90 percent.

• The nation must dramatically reduce its dropout rate and seventy-five percent
of those students who do drop out will successfully complete a high school degree
or its equivalent.

• The gap in high school graduation rates between American students from
minority backgrounds and their non-minority counterparts will be eliminated.
(White House; 1990, p. 3)

This goal sounds suspiciously similar to the national goal voiced by President
Reagan in 1984 and similarly suggests nonrecognition of students with disabilities.

The press release discussion of this goal suggested that the goal could be met by fundamentally restructuring the public school system and that "efforts to restructure education must work toward guaranteeing that all students are engaged in rigorous programs of instruction designed to ensure that every child, *regardless of* background or *disability*, acquires the knowledge and skills necessary to succeed in a changing economy" (White House, 1990, p. 7; emphasis added). It is doubtful that this suggestion reflected a recognition of students with disabilities, given that no attempt was made to define "knowledge and skills necessary to succeed" in a broad enough way to include students with serious emotional disabilities, severe mental retardation, or multiple physical disabilities, for example. Nor did this goal address how the high school graduation rate could reach 90 percent if students with disabilities were included in the student count. Would different graduation standards therefore be needed for students in special education programs? And would varying standards fly in the face of calls for stiffer graduation requirements?

The notion of dramatically reducing the dropout rate reflects the flip side of the coin and thus encounters the same difficulties. Indeed, the nation's governors, along with many others, may not have even begun to recognize the extent to which dropping out of school is a problem in the special education population. For some time, an implicit assumption held that students in special education were less likely to drop out of school because they were already receiving the extra attention they needed. But recent evidence suggested that "youth with handicaps, who are entitled to receive appropriate pubic education until they complete a high school degree or until age 21, also drop out of school at high rates" (Wolman, Bruininks, & Thurlow, 1989, p. 6). In fact, relatively "controlled" studies have generally reported that students with handicaps, whether they attend special education schools or are mainstreamed, are more likely to drop out of school than are students without handicaps (e.g., Bruininks, Thurlow, Lewis, & Larson, 1988; Owings & Stocking, 1986; Stephenson, 1985).

If students in special education are already in programs and receiving services much like those now identified as effective for dropout prevention, what must be done to prevent students in special education from dropping out of school? Although this major question was receiving attention as the 1990s began, that attention did not come from the national education goals and the programs identified as reflecting "best practice" for dropout prevention in educational reform.

School Achievement and Citizenship

Broad notions of achievement and citizenship come together in the third educational goal and the five objectives associated with it.

- *Goal 3:* By the year 2000, American students will leave grades four, eight and twelve having demonstrated competency in challenging subject matter including English, mathematics, science, history, and geography; and every school in America will ensure that all students learn to use their minds well, so they may be prepared for responsible citizenship, further learning, and productive employment in our modern economy.

• The academic performance of elementary and secondary students will increase significantly in every quartile, and the distribution of minority students in each level will more closely reflect the student population as a whole.

• The percentage of students who demonstrate the ability to reason, solve problems, apply knowledge, and write and communicate effectively will increase substantially.

• All students will be involved in activities that promote citizenship, community service, and personal responsibility.

• The percentage of students who are competent in more than one language will substantially increase.

• All students will be knowledgeable about the diverse cultural heritage of this nation and about the world community. (White House, 1990, pp. 3–4)

This goal focuses on demonstrating competency in various content areas and on learning how to use the mind to foster responsible citizenship, further learning, and productive employment. Two of the objectives indicate that the percentage of students will be increased. For example, the percentage of students demonstrating specific abilities and the percentage of students showing competence in use of another language are targeted for increases. These objectives can be viewed as reasonable regardless of whether students with disabilities are included in the computations. Other objectives under goal 3, however, seem to provide another indication that special education was discounted as the objectives were formulated. The objective that "all students will be involved in activities that promote citizenship, community service, and personal responsibility" can be viewed as possible only within an inclusive environment where people with disabilities participate along with people without disabilities. The suggestion that "all students will be knowledgeable about the diverse cultural heritage of this nation and about the world community" may not even be possible for some people with severe mental disabilities.

Goal three and its objectives reflected a move toward national and state-by-state assessments of educational indicators such as the National Assessment of Educational Progress. Consideration of the development of a national test for all students similarly reflected this move toward better educational accountability. But the push toward assessment of outcomes created many additional questions for educators responsible for students with disabilities. How many students with disabilities, and which ones, should be included in statewide assessments? Is it fair for one state to exclude all students with emotional and learning disabilities from its testing program when another state includes all except those who would be detrimentally affected by the testing experience (in the opinion of a designated team)? (These issues and many others that arise in relation to demonstrating competency are discussed in greater depth in Chapter 9.)

Science and Mathematics

The fourth goal and the accompanying three objectives address two specific content areas in the general school curriculum: science and math.

- *Goal 4:* By the year 2000, U.S. students will be first in the world in science and mathematics achievement.

- Math and science education will be strengthened throughout the system, especially in the early grades.

- The number of teachers with a substantive background in mathematics and science will increase by 50 percent.

- The number of U.S. undergraduate and graduate students, especially women and minorities, who complete degrees in mathematics, science, and engineering will increase significantly. (White House, 1990, p. 4)

This fourth goal targets two specific content areas for emphasis because of their significance in international business competition. This concentration is not reasonable for all students unless math is broadly defined as consumer skills or science connotes knowing one's place in the world. This issue and related issues form another pervasive question in special education—what should be the content of instruction? (See Chapter 8 for further discussion.)

The fourth goal is also an example of a focus on some educational processes (expertise of teachers, strength of the educational program), rather than on student outcomes. This emphasis is fine, but its implications for special education are unclear. Does it mean that special education teachers also have to increase their expertise in science and math? Will general education math teachers have to become better trained at working with students with disabilities?

Adult Literacy and Lifelong Learning

The fifth education goal and its five objectives move the focus more clearly beyond the school setting to focus on postschool outcomes.

- *Goal 5:* By the year 2000, every adult American will be literate and will possess the knowledge and skills necessary to compete in a global economy and exercise the rights and responsibilities of citizenship.

- Every major American business will be involved in strengthening the connection between education and work.

- All workers will have the opportunity to acquire the knowledge and skills, from basic to highly technical, needed to adapt to emerging new technologies, work methods, and markets through public and private educational, vocational, technical, workplace, or other programs.

- The number of quality programs, including those at libraries, that are designed to serve more effectively the needs of the growing number of part-time and mid-career students will increase substantially.

- The proportion of those qualified students, especially minorities, who enter college; who complete at least two years; and who complete their degree programs will increase substantially.

- The proportion of college graduates who demonstrate an advanced ability to think critically, communicate effectively, and solve problems will increase substantially. (White House, 1990, pp. 4–5)

This goal can be broadly interpreted to cover a goal for successful transition from school to work that has been espoused for students with disabilities (Johnson, Bruininks, & Thurlow, 1987; Rusch & Phelps, 1987; Will, 1984). Yet the press release discussion of this goal spoke only of jobs that required more than a high school education, coordination of policies and programs to promote literacy, and greater access to college educations for qualified students. These objectives are reasonable under certain assumptions, but they do not ask, for example, what makes a student qualified for access to a college education. This is a crucial consideration given that youths with disabilities are less likely to enroll in postsecondary education programs than are their peers without disabilities (Fairweather & Shaver, 1991), despite increases in the number of two- and four-year colleges providing services for students with disabilities (Vogel, 1982). Even though students with certain disabilities (such as speech, physical, visual, or hearing impairments) may be more likely to enroll in postsecondary education than students with learning or emotional difficulties, the enrollment of such students is still much lower than for students without disabilities.

Safe, Disciplined, and Drug-Free Schools

The sixth goal and three related objectives address the school environment.

- *Goal 6:* By the year 2000, every school in America will be free of drugs and violence and will offer a disciplined environment conducive to learning.
- Every school will implement a firm and fair policy on use, possession, and distribution of drugs and alcohol.
- Parents, businesses, and community organizations will work together to ensure that schools are a safe haven for all children.
- Every school district will develop a comprehensive K–12 drug and alcohol prevention education program. Drug and alcohol curriculum should be taught as an integral part of health education. In addition, community-based teams should be organized to provide students and teachers with needed support. (White House, 1990, p. 5)

This broad goal, which is directed primarily at the content and process of education, is appropriate for all students as long as those with disabilities are included in the health education program. But this goal's actual acknowledgment of the needs of or programs for students with disabilities is questionable. This has been the case in many aspects of the school reform movement. Much of what is proposed would be appropriate if adapted to meet the needs of a broad array of students, not just those preparing for college or those at risk for academic failure.

Programs to Meet the National Education Goals

One year after the goals had been identified and voiced to the nation, President Bush reported to the governors on the ways in which the goals had been "woven

Gallup Poll Results on the Issue of National Goals for Education

People strongly believe in the six education goals for the Nineties announced last February, with appropriate fanfare, by President George Bush and the 50 state governors. They believe in them so strongly that they would like to vote for political candidates who support these goals. But people are also profoundly skeptical about the possibility that the goals can be reached within this decade, which was part of the plan put forth by the President and the governors.

These conclusions are drawn from answers to three key questions asked in the 22nd Annual Poll of the Public's Attitudes Toward the Public Schools, sponsored by Phi Delta Kappa and conducted by the Gallup Organization in April and May 1990.

More than three-quarters of the 1,594 adults interviewed for the poll attach very high or high priority to all six of the national goals for education. They give highest priority to the last goal: to free every school in America from drugs and violence and offer a disciplined environment conducive to learning. But only 5% of the respondents think it very likely that we will achieve this goal by the year 2000, and 36% think it very *unlikely* that we will. The only goal among the six that even 50% of the people think we might reach in this decade is that of readying children to learn by the time they start school.

This pessimism echoes the judgment of many experts, some of whom, like Dorothy Rich, president of the Home and School Institute and a member of the governing board for the National Assessment of Educational Progress, regard the goals as political pabulum. "They are too big to be doable," she asserts. "It's like saying, 'No one will be killing each other in automobile accidents by the year 2000.' "

SOURCE: Results from the 22nd annual Gallup Poll of the public's attitudes toward the public schools (Elam, 1990), p. 42. Elam, S. M. (1990). The 22nd annual Gallup Poll of the public's attitude toward the public schools. *Phi Delta Kappan, 72*(1), 41–55

into the fabric of our efforts to restructure and revitalize American education" (White House, 1991 n.p.). This 107-page report (not counting many pages of appendices) presented the important steps that the nation had taken in the reform of American education and did make mention of programs supported by the Office of Special Education and Rehabilitative Services and students with disabilities. The number of special education activities and the programs identified are summarized in Table 6.4. Clearly, policy makers in special education were attending in many ways to the nation's educational goals.

TABLE 6.4   Special education activities to reach national education goals, 1990–1991

Goal	Special Education Activity
Readiness for school (49 activities; 12.2 percent for special ed)	Department of Education's Preschool Grants program, serving an estimated 360,000 children with disabilities aged three through five offers a head start to children with disabilities who are preparing for school. Program identifies and provides training, diagnostic assessments, and physical therapy so that children may enter school ready to learn.
	Office of Special Education and Rehabilitative Services supports various discretionary grants to improve the quality and availability of early intervention services for children with disabilities from birth through age three. For example, the Singer Research Institute is developing and testing intervention strategies to improve the integration of children with disabilities into regular preschool, prekindergarten, and kindergarten programs.
	Office of Special Education and Rehabilitative Services is emphasizing in its Early Childhood Education Program the problem of children disabled through maternal drug abuse. As part of this effort, department will fund new demonstration projects for children with disabilities born with human immunodeficiency virus (HIV) infection or drug addiction and children with disabilities born to teenage mothers.
	Office of Civil Rights has issued formal policy guidance on the requirements of school districts to educate children with HIV infection and has also advised all chief state school officers of their legal responsibility to provide an appropriate education to children born with drug addiction and to homeless children with disabilities.
	Department of Education is concentrating work on readiness among special populations. Working with other federal agencies, the department is preparing an inventory of readiness programs serving special populations with emphasis on limited-English-proficient, disabled, and at-risk populations.
	In fiscal year 1991, Office of Special Education and Rehabilitative Services will establish a new early childhood research institute that will focus specifically on children prenatally exposed to drugs and alcohol. A second institute will examine state eligibility policies and the availability of early intervention and special education programs for infants with disabilities, including drug-exposed infants. Model demonstrations will invite projects that develop innovative programs for drug-exposed children three to five years old.
High school completion (35 activities; 11.4 percent for special ed)	Office of Special Education and Rehabilitative Services and the Department of Justice are jointly funding a comprehensive training program for counselors of state vocational rehabilitation agencies involved with fourteen- to eighteen-year-old youths who have been drug dependent.

TABLE 6.4 (cont.)

Goal	Special Education Activity
High school completion (35 activities; 11.4 percent for special ed) (*cont.*)	Office of Special Education Programs (OSEP) is sponsoring multiple program demonstrations for junior high school students with serious emotional disturbance and learning disabilities who are at risk of dropping out of school. These demonstrations are aimed at developing educational programs and practices that encourage these students to stay in school and graduate.
	OSEP's state-reported data system has been collecting dropout and other high school exiting data for more than five years. Additionally, the National Longitudinal Transition Study (NLTS) has collected dropout data on a sample of students aged fourteen to twenty-six. Both sources report that the dropout rate for students with disabilities is at least 10 percent greater than that for nondisabled students. These national-level data have prompted states to undertake state and local analysis of the dropout problem, leading to special dropout projects aimed at correcting the problem.
	OSEP is supporting an extension of the NLTS to gain more information about factors that contribute to high dropout rates for students with disabilities and about ways that completion rates can be improved.
Student achievement and citizenship (67 activities; 3.0 percent for special ed)	Department of Education is providing support programs for those most in need, such as Chapter 1 compensatory education, special education and services, bilingual education, migrant education, education for the homeless, and students services programs to promote entry into postsecondary education for the neediest students. The department is committed to a more extensive dissemination of information about "what works" to improve the educational performance of at-risk students.
	OSEP's Technology, Educational Media, and Materials for the Handicapped Program provides grants to institutions of higher education, state and local education agencies, and other agencies to assist public and private industry in developing and marketing new technology, media, and materials for persons with disabilities. Although the majority of these students are cognitively competent, many require special technology to learn. This program designs and adapts such instructional technology for students eager to compete in challenging subject matter.
Science and math (86 activities; 2.3 percent for special ed)	Through the Office of Special Education and Rehabilitative Services, work will continue on two three-year projects initiated in 1989 (for mathematics) and 1990 (for science) to develop curriculum guides and alternative curricular proposals for integrating students with disabilities into regular classroom work in these subjects.
	Department of the Interior signed an agreement with Gallaudet University in Washington, D.C., designed to enhance opportunities for employment in the science fields for people with hearing impairments and other disabilities.

(continued)

TABLE 6.4   Special education activities to reach national education goals, 1990–1991 (cont.)

Goal	Special Education Activity
Adult literacy and lifelong learning (71 activities; 2.8 percent for special ed)	Office of Special Education supports innovative models for providing postsecondary students and adults who have disabilities with vocational and independent living skills that are essential for entering the workplace, maintaining employment, and becoming active citizens in their communities.
	Department of Labor launched a school-to-work transition program for disabled youths in October 1990. The project will seek to integrate education, rehabilitation, the Job Training Partnership Act, and employer resources in a community-based network of effective services and opportunities leading to greater participation of youths with disabilities in the labor force.
Safe, disciplined, and drug-free schools (61 activities; 0 percent for special ed)	(No activities are listed for special education.)

SOURCE: Based on White House. (1991, February 4). *The National education goals: A second report for the nation's governors.* Washington, DC: Author.

Reform, Restructuring, and Excellence in Special Education?

At about the time that the governors and President Bush were discussing the nation's goals for education, the National Council on Disability was preparing a report for the president entitled *The Education of Students with Disabilities: Where Do We Stand?* This report noted that "for the most part school reform efforts have not been directed toward addressing the special challenges that students with disabilities face. There is a perception that students with disabilities have a separate system, called special education [in which they are] better provided for than many other groups of students" (1989, p. 2).

Based on a year-long study, the Council argued that it was time to shift the focus of concern from access to education to the quality of education and student outcomes. The Council found many problems in current educational practice for students with disabilities and reported twenty-eight findings that indicated a need for reform. (These findings are presented in Table 6.5.) These findings led the Council to call for the establishment of a national commission on excellence in the education of students with disabilities to continue an assessment of the status of the education of students with disabilities and to make recommendations about how the quality of education for these students could be enhanced and how improved student outcomes could be realized. Twenty questions to be addressed by the commission were identified (National Council on Disability, 1989):

TABLE 6.5   Findings on educational practice with students with disabilities

1. Parent-professional relationships too often are strained and difficult, and parents and professionals frequently view one another as adversaries rather than as partners. (p. 15)
2. Some parents have difficulty finding appropriate services for their children. (p. 16)
3. Parents and students report that some schools have low expectations for students with disabilities and establish inappropriate learning objectives and goals. (p. 19)
4. Services often are not available to meet the needs of disadvantaged, minority, and rural families who have children with disabilities. (p. 21)
5. Families in the military are not universally entitled to the services or the protections guaranteed under P.L. 94-142. (p. 22)
6. There is a perception that the outcomes of due process hearings are biased in favor to the schools. (p. 24)
7. Many parents are uninformed about their rights under the law. (p. 24)
8. Due process hearings are costly. (p. 25)
9. There is a paucity of attorneys with expertise in special education law available to represent parents. (p. 25)
10. There are no standard qualification or training requirements for hearing officers. (p. 26)
11. There is no national database that includes the routine collection of data regarding due process hearings. (p. 26)
12. There are several commonly agreed upon characteristics to describe what constitutes an effective school. (p. 27)
13. Most school reform initiatives appear to be a response to declining academic achievement, rather than efforts to find ways for schools to meet the diverse needs of all students. (p. 27)
14. An essential aspect of school reform is the professionalization of teaching. (p. 28)
15. School reform efforts have not specifically addressed the diverse needs of students with disabilities. (p. 28)
16. Evaluation procedures, disability classifications, and resulting placement decisions vary greatly among school districts and States, and they often are not related to students' learning characteristics. (p. 29)
17. A highly emotional discussion is taking place about the role of separate schools and the unique instructional needs of students with specific disabilities such as deafness. (p. 31)
18. Special education is a relatively separate system of service delivery. (p. 34)
19. In practice, special education has been defined more as an organizational approach to delivering instruction—as part of a placement continuum—than as a specific body of professional expertise. (p. 35)
20. Current pedagogy regarding effective schools and teaching practices can facilitate the integration of special needs students into general classrooms. (p. 36)
21. A strong Federal role in educating students with disabilities is essential. (p. 38)
22. The Federal government has not fulfilled its promise of 40% funding of the cost of providing education to students with disabilities. (p. 39)
23. Federal monitoring is an essential aspect of the Federal-State partnership. (p. 39)
24. Upon leaving school, students with disabilities and their families often have a difficult time accessing appropriate adult services and/or postsecondary education and training programs. (p. 40)
25. Effective transition planning for high school students with disabilities can facilitate their success in adult life. (p. 41)
26. Graduates with disabilities are more likely to be employed following school if (1) comprehensive vocational training is a primary component of their high school program and (2) they have a job secured at the time of graduation. (p. 42)
27. There are insufficient partnerships between the business community and schools for the purpose of enhancing employment opportunities for students with disabilities. (p. 43)
28. Parent participation during high school facilitates the successful transition of students with disabilities from school to adult life. (p. 44)

SOURCE: National Council on Disability. (1989). *The education of students with disabilities: Where do we stand?* Washington, DC: Author. Used with permission.
NOTE: The report has three additional findings not presented here that reflect an international perspective.

1. How can the special education community join the general education community in a partnership to assure that the goals of equity and excellence are pursued simultaneously in national school reform efforts? (p. 49)

2. How can the special education community and the general education community collaborate to further consolidate the special education and general education systems for the benefit of all students? (p. 51)

3. What steps can be taken to assure that the movement toward providing services for students with disabilities in their neighborhood schools continues and that the services are appropriate? (p. 52)

4. How can the pedagogy associated with special education be brought to bear in general education classrooms? (p. 52)

5. What is the relationship between the educational setting and student outcomes? (p. 53)

6. In the 1990s what is the appropriate Federal role in the education of students with disabilities as we continue to focus on developing excellence in education services for students with disabilities? (p. 53)

7. What can be done to further enhance the Federal-State partnership that is so critical to the effective implementation of P.L. 94-142? (p. 54)

8. How can Federal compliance monitoring for P.L. 94-142 be improved to (1) more meaningfully involve parents, (2) be more timely, and (3) ensure full compliance with the law? (p. 54)

9. How can effective parent-professional relationships be established and maintained as a component of an appropriate educational program for students with disabilities? (p. 54)

10. What steps can be taken to assure that students with disabilities in minority, rural, and disadvantaged communities have full access to appropriate educational services? (p. 55)

11. How can students with disabilities whose parents serve in the military be afforded the same equal educational opportunity as all other eligible students? (p. 55)

12. What steps can be taken to assure that all parents of students with disabilities are fully informed of and understand their rights under P.L. 94-142? (p. 56)

13. What are the minimum competencies and training requirements for due process hearing officers? (p. 56)

14. How can information about the due process system, including outcomes of due process hearings and relevant court decisions, be disseminated nationally to parent organizations, State and local policymakers, and other entities concerned with the education of students with disabilities? (p. 56)

15. Is there an expanded role for institutions of higher education in the development of innovative personnel preparation programs that prepare educators to work with students who have a range of diverse needs? (p. 57)

16. How can schools provide an individualized transition plan for every high school student with a disability and ensure coordination between the school and adult service agencies or postsecondary education and training programs? (p. 57)

17. What steps are necessary for schools to provide (1) a comprehensive curriculum that includes extensive community-based vocational experiences as a primary component of each high school student's individualized educational program and

(2) job placement at the time of graduation for all students who want to work? (p. 58)

18. How can schools and businesses effectively form partnerships, particularly at the local level, to collaborate on employment-related curriculum and training programs for students with disabilities? (p. 59)

19. How can the special education community take the lead in educating the business community about the abilities and talents of students with disabilities and the contributions they do and can make in the workplace? (p. 59)

20. How can the United States best coordinate with other countries in sharing information and resources regarding effective educational practices for students with disabilities? (p. 59)

These questions were not related to the nation's six education goals because the goals did not exist at the time these questions were posed. Even though the questions were in line with those being voiced in general education, the recommended commission was not established. Nevertheless, the National Council on Disability did announce a request for proposals for the establishment of a project to study the outcomes of elementary and secondary educational programs for students with disabilities. In its request, the Council indicated that information was needed on the effectiveness of education for children with disabilities on three "national objectives": academic achievement for the majority of students, work "readiness," and improved ongoing quality of life.

Reform and restructuring in general education necessarily had (and continue to have) an impact on special education. But ideas for reform and reform movements in general education continued to occur without much input from special education. Kaufman, Kameenui, Birman, and Danielson suggested that special education had to change this situation by becoming a master of educational reform:

> In order to be a master of educational reform and not become its victim, special education must not be complacent with the impressive and significant achievements of the past 15 years. Special education must do more than focus on issues of access and inclusion for children with disabilities during these times of reform and change. In order to achieve better results, special educators and parents must assertively seek the knowledge and innovations needed to expand the provision of effective educational experiences and support not only through special education but in regular education, at home, and in the community. It is critical that educational reform and change be viewed as an open-ended journey. The nature of the journey will depend on our inquisitiveness and our resolve to inquire and act. (1990, p. 110)

At the beginning of the 1990s, comprehensive general education reforms were getting well under way, with as yet unidentified effects, as some of the examples in the next section indicate.

General Education Reforms and Their Effects

For the most part, educational reform proceeded on a piecemeal basis, with more talk than action. Local districts sometimes made what they considered dramatic changes in their programs (e.g., whole language approach to reading) in the name of reform. States commonly participated in reform by gathering task force groups to determine how to raise their standards for graduation or to develop a minimum competency test that students had to pass to graduate. In a few places, however, large-scale reforms were enacted by states. Two of these are described in brief here, along with their possible ramifications for students with disabilities.

Choice in Education

In 1985, only those students who had their own (or their parent's) financial resources and those students who resided in a school district with a magnet school program could choose where they received their elementary or secondary education. School placement was determined by where a student lived unless the student or parents could pay for a private school or unless the student lived in a school district that had designed school programs to attract a variety of students, usually in an attempt to meet desegregation goals. By the late 1980s, this had changed dramatically.

Minnesota was the first state to enact a statewide open enrollment law, which was one in a series of choice-in-education policies legislated in this state (programs of excellence; postsecondary enrollment option program, high school graduation incentives program, area learning centers; educational program for pregnant minors and minor parents). The open enrollment law allowed parents of students attending school in Minnesota to enroll their children in any district in the state unless there clearly was not enough space or enrollment would interfere with desegregation activities of either the sending or the receiving district. State moneys followed students who used this option.

Open enrollment was one of the most comprehensive and far-reaching educational reform efforts undertaken by a state. At about the same time, President Bush declared that "expanding parents' rights to choose public schools is a national imperative" (*Education Week*, January 18, 1989, p. 1). Within a year of the Minnesota enactment, Nebraska, Iowa, and Arkansas had passed open enrollment legislation.

Arguments were made both for and against open enrollment as well as for other "choice" options. The gist of most of the arguments for choice was that no single educational program was best for all children and that parents and schools together had to address the different ways that students learn and how schools could provide the best education for all children (see Boyd & Walberg, 1990; Nathan, 1989). Arguments against choice concentrated on its perceived "real purposes," such as the National Education Association's argument that it would compromise a commitment to free, equitable, universal, and quality public education for every student (Olson, 1989). In all these arguments, little or no mention was made of students with disabilities and the potential impact of an open enrollment policy on this group.

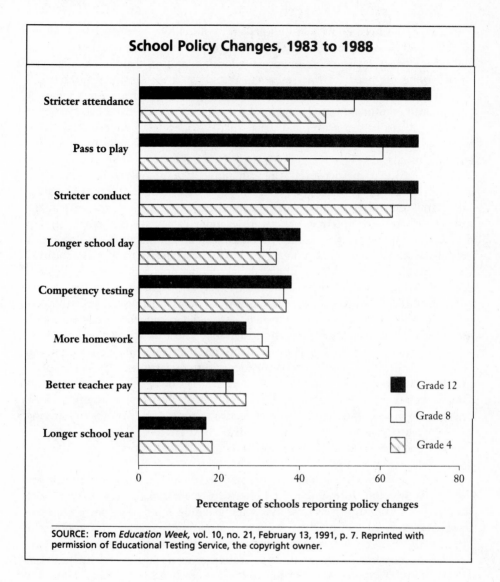

School Policy Changes, 1983 to 1988

Stricter attendance

Pass to play

Stricter conduct

Longer school day

Competency testing

More homework

Better teacher pay

Longer school year

Grade 12

Grade 8

Grade 4

0   20   40   60   80

Percentage of schools reporting policy changes

SOURCE: From *Education Week,* vol. 10, no. 21, February 13, 1991, p. 7. Reprinted with permission of Educational Testing Service, the copyright owner.

A major research effort was undertaken by Ysseldyke, Thurlow, and Algozzine in 1990 to begin collecting some data on the effects of a statewide open enrollment policy on students in special education and on their school districts. In proposing the need for this research, Ysseldyke et al. identified three broad issue areas: issues for those students who transfer from one district to another as part of open enrollment, issues for those who do not transfer from one district to another, and issues that arise for districts that provide special education services, particularly those that experience large increases in special education student enrollments.

Some say that district-level issues should not be a concern since it is the effect on the students that is important. But potential district-level effects are important to consider because such effects ultimately affect the students in the district. When these potential effects are examined in relation to students with disabilities, questions arise about special education staffing (will staffing needs become so variable from one year to the next that a consistent special education staff cannot be maintained?), financing (how will districts handle excess program costs for students attending different districts?), and transportation (will transportation difficulties limit the choices open to students with disabilities?). Effects on districts also may appear in the form of changed demands for special education assessment and reevaluations, which in turn may affect how well they are done. Further, districts chosen by many students on IEPs may find it necessary to change their definitions and criteria for identification of students as handicapped in order to keep the numbers reasonable in the eyes of the federal government. One of the premises behind open enrollment is that schools will attempt to draw students by making themselves more attractive in some way, perhaps by offering an advanced science program. Will any districts strive to earn the reputation of having a good educational program for students with disabilities, especially those with severe emotional and behavioral problems?

Some students with disabilities will transfer under the open enrollment option. It is important to examine the reasons for their transfer. Are they seeking better special education services? Are they avoiding more stringent graduation requirements in their district of residence? It is also important to examine the information that transferring students or their parents had before making the decision to transfer. For students with disabilities who transfer, the amount and quality of interdistrict communication will be extremely important. But if it means additional time and paperwork for already overburdened teachers, will it occur? Eventually, we need to have a good data base on the effects of transfer on student and family involvement in education, student academic engaged time in the classroom, and student achievement.

Some students with special learning needs may choose not to transfer under the open enrollment option. For these students, it will be important to make sure that remaining in the district of residence is not a result of coercion. Also, it will be important to examine whether certain schools become repositories for students who are poor, minority, and/or handicapped and who demonstrate significant behavior problems.

A summary of some of the pertinent issues are presented in Table 6.6, which includes a short explanation of each issue. Although the issues presented in the table are all real, it sometimes helps to think about them in terms of scenarios that have occurred or conceivably could occur from an open enrollment policy. For example:

• To a family desiring to protect their member with Down's syndrome from teasing and ridicule, the open enrollment policy means that the student can be enrolled in a district where mainstreaming will not be a required part of programming.

• To one administrator in a small urban school district surrounded by many rural school districts, the consumer orientation of the open enrollment plan could very likely mean that her school will become the favorite school serving students with emotional and behavioral disorders in the state. The school has an excellent program for students with emotional and behavioral disorders, and the principal envisions the onslaught of students whose parents want them to benefit from this program. She does not envision the school district's declaring the program "full" anytime in the near future.

• To a mother in a small district in northwestern Minnesota, the choice is more apparent than real because she feels coerced by her local school district to keep to son in their program for students with mental retardation. If her son leaves, the program will not have enough students, and one special education teacher will have to be dismissed.

• To a young woman of sixteen who has barely been making it in her school district, a move to a district not too far away means that she will be subject to more lenient graduation criteria and will no longer be labeled as handicapped. She sees both of these changes as beneficial for future employment.

• To a father in a suburban school district, the new, more stringent graduation requirements being implemented in his son's school district will result in significant programming changes. So while the learning disabilities program will continue to help his son to acquire some basic skills, regular classes in the district now will be paced much too fast for him, and he will face failure in any mainstream setting where previously he would have been okay.

At the time that Minnesota, Nebraska, Arkansas, and Iowa enacted their open enrollment legislation, there were no data about the effects of the policy for students with handicaps. In fact, there was no significant mention of the possibility of an effect on students with disabilities or on the districts providing services to them. It was not until after the legislation was enacted that anyone even addressed the issue. A book edited by Boyd and Walberg (1990) first mentioned the possibility of effects on students in special education. In this book, Finn (1990b) argued that any problems that might arise were solvable. He further noted that funding was an issue because federal policies directed the money to school districts based

TABLE 6.6   Issues for students with handicaps and for school districts

Issue	Explanation
For students who are handicapped and who transfer	
1. Variation in the kinds of families whose children participate	Some groups of parents or students may be more attracted than others to transferring districts. Certain families may choose certain districts, and certain districts may be more attractive to certain families.
2. LRE issues	Structure of special education programs may vary in terms of being more or less integrative and may be selected by parents on this basis.
3. Credits and graduation requirements	Districts have different requirements for students with handicaps in regard to credits and graduation.
4. Provision of information	Parents with children who are handicapped need to have specific information on different districts' criteria for identification of handicapped as well as information on services that are offered to students with special needs.
5. Transportation	Sending districts are not required to transport students, and receiving districts are required to transport only from the district border. Parents in poverty can be reimbursed by the nonresident district for the costs of transportation to the district border. Does this apply to special forms of transportation that may be required for students with handicaps?
6. Interdistrict communication	Guidelines for the provision of information about students are not specified.
7. Coercion	Coercion can occur when parents talk to their district about transferring. This may be a bigger problem for parents of students with handicaps.
8. Effects on academic performance	Students with mental handicaps may move to schools where they believe they will be provided a greater degree of freedom. Students may also move to schools where they feel they will receive better instruction.
9. Effects on student behavior	Students' behavioral problems may improve or deteriorate after movement to a selective school or after continuation in a nonselective school as a function of the behavior of other students.
10. Reasons for movement	Reasons for movement may include opportunity to participate in wider school activities, better programs, or more convenient school location.
11. Participation by specific categories of students	Certain categories of students with handicaps may participate more often in open enrollment than others.
12. Parental satisfaction	Parents may be more involved, supportive, and satisfied with districts they have chosen.
13. Parent involvement	Proponents of choice argue that open enrollment will expand parental involvement.
14. Dropout	Proponents of choice argue that open enrollment will decrease student dropout rate.

TABLE 6.6   (cont.)

Issue	Explanation
For students who are handicapped and who do not transfer	
1. Raising standards to attract students from other districts	When districts raise their standards to attract students, students who are already having difficulty in school may find school standards impossible to meet.
2. Dropout	Dropout rates are generally higher for students with handicaps. Will they increase for students who do not transfer?
3. Effects on academic performance	Effects on academic performance could result from either a decrease or an increase in students with handicaps and the types of students entering or leaving the nonparticipant's district.
4. Effects on student behavior	Changes in the behavior of other students may cause a student to be viewed as more of a problem or less of a problem.
5. Subtle coercion	Students must meet with someone in their district before transferring. At this point, they may be exposed to coercion to stay in the district.
6. Parental and student reasons for nonparticipation	Parents and students who do not participate in open enrollment may do so for specific reasons or for lack of knowledge about the option.
7. Nonparticipation by specific categories of students with handicaps	Nonparticipation may result for many reasons (e.g., parents satisfied with an MR program, parents not satisfied with an LD program).
8. Parental satisfaction	Parental satisfaction may be a reason for nonparticipation. Parental satisfaction for nonparticipants may change because of the nature of changes resulting from open enrollment.
For districts	
1. Criteria for approving between-district transfer of students with special needs	Guidelines, and probably who will be accepted for transfer, will vary between districts. Although guidelines will not include handicapping conditions, previous academic achievement, or disciplinary proceedings, they may include the capacity of a program or building. It will be important to look at *actual* guidelines.
2. Planning	Districts attractive to large numbers of students will know the nature of their enrollment (characteristics of students) earlier than will districts losing students. This will affect instructional planning, especially for those students with handicaps requiring very expensive programming.
3. Gain and loss of teachers	Federal and state money follows students when they change districts. Staffing needs change as the number of students with handicaps changes.
4. Excess program costs	Excess program costs for students with handicaps must be paid by the resident district.
5. Native American schools	School districts in northern Minnesota frequently follow reservation boundaries, and use of open enrollment options may be different in these areas.

(Continued)

TABLE 6.6   Issues for students with handicaps and for school districts (cont.)

Issue	Explanation
For districts	
6. Small rural school districts	Open enrollment may result in widespread movement of students with special needs from small rural school districts to larger districts where there are more program options. This may make it nearly impossible to carry on viable special education programs in rural districts.
7. Provision of information	Providing information to parents and students about open enrollment options is an important part of advancing their equitable use but may vary by different districts.
8. Local control	Some argue that open enrollment will harm small schools and districts because they will not be able to provide expensive services, and thus they will lose students and be closed, thereby decreasing local community input on schools. Others argue that schools will become more responsive to community desires to keep up enrollment, and thus local control will increase.
9. Changes in excess levies	Districts accepting students under open enrollment receive reimbursement from the state but not for any excess levies that they may have imposed for their districts' schools.
10. Transportation	Sending districts are not required to transport students, and receiving districts are required to transport only from the district border. Parents in poverty can be reimbursed by the nonresident district for the costs of transportation to the district border. Does this apply to special forms of transportation that may be required for students with handicaps?
11. Criteria for identifying students as handicapped	There are differences among districts in the criteria used to identify students as handicapped. Districts may modify their criteria to limit or encourage students who are handicapped to participate in open enrollment.
12. Mainstreaming	The initiative toward mainstreaming students with handicaps may influence parental decisions about changing districts, and this in turn may influence the mainstreaming initiative.

on counts of students in special education, rather than distributing funds student by student so that they could follow the student from one school or district to another. In the same book, Moore and Davenport reported on the findings from a two-year research study (Designs for Change) on school choice at the high school level in New York, Chicago, Philadelphia, and Boston. They found that this type of within-district choice was "a new improved method of student sorting" that "students with low achievement, students with absence and behavior problems, handicapped students, and limited-English-proficient students have very limited opportunities to participate in popular-options high schools and programs" (1990, p. 188). Although the form of choice they studied is different from the more dramatic statewide open enrollment plans, which in most cases are set up to

---

Seymour Sarason on "Obstacles to Change"

How, when, and why new ideas gain currency, get accepted and institutionally implemented, are questions far beyond the purposes of this book. A modest-sized library could be easily filled with the books written on the subject. A fair proportion of these books would be disheartening to read because they chronicle new ideas that have all of the transitory and superficial features of fads and fashions. That is clearly the case in the educational arena, where new ideas have not been in short supply among those within and without the educational establishment. And, in too many cases, where the new ideas deserved consideration, the processes through which they were implemented were self-defeating. Ideas whose time has come are no guarantee that we know how to capitalize on the opportunities, because the process of implementation requires an understanding of the settings in which these ideas have to take root. That understanding is frequently faulty and incomplete. Good intentions married to good ideas are necessary but not sufficient for action consistent with them. In accordance with Murphy's Law, if anything can go wrong it will. The world is not organized in ways that permit it passively to conform to our needs or good ideas, and when that fact interacts with our capacity to oversimplify, and even to delude ourselves, disappointment is not far down the road. That explains Sullivan's Law: Murphy's Law is a gross underestimation.

SOURCE: Sarason, S. B. (1990). *The predictable failure of educational reform: Can we change course before it's too late?* San Francisco: Jossey-Bass, pp. 99–100.

---

eliminate the possibilities for discrimination in determining acceptable transfer students, the results are nevertheless disturbing.

Comprehensive Restructuring of Education

Not all states have pushed forward on educational reform; some have been forced to change. In 1989, the Kentucky Supreme Court declared the entire state education system to be unconstitutional. Superintendents, local school boards, the state Department of Education, and essentially all educators were identified as part of the problem. The court ordered the revision of every aspect of the school system. Kentucky's response was to form a special task force and several working committees to make recommendations. Legislators put together a school reform bill that was called a "roadmap to reform" and "one of the most comprehensive restructuring efforts ever undertaken by a legislature" (Walker, 1990, p. 1). Features of the Kentucky reform, which was signed into law in April 1990, included:

• System of rewards and sanctions for schools based on performance. Successful schools receive monetary rewards. Unsuccessful schools are publicly identified and helped. Parents may use "choice" enrollment options to move their child out of an unsatisfactory school.

• Outcomes-based focus. New techniques will be used to assess student achievement. Schools will be assessed on student health, dropout and retention rates, and attendance, as well as on student achievement.

• Site-based management. Each district will have at least one site-based management school immediately, with all other schools phasing in by 1996.

• Staff development increases, with financial backing to increase to a $25 per student formula.

• Family resource centers in areas with a 20 percent free school lunch population.

• Nepotism ban. School-board members, superintendents, and principals cannot hire relatives to work in schools within their jurisdiction.

• Complete governance change. New state department personnel and a new state school board are being hired.

Most changes started in July 1990. Some are being phased in over several years. These massive changes permeate the entire system. A noteworthy aspect of the Kentucky reform is that it incorporates an emphasis on performance-based outcome assessment that is to be applicable to all students, including those in any program from early childhood education to postsecondary education, and those of any ability level ranging from students with mental disabilities to those considered gifted. It focused on capacities and goals covering all aspects of child development from academics to physical and mental well being. A critical part of Kentucky's approach is the identification of appropriate measurable student outcomes; expected completion date for this task was 1994. Many states were grappling with the issue of how to identify appropriate student outcomes without trying to make them apply to *all* students in the educational system. These issues are discussed in greater detail in Chapter 9.

Almost all states have made some type of changes considered to be "reforms" during the 1980s. Many of these were summarized by the ETS Policy Information Center (1990).

Change in Education

The Kentucky experience represents a dramatic approach to school reform and the implementation of change in education. Its promise of success leads to the question of whether other states will deem it appropriate to proceed in the same

Gallup Poll Results on the Issue of Improvement in the Schools

On two occasions—first in 1988 and now in 1990—Gallup interviewers have asked people whether they think the public schools in their communities have improved, gotten worse, or stayed about the same over the preceding five years. This question is intended to determine whether people believe the current wave of school reform has been successful. Evidently, not many people do. Whereas 29% of those surveyed in 1988 saw improvement over the preceding five years, only 22% did so this year. This finding seems congruent with the opinions people offered about the education goals announced by President Bush and the 50 governors last fall, which were discussed earlier in this report. Not only does a sizable group of respondents think that the schools haven't gotten better recently, but they also think that no great improvement is likely to occur within the current decade.

This preponderantly negative opinion is fairly evenly distributed among the major demographic groups that the Gallup Organization defines. However, the pessimism seems stronger in large cities, in the South and the West, and (ominously) among 18- to 29-year-olds. In cities of a million or more people, only 17% think their public schools have improved, while 35% think they have gotten worse. However, in communities of 50,000 and under, more people believe that their schools have improved than believe that they have deteriorated.

SOURCE: Results from the 22nd annual Gallup Poll of the public's attitude toward the public schools (Elam, 1990), pp. 52–53.

manner. Two other issues emerge in relationship to this approach and to others as well. First, to what extent will programs or reforms that are successful in one place generalize to another; to what extent will programs of reforms that are successful with one population generalize to another? Second, how rapidly can change proceed? And, what do we know about the change process that can promote quicker and more effective adoption of changes?

Many individuals have written about the process of change and innovation in education. Some approach the issue from a logical perspective emphasizing technical, rational, and mechanistic characteristics, while others approach it from a sociological perspective emphasizing either a cultural or political point of view (Bennis, Benne, & Chin, 1969). Several writers have addressed change in relationship to specific content areas, such as mathematics (Willoughby, 1990) or specific educational processes, such as staff development (Joyce, 1990). At this time, some professionals also began to question the possible success of planned educational reforms. For example, Sarason (1990) wrote:

Schools have been intractable to change and the attainment of goals set by reformers. A major failure has been the inability of reformers to confront this intractability. As a result, each new wave of reform learns nothing from earlier efforts and comes up with recommendations that have failed in the past. What is called reform is based on an acceptance of the system as it has been and is. (pp. xiii–xiv)

This analysis applies to special education as well as to general education.

While special education clearly was attempting to position itself to participate in general education reform that was occurring around it, it had its own barriers to change and educational reform. Special educators formed their own factions and were unable to reach consensus on such issues as defining categories of disability, accepting the regular education initiative and mainstreaming, and appropriate instructional interventions for specific types of disabilities. These and other issues are the substance of the remaining chapters in this book. In many ways, these same issues result in special education's being divided into various forces that are unable to bring about enough consensus to have an influence on general education.

Discussion Questions

1. What reform activities are currently taking place at the national, state, or local level? To what extent do these activities acknowledge or apply to special education?

2. How might the six national goals be restated to show that they are goals for all students, including those with disabilities?

3. Prepare an argument for or against open enrollment as a policy for special education.

4. What would be a "road map to reform" for special education today?

Issues in Assessment

You can weigh horse manure on a jewelers scale and you can slice baloney with a laser beam, but in the end you've still got horse manure and baloney.

—*University of Minnesota criminologist Hans Mattick*

More than 250 million standardized tests are administered each year to the forty-four million students who attend American elementary and secondary schools. In addition, teachers and educational support personnel regularly collect data on students through classroom tests, classroom observations, and interviews with students' family members or care-givers. Clearly, assessment, especially the testing dimension of it, is a major activity in America's schools.

Many issues arise regarding assessment of students, specifically those who are disabled, and they are primarily the result of the considerable importance attributed to testing and test results in America's schools and American society. Consider for just a moment the decisions made about people using tests. Eleanor is not allowed to enter school because her performance on a test indicates that she is not yet "ready" to do so. Heidi is told to repeat second grade because her performance on a set of tests indicates she has not yet mastered second grade content. Jose is assigned to a class for gifted students, while Zeke is placed in a class for students who are learning disabled. Both placements were dependent on how the students performed on a set of tests. Ariel is admitted to Florida State University, but Clem is denied admission because his test scores are too low. Mark, an all-city basketball player, cannot attend a Division I college because his test scores are too low, even though his grades are high enough. Kate earns a high score on a selection test; Esther does not. Kate gets a position with General Mills; Esther does not. When society uses test results to make decisions that have a significant effect on people's life opportunities, it is little surprise that how tests and test results are used generates controversy.

Current Decision-Making Practices

Although tests are administered to students for one or more purposes, testing is only one part of the broader conception of assessment. Testing refers to the sampling of behaviors in students to obtain quantitative indexes (that is, scores) of relative standing. Assessment can be described as a process of collecting data to make decisions about students (Salvia & Ysseldyke, 1991). Assessment data are obtained, in part, from norm-referenced and criterion-referenced tests, observations, interviews, searches of school records, medical evaluations, and social histories.

Salvia and Ysseldyke (1991) identified five kinds of decisions regarding students—evaluation of the individual, program evaluation, screening, placement, and intervention planning—made on the basis of assessment data. These data are supposed to facilitate correct decision making, although the misuse of assessment data can lead to inappropriate decision making and adverse effects on students' life opportunities. Current practice is heavily biased toward collection of information using tests. Table 7.1 lists the decisions made using tests, briefly describes the decisions, and lists examples of tests used for each of the decisions.

Evaluation of Individual Progress

School personnel regularly gather data to evaluate the extent to which individual students or groups of students are making progress in the instructional programs to which they are assigned. These data also give information about the school's effectiveness. If students make progress, the school is judged to be effective. Parents, teachers, and students themselves have both a right and a need to know whether and how much progress is being made. Parents, at the time of annual or semiannual parent-teacher conferences, are often given test scores as indexes of their children's progress.

School personnel regularly administer group achievement tests to obtain comparative data (Have the students under one teacher made as much progress as the students under a different teacher? Have the students in one school or school district progressed as much as students in comparable administrative units?) and to measure the progress of individuals, thereby detecting students who, for any number of reasons, may not be profiting from instruction.

Program Evaluation

Schools use tests to evaluate the effectiveness of instructional programs. When school personnel observe that students in their school profit more from instruction in one year than do students in other schools, they tend to be proud of their instructional programs. When they observe that pupils in their school profit less on the average than do students in other schools, they search for reasons. When low scores are earned, school officials may become concerned about the quality of instruction in their schools, or they may attribute the observed differences to the inferior quality of their students.

At a curricular level, tests are often used to evaluate the effectiveness of specific instructional interventions. In the simplest form, school personnel give tests before and after instituting new teaching methods or materials, and they compare the gain in achievement with the gain that followed some other intervention. Using data obtained from such tests, administrators try to sort "good" from "bad" programs.

Screening and/or Selection

Tests are administered regularly to students to assist in admission decisions. College admissions officers use test data (from the Scholastic Aptitude Test or

TABLE 7.1   Decisions made using tests

Purpose of the Decision	Nature of the Decision	Examples of Tests Used for the Decision
Evaluation of individual progress	To let parents and teachers know the extent to which a student is profiting from instruction	Stanford Achievement Test Iowa Tests of Basic Skills Metropolitan Achievement Test Curriculum-based measures Wide Range Achievement Test Peabody Individual Achievement Test
Program evaluation	To evaluate the general effectiveness of the school's instructional program	Stanford Achievement Test Iowa Tests of Basic Skills Metropolitan Achievement Test
Screening	To spot students who are experiencing difficulty in school	Kaufman Test of Educational Achievement Basic Achievement Skills Individual Screener Detroit Tests of Learning Aptitude—2 Gates-MacGinitie Reading Test Test of Mathematical Abilities Woodcock-Johnson Psychoeducational Battery
	To provide data for use in making decisions about entrance/admissions to kindergarten, college, graduate school	Metropolitan Readiness Test Preschool Inventory Graduate Record Examination American College Testing Program (ACT) Scholastic Aptitude Test
Eligibility/ classification placement	To identify students who are eligible for special education and related services so as to classify them or place them in special education.	Stanford-Binet Intelligence Scale IV Wechsler Intelligence Scale for Children—Revised Woodcock-Johnson Psychoeducational Battery
Instructional planning	To plan an instructional intervention for an individual or a group	System to Plan Early Childhood Services The Instructional Environment Scale Stanford Diagnostic Mathematics Test Stanford Diagnostic Reading Test Key-Math BRIGANCE Diagnostic Inventories Test of Language Development Woodcock Reading Mastery Test

the American College Testing Program) to assist them in deciding which applicants should and should not be accepted, and graduate school personnel use test scores (from the Graduate Record Examination or the Miller Analogies Test) as one criterion for admission to graduate school.

Assessment data are used in elementary and secondary schools to identify students who are not profiting from educational programs. School personnel regularly review pupil performance on routinely administered group tests to identify students who may need remediation or who should be referred for additional assessment because they may be eligible for special education intervention. Much as routine vision and hearing screenings are used to discover students with possible vision or hearing difficulties, the results of screening tests that assess learning aptitude, academic achievement, or perceptual-motor functioning are used to discover students with potential difficulties in these areas.

School personnel also screen students at the preschool level to identify those with potential problems. Under PL 99-457 schools are required to identify infants, toddlers, and preschoolers who are handicapped.

Eligibility, Placement, and/or Classification

Decisions as to whether students are eligible for special or remedial education services, can be classified as handicapped, and should be placed in special education programs can have the profoundest effect. It may be advantageous to distinguish among these three decisions, although in practice it is nearly impossible to do so. Ysseldyke, Algozzine, and Thurlow (1980) reported that most teams make eligibility, classification, and placement decisions concurrently.

Intervention Planning

Assessment practices in schools are beginning to change, though slowly. Practices have moved away from a relatively narrow prediction orientation in which the focus was on giving tests to students for the purpose of predicting how well they would do in school. Beginning in the late 1960s and early 1970s, assessors engaged in more comprehensive and extensive qualitative analysis of assessment results and in differentiation of student strengths and weaknesses. They began to write about relatively specific "instructional prescriptions" (Newland, 1980), about "diagnostic-prescriptive teaching" (Ysseldyke, 1973), or of "differential diagnosis and prescriptive teaching" (Arter & Jenkins, 1979). More recently, assessors have been viewing their activities more broadly. They are taking into account the many contextual factors (school and school district policies and practices, home and family factors, in-class instructional factors) that interact to influence instructional outcomes for individual students (Norby, Thurlow, Christenson, & Ysseldyke, 1990; Ysseldyke, Christenson, & Thurlow, 1987).

Early assessment practices occurred at the level of disposition. Assessors described the pathology, conditions, and dispositional states of individual students referred by classroom teachers. Such practices received widespread criticism, which resulted in shifts to procedures such as prereferral intervention (Graden, Casey, & Christenson, 1985), curriculum-based measurement (Deno, 1986), functional assessment of the academic environment (Lentz & Shapiro, 1986), direct assessment of academic performance (Howell, 1986), and assessment of instructional environments (Ysseldyke & Christenson, 1987). Newer procedures have evolved in direct response to the contention that assessment activities ought to be instructionally relevant (Fuchs & Fuchs, 1986; Heller, Holtzman, & Messick, 1982). Despite more frequent use of new assessment approaches, many of which account for the effect of contextual factors on student performance, school assessment practices still emphasize dispositional description and tend to view a student's learning and behavioral difficulties as a within-student (internal) problem.

Teacher Competence

Most states have recently implemented teacher competency testing programs designed to ensure that students are taught by teachers who are literate in reading, math, writing, and spelling. Ramsey and Algozzine (1991) surveyed state departments of education and reported that 48 of 50 states had such practices in place and that 25 states were developing or administering tests in specific subject areas to include special education. Ramsey and Algozzine identified the competencies tested, raised issues about the practices, reported that litigation had been filed in Georgia and Alabama charging invalid uses of teacher competency tests, and asked the following questions about the practice:

• Are states testing to appease the public, or is quality education the real goal?

• Will higher standards increase the pool of minority candidates, or will other factors relating to job attraction outweigh the standards issue?

• What tests are most appropriate for assessing teacher competence?

• Will national teacher competence testing be the eventual result?

• How can the validity of tests used to measure teacher competence be guaranteed?

Contemporary Influences on Assessment Practices

In this section we describe three factors that are having an influence on assessment practice—law, outcomes-based education, and the push for a national achievement test.

Law

The assessment practices used with students are influenced by PL 94-142, PL 99-457, and PL 101-476. In these laws Congress specified a set of rules about assessment activities. For example, PL 94-142 specified a set of Protection in Evaluation Procedures (PEP) provisions. According to these provisions, assessment practices must be fair, with no racial or cultural bias.

Procedures to assure that testing and evaluation materials and procedures utilized for the purposes of evaluation and placement of handicapped children will be selected and administered so as not to be racially or culturally discriminatory. Such materials or procedures shall be provided and administered in the child's native language or mode of communication, unless it clearly is not feasible to do so, and no single procedure shall be the sole criterion for determining an appropriate educational program for a child.

There are specific rules and regulations for implementation of the PEP provisions:

• A full and individual evaluation of a student's needs must be made before the student is placed in a special education program.

• Tests must be administered in the student's native language or other mode of communication.

• Tests must be valid for the purposes for which they are used.

• Tests must be administered by trained personnel following the instructions provided by the test's producer.

• Tests and other evaluation materials must be relevant to specific areas of educational needs and must not be designed to yield a single general IQ.

• The results of tests administered to students who have impaired sensory, manual, or speaking skills must reflect aptitude or achievement, not impairment.

• Special education placement cannot be determined on the basis of a single procedure.

• Evaluations for special education placement must be made by a multidisciplinary team.

• Students must be assessed in all areas related to their suspected disability, including general health, vision, hearing, behavior, general intelligence, motor abilities, academic performance, and language skills.

PL 99-457 was a downward extension of PL 94-142; it extended the assessment rules to infants and toddlers. According to this law, school personnel must develop for preschool children with disabilities an individualized family service plan (IFSP) that includes a statement of the child's present level of cognitive, social, speech and language, and self-help development. The IFSP must also specify criteria, procedures, and timelines for measuring progress toward major outcomes.

On October 30, 1990, President Bush signed into law the Education of the Handicapped Act Amendments (PL 101-476), which brought about changes in PL 94-142. Specifically, the title of the law was changed to Individuals with Disabilities Education Act, two new categories of disability (autism and traumatic brain injury) were added, the definitions of "related services" and "individualized education program" were clarified, and transition services were added.

In Section 504 of PL 93-112 (the Rehabilitation Act of 1973) Congress declared illegal discrimination against people with handicaps solely on the basis of their handicaps. This law led to increased assessment of vocational skills and to assessment of the extent to which college students needed special support services.

Outcomes-Based Education

The push to evaluate educational accomplishments in terms of outcomes, rather than processes, has led to efforts to specify domains of outcomes and outcomes indicators to be assessed. As government officials and school personnel have sought to establish and evaluate accountability for schools and programs, they have had to specify ways in which outcomes and progress toward major objectives will be measured.

The Push for a National Achievement Test

As this text was going to press, there was a major national debate emerging as to whether the United States should have a national achievement test. Members of President Bush's advisory committee on education policy proposed the creation of national standards for pupil performance and tests to measure the extent to which students were meeting those standards. It was being proposed that every U.S. high school senior take such a test in the fall of the senior year and that scores earned be published so that everyone could see school by school, district by district, and state by state how students were performing. Those who proposed a national test argued that it would motivate students and teachers to perform better. Those who opposed the practice argued that development and administration of such a test would be a major waste of time and money and that such a test would result in a national curriculum driven by the test. They argued that teachers would teach to the test, rather than teaching students to think critically.

Issues Regarding Who Is Assessed

At the beginning of this chapter we noted that about 250 million standardized tests are administered annually to students in school settings. Routine achievement tests account for a substantial number of the measures administered, but many—perhaps too many—of the assessments take place under the umbrella of "special education planning." In trying to describe the magnitude of assessment activities, Thurlow and Ysseldyke (1979) surveyed forty-four federally funded model programs for students with learning disabilities. They found that the model programs used different tests to decide whether students were eligible for special education services and individually appropriate instructional interventions. Often tests that were developed and intended for one purpose were diverted to other purposes.

Similar findings were reported by Ysseldyke, Algozzine, and Thurlow (1980) in their study of decision making by placement teams and by Ysseldyke, Algozzine, Regan, Potter, Richey, and Thurlow (1980) in their computer simulation study of the decision-making process. In their report of a longitudinal study of the assessment and decision-making process in eight individual cases, Ysseldyke and Thurlow (1980) found that although the actual number of tests used in making the decisions varied considerably, much time was spent assessing students and deciding what to do for or about them.

In some cases, assessment and decision making may require as much as 13 to 15 hours of professional time. If we estimate an average charge of $30 per hour by each professional, then the costs of assessment are obviously very high. Mirkin estimated in 1980 that it cost as much as $1,800 to assess and make decisions for one student; costs would be much higher today. And the practical knowledge gained from such activities is marginal at best. The cost of assessing students looks especially high in comparison to figures recently published by Stanford Research Institute showing the cost of providing basic training to soldiers. The institute reported that costs for basic training were $16,100 for the marines (twelve weeks), $13,000 for the army (eight weeks), $5,000 for the navy (eight weeks), and $4,600 for the air force (six weeks).

When we look at the magnitude of the assessment process, at the large numbers of tests administered to students, we repeatedly ask, "Why?" Why is it that school personnel administer so many tests to make decisions about students? Is it because they learn so much about the students and how to teach them? Apparently, educational personnel believe so. We think, however, that there is much evidence to indicate that assessors learn very little about students from the students' performances on standardized tests. Ysseldyke, Algozzine, Richey, and Graden (1982) investigated the correspondence between decisions made by placement teams and the extent to which the data supported the decisions, and they reported very little correlation (range: $-.13$ to $+.29$) between the team decision and the empirical support for the decision. Why, then, do decision makers expend so much energy on assessing students? Sarason and Doris addressed this same question in relation to the assessment of students with mental retardation. To them, "diagnosis is a pathology-oriented process activated by someone who thinks something is wrong with somebody else" (1979, p. 39), and they described the assessment process as follows:

> The diagnostic process is always a consequence of somebody saying that someone has something wrong with him. We put it this way because frequently it is not the individual who decides to initiate the process. This is the case with children, but there are also times when adults are forced by pressure from others or by legal action to participate in the process. In all of those instances people individually or society in general communicate four ideas: something may be wrong with someone; our lives are being affected; we should find out the source of the trouble; and we should come up with solutions to alter the individual's status and allow us to experience our lives in the way we wish. (p. 16)

Although the assessment process is problematic, teachers refer very large numbers of students for evaluation because they think that "something is wrong," either academically or socially, and that the students are not performing as expected. The professionals who assess students presume that something is wrong with them, and tests are administered until the professionals are able to identify some pathology, which they nearly always can.

Giving Students with Disabilities Standardized Achievement Tests

Educators regularly disagree about whether students who are handicapped should be given the same tests as those who are not. One argument holds that the standards set for students should be applied to all students and that a district does not have good evidence of how it is doing instructionally if it does not regularly assess students who are handicapped. When such a position is taken, students who are handicapped take the district's achievement tests along with students who are not handicapped. The converse argument is that standards for students who are handicapped should be adjusted to meet their particular needs and that any testing should be specific to the instructional needs of the student. When this argument is applied, students who are handicapped do not participate in district-wide testing programs, other tests may be used to document their educational progress, or they may be excluded entirely from testing.

The Exclusion of Students with Disabilities from National Norms

One of the fundamental assumptions in norm-referenced assessment is that students' performances will be evaluated relative to those of others who have had comparable acculturation (Salvia & Ysseldyke, 1991). Yet students with disabilities are often excluded from the norming population for standardized tests. Fuchs, Fuchs, Benowitz, and Barringer (1987) systematically examined the extent to which students with handicaps were included in the development of test norms, items, and indexes of reliability and validity. They reported widespread failure among test developers to clarify the nature of the populations on whom they developed their tests and to establish the reliability and validity of standardized tests for use with students with handicaps. In most instances, the use of norm-referenced tests to evaluate pupil performance consists of comparison of students to those who are nonhandicapped, and there is little demonstrated validity for making decisions about students with disabilities on this basis. This practice, of course, runs contrary to federal laws, according to which tests must have demonstrated validity for the purposes for which they are used. The inclusion of students who are handicapped in norm groups is critical because specific kinds of tests discriminate against specific kinds of students with disabilities (Fuchs, Fuchs, Power, & Dailey, 1985).

Issues Regarding What Is Assessed

Student Characteristics versus Instructional Diagnosis versus Assessment of Instructional Environments

Assessment can follow three fundamentally different approaches: to diagnose the learner, to diagnose instruction, and to assess the learning environment. Those who conduct assessments tend to concentrate their efforts on one of the three approaches and in most instances the focus is on diagnosing the learner. Tests, or test batteries, are given in an effort to identify what is wrong with students who are first referred by teachers. Elaborate classification systems are used, and varied labels result. When professionals focus on diagnosing instruction, they break it down into component parts, identify specific skill development strengths and weaknesses, and highlight specific instructional needs. According to Engelmann, Granzin, and Severson, "The purpose of instructional diagnosis is to determine aspects of instruction that are inadequate, to find out precisely how they are inadequate, and to imply what must be done to correct their inadequacy" (1979, p. 361). Engelmann et al. argued that "accurate conclusions about the learner . . . can only be reached after an adequate diagnosis of instruction" (p. 356). This type of diagnosis results in a description or an inventory of instructional strengths and needs.

Ysseldyke and Christenson (1987) developed a comprehensive methodology for analyzing the instructional environment—"the interaction of student characteristics, the assigned task, and the teacher's instructional or management strategies" (Christenson & Ysseldyke, 1989, p. 415)—for an individual student. They argued that the instructional environment consists of many factors in addition to curriculum and instructional materials. These factors include the nature of instructional planning, classroom management, instructional presentation, methods and techniques for motivating the learner, clarity of directions, the extent to which teachers check for student understanding, provision of opportunities for practice, feedback, and techniques used to monitor student progress. Ysseldyke and Christenson developed The Instructional Environment Scale to enable practitioners to account for these factors in assessment.

In practice, it is probably difficult to identify diagnostic personnel who exclusively use one of the three approaches. It is, however, possible and desirable to characterize specific assessment activities as consisting of one of the three approaches.

The Use and Misuse of Screening Tests

Screening tests have often been misused, and much of the misuse has been in screening students for referral to and potential placement in special education. For example, in the 1960s researchers discovered a relationship between pupil performance on perceptual-motor tests and reading performance. It was therefore presumed that perceptual-motor problems led to or caused reading problems. Schools set up elaborate procedures to screen all entering students, or all kindergartners, using perceptual-motor tests. They identified students who scored low as in need of remedial perceptual-motor training. Only after some time did further research show that such training was not a necessary prerequisite for learning how to read (Ysseldyke, 1973, 1978; Ysseldyke & Salvia, 1974).

Screening tests are also misused when the data obtained from the tests are applied to diagnostic decisions. Screening tests are designed to provide molar data; they do not have the precision of diagnostic measures. The data obtained from screening measures cannot be used to make decisions about specific strengths and weaknesses; they cannot be used to decide what to teach.

Another misuse of screening measures is in the labeling of students. When on the basis of screening data students are identified and formally labeled as handicapped at very early ages, this may lead to stereotyping and to expectations of low performance on kindergarten entrance.

Screening is not restricted to kindergarten screening. About once a year an article appears in the local newspaper about the misuse of a screening measure. Usually the article has to do with administration of verbal paper and pencil tests to predict performance on manual jobs (like assembly of parts). Sometimes the reverse is true. The article we remember best was one reporting the use of a physical measure (lifting weights) to screen people for clerical positions. A factory had a practice of testing all potential employees with the same screening test, whether they were applying to drive a forklift truck or file memos.

Very young children exhibit considerable variability in the performance of tasks. An issue that arises in the use of screening measures is the practice of making yes-or-no, hit-or-miss decisions when there is such variability in performance.

Using Tests to Classify and Place Students

On paper at least, eligibility, classification, and placement decisions are made on the basis of assessment data. All states have special education rules and regulations that specify eligibility criteria for special education services. The criteria differ considerably among states (Mercer, Forgnone, & Wolking, 1976), and within states there is typically considerable variation in the extent to which local education agencies use the state criteria. Ysseldyke, Algozzine, and Mitchell (1982) tried to identify the kind(s) of decisions made at special education team meetings by videotaping thirty-two meetings and carefully analyzing the contents. They reported that it was impossible to specify the decisions made by the teams. In addition, at the conclusion of meetings the teams did not regularly state or formally write down the decisions they had reached.

There is considerably variability among states in the numbers of students who are served in the various categories. Hallahan, Keller, and Ball (1986) reported variability among states in the numbers of students classified in the various conditions during the 1983–1984 school year. This variability is shown in Table 7.2. Algozzine & Ysseldyke (1987) argued that the variability among states reflected the vagueness with which the conditions were defined. More current figures on variability were included in Ysseldyke & Algozzine (1990).

The Use and Misuse of Intelligence Tests

The use of intelligence tests has been banned in some school districts and in some states. For example, as a result of rulings in the *Larry P.* v. *Riles* court case in San Francisco, school districts in California were not allowed to administer intelligence tests in the process of declaring black students eligible for enrollment in classes for the mentally retarded. The decision was expanded so that use of intelligence tests to assess any students for the purpose of placing them in special education classes in California was rendered illegal.

Typically, the argument against the use of intelligence tests is twofold. Opponents maintain that the tests are biased against specific types of students and that the information obtained from the tests is of little or no value in planning instructional interventions.

Issues in Ascertaining Student Gain in Achievement

Assessment information is regularly used to measure gain in achievement. In fact, many school districts report in local newspapers either test scores or gains in achievement for their districts as a whole or for specific buildings within the districts. The use of gain scores, however, has been repeatedly criticized in the professional literature (Cronbach & Furby, 1970). Arguments against the use of gain scores have typically focused on issues of reliability and regression toward the mean. Psychometricians have been able to show that on repeated administrations of a test, the student will probably score closer to the population average. With students who are handicapped these arguments take on special meaning because these students typically earn low scores on aptitude and achievement tests. Because there is a higher probability of low scores regressing to the mean as a function of chance, there is then a high probability that these students will evidence as least some gain as a function of chance.

The Directness and Nature of Assessment

Assessment activities differ in their directness and in the nature of inferences made. Sometimes assessors engage in direct measurement of pupil performance. They use terms such as *direct and frequent measurement* to reflect the practice of assessing student performance in the day-to-day activities of instruction. They measure reading to describe pupil performance in reading, they measure math to describe performance in math, and they observe and record interactions with

TABLE 7.2   Special education prevalence percentages by category for the 1983–1984 school year with the mean, variances, and standard deviations for each category

State	Category[a]										
	SLI	LD	MR	ED	OHI	OI	MH	DHI	VI	DB	Total
AL	2.39	3.35	4.77	.69	.08	.06	.14	.15	.06	.01	11.70
AK	3.01	6.53	.67	.30	.09	.23	.23	.19	.05	.02	11.32
AZ	2.19	5.14	1.14	1.06	.15	.11	.18	.21	.08	0.00	10.26
AR	2.36	4.77	3.50	.15	.06	.08	.15	.15	.06	0.00	11.28
CA	2.13	4.76	.67	.21	.30	.17	.11	.17	.05	.01	8.58
CO	1.44	3.73	1.02	1.47	0.00	.17	.33	.18	.06	.01	8.41
CT	2.73	6.28	1.20	2.76	.19	.07	.12	.20	.15	0.00	13.70
DE	2.07	7.78	2.10	3.45	.09	.28	.10	.35	.15	.04	16.41
DC	1.88	3.39	1.51	.84	.13	.05	.10	.09	.07	.04	8.10
FL	3.23	3.90	1.84	1.20	.11	.13	0.00	.13	.05	.01	10.60
GA	2.46	3.34	2.54	1.70	.03	.08	.01	.16	.05	0.00	10.37
HI	1.41	4.82	.85	.27	0.00	.18	.09	.18	.05	.01	7.86
ID	2.14	4.11	1.43	.26	.18	.14	.14	.21	.08	0.00	8.69
IL	4.09	5.19	2.32	1.65	.10	.24	0.00	.22	.08	.01	13.90
IN	4.21	3.06	2.44	.32	.02	.08	.14	.14	.06	0.00	10.47
IA	2.92	4.28	2.46	1.08	.04	.19	.14	.20	.04	.01	11.36
KS	3.26	4.06	1.59	1.01	.09	.14	.19	.18	.07	0.00	10.59
KY	3.89	3.31	3.23	.38	.07	.13	.22	.20	.08	.01	11.52

TABLE 7.2 Special education prevalence percentages by category for the 1983–1984 school year with the mean, variances, and standard deviations for each category (cont.)

State	Category[a]										Total
	SLI	LD	MR	ED	OHI	OI	MH	DHI	VI	DB	
LA	2.71	5.13	1.73	.52	.22	.10	.16	.20	.07	0.00	10.84
ME	3.07	4.51	2.33	1.97	.17	.20	.37	.21	.07	.01	12.91
MD	3.61	6.89	1.12	.60	.10	.13	.51	.22	.09	.01	13.28
MA	3.65	5.72	3.38	2.18	.23	.17	.14	.22	.10	.07	15.86
MI	2.49	3.39	1.50	1.23	.01	.26	.01	.19	.05	0.00	9.13
MN	2.70	5.05	1.89	.96	.11	.18	0.00	.24	.06	0.00	11.19
MS	3.77	3.94	2.94	.09	0.00	.08	.06	.12	.05	.01	11.06
MO	3.98	4.62	2.36	.92	.11	.10	.08	.12	.06	.01	12.36
MT	3.09	4.83	.93	.50	.09	.07	.26	.16	.12	.01	10.06
NE	3.29	4.52	2.08	.84	0.00	.21	.15	.22	.07	0.00	11.38
NV	2.09	4.77	.67	.58	.27	.19	.25	.15	.04	0.00	9.01
NH	1.69	5.57	.83	.78	.17	.10	.13	.23	.08	.01	9.59
NJ	5.24	5.72	.98	1.31	.08	.08	.74	.16	.12	0.00	14.43
NM	2.87	4.47	.95	.93	.03	.13	.45	.17	.05	0.00	10.05
NY	1.49	4.99	1.33	1.69	.30	.14	.30	.19	.07	0.00	10.50
NC	2.46	4.77	2.72	.59	.12	.08	.16	.20	.06	0.00	11.16
ND	3.33	4.08	1.65	.31	.03	.19	.02	.19	.07	0.00	9.67
OH	3.08	3.97	3.05	.36	0.00	.19	.18	.14	.05	0.00	11.02
OK	3.44	4.80	2.07	.20	.04	.07	.24	.14	.05	.01	11.06
OR	2.57	5.48	1.02	.58	.13	.20	.03	.30	.15	.01	10.47

TABLE 7.2   Special education prevalence percentages by category for the 1983–1984 school year with the mean, variances, and standard deviations for each category (cont.)

State	SLI	LD	MR	ED	OHI	OI	MH	DHI	VI	DB	Total
PA	3.49	3.86	2.58	.94	0.00	.12	0.00	.23	.09	0.00	11.31
RI	2.29	8.73	1.06	.87	.11	.17	.02	.17	.05	.01	13.48
SC	3.30	3.72	3.50	.97	.03	.12	.06	.20	.08	0.00	11.98
SD	3.95	3.26	1.29	.31	.05	.18	.33	.20	.07	.01	9.65
TN	3.82	5.28	2.30	.38	.18	.14	.21	.25	.09	0.00	12.65
TX	2.30	5.21	.98	.61	.24	.13	.17	.17	.07	.01	9.89
UT	2.39	3.63	.83	3.13	.06	.08	.41	.22	.09	.01	10.85
VT	2.84	3.64	2.82	.39	.21	.10	.20	.29	.44	.01	10.94
VA	3.20	4.15	1.62	.73	.09	.07	.43	.15	.19	0.00	10.63
WA	1.92	4.53	1.24	.50	.23	.16	.26	.19	.05	.01	9.09
WV	3.44	4.24	2.86	.45	.07	.10	.16	.12	.08	0.00	11.52
WI	2.18	3.80	1.72	1.33	.08	.11	.10	.15	.06	0.00	9.53
WY	3.40	5.37	.95	.93	.25	.18	.10	.14	.06	.01	11.39
Means	2.88	4.68	1.85	.93	.11	.14	.18	.19	.08	.01	11.04
Variance	.65	1.30	.85	.54	.01	.00	.02	.00	.00	.00	3.25
SD	.80	1.14	.92	.74	.08	.06	.15	.05	.06	.01	1.80

SOURCE: Hallahan, D. P., Keller, C. E., & Ball, D. W. (1986). "A comparison of prevalence rate variability from state to state for each of the categories of special education." *Remedial and Special Education* 7(2): 8–14. Copyright © 1986 by PRO-ED, Inc. Reprinted by permission.

a. SLI = Speech and Language Impairment; LD = Learning Disabilities; MR = Mental Retardation; ED = Emotional Disturbance; OHI = Other Health Impairment; OI = Orthopedic Impairment; MH = Multiple Handicaps; DHI = Deaf and Hearing Impairment; VI = Visual Impairment; DB = Deaf and Blind.

others as a measure of interactions with others. In contrasting direct and indirect approaches to measurement, Ysseldyke and Marston reported that

> direct measures are those that measure precisely the same skills as have been taught and often use the same response mode as was employed in teaching the skills initially. Indirect measures are those in which test items are usually sampled from a larger domain and are not necessarily the items that have been taught. Success on the sampled items is viewed as indicative of mastery of the behaviors from which the samples were taken. (1990, p. 664)

Sometimes assessors engage in projective assessment. They do not sample behaviors directly but instead make large inferences. Such approaches are employed under the assumption that direct assessment may be threatening or that it may result in an inaccurate picture of the student's thoughts, feelings, or behaviors. Students are shown pictures and asked to describe what they think is happening in the pictures. The examiner infers from the student's "story" aspects of how the student feels.

Examiners and educators differ in their positions on what should be assessed. Sometimes the focus is on assessment of student characteristics, traits, or attributes. The assessor administers tests as measures of student intelligence, visual perceptual processing, auditory processing, psycholinguistic processing, attitudes, and so on. The list of possible attributes or characteristics to be assessed is very long. Such attributes or characteristics are assessed under the assumption that the assessment provides important information relevant to pupil performance in school. But those who engage in assessment of student characteristics are forever having to defend their actions and demonstrate the relevance to instruction of their assessment activities.

Sometimes assessment is focused on assessment of pupil progress within the curriculum. Assessment is direct and focused on provision of data on skills acquired and progress toward completion of specific objectives. At other times, assessment does not monitor progress on a direct, frequent basis but instead repeatedly measures the extent to which the student has accomplished specified outcomes. As can be seen from these examples, a number of differing perspectives exist on the goal or focus of assessment.

Curriculum progress   The predominant approach in assessment focuses on assessment of student progress in the curriculum. Sometimes this is accomplished by informal recording of pupil completion of assignments, sometimes by collection of the products of pupils' work. Often teachers document progress through the curriculum by using unit mastery tests, especially in basic skills areas such as reading and math. Sometimes data are collected using norm-referenced achievement tests.

Student characteristics   Many practitioners hold firmly to the perspective that students who experience difficulty in academics do so because of fundamental within-student deficits and deficiencies. Thus, these practitioners advocate collection of data on pupil characteristics (performance on aptitude measures, ability measures, personality measures) and the use of those data in planning interventions for students.

Pupil performance Still other educators advocate collection of data on pupil performance, rather than on pupil characteristics. They argue that it is more important to know what students do—what they produce—than to know their characteristics. The focus on collection of data on pupil performance is clearly reflected in the work of those who advocate performance assessment.

Pupil outcomes/broad systems indicators Many practitioners now focus heavily on broad systems indicators in the assessment of students with disabilities. We have seen a real push to move away from demonstrations that services have been delivered and move toward a focus on the outcomes of service delivery (Finn, 1990). The National Council on Disability (1989) argued that it is time to concentrate on the quality of educational experiences for children and youths with disabilities. To make judgments about educational quality, educators need indexes by which to judge quality.

Another impetus for developing a set of indicators for special education is that general education is proceeding with its own agenda to raise expectations for students and to identify outcomes for "all" students. Although it is clear that educational indicators are needed, there is no consensus on their definition, their uses, and their types. Smith suggested that "most commonly, an educational indicator either assesses or is related to a desired outcome of the educational system or describes a core feature of that system" (1988, p. 487). As is no doubt obvious, many views obtain on which data should be used as outcomes indicators. Should indicators be cognitive or affective? Should they focus on mastery of subject matter content, on acquisition of learning and adjustment skills, or on development of positive attitudes and positive self-perceptions? Many different outcome indicators are currently used by states. The National Center on Educational Outcomes for Students with Disabilities, which is funded by the U.S. Department of Education, housed at the University of Minnesota, and directed by James Ysseldyke, is engaged in collecting data from states, developing a conceptual model of outcomes indicators, achieving consensus among states on outcomes indicators, and developing a comprehensive system of assessing outcomes for children and youths with disabilities.

Issues Regarding Assessment Techniques and Procedures

Even though assessment data may be collected through various methods, the primary focus in assessment is on testing. This focus gives rise to many issues about the techniques and procedures used in assessment.

Bias in Assessment

A major, and legitimate, issue in assessment is bias. This concern arises directly out of the ways in which American society evaluates the worth of the individual on the basis of presumed intelligence. The IQ has become a very potent yardstick: educators become concerned when a student's achievement is not commensurate with his or her intelligence, parents repeat their children's IQ scores as if they were measures of worth, and society tries to limit immigration, advocate sterilization, and explain criminal tendencies, mental and physical defects, and degeneracy on the basis of IQ. According to Kamin, "Since its introduction to America, the intelligence test has been used more or less consciously as an instrument of oppression against the underprivileged—the poor, the foreign born, and racial minorities" (1974, p. 1). Kamin illustrated his argument by repeating quotations from early psychologists and congressional witnesses in support of limiting immigration.

This issue of bias also grows out of the different average intelligence test scores achieved by different racial groups. This variance has been fashioned into an instrument of oppression, according to Kamin (1974), and it has also kindled considerable professional controversy over the reason for the observed differences.

Bias is also an issue in the disproportionate representation of minority students in special education classes; this concern is apparent in both litigation and legislation (see Chapter 12), even though neither has changed the situation. Tucker (1980) reported on an eight-year study in the Southwest in which he demonstrated that the number of students in the total special education population had increased by 10 percent and that the placement of minority students, especially blacks, in special education classes, particularly for learning disabilities, had continued in disproportionate numbers despite national preventive efforts.

Given the legitimate and necessary concern of professionals with bias in assessment, let us look at how educators and psychologists have addressed the problem. Early observations that minority students earned lower scores on the average than did nonminority students led to long and heated debates on the relative contributions to intelligence of genetic and environmental factors (Bayley, 1965; Bereiter, 1969; Bijou, 1971; Bloom, 1964; Cronbach, 1969; Elkind, 1969; Gordon, 1971; Hirsch, 1971; Jensen, 1967, 1968a, 1968b, 1969b). The debate still goes on, the observed differences continue to exist, and children continue to fail in school.

Observed differences between groups also led to investigations of test fairness. These investigations included large-scale comparative studies of the performances of groups on specific tests (Goldman & Hewitt, 1976; Hennessey & Merrifield, 1976; Jensen, 1976, 1979; Matusek & Oakland, 1972; Mercer 1973). Studies of group differences in performances on psychometric devices persuaded other investigators to examine the fairness of specific items used with members of minority groups (Angoff & Ford, 1971; Newland, 1973; Scheyneman, 1976). Specific tests and test items were examined for linguistic bias (Berry & Lopez, 1977; Matluck

& Mace, 1973; Vasquez, 1972) and for sex bias (Dwyer, 1976; Tittle, 1973; Tolor & Brannigan, 1975). But major measurement experts have been unable to agree on a definition of a fair test, let alone a test that is fair for members of different groups.

This nation and its researchers have invested considerable effort, time, and financial resources in attempts to develop or identify assessment devices that are not biased against members of racial or cultural groups. Given the history of psychologists' efforts to address the concept of fairness and their generalized lack of success, it troubles us to see educators these days trying to find *the* fair test to use with specific groups, arguing about the fairness of specific test items, and generating state-approved lists of fair tests. What would it mean if *the* fair test was found? Would bias and abuse in assessment and decision making cease to exist? We think not. Even given a fair test or set of tests, there is considerable evidence that the bias in decision making would not be ameliorated. Indeed, review of testimony before the congressional committee on the Protection in Evaluation Procedures Provisions of PL 94-142 revealed a broader concern with the subject of abuse in the entire process of assessment. Such abuse includes inappropriate and indiscriminate use of tests, bias in the assessment of children with handicaps and in the identification of children as handicapped who are not, bias throughout the decision-making process, and bias following assessment. An excerpt from a Senate report on the matter illustrates the depth of concern:

> The Committee is deeply concerned about practices and procedures which result in classifying children as having handicapped conditions when, in fact, they do not have such conditions. At least three major issues are of concern with respect to problems of identification and classification: (1) the misuse of appropriate identification and classification data within the educational process itself; (2) discriminatory treatment as the result of the identification of a handicapping condition; and (3) misuse of identification procedures or methods which results in erroneous classification of a child as having a handicapping condition. . . . The Committee is alarmed about the abuses which occur in the testing and evaluation of children; and is concerned that expertise in the proper use of testing and evaluation procedures falls far short of the prolific use and development of testing and evaluation tools. The usefulness and mechanistic ease of testing should not become so paramount in the educational process that the negative effects of such testing are overlooked. (U.S. Senate, 1975, pp. 26–29)

Norm-Referenced Assessment

In norm-referenced assessment the pupil's performance is evaluated in reference to the performance of others who are like him or her. Standardized measures are used, and the pupil's performance is compared to the performance of those in the norm group. Those who support norm-referenced assessment argue that it is necessary to know where pupils are in reference to their peers and that this knowledge assists teachers in picking the level at which to instruct students and in grouping students for instructional purposes. Those who call attention to the limits of norm-referenced assessment argue that knowledge of relative standing does not help a teacher decide *how* to teach. They contend that instructional decisions are best made by using curriculum-based approaches or by teaching students and monitoring progress toward objectives.

Professionals who assess students so as to make decisions about them use technically inadequate data-collection procedures. We stress this fact because the decisions can have profound effects on the students' lives. Educators are purported to have the best interests of the students at heart when they make decisions, though they often base the decisions on data from technically inadequate tests. Three characteristics determine the technical adequacy of tests: norms, reliability, and validity.

Norms   Norms are standards of comparison. A norm-referenced test is developed by standardizing it on a sample of students that actually represents the population on which the test will be used. The performance of an individual on the test can then be compared with, or evaluated according to, the performance of other members of the population. The nature of the norm group, the group with whom a person is being compared, is important because the norm group's performance is the standard against which the quality of the individual's performance is judged.

To be representative the sample has to be made up of correct proportions of people in the total population—that is, "the various kinds of people should be included in the same *proportion* in the sample as in the population" (Salvia & Ysseldyke, 1981, p. 115). The test's norms also must be current. A joint American Psychological Association–American Educational Research Association committee recommended that tests be revised at regular intervals, usually at least once every fifteen years.

Inadequately constructed or described norms skew the judgments educators make about the quality of a pupil's test behavior; the pupil is then being evaluated in reference to an unknown and/or unrepresentative norm group. Some of the most widely used measures of intelligence, achievement, personality, and perceptual-motor functioning were standardized on inadequately constructed and/or described norms (Salvia and Ysseldyke, 1991).

Reliability   Reliability refers to consistency in measurement. Assessment instruments are said to be reliable when students achieve approximately the same score whenever they take the test. Evaluation of pupil performance depends, in part, on the obtaining of a reliable index of performance. As part of the process, test developers do provide evidence that their tests are reliable. But when Salvia and Ysseldyke (1991) evaluated the evidence for reliability in each test they reviewed, they concluded that there was insufficient evidence of reliability for many tests.

There are standards for reliability, but they change according to the decision being made. Salvia and Ysseldyke (1991) indicated that tests should have reliability coefficients in excess of .60 when the scores are to be used for administrative

---

The Hypothetical Typing Test

Suppose that you are the personnel manager for a large industrial firm and that part of your job includes hiring typists. You regularly require applicants for positions as typists to take a typing test, which you score for both speed (number of words per minute) and accuracy. You usually try to hire those applicants who are the fastest and most accurate. But how do you know that you are hiring the best possible typists? You do not unless you have a standard according to which the applicants can be evaluated. Hence, you decide to develop a typing test that requires applicants to type from both handwritten copy and dictation. But even if you give every applicant the same test, you will still need some basis for evaluating the performance. So you decide to standardize your test— that is, develop a set of norms according to which applicant performance can be consistently evaluated.

The way in which you standardize the typing test will affect the evaluation of each applicant's performance. There are several groups on which the typing test can be standardized:

1. All high school seniors in your local school district

2. All high school seniors in your local school district who have been enrolled in a business curriculum and who have taken at least one full year of typing classes

3. A representative national sample of high school seniors who have been enrolled in a business curriculum and who have taken at least one full year of typing classes

4. All those persons who, over a three-year period, have applied for employment with your company

5. All those persons who, over a three-year period, have applied for employment as typists with your company

---

purposes and when test data are to be reported for groups of individuals. When, however, tests are to be used to make decisions regarding individuals, they must have reliability coefficients greater than .90.

Validity   Validity refers to how much a test measures what it purports to measure. Evidence for validity is not only considered essential by the *Standards for Educational and Psychological Testing* (American Educational Research Association, American Psychological Association, and National Council on Measurement in Education, 1985) but is also required by law. According to the regulations for PL 94-142, "Tests must have demonstrated validity for the purpose(s) for which

6. Persons currently employed as typists in your company who have better than "satisfactory" performance evaluations from their immediate supervisors

The nature of the norm group you select will influence your judgment of an applicant's typing skills. An applicant can look very good compared with high school seniors but very poor compared with currently employed, successful typists. In addition to the test score and norms for evaluating that score, you will still need to know the nature of the norm group. Because the decision to hire or not to hire a person will be influenced by his or her performance relative to the norm group, your decision may well be in error if you do not know the nature of the group on which the test was standardized.

Psychological and educational assessment assumes that the acculturation of the person being assessed is comparable to, although not necessarily identical with, that of the people on whom the test was standardized (Newland, 1980; Salvia & Ysseldyke, 1981). Acculturation refers simply to a person's background experiences and opportunities. This assumption is typically addressed by test developers when they select a sample representative of the population of concern. Representativeness in the testing industry is usually achieved by stratifying a norm sample on a number of characteristics specified in the *Standards for Educational and Psychological Tests* (APA, 1974; see also Salvia & Ysseldyke, 1981). These characteristics include age, grade, sex, acculturation of parents (as usually indicated by some combination of socioeconomic status, income, occupation, and education), geographic region, and race. For achievement tests, the cognitive functioning (intellectual level) of the norm group is also a significant consideration.

they are used." In addition, test developers must provide consumers with evidence of test validity; tests are considered invalid when they provide inappropriate information for decision-making purposes.

The technical adequacy of tests currently used to make decisions on students has been evaluated in several investigations. Thurlow and Ysseldyke (1979) evaluated the technical adequacy of tests used in forty-four model programs for learning disabled students, the Child Service Demonstration Centers. They found that of thirty tests used by three or more centers, only five (16.7 percent) tests had technically adequate norms. Only ten (33.3 percent) of the thirty tests had reliability adequate for decision making, and only nine (30 percent) had technically adequate validity. The model programs—among the very best special education programs in the nation—made decisions about students by using tests that for the most part were technically inadequate.

Much abuse can follow from the use of norm-referenced assessment data to make decisions regarding students. Abuse results from the use of tests for purposes other than those for which they were designed, from comparisons of students who differ systematically in several characteristics, and from the use of technically inadequate tests to collect data on students.

Criterion-Referenced Assessment

Rather than indicating a person's relative standing in skill development, criterion-referenced tests measure a student's mastery of specific skills. These tests give teachers a measure of the extent to which individuals or groups have mastered specific curriculum content. The tests are developed by specifying the objectives or criteria to be mastered, usually in basic skill areas, and then by writing items to assess mastery of those objectives or criteria. Two critical issues in criterion-referenced assessment are the establishment of the criteria and the setting of the level of mastery. When the extent to which students have mastered curriculum content is measured, the precise content to be mastered has to be specified. This act is heavily influenced by the biases and values of the committee, group, or individual who is responsible for setting criteria.

In criterion-referenced assessment the level of mastery to be demanded also has to be specified. This in turn is usually a function of how important the content is. School personnel usually contend that very important material ought to be learned to high degrees of mastery (80–100 percent correct), whereas less important material requires only limited degrees of mastery (50–80 percent). Of course, debate abounds as to the relative importance of various contents.

Curriculum-Based Assessment

Curriculum-based assessment, which is sometimes called task analytic mastery measurement (Fuchs & Deno, 1991), is "a procedure for determining the instructional needs of a student based on the student's ongoing performance within existing course content" (Gickling & Havertape, 1981, p. 55). This assessment includes direct observation and analysis of the learning environment, analysis of the processes students use to approach tasks, examination of students' products, and control and arrangement of tasks for students. School personnel break complex tasks into their component parts and analyze the extent to which the student can master each of the components. They teach those components that have not been mastered and integrate the components to teach the complex skill. Assessment consists of setting terminal objectives and enabling objectives, writing items designed to measure mastery of enabling objectives, administering minitests to students, and charting pupil performance on the tests. Those opposed to the use of these measures argue that the approach is labor intensive and fractionated and that performance on the small tests does not generalize to performance in the broader domain of behaviors that can be assessed.

Curriculum-Based Measurement

Curriculum-based measurement is a specific form of curriculum-based assessment devised by Deno and his colleagues at the University of Minnesota. Curriculum-based measurement is characterized by standardized direct measures of the pupil's skills in the content of the curriculum. The measures meet the following criteria: "(1) tied to a student's curricula, (2) of short duration to facilitate frequent administration by teachers/educators, (3) capable of having many multiple forms, (4) inexpensive to produce in terms of time in production and in expense, and (5) sensitive to the improvement of students' achievement over time" (Marston, 1989, p. 30).

Those in favor of the use of curriculum-based measures point out that the measures give valid indications of the student's performance in the curriculum of interest, focus on the broad goals of the curriculum, and enable teachers to monitor student skill development across an entire school year without shifts in measurement devices and procedures. Those against the use of these measures maintain that their curriculum specificity limits their use to the specific curriculum being measured.

Performance-Based Assessment

Assessors are now attempting to move away from assessment that focuses on pupil performance on multiple-choice tests and memorization. They are looking at problem-solving ability and are gathering data on pupil performance over longer periods of time. Such assessment may consist of measurement of student performance on tasks that may take as long as a semester to complete, and students may be asked to work individually or in groups to solve major problems. This form of assessment requires students to frame problems, collect data, and analyze and report the results. Students may be asked, for example, to study the prices at two supermarkets and determine which supermarket has the lower prices. Performance is evaluated on the bases of how well students work as a group, how well they use math to solve the problem, and so on. This kind of assessment is most often called performance-based assessment, though the terms "alternative assessment" and "authentic assessment" are also used.

Several applications of performance-based assessment are currently being conducted. For example the Connecticut Department of Education is directing a project in which science and mathematics teachers from Connecticut, Michigan,

Convention Highlights Reading Assessment Changes

During the 1990 IRA Annual Convention, the focus of sessions relating to assessment varied, but the central theme was "change." The snapshot testing paradigm, where a score on a contrived task is assumed to represent reading skill, is being replaced with more authentic measures of the process of reading.

According to Karen Wixson of the University of Michigan, this change is being fostered as more educators begin to view reading as an active-constructive process where the application of skills and strategies varies as the demands of the reading situation change. Thus, skills and strategies are dynamic, rather than static, and must therefore be measured in a variety of reading contexts. Wixson pointed out that "instructional changes [based on this interactive definition] have outpaced assessment."

No longer is static assessment of subskill mastery viewed as a measure of reading comprehension. Researchers and teachers are looking for "authentic" activities that measure the process of meaning construction. Wixson warned that "anything subject to 'silly coaching,' such as skill and drill activities, is not authentic and does not promote active-constructive reading." Literacy is now viewed as complex and variable, thus requiring process-oriented assessments.

As assessment is redirected, state and national assessments are attempting to reflect these new directions. Michigan and Illinois have included measures of prior knowledge and strategic reading behaviors along with longer, more authentic story selections in their assessments. Also, Vermont is developing a system of portfolio assessment to be implemented *statewide*.

Changes in assessment extend to the national level as well. Barbara A. Kapinus of the Maryland State Department of Education reported that the National Assessment of Educational Progress Planning Committee was recommending open-ended response items that use holistic scoring criteria and a special study of classroom portfolios.

Although these are welcome indicators of change, conferees were most interested in forms of assessment that could be implemented in their classrooms. Three new forms of assessment were highlighted at the conference: portfolio assessment, instruction as assessment, and student self-assessment.

Portfolio Assessment

Portfolios contain multiple samples of classroom work over an extended period of time. According to Sandra Murphy of San Francisco State University, the "power of portfolios is the contextualized base of assessment" they offer, since the samples illustrate the process of learning as well as the content learned.

Presently, there is wide variation in what is included in a literacy portfolio, but Donald H. Graves of the University of New Hampshire and Denny Taylor of the Institute of Urban and Minority Education, Teachers College, maintain that the reflective process of choosing what is included offers the most authentic evidence of students' learning. When choosing what to include, students must reflect on their own literacy development, evaluate their learning, and set new goals. Thus, portfolios become integrated within the curriculum and serve as a mirror of the process of learning in the classroom.

Instruction as Assessment

Instruction and assessment can interface so that information gained from instruction becomes a form of assessment. When using this assessment strategy, the teacher finds a situation in which the student responds positively to instruction, and then watches and listens to how the student constructs meaning during the lesson.

This type of assessment often is referred to as dynamic assessment. It stems from the Vygotskian notion that every learner has a zone of proximal development where he or she can achieve more complex intellectual activity under the guidance of a more capable learner—the teacher. As the teacher varies the explicitness of the task, the student's growth under various conditions is measured.

When conducting this kind of assessment, Jeanne Paratore of Boston University includes a description of the intervention. The assessment then becomes instructionally valid. According to Sharon Kletzien of the Springfield (PA) School District and Maryanne Bednar of LaSalle University, measuring the difference between initial placement and placement after instruction provides an index to gauge the student's zone of reading potential.

Self-Assessment

According to Peter Johnston of the State University of New York at Albany, one of the conditions of self-assessment is the "sensible and noncompetitive context of evaluation." The students themselves, not tests, evaluate their ongoing literacy development. As students examine their own learning, their involvement in that learning increases.

Susan Mandel Glazer of Rider College recommends that students assess themselves before and after completing tasks. The students write out on weekly sheets: "Things I can do. Things I'm working on. Things I want to learn." This offers a consistent and visible plan for each student. As students complete literacy tasks, they evaluate their own literacy using checksheets related to the task.

(continued)

Convention Highlights Reading Assessment Changes (cont.)

In content area classrooms, Susan McMahon and Taffy Raphael of Michigan State University suggest having students ask themselves, "What did I learn about sharing my ideas, putting my ideas together, using different sources of information, and the topic in general?" Thus, self-assessment is like having a conversation with yourself about your learning.

Summary

In these three forms of assessment, evaluation is more contextualized than in "snapshot testing." However, the move toward these types of assessment means not only that assessments should use authentic literacy tasks and be instructionally valid, but also that teachers and students, rather than tests, should be used to evaluate learning.

According to Johnston, in these types of assessment "teachers begin to know students and instruction in a personal way." They spend more time listening to children. In essence, teachers become increasingly reflective, and their professional development must include ways to enhance their reflections about literacy and children.

SOURCE: Walker, B. J. (1991). Convention highlights reading assessment changes. *Reading Today, 8*(4) (February/March), 20.

Minnesota, New York, Texas, Vermont, and Wisconsin, are being trained in the writing and implementation of performance-based student assessments. The project, called the Connecticut Multi-State Performance Assessment Coalition Team Project, is designed to train teachers to develop performance tasks in which students must think critically, use their knowledge, and use creative problem solving to apply math and science to the solution of real-life problems. The teachers measure student performance on a series of tasks that may take as long as a semester to complete. Students work individually and in groups to frame problems, collect and analyze data, and report results. Students are required to use knowledge to solve new problems and are evaluated on the basis of how well they do so.

The practice of performance-based assessment is spreading. For example, as part of a new law restructuring the state's public education system, Kentucky is to "develop and implement a state-wide, primarily performance-based assessment program as early as the 1993–94 school year but no later than the 1995–96 school year." Vermont has approved funding for statewide portfolio assessments, initially in the areas of writing and math; students will be evaluated on the basis of progress evidenced in their portfolios as well as on the "best piece" they develop. In Arizona educators are developing performance-based assessments in reading, math, and writing to evaluate student achievement in areas of the curriculum shown to be untapped by use of the state-adopted standardized achievement test.

Major arguments are raised for and against performance-based assessment. Those in favor point out that current standardized measures really measure only recognition and retention, which is not enough. Resnick (1990) argued that performance assessment measures the "thinking curriculum," not the "remembering curriculum," and that such measures are more closely aligned to the context of instruction; others say that performance assessments let students know what the goals of schooling are. Shavelson (1990) argued that performance assessment is teaching as well as assessment, and Baron (1990) contended that performance assessment, because it is so closely tied to instruction, has more ecological or face validity.

Those who argue against these assessments typically question the technical adequacy of the measures (Porter, 1990, Cross, 1990), the assumption that the teacher has more expertise than can be demonstrated (Linn, 1990; Reddaway, 1990), and point to the extensive time and expense demands placed on the teacher (Linn, 1990). And because students often select the task they will use to demonstrate their expertise, the equivalence of measurement necessary for comparative judgments is difficult. Opponents also argue that the use of such measures requires considerable input from teachers, administrators, and parents, all of whom are pretty busy already, and that the local scoring requirement adds to teachers' burdens. Opponents also question what ought to be assessed: what is taught or what should be taught.

The jury is still out on the use of performance-based tests. Clearly, the tests will be used extensively during the 1990s. Time will tell if they become a major part of the assessment activities that go on in schools. And time and use will help practitioners to evaluate the extent to which these instruments are viable for use with students with disabilities.

The Use of Clinical Judgment

A discussion of issues in assessment techniques would be incomplete without a discussion of clinical judgment. Many assessors argue that they do not rely on test scores in making decisions about students; they rely on clinical judgment. They contend that they take into account pupil performance on many tests, rather than on single tests; integrate this with what they learn through interviews and observations; and make diagnostic judgments based on their own clinical experience and expertise. Epps, Ysseldyke, and McGue (1984) reported the results of an investigation in which they provided test scores to teachers and psychologists and asked them to use clinical judgment to decide whether students were learning disabled; judges were correct about 50 percent of the time.

Issues Regarding Who Performs Assessment

Many different disciplines are involved in the assessment of students with disabilities. Classroom teachers, resource room teachers, school social workers, remedial reading specialists, school psychologists, counselors, occupational therapists, and others administer tests in the process of planning instructional interventions and making other decisions about students. As might be expected, there is disagreement about who ought to administer and interpret which tests.

In some states some assessment activities are governed by licensure and credentialing agencies. For example, in some states a licensed psychologist administers intelligence tests to students. In such cases, deciding who should give which tests should be a relatively simple matter: reading specialists administer reading diagnostic measures, speech and language personnel give and interpret language tests, and so on. But such simplistic reasoning assumes one-to-one correspondence between professional title and professional competence. We have learned that no such correspondence exists. In some districts the best person to give language measures is the speech and language pathologist. In other districts that person does not have the expertise, but the counselor or school psychologist does. We firmly believe that tests ought to be given and interpreted by people who have the necessary competence, regardless of professional title, to give and interpret the measures.

Interdisciplinary Cooperation

Until quite recently it was not unusual for an individual school psychologist, counselor, social worker, administrator, or teacher to make an assessment decision unilaterally. On occasion this still happens today, and for that reason it becomes an issue. The problems students bring to school are so complex that they are not going to be solved by a single individual or a single discipline operating in isolation. Rather, they are going to require interdisciplinary appraisal and cross-disciplinary collaboration and cooperation (Norby, Thurlow, Christenson, & Ysseldyke, 1990).

The Use and Misuse of School Psychologists

School psychology is a profession long associated with psychoeducational assessment, and many school psychologists have become psychometric robots. They test and classify children to declare them eligible for programs and to quality schools for dollars. According to Bardon, "If you ask teachers or parents what school psychologists do, chances are good that you will get one of three responses: they will not know what a school psychologist is; they will say that school psychologists give tests to atypical children; or they will describe functions commonly attributed to psychiatrists or clinical psychologists (1982, p. 3). Bardon went on to state that when school psychologists were asked what they actually did, they described functions that required "substantial attention to the administration of individual tests to children referred by school personnel either for special education classification or because of untoward behavior or poor school performance in a classroom" (p. 3).

Ysseldyke, Reynolds, and Weinberg (1984) argued for a necessary transformation in the practice of school psychology that would change the psychologist's role from a psychometrician to a provider of indirect service, prereferral intervention, collaborative consultation, and general intervention. The school psychologist would focus on creating environments in which effective instruction and learning were the key concerns and activities of the school. This would mean applying all relevant knowledge about the improvement of instruction.

Other issues arise in the use of school psychologists as assessors. Many school psychologists have no training or in-depth experience in curriculum and hence are reluctant to use curriculum-based assessment or curriculum-based measurement approaches. They fall back on their expertise as psychometricians. They are also often employed in a semiadministrative role: because they are responsible for making decisions about interventions for students, they must also participate in making decisions about staffing, which may be a conflict of interest.

Relevance to Intervention

A major issue in assessment is the link between assessment information and instruction. Heller, Holtzman, and Messick maintained that "the purpose of the entire process—from referral for assessment to eventual placement in special education—is to improve instruction for children. Valid assessment, in our view, is marked by its relevance to and usefulness for instruction" (1982, pp. x–xi). According to Christenson and Ysseldyke, assessment activities should shift away from a simple prediction orientation and toward a broader perspective in which information from multiple sources (the student, the family, the instructional environment, the community) is integrated for the primary purpose of designing appropriate interventions. "Assessment practices in schools would be dramatically improved if (a) student performance were assessed within the context of classroom and home influences, and (b) educators viewed the primary purpose of assessment as intervention planning—or finding ways collaboratively with parents and teachers to teach the child" (1989, p. 410). Unfortunately, much that goes on in the assessment of students with disabilities has very limited relevance to intervention. Our hope is that such activities will diminish and that data collection will be restricted to what is absolutely necessary for planning interventions.

Assessment is a process of collecting data for the purpose of making decisions about students. To the extent that the decisions that are made are viewed as harmful, inappropriate, biased, or limiting students' life opportunities assessment practices get blamed. In this chapter we have reviewed issues that arise when decisions are made about whom to assess (or whom to exclude from testing), what to assess, the specific techniques and procedures to use, and who should perform assessments. The bottom line in assessment is relevance to intervention. Assessment activities are useless if they do not result in improved instructional opportunities for students.

Discussion Questions

1. There is currently much debate about developing and using a national achievement test. What do you believe will be the major benefits gained by using such a test? Are the costs of developing such a measure (about $300 million) worth the benefits?

2. Do you believe students with disabilities ought to participate in standardized testing? If so, what are the major technical difficulties in ensuring appropriate testing of these students? If not, where do school personnel draw the line in making decisions about the kinds of students who will participate? How severe must a student's handicap be to be excluded from testing?

3. There is currently a major effort toward outcomes-based education. Should outcomes for general education and special education students be different?

CHAPTER 8

Issues in Instruction

We evaluate the progressivism of a public school system by the number of new things it is doing, rather than concerning ourselves with whether it is doing any of them well.

—Trachtman, 1981

What is special about special education? Do students who are exceptional require instruction that is different from that received by students who are not considered exceptional? Who is responsible for teaching and who is best equipped to teach students who are handicapped? Do students who are exceptional profit from instruction only when it is delivered by teachers who are specifically trained to teach them? What should be the content of instruction for children and youths with disabilities? These and other instructional issues are addressed in this chapter.

Despite considerable disagreement over what should be taught in schools, there is a national consensus that the primary function of schools is to teach students. Thus, educators develop curricula with the general goal of educating all students to their maximum potential, and the curricula are typically designed to meet the assumed capabilities of the majority of students. Because schools are organized according to the students' age or grade, a general core curriculum is made up for each grade. It is the responsibility of the school personnel to adapt these core curricula according to the appropriate emphases for all or for select groups of students. If students fail to profit from the core curricula developed for their ages and grades, they are given special or remedial programs or interventions.

The critical issues in special and remedial instruction are reviewed in this chapter. We begin with a review of alternative perspectives on students and on what schools are charged with doing to/for them, and we consider alternative views on why students fail in school. In the remainder of the chapter we discuss issues regarding where and when intervention should take place, what to teach, how to teach, and whether instruction occurred.

Views of Causality and Their Relationship to Treatment Approaches

Significant numbers of students fail to profit from the experiences they receive in general education. Educators develop remedial or compensatory interventions or provide alternative schooling for students who fail to profit. The nature of these interventions is very often a direct function of the views that educators hold on the causes of failure.

Attributions for Failure

There are three views of the causes of failure. The first view holds that the schools are doing an inadequate, perhaps deplorable, job of educating students and indeed that the schools are not designed to teach. Baer and Bushell (1981, p. 262) developed this premise after taking a careful look at why students who are poor do not perform well in school. American public schools, they stated, direct considerable time, effort, and energy toward the following societal functions: providing day care for young children, delaying the entrance of adolescents into the labor market, posing difficult problems that children must learn to solve for themselves, and sorting and sifting children into different social positions according to how well they teach themselves to solve academic problems.

The Research and Policy Committee of the Committee for Economic Development took a similar position in its report *The Unfinished Agenda: A New Vision for Child Development and Education*. In that report the committee stated, "Our society has undergone profound economic and demographic transformations, but the social and educational institutions that prepare children to become capable and responsible adults have failed to keep pace" (1991, p. 1).

The second view argues that the schools are designed to teach, that teachers are prepared to do an adequate job of teaching, but that many students simply have too many defects, deficiencies, or disabilities to profit from instruction. These educators contend that students enter school with so many deficiencies that the schools can hardly be expected to overcome them. They maintain that the home situations from which such students come are so problematic that they make it impossible for the students to learn.

The third view attributes student failure to a combination of internal constraints, external pressures, and unattainable objectives; in other words, the schools are being asked to do too much. Given the nonoperational nature of many educational goals (for example, to develop self-realization) and society's unwritten goals (for example, to eradicate poverty), the argument says that it is impossible to demonstrate how many, if any, students achieve them. Broudy (1978), for example, noted that education cannot possibly eradicate poverty, unemployment, and war; most people agree with this appraisal of what education can do.

Despite the identification of these three explanations for failure, most educators attribute failure to deficiencies in the students and/or their home environments. In 1979 the research staff of the National Education Association conducted a poll that asked teachers why children did poorly in school. Of the responses, 81 percent blamed the students' home lives, and 14 percent blamed the students themselves; only 1 percent attributed the cause to teachers, and 4 percent blamed the schools. Thus, a total of 95 percent of teachers blamed the students' poor performance on either the students themselves or the students' home lives.

The Causes of Disability

In a survey of assessment and intervention practices for students with handicaps, Quay (1973) said that these practices varied according to the educators' views regarding the causes of handicapping conditions. He broke these causal explanations down into four general categories: process dysfunctions, experiential defects, experiential deficits, and interaction.

Process dysfunctions The many educators who believe that the causes of failure reside within the students themselves generally attribute school problems and failure to either process dysfunctions or experiential defects. Quay (1973) described the process dysfunction view as the belief that problems in sensory acuity (for example, deafness), response capability (for example, motoric responses), or internal processes (for example, short attention span, poor visual sequential memory) are the reason for students' academic difficulties. In this view, process dysfunctions are either expressed (for example, deafness or blindness) or implied (for example, minimal brain dysfunction). Until recently, many believed that process dysfunctions were unremediable and that they either had to be compensated for or bypassed (for example, teaching deaf students to use manual communication). Since the early 1950s, there have been extensive efforts in special education to remediate certain process dysfunctions (for example, perceptual-motor or psycholinguistic deficits) or symptoms of process dysfunctions (for example, inadequate eye-hand coordination).

Mann traced early views about processes and process dysfunction to the early writings of the Greeks, who attributed specific functions, or appetites (for example, practical, vegetative, speculative, mechanical, and intellectual), to the soul. These functions or appetites were believed to guide behavior. According to Mann:

> Behavioral or psychological processes are, whatever their validity, hypothetical "inner" events or entity constructs. They are usually used to explain behavior, i.e., presumed to cause behavior. While there is nothing that precludes process theorists from identifying their processes with numerical codes, say 45D, they have usually chosen to name their constructs in a commonsense way—as would the man on the street; the name of a process is usually assigned to it on the basis of the behavior it is presumed to generate. "Intelligent behavior" is the result of intelligence. "Remembering" is brought about by memory; we "perceive" with our perceptual abilities. The famed Roman medical authority Galen (130–200) noted a given faculty "exists only in relation to its own effect." . . . Earlier, Aristotle had attempted a similar operational definition: "Mind must be related to what is thinkable as sense is to what is sensible." Frostig similarly defined perceptual processes, centuries later. (1979, p. 14)

Early thinking about the causes of conditions now associated with special education can be seen in Howe's attribution of idiocy to the violation of natural laws:

> Idiocy is found in all civilized countries, but it is not an evil necessarily inherent in society; it is not an accident; and much less it is a special dispensation of Providence; to suppose it can be so, is an insult to the Majesty of Heaven. No! It is merely the result of a violation of natural laws, which are simple, clear, and beautiful; which require only to be seen to be known, in order to be loved; and which, if strictly observed for two or three generations, would totally remove from any family, however strongly predisposed to insanity or idiocy, all possibility of its recurrence. (1848, p. 2)

Mann described process training activity as follows:

> During the decade leading up to America's bicentennial, there was a process explosion as new areas of psychological investigation proliferated. Witness Neisser's (1967) list of cognitive processes. The visual area includes transient iconic memory, verbal coding, perceptual set, span of apprehension, displacement and rotation in pattern recognition, backward masking, template matching, decision time, visual search, feature analysis, focal attention, preattentive control, figural synthesis, and perceptual defense. In the auditory area, Neisser lists segmentation, auditory synthesis comprises, among others, recoding, slotting, decay, linguistics, gestalts, and grammatical structure. (Mann, 1979, p.14)

People who believe that exceptionality is caused by process dysfunctions search for the causes of disorders by studying heredity, nutrition, biochemistry, brain function, and so on (Ullmann & Krasner, 1969). To them, remediation is dependent on advances in biochemistry, physiology, pharmacology, and genetic engineering.

Educators have spent a considerable amount of time, effort, and money developing instructional interventions to remediate process dysfunctions. They designed remedial programs to alleviate or ameliorate visual-perceptual, auditory-perceptual, and psycholinguistic deficits, believing that such deficits caused academic difficulties and that children would not (indeed, could not) learn to read, write, and compute until such presumed deficits were overcome. Nevertheless, the history of such efforts consists of a set of pretty dismal findings. Educators have been unable to demonstrate that remediation of process deficits or dysfunctions leads to improved school performance. Those who have reviewed the research on process training or ability training have concluded that there is little empirical evidence to support the efficacy of these practices (Arter & Jenkins, 1977; Ysseldyke, 1973; Ysseldyke & Marston, 1990).

Educators often rely on medical findings to create still other interventions. Evidence suggesting the importance of nutrition to development and learning led to the establishment of school lunch programs, breakfast programs, and vitamin therapy. An entire industry has grown up and prospered in response to the belief and evidence that some conditions of behavioral deviance result from abnormal levels of specific body chemicals.

Mann reviewed the history of efforts to identify and train processes or abilities. He summarized the repeated return to process deficits to explain learning or behavior problems. Mann stated that

> processes come and go; they are evoked or evolved to explain phenomena of interest and then discarded to die or disappear if no one any longer cares about the phenomena they "explain." They are often absorbed into other, newer processes or assume new names according to the changing times or fashions. Frequently they are reinterpreted and given new meanings. Many of the old processes are no longer with us. Where have they gone? Where were the newest of today's processes when we needed them years ago. (Mann, 1979, p. 14)

The idea that academic problems are caused by process dysfunctions leads educators either to give up on efforts to resolve problems (as when educators abandon the education of children who demonstrate cognitive deficits in the belief that intelligence is innate) or to design and implement remedial interventions to alleviate unseen but assumed dysfunctions (for example, visual sequential memory deficits).

Experiential defects   The view that exceptionality is caused by defective experience has led to the investigation of emotional disturbance; these investigations are replete with examples of situations in which researchers hypothesize that "deleterious early experiences (e.g., overinhibition of a child's behavior) produce conditions within the child (e.g., fear and anxiety) that interfere with learning"

(Quay, 1973, p. 166). People who ascribe to this view do recognize that certain process dysfunctions or defects (for example, minimal brain dysfunction) exist, but they regard these dysfunctions as the result of experiential defects. Entire special education remedial programs have been developed on the presumption that defective experience (for example, failing to creep and crawl appropriately) causes brain dysfunction and results in academic difficulties. The programs are designed to undo the harm caused by the defective experience.

Experiential deficits   The view that educational difficulties are the result of deficient, rather than defective, experiences arises from the belief that although students have intact learning apparatus, they have limited behavioral repertoires, which create difficulties. Much has been written on the "disadvantaged" or the "deprived" child and on the effects of deficient early experience on later intellectual, academic, and social development. Educators today believe that deficient experience is a major cause of school difficulties. The Research and Policy Committee of the Committee on Economic Development indicated that "when multiple risk factors, such as poverty, family structure, and race are taken into account, as many as 40 percent of all children may be considered disadvantaged" (1991, p. 3). Whiteman and Deutsch described the view that experiential deficits cause difficulties as follows:

> The child from a disadvantaged environment may have missed some of the experiences necessary for developing verbal, conceptual, attentional, and learning skills requisite to school success. These skills play a vital role for the child in his understanding of the language of the school and the teacher, in his adapting to school routines, and in his mastery of such a fundamental tool subject as reading. (1968, p. 87)

In this view, the locus of the problem is outside the student; even when teachers view the problem as within the student, they consider it caused by outside factors. That is, the student's deviant social behavior, limited vocabulary, and limited reading skills, for instance, are caused by deficient experience and environmental disadvantages. This view is often called the sociological perspective because various social explanations for the development and existence of deviant behavior have been proposed. Each explanation points to rules of social conditions as the source of the problems. For example, social disorganization theory emphasizes differences among communities as the basis for differing levels of abnormal behavior. Levy and Rowitz (1973) reported that the highest rates of mental illness are found in cities' central sections and that the crime rate is likely to be higher in disorganized than in organized communities. Other sociological theorists believe that deviance or dullness is learned through association with deviant or dull people. Proponents of such cultural transmission theories were influential in the early history of American education.

When academic and social problems, school failure, declining achievement, and high dropout rates are viewed as the result of deficient experience, the people holding this view too often limit their explanations to out-of-school environments. As we observed earlier, 95 percent of the teachers who responded in a recent survey attributed problems to home environments and to the children themselves. Nevertheless, more and more blame is now being placed on the schools.

Hall, Greenwood, and Delquadri quoted a statement by the Reverend Jesse Jackson:

> "We keep saying that Johnny can't read because he's deprived, because he's hungry, because he's discriminated against. We say that Johnny can't read because his daddy's not in the home. Well, Johnny learns to play basketball without daddy. We do best what we do most, and for many of our children that is playing ball. One of the reasons Johnny doesn't read well is that Johnny doesn't practice reading." (1979, p. 14)

Interaction   The view that handicaps, disorders, or disabilities may result from the interaction of process dysfunctions, experiential defects, and experiential deficits (including inadequate teaching) has yielded a closer look at the selective, rather than the general, effects of both nature and environment. Sarason and Doris, for example, stated, "Not all abusive parents abuse all of their children, and not all parents with characteristics of abusive parents have abused their children" (1979, p. 21). Likewise, referrals for psychological evaluations occur at varying rates for children with similar and different characteristics, children who exhibit the same behaviors often do not receive the same school experiences; and problem behaviors occur in normal as well as deviant children. Sarason and Doris suggested that a "transactional approach" (Sameroff & Zax, 1973) may be useful in explaining such outcomes:

> [From the transactional perspective,] heredity and environment are never dichotomous. It can even be misleading to say they "interact" because that is more often than not interpreted in terms of effects of heredity on environment just as for so long we have paid attention to the effects of parents on children and virtually ignored the influence of children on parents. The transactional approach is always a two-way street. There is nothing in the transactional formulation that denies the existence and influence of genetic processes or the existence of a socially structured context populated by diverse people. (Sarason & Doris, 1979, p. 25)

A similar transactional, or ecological, perspective was suggested by Rhodes (1967, 1970) to explain emotional disturbance. Algozzine, Schmid, and Mercer described this theory as follows:

> Ecological theorists believe that deviance is as much a function of where and with whom a child interacts as it is the nature of the interaction in terms of behaviors which are exhibited by the child . . . ; to these theorists emotional disturbance is in the "eye of the beholder" and is generated or develops when an individual's behavior is viewed as disturbing or bothersome by others with whom interaction occurs. Deviance, then, is as much a function of reactions to behavior as it is the behavior in and of itself. (1981, p. 168)

An interesting application of ecological theory was suggested by Sarason and Doris in their discussion of iatrogenic retardation:

To the extent that it is appropriate to view the common school as a prescribed cure for the ills of society, we maintain that a considerable proportion of mental retardation encompassed by the term "educably retarded" can be viewed as an iatrogenic disease. By that we mean, just as the administration of certain medications in the treatment of physical disease can cause the appearance of new disease related to the nature of the medication and to the patient's idiopathic response to it, irrespective of its effect upon the original disorder for which it was prescribed, so, in like manner, a considerable part of the problem of educably retarded children derives from the way in which we have devised our educational system. To the extent that we have ignored cultural differences, differences in patterns and tempos of learning, social and affective differences in the temperaments of children, to the extent that we have set goals of achievement for individual children that are either unrealistically high or low, we have ensured the development of that educationally disordered child, with cognitive and social handicaps, that we relegate to the special classroom.

This is not to deny a continuum of competence that may be based on genetic and environmental factors acting together and independent of the educational environment in which society attempts to develop and measure competence. It is to state that the continuum of competence, cognitive and social, existing prior to entry into school becomes distorted by the very system that society has devised for the development and measurement of competence. And that the distortion is of such a nature that individual and social and ethnic class differences interact with the categorical rigidities of curriculum, methods of instruction, and administrative organization to sort out the children not solely in terms of the constitutional and environmentally determined differences existing prior to school entry, but to a large extent independently of such preschool individual differences. (1979, pp. 154–155)

From this point of view, retardation is not simply the consequence of the child's nature or the school's environment; rather, it is the product of transactions between the child's characteristics and school environments, each in response to the other.

Issues Regarding Where and When Intervention Should Take Place

Most special and remedial instructional interventions are developed to accommodate learners observed or alleged individual differences. Educators have usually assumed that individual differences in rates of learning or in the extent to which students profit from instruction are due to individual differences in learning ability.

Where Should Instruction Take Place?

In early American educational history, a dual-track system compensated for such differences: a student either received and profited from instruction in lockstep graded classes or was educated in a special school or class. To tailor instruction to the learner's needs, educators placed students in homogeneous groups, assuming that those with similar characteristics should be taught using the same instructional methods or techniques. Special education classrooms were self-contained. Classes for students who were deaf, blind, and mentally retarded (as defined by performance on standardized tests) were established according to the considerable research on the learning characteristics of those children.

In the late 1950s and early 1960s, the efficacy of self-contained special classrooms for students with handicaps was seriously and continually challenged. Investigators demonstrated again and again that students who received special education services did not improve academically and socially over those peers with disabilities who were kept in regular classrooms and were not offered special educational interventions. Although early efficacy studies were plagued with methodological problems (for example, failure to demonstrate that the groups were comparable), they did cause educators to question the efficacy of self-contained programs for students who were handicapped.

At the same time that educators were questioning the benefits of special education, especially of self-contained classrooms, they recognized that there were as many variations within categories of students as among them. This recognition returned the focus of education to individual differences, rather than to categories, and instruction was tailored to the learner's own needs.

Special education has evolved to the point that today educators speak of "continua of placements" and of a "variety of alternative placements and services" in a continuum from regular class placement with tutorial or resource teacher assistance to isolation from the regular classroom program. Deno (1970) pictured the continuum of placements as in Figure 8.1. Reynolds (1978) elaborated and refined Deno's cascade model by developing a triangular conception with regular class placement as the base (Figure 8.2). Reynolds considered abnormal anything other than regular class placement. In Deno's conception, students with special needs are sifted out of the regular classroom to settle downward in a variety of increasingly restrictive environments. In Reynold's triangular conception, students move individually and deliberately up from regular classroom placement, with the goal of returning as soon as possible to regular classroom placement. Reynold's triangular conception goes beyond the "places" where instruction occurs to consider how instructional services are delivered.

PL 94-142, the Education for All Handicapped Children Act of 1975, specified that all students with handicaps have the right to a free appropriate public education to meet their particular needs. Simply placing students in classes or programs for students with handicaps is not enough; schools must ensure that the instruction delivered is appropriate to the needs of each learner. To match instruction to the learners' needs, schools have adopted a variety of assessment-intervention approaches.

Prereferral Intervention

Large numbers of students experience difficulty in school, and many who do are referred for psychoeducational evaluation. Very recently educators and related-services personnel have instituted prereferral interventions to avert placement in set-aside structures for students who can profit from regular education placement.

FIGURE 8.1   Cascade model of special education service

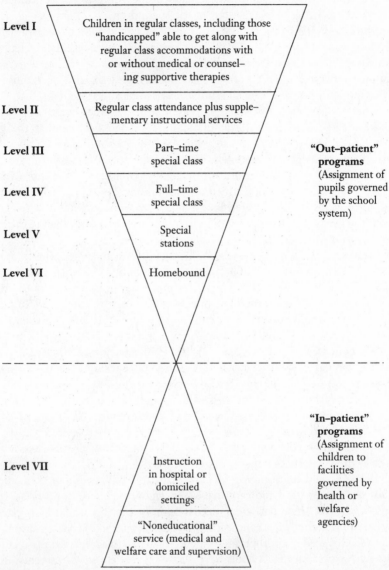

Level I — Children in regular classes, including those "handicapped" able to get along with regular class accommodations with or without medical or counseling supportive therapies

Level II — Regular class attendance plus supplementary instructional services

Level III — Part–time special class

Level IV — Full–time special class

Level V — Special stations

Level VI — Homebound

"Out–patient" programs (Assignment of pupils governed by the school system)

Level VII — Instruction in hospital or domiciled settings

"Noneducational" service (medical and welfare care and supervision)

"In–patient" programs (Assignment of children to facilities governed by health or welfare agencies)

SOURCE: From Special education as developmental capital by E. Deno. *Exceptional Children, 37,* 1970, 229–237. Copyright 1970 by The Council for Exceptional Children. Reprinted with permission.

FIGURE 8.2   Reynolds's triangular conceptualization of instructional alternatives

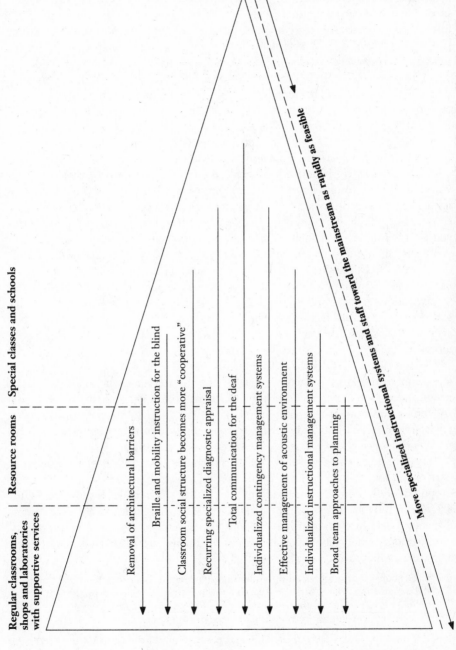

SOURCE: Reprinted from M. C. Reynolds. Final notes. In J. Grosenick & M. Reynolds (Eds.) *Teacher education.* Minneapolis: University of Minnesota Leadership Training Institute/Special Education, 1978. Reprinted with permission.

According to Carter and Sugai, prereferral interventions are required in twenty-three states and recommended in eleven others. "The purpose of the prereferral intervention approach is to reduce the number of inappropriate special education placements while identifying interventions which will enable students to remain in the least restrictive setting, usually the regular classroom" (1989, p. 299).

The prereferral intervention model is usually an indirect form of service in which school resource personnel provide resources or assistance to classroom teachers at the point of referral to help the teachers cope with students' difficulties. Fuchs (1991) identified four characteristics of prereferral intervention. First, it is consistent with the LRE doctrine set forth in law; efforts are made to maintain the student in the least restrictive environment. Second, the model is preventive; efforts are made to prevent educational failure at the same time that personnel work to prevent more intensive treatment. Third, prereferral intervention is implemented or coordinated by one or more special service personnel working as consultants. While this typically is the case, new forms of prereferral intervention consist of groups of regular education teachers helping one another to solve problems; such efforts often come under the title of "teacher assistance teams" (Phillips & McCullough, 1989). Fourth, prereferral intervention encourages use of an ecological perspective in which problems are viewed as resulting from an interaction among the individual, instructional approaches, school organization, and home and family factors. The approach downplays a focus on student characteristics and on the assumption that school problems reside within the individual.

Fuchs also identified three factors that have led to the focus on prereferral intervention: the large increase in the number of students who are identified as handicapped, the increased frequency of teacher referrals, and the "arbitrariness and precipitousness of teacher referral" (1991, p. 242). In short, people attempt prereferral interventions in an effort to stem the tide of the large increase in the provision of special education services in set-aside structures.

There are many models of prereferral intervention. One of the easiest to understand and follow, and one of the few on which there are data, is the model proposed by Graden, Casey, and Bonstrom (1985). This model is shown in Figure 8.3. A carefully articulated set of steps is followed in an effort to alleviate student difficulties and prevent further failure. The important features of prereferral intervention, which have been identified by Fuchs, are illustrated in the figure and are as follows:

1. School systems interested in implementing prereferral intervention must build the activity into the job descriptions of the people they want to implement it. School personnel have other important things to do, and implementation will be facilitated (or even only accomplished) through mandate.

2. Someone must assume leadership and provide overall direction for the prereferral effort.

3. Consultants must receive adequate training in the process of consultation and in implementation of prereferral interventions.

FIGURE 8.3 Prereferral intervention

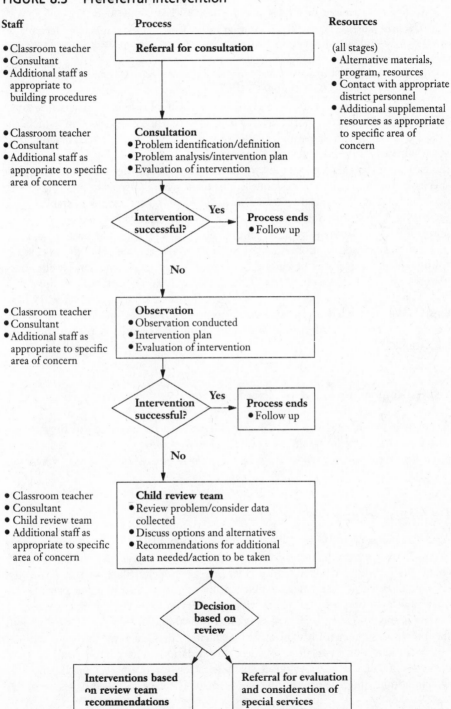

Staff

- Classroom teacher
- Consultant
- Additional staff as appropriate to building procedures

- Classroom teacher
- Consultant
- Additional staff as appropriate to specific area of concern

- Classroom teacher
- Consultant
- Additional staff as appropriate to specific area of concern

- Classroom teacher
- Consultant
- Child review team
- Additional staff as appropriate to specific area of concern

Process

Referral for consultation

Consultation
- Problem identification/definition
- Problem analysis/intervention plan
- Evaluation of intervention

Intervention successful? — Yes → **Process ends** • Follow up

No

Observation
- Observation conducted
- Intervention plan
- Evaluation of intervention

Intervention successful? — Yes → **Process ends** • Follow up

No

Child review team
- Review problem/consider data collected
- Discuss options and alternatives
- Recommendations for additional data needed/action to be taken

Decision based on review

Interventions based on review team recommendations

Referral for evaluation and consideration of special services

Resources

(all stages)
- Alternative materials, program, resources
- Contact with appropriate district personnel
- Additional supplemental resources as appropriate to specific area of concern

4. The consultation process must be efficient, yet corners must not be cut.

5. The interventions used must be acceptable to classroom teachers.

6. There must be provision for ensuring the "fidelity" of the classroom interventions. Consultants must check that interventions are implemented as they were intended.

7. Data on student or teacher behavior should be collected at multiple points in the prereferral intervention process. (1991, p. 263)

Prereferral intervention is catching on in most states and districts (see box). Yet there is limited support for the practice. In those instances in which the practice has been implemented extensively, it has not always been documented and evaluated. The New Jersey Department of Education has had in place since the early 1980s a project designed to assess and improve the quality of the state's special education delivery system. In thirteen school districts, building-based, decision-making teams known as school resource committees were established in each school to strengthen the capacity of regular education personnel to serve nonhandicapped students with learning problems. The state has been engaged in pilot studies of modifications to the assessment system, operation of child study teams, and modifications of eligibility criteria for special education. Preliminary results indicate that the outcomes of the pilot study have been very positive.

What are the outcomes of prereferral intervention? Graden, Casey, and Christenson (1985) reported that prereferral intervention resulted in lower referrals for testing, less testing, and a lowering in the number of students placed in special education.

Issues Regarding What to Teach

Those who teach students must decide what to teach. In doing so, they design treatments and decide what the content of instruction will be. These decisions often generate controversies, as do curriculum overload and the use of aversive treatments.

Derivation of Interventions

Any discussion of the critical issues in intervention should start by analyzing the assumptions underlying intervention and the many ways in which educators conceptualize the purposes of intervention. Cromwell, Blashfield, and Strauss (1975) described assessment and intervention as parts of an ongoing process and identified four categories of diagnostic and intervention data, which they labeled A, B, C, and D. Category A consists of historical and/or etiological information, the precursors of currently observed behavior or characteristics (for example, phenylketonuria as a precursor of mental retardation). Category B is made up of data on currently assessable pupil characteristics (for example, "intelligence" or skill in adding single-digit numbers). Category C refers to specific treatments or interventions (or levels of such), and category D comprises the outcomes that result from particular interventions. Use of these four categories enables the interrelations of historical-etiological information, currently assessable pupil characteristics, specific interventions, and the outcomes of those interventions to be examined. The assessment-intervention paradigms proposed by Cromwell, Blashfield, and Strauss are sketched in Table 8.1.

This conceptualization of assessment-intervention programs is useful because it helps to describe the current interventions used in special and remedial instruction and it helps to differentiate valid from invalid assessment-intervention approaches. According to Cromwell and his colleagues, assessment-intervention approaches that include both C and D data (ACD, BCD, CD, and ABCD) are valid because they include treatments on the basis of known outcomes. The three approaches that do not pertain to interventions (AD, BD, and ABD) are not useful in helping to establish a science of instruction. Four approaches (AB, AC, BC, and ABC) have little value for the educator because they describe relationships among historical-etiological data, pupil characteristics, and treatments but pay no attention to the outcomes of differential treatment. Many instructional interventions (AC, BC, and ABC) now used in schools are invalid, assigning students to interventions or treatments with no evidence of their effectiveness or outcomes.

Mercer and Ysseldyke (1977) described five models used by educators in developing interventions: medical, social system (deviance), psychoeducational process, task analysis, and pluralistic. These models are helpful in considering the kinds of instructional interventions employed in schools, and they are outlined in Table 8.2.

Each of the five models has a different definition of abnormality, or perception of deviance from "normal" behavior. In the medical and psychoeducational process models, disorders are traced to pupil disease or dysfunction. Normality is defined as the absence of disease or dysfunction and abnormality as the presence of pathology or process ability deficits. In the other three models, abnormality is traced to environmental (including school) influences on the student. In the social system model, abnormal behavior is perceived as behavior that deviates from society's expectations. In the task analysis model, normal or abnormal behavior is not defined but is viewed as normal or abnormal only in accordance with the context in which it occurs. In this model, "abnormality is the sort of deviance that calls for and sanctions the professional attention of psychiatrists, clinical psychologists and other 'mental health' professionals" (Ullman & Krasner, 1969, p. 1).

The models for perspectives on intervention programs differ in their assumptions of what causes difficulty and thus lead to the design of different interventions. The medical model views symptoms, difficulties, or problems as originating in the individual's biological condition. The psychoeducational process model sees difficulties as the direct result of underlying process dysfunctions. The social system model assumes that normality and abnormality are role and system specific. The task analysis model views academic performance as the function of an

CONNECTICUT'S EARLY INTERVENTION PROJECT: ALTERNATIVES TO REFERRAL, 1991–1992

Q: What is the Early Intervention Project: Alternatives to Referral?

A: The Early Intervention Project (EIP) is an innovative effort initiated by the Connecticut State Department of Education in 1985 to address the misclassification of students as disabled. Since 1985, five urban districts have participated: Bridgeport, Danbury, Hartford, New Britain, and New London. Nonurban districts have also joined the project over the past several years: Bloomfield, Greenwich, Milford, North Haven, Orange, Oxford, Shelton, Trumbull, and Woodbridge. Ten additional school districts will participate beginning with the 1991 to 1992 school year. Since 1988, the EIP has been administered by the Special Education Resource Center (SERC). The project is a pilot program and participation is voluntary based on cooperation between the local district and SERC. The project primarily addresses two emerging issues in special education: (1) the apparent overrepresentation of minority students in certain categories of special education and (2) the increasing numbers of children being inappropriately diagnosed as disabled and placed in special education. The project also represents an initiative to more effectively integrate programs and services between general and special education.

Q: What is the purpose of the Early Intervention Project: Alternatives to Referral?

A: The Early Intervention Project is designed to provide classroom-based services for at-risk students, particularly minority students, experiencing academic or social/behavioral problems. These classroom-based services are provided prior to consideration or referral to the Planning and Placement Team for possible placement in special education. It provides early referral and intervention that focus support in the regular education classroom.

Q: What outcomes can districts anticipate from participation in the Project?

A: Through long-term training and ongoing technical assistance provided by SERC, districts involved in the Project will

• Develop a systematic intervention process to be initiated by the regular classroom teacher or others seeking assistance for students experiencing academic or social/behavioral problems;

• Establishing a non–special education building team specifically trained to assist classroom teachers in designing alternative strategies within the least restrictive environment of the regular classroom;

• Develop least biased, nonstandardized assessment techniques that provide information about the student's performance in the specific curriculum and within the specific classroom placement.

Q: What training will participating district teams receive and what competencies will participants develop?

A: SERC will provide initial core team training to selected district teams during the 1991 to 1992 school year through a comprehensive program. It is anticipated that on completion of the core team training program, participants will be able to

•Delineate the rationale, purpose, and objectives of Connecticut's Early Intervention Project: Alternatives to Referral;

• Utilize various assessment techniques (i.e., curriculum-based assessment, observation-based assessment, classroom-management assessment);

• Recommend and utilize intervention skills regarding instructional and social/behavioral problems;

• Demonstrate skills and techniques necessary to collaborate and work effectively with colleagues.

Q: What personnel will participate in core team training?

A: Each district will designate one building in which to initiate the EIP. The core team from that building must total four to five members and consist of the building principal, two general educators, and a pupil personnel specialist or special educator. Districts may identify additional educators within their building to be members of their EIP team, although these educators will not participate in SERC's core team training. Additional team members are to be trained by the district's own core team.

Q: In addition to core team training, what other resources will SERC provide to selected districts?

A: On-site technical assistance will be provided to assist districts in preparing their teams to conduct prereferral initiatives. Technical advisors will provide approximately two days of technical assistance per month on site. In subsequent years, SERC provides ongoing training programs to participating districts in order to strengthen and refine necessary skills.

Q: What are the results of past EIP efforts?

A: Statewide data compilation from the project has demonstrated that a minimum of 75 percent of all referrals within each building were either resolved to the teacher and team's satisfaction or continued with assistance within the regular classroom without the need to refer the child for special education evaluation. Additionally, 85 percent of all students referred to the EIP either achieved satisfactory resolution or were continued with support in the least restrictive environment of the regular classroom. This indicates a reversal of the typical referral pattern wherein approximately 70 percent of all referrals result in identification and placement in special education.

SOURCE: Special Education Resource Center, 25 Industrial Park Road, Middletown, CT 06457, (203) 632-1485. Marianne Kirner, director of the Special Education Resource Center, is project director. Nancy Krafcik is project coordinator.

TABLE 8.1   ABCD assessment-intervention paradigms

Paradigm	Nature of the Paradigm
AB	Describes relationships between historical events or etiologies and current pupil characteristics or behaviors without considering treatment or its outcomes
AC	Describes relationships between historical events or etiologies and particular treatments or interventions without considering pupil characteristics or treatment outcomes
AD	Links generalized outcomes to etiology without considering differences among pupils or treatments
ABC	Plans interventions for students according to their history-etiology and current characteristics without evidence of the effectiveness of the outcomes
ABCD	Prescribes treatments with known outcomes or effects according to etiology and current pupil characteristics
BC	Assigns pupils to treatments according to their current characteristics without evidence regarding known treatment outcomes
BCD	Assigns pupils to interventions with known outcomes on the basis of their current characteristics without considering the etiology or historical development of their conditions
CD	Describes relationships between treatments and outcomes without considering etiology or current characteristics
BD	Investigates relationships between student characteristics and instructional outcomes without considering the etiology of the characteristics or the differences in treatment programs

SOURCE: Adapted from Cromwell, R. L., Blashfield, R. K., & Strauss, J. S. (1975). Criteria for classification systems. In N. Hobbs (Ed.), *Issues in the classification of children: A sourcebook on categories, labels, and their consequences.* Vol. 1. San Francisco: Jossey-Bass.

interaction between the particular set of background experiences an individual brings to the learning setting and the demands of the tasks he or she is asked to perform.

In terms of interventions, proponents of the medical model design interventions to treat the biological organism; when disorders cannot be treated by medical (pharmacological or surgical) intervention, educational programs are designed to compensate for or bypass them. Those who support the social system model and who believe that specific behaviors are abnormal only in that they deviate from role or system expectations design treatments to teach students socially expected behaviors. Advocates of the psychoeducational process model design interventions to remediate or compensate for underlying causes (process dysfunctions) of behavior; treatment consists of ability training. The task analysis model emphasizes the teaching of enabling skills, which are subskills necessary to perform more complex behavior.

The perspectives or models of the assessment-intervention process formulated by Cromwell and his colleagues, Mercer and Ysseldyke, and Quay have much in common, and all can be used to analyze the assessment-intervention process and

TABLE 8.2   Different assessment models

Elements of the Models	Medical Model	Social System (Deviance) Model	Psychoeducational Process Model	Task Analysis Model	Pluralistic Model
Definition of abnormal	Presence of biological symptoms of pathology.	Behavior that violates social expectations for specific role.	Psychoeducational process and/or ability deficits.	No formal definition of normal or abnormal. Each child is treated relative to himself and not in reference to a norm.	Poor performance when sociocultural bias controlled.
Assumptions	Symptoms caused by biological condition. Sociocultural background not relevant to diagnosis and treatment.	Multiple definitions of normal are role and system specific. Biological causation not assumed.	Academic difficulties are caused by underlying process and/or ability deficits. Children demonstrate ability strengths and weaknesses. Processes or abilities can be reliably and validly assessed. There are links between children's performance on tests and the relative effectiveness of different instructional programs.	Academic performance is a function of an interaction between enabling behaviors and the characteristics of the task. Children demonstrate skill development strengths and weaknesses. There is no need to deal with presumed causes of academic difficulties. There are skill hierarchies; development of complex skills is dependent upon adequate development of lower-level enabling behaviors.	Learning potential similar in all racial-cultural groups. Tests measure learning and are culturally biased.
Nature of treatments or interventions	Treat biological organism. ABCD-type constructs.	Teach child socially expected behaviors. BCD- and BD-type constructs.	Compensatory or remedial ability training. BD-type constructs.	Test-teach-test. Teach enabling behaviors. BC(D)-type constructs.	Nonspecific estimate of performance level. ABD- and BD-type constructs.

SOURCE: Reprinted with permission from J. Mercer & J. E. Ysseldyke. Designing diagnostic-intervention programs. In T. Oakland (Ed.), *Psychological and educational assessment of minority children.* New York: Brunner/Mazel.

to better understand the interventions used in schools. At issue is the extent to which the alternative approaches have merit and whether schools ought to subscribe to instructional approaches for which there is limited empirical support.

Factors That Influence Intervention Decisions

Educators decide to use certain interventions because they believe these interventions will improve students' academic and/or social functioning. No food and drug administration controls this process: any intervention can be used by anyone, and interventions are selected and used as a result of a "bandwagon effect," tradition, cash validity, a "doctor-tested" claim, a recommendation by the Joint Dissemination Review Panel (JDRP), research findings, or for no known reason.

Bandwagon effect   The bandwagon effect is probably more often the source of most special and remedial interventions than any other base.

> The bandwagon effect, wherein an idea or a cause suddenly becomes popular and gains momentum rapidly, may not have been invented in this country, but we have surely perfected it. Our propensity for faddism extends from diets, fashions, and games to major political, educational, or sociological movements. We also tend frequently to be more concerned with the appearance of things than with the substance of things. This is the issue of form versus content. Thus, I wrote elsewhere, "we live in a society which tends to evaluate its devoutness by counting the number of people who go to church rather than the number of people who believe in God. We promote university professors on the basis of the number of publications they have authored, with little consideration for the quality of the contents. We evaluate the progressivism of a public school system by the number of new things it is doing, rather than concerning ourselves with whether it is doing any of them well." . . . The form versus content issue interacts with the bandwagon effect to produce hastily conceived, poorly implemented innovations or programs, the failure to achieve anticipated goals, and consequent disillusionment with the original idea, or backlash. In turn, backlash may lead to equally precipitous abandonment of meritorious programs and ideas which have not been adequately conducted or sufficiently tried. This situation establishes a state of readiness for the next bandwagon and places us constantly at the mercy of what Hyman (1979, p. 1024) called the panacea mongers. (Trachtman, 1981, pp. 140–141)

Parents have been instrumental in encouraging, and indeed sometimes nearly forcing, educators to get on a variety of bandwagons. To strengthen the bandwagon, parents form clubs or organizations to popularize, promote, and push specific treatments or interventions, and in the process of doing so they push educators to adopt the interventions. Educational fads come and go and are usually adopted with no regard for the empirical evidence of their effectiveness. Then each in turn is replaced by a new, equally untested fad.

Tradition and precedent   In special and remedial education, many practitioners choose to use specific interventions either because of tradition ("We've always done it this way") or because of history ("The treatment worked before"). Some educators employ the same intervention with all students who have academic and social problems simply because they have always used it, and others prescribe a program just because it once worked for another student.

Cash validity   Many educational interventions are adopted because they have "cash validity"—that is, they sell well. Just as school systems use specific group tests because other school districts use them, personnel select interventions because they can be sold. This is one way that bandwagons begin rolling.

Unfortunately, when there is little information on how to treat specific educational difficulties and parents and teachers are looking for simple solutions to complex problems, the environment is ripe for someone to come up with a panacea. Thus, because their developers are looking for profits, many instructional interventions are developed and marketed with no evidence of their effectiveness. Lynn illustrated cash validity by using a statement attributed to one Mel Levine:

> I would like to call Doubleday and have them come over here, tell them I'm a Harvard professor and that I've found out, from seeing lots and lots of patients, that air pollution causes learning disabilities and that I'd like to write a book about it. I could have that book done in a few months' time, full of anecdotal evidence about how it hits the kid nearest the city, or tell stories about a kid who lived near a factory and when he moved there his schoolwork got worse, and when he moved away it got better and how that got me thinking. . . .
>
> This book would sell a million copies.
>
> I would then go to Arthur D. Little, which is a consulting firm, to see what they could do about designing me a mask for kids to wear that will filter the air they breathe. Let them design that mask for me, put activated charcoal in the mask so they'll breathe pure air, and then sell these for $15.95 each—you can send away for them—to parents of LD children.
>
> I'll say have them wear the mask at least eight hours a day; kids will go to school with their masks on. I'll have a following around the country—the "Levine Dyslexia Society." It will be extraordinary, with parents who can provide abundant testimony as to how their child's whole life was changed when they started using the Levine method. I'll be famous; I'll get on the "Today" show with my mask; and I'll continue to make money because we'll patent it and sell replacement cartridges that you have to get for $6.95 every six months.
>
> No problem. It will be antitechnological, which is in the spirit of the times; antiauthoritarian (it's those big boards of directors that are poisoning our kids' brains). . . . I'll guarantee you that my air pollution idea will come up within the next three or four years. (1979, pp. 116–117)

Interestingly, Levine may have shown considerable foresight, as we note that today residents of the Three Mile Island region in Pennsylvania are claiming that the leakage of the Three Mile Island nuclear power plant may be affecting the learning and behavior of youngsters in that region.

"Doctor tested"   A well-known remedy for hemorrhoids has been advertised as "doctor tested, found effective in many cases." Other medical products use slogans like "Four out of five doctors surveyed recommend . . ." Of course, such statements do not provide evidence of the effectiveness of a product; they merely try to convince consumers that if a product is doctor tested and used or recommended by a physician, then it is something the consumer should buy. Educators have used many interventions simply because they were "doctor tested"—that is, their use was urged, and no evidence for their effectiveness was provided.

JDRP recommendation   In all our years of reading the final reports of projects funded by the old U.S. Office of Education, we never came across a project intervention that did not work. Investigators whose intervention studies are funded by the government somehow always manage to present evidence that, they say, supports the effectiveness of their particular interventions. They just do not tell the sponsoring agencies that the funded programs were ineffective. How then does the consumer select from all these "effective" interventions those that actually have merit and ought to be adopted?

In the mid-1970s, the U.S. Office of Education established a mechanism for reviewing educational interventions and identifying those that were worthy of dissemination. In the belief that the government should encourage schools to adopt only "validated" educational interventions, the Joint Dissemination Review Panel was formed. Educators evaluate the effectiveness of their specific interventions, and submit their findings to the JDRP for review and endorsement. Only after JDRP endorsement has been received are projects, programs, or interventions disseminated for adoption in new settings. The idea is a good one, but unfortunately many inadequate and technically and methodologically unsound interventions have been validated and recommended for dissemination.

Research   Decisions to use particular interventions should be based on evidence that they are effective. Unfortunately, there are few research findings to support specific interventions. Joyce and Weil stated:

> There have been several hundred studies comparing one general teaching method to another, and the overwhelming portion of these studies, whether curriculums are compared, specific methods for teaching specific subjects are contrasted, or different approaches to counseling are analyzed, show few if any differences between approaches. Although the results are very difficult to interpret, the evidence to date gives no encouragement to those who would hope that we have identified a single, reliable, multipurpose strategy that we can use with confidence that it is the best approach. (1972, p. 4)

Although we do not have evidence that specific curricula are universally effective, many data support the contention that interventions must be designed for the individual and must be monitored frequently to ensure their effectiveness. Intervention is equivalent to research and is therefore a process of hypothesis testing:

> At the present time we are unable to prescribe specific and effective changes in instruction for individual pupils with certainty. Therefore, changes in instructional programs which are arranged for an individual child can be treated only as

hypotheses which must be empirically tested before a decision can be made on whether they are effective for that child. (Deno & Mirkin, 1977, p. 11)

The Content of Instruction

The curriculum may or may not be modified for students who are exceptional. And instructional modifications may take on many forms. For some students with disabilities, the goals are academic, whereas for others the goals are primarily social and/or vocational. Educators regularly debate, with little clear conclusion, the extent to which students who are exceptional should be enrolled in academically oriented curricula and whether they should be taught in the same ways as regular education students.

How do educators decide the level of content for students? Some educators merely use the results of a standardized test to decide where to place the student in the curriculum. Others advocate sampling pupil performance using curriculum-based measures; these educators argue that doing so enables them to spot the level of pupil performance within the curriculum and the deficits in skill development that must be remediated.

Strategy Training Versus Content Instruction

One way in which educators have attempted to intervene with students who experience failure is through training in the use of specific cognitive strategies. Even though the term *cognitive strategy training* has various meanings, Deshler and Schumaker's (1988) Strategies Intervention Model (SIM) is the approach used most often. In the SIM, regular and special education teachers work cooperatively to improve the instruction of difficult-to-teach students. The regular education teacher works on delivering content, while the special education teacher works on teaching students how to learn and how to succeed in the mainstream class. (An example of the SIM is shown in the box.) A number of methodologies are used to teach strategies, including cooperative group instruction, peer tutoring, special feedback systems, and visual and verbal cueing methods (Schumaker, Deshler, & McKnight, 1991). The SIM also includes routines for teaching content, including the advance organizer routine, the concept teaching routine, the survey routine, factual enhancement routines, and integrative approaches. Some argue that even though strategy training may be effective, it is too difficult for teachers to implement. Indeed, Schumaker, Deshler, and McKnight indicated that following development of the University of Kansas Institute for Research on Learning Disabilities (KU-IRLD) strategy training interventions, classroom implementation rates were "abysmally low." In response, they began working with commercial publishers to include in teachers' manuals examples of strategies to implement and they provided inservice training to teaching staffs. They reported that

> to ensure the adoption of complex educational innovations, training must be offered over a sustained period of time rather than as a one-shot event. Sustained training efforts allow time for modeling, practice, feedback, and questions. In

---

An Example of the Strategies Intervention Model

An example of how a SIM program might work for a student under certain circumstances illustrates some of the processes that have been activated in school districts across the nation. Suppose that in a school in which teachers, support staff, and administrators have worked together to promote a SIM program, the school psychologist has determined that students have to be able to memorize lists of items to succeed on a particular biology teacher's tests. A student enrolled in the learning specialist's support class also is enrolled in the targeted biology class. The learning specialist works with the student to determine whether he or she wants to learn a strategy that will help with this class demand. First, a pretest is given to determine how well the student can organize and memorize lists. Next, the results of the pretest are shared with the student, who decides whether to try to learn a strategy to help memorize lists. Upon deciding to learn the strategy, the student writes a goal to that effect. Then the learning specialist teaches the students (and others who have written a similar goal) the FIRST-Letter Mnemonic Strategy (Nagel et al., 1986), a strategy for (a) organizing the information into list form, (b) memorizing the information, and (c) utilizing the information to answer test questions. After working hard over a period of about 3 weeks, the student masters the strategy so that it can be applied to the textbook used in the biology class and the notes taken in that class.

Meanwhile, the learning specialist and the biology teacher work together to ensure that the biology teacher understands the strategy the student (and other students in the class) is learning in order to be better able to facilitate the student's use of the strategy. Whenever possible, the biology teacher presents lecture information in list form and, in addition to writing lists on the board, cues students when lists must be memorized for tests. When time permits, students are helped in design-

---

addition, teachers need the opportunity to try out the new procedure . . . in their classroom and to debrief with the trainer(s) on problems encountered. Finally, following the formal training session(s), teachers must have the opportunity to receive ongoing support in their efforts to implement the new procedure. (p. 489)

The key, according to Deshler, Schumaker, and their colleagues, is effective use by mainstream teachers of a host of validated teaching routines and devices that can facilitate students' understanding and retention of content information.

Enrichment, Acceleration, and Separation

Historically, gifted and talented students have been served through three educational approaches: enrichment, acceleration, and separation. Enrichment means

ing a mnemonic device for a given list or they are asked to work cooperatively to design the devices themselves. When the biology teacher reviews information the day before a test or when he or she gives students a study guide, the necessary information is provided in list form. The day before the test, the students who have learned the strategy are reminded to use the FIRST-Letter Mnemonic Strategy as they study for the test.

Throughout instruction on each new biology unit, the target student builds up a file of 3″ × 5″ cards containing important lists. The night before a test, in a study session supported by his or her parents, the student applies the FIRST-Letter Mnemonic Strategy to lists taken from lectures as well as other lists derived from the assigned textbook chapter to ensure that he or she has memorized the necessary information. As he or she takes each test, the student recalls information through use of the memory devices he or she has designed.

Our target student receives grades of As and Bs on tests. After learning and integrating several strategies like this and applying them to several courses, the student graduates from high school. By working with a mentor, he or she later enrolls in junior college courses, taking biology and other courses at the local junior college and continuing to apply the strategies learned in high school. The support class student has become an independent learner and performer.

SOURCE: Schumaker, J. B., Deshler, D. D., & McKnight, P. C. (1991). Teaching routines for content areas at the secondary level. In G. Stoner, M. Shinn, & H. Walker (Eds.), *Interventions for achievement and behavior problems* (pp. 478–479). Silver Springs, MD: National Association of School Psychologists. Used with permission.

enhancing the educational experiences of students without changing the setting in which they are educated. Early efforts to educate gifted and talented students consisted entirely of enrichment programs. One of the earliest was established in the Cleveland public schools in 1922; students identified as gifted or talented stayed in the regular classroom in the same grade as their agemates but were given advanced or extra work.

Today enrichment can mean more than within-class tinkering with the curriculum. Students who are gifted can attend special programs at other schools, or they can enroll early in university programs. In Minnesota, for example, the Postsecondary Enrollment Options Program enables students to attend colleges and universities for the purpose of taking advanced coursework. Others participate in after-school coursework in specific subject areas at universities, colleges, or in high school settings.

Students also have been treated by acceleration, sometimes called double promotion or the skipping of a grade. Students who are gifted are also sometimes placed in self-contained classes. At issue here is the most effective way to deliver advanced, enriched instruction to students who have already demonstrated competencies that are being taught to their age-level peers in regular classrooms.

Curriculum Overload

Teachers often complain of curriculum overload, by which they mean the repeated adding on to the curriculum of new areas of instruction and new content. Each time society experiences a major issue, like drug abuse or AIDS transmission, it is suggested that there ought to be coursework on the topic. Schools and school personnel are held responsible for addressing these issues, but in an additive manner. That is, nothing is removed from the content of the curriculum, and new material is added. School personnel now are not only responsible for inculcating the culture; they are expected to assist in the elimination of poverty, war, the use of drugs and alcohol, racism, sexism, and AIDS.

Aversive Treatments

The appropriateness of using aversive treatments with students who are handicapped has been a hotly debated topic in special education and one on which major organizations have taken firm positions. Some individuals and associations have argued for a moratorium on the use of behavior reduction procedures (The Association for Persons with Severe Handicaps, 1981; Donnellan, Negri-Shoultz, Fassbendes, & LaVigna, 1988; Guess, 1988), whereas others (Martin, 1975; Association of Advancement of Behavorial Therapy; Favell et al., 1982; Council for Exceptional Children, 1990; Council for Children with Behavior Disorders, 1990) have argued that the judicious use of behavior reduction may be necessary or even imperative. For example, the Council for Exceptional Children has policies on physical intervention and on corporal punishment, which are as follows:

> *Physical Intervention.* The Council recognizes the planned use of aversive stimulation and negative reinforcement when these options are the treatment of choice, provided that the situations in which they are used are planned between the teacher and the teacher's supervisor, made known to the parent or guardian, applied prudently, and evaluated and modified in terms of the results. The Council also recognizes that at times staff members must physically intervene immediately in the behavior of a child to protect health, safety, or property.
> *Corporal Punishment.* The Council for Exceptional Children supports the prohibition of the use of corporal punishment in special education. Corporal punishment is here defined as a situation in which all of the following elements are present: An authority accuses a child of violating a rule and seeks from the child an explanation, whereupon a judgment of guilt is made, followed by physical contact and pain inflicted on the child. The Council finds no conditions under

which corporal punishment so defined would be the treatment of choice in special education. (1990, Sections 8.315 and 8.316)

One of the major difficulties in the formulation of clear positions on the use of punishment or aversives, according to Skiba and Deno (1991) is that the terms have multiple meanings, are not clearly defined, and carry with them misconceptions, misunderstandings, and confusions. They argued for replacing the terms *punishment* and *aversive* with more value-neutral terms because doing so would lead to careful collection of data on methods of behavior reduction and use of the data to make decisions about appropriate behavior reduction procedures.
students, and the severity of the student's difficulties.

Issues Regarding How to Teach

Perhaps the most fundamental issue in instruction of students with disabilities is the issue of teacher responsibility for instruction. Even though it would be easy to argue that no one wants to teach students with disabilities, this is an overstatement. Both regular and special education teachers do want to assume responsibility for teaching certain kinds of students with disabilities, yet at the same time there are some students whom no one wants to teach. Salvia, Ysseldyke, and Algozzine (1984) argued that no one wants to teach difficult-to-teach students. Braaten, Kauffman, Braaten, Polsgrove, and Nelson (1988) argued that only some students with behavior disorders are the responsibility of general education teachers, whereas others are the responsibility of special educators.

Many factors influence teachers' perceptions of responsibility for providing instruction. Among these are the nature of the handicapping condition, the presumed cause of the condition, teacher expectations, presumed impact on other students, and the severity of the student's difficulties.

Nature of the Disability

Some disabilities are more acceptable than others to all teachers. Yet there is good evidence to suggest that teachers differ in the kinds of students they like to teach and/or will tolerate. At the same time, the stimulus properties of conditions vary; some characteristics are more obvious than others. For example, it is relatively easy to distinguish among racial groups in America. The differentiation is usually made on the basis of one or two obvious characteristics, such as skin color or physical features. But sorting people into groups according to handicapping conditions is less simple because not all people who have a handicap act the same, nor are they differentiated by a simple set of features.

People behave differently toward different kinds of individuals with handicaps largely because of their own reactions to physical or behavioral features. Therefore, specific conditions seldom produce consistent reactions among all people. Some people do not like to interact with individuals who are cerebral palsied, whereas others are not bothered by that condition but prefer to associate with students who are gifted. Still others believe that their compassion for others is displayed when they have a friend who is blind or who has cerebral palsy.

Most teachers express a reluctance to teach students with behavior disorders. In major research projects in which we have tried to integrate into general education students with disabilities, general education teachers have told us that they "should not have to tolerate the crap they take from these students." We have found that teachers are more willing to assume responsibility for instructing students who are mildly mentally retarded, who evidence mild learning problems, or who evidence physical disabilities. They are willing to assume responsibility for educating students with sensory impairments provided they do not have to make major modifications in their lessons. One factor that influences assumption of responsibility for instruction and willingness to have exceptional students in the class is the extent to which the teacher must personally design or redesign instruction. Many teachers indicate a willingness to integrate into their classrooms students with relatively severe physical disabilities. Yet further inspection often reveals that these kinds of students come with their own teacher or with a paraprofessional who assumes instructional responsibility. Teachers are often willing to integrate into their classes students with disabilities provided that someone else is responsible for teaching them.

Presumed Cause

The cause of the condition of exceptionality influences the actions and reactions that result from it. When reactions to categories are compared, organic impairments (those believed caused by physical ailments) are seen as more acceptable than functional impairments (those with unknown causes but obvious effects). Many teachers are more accepting of student learning problems (and more willing to work on remediating problems) if they think think the difficulties are beyond the control of—or not "the fault of"—the student.

Teacher Expectations

Past experiences help to form teachers' expectations about how students will act or behave. Indeed, expectations are useful for making predictions about what will happen relative to some of those experiences. The relationship between expectations and behavior is cyclical—past actions influence expectations, and expectations influence future behavior—and teachers' expectations can affect students' personal expectations for their own success or failure and, most important, for their own performance.

Teachers are willing to assume responsibility for some students but not for others. Often this assumption of responsibility for instructing students is a direct function of the teachers' expectations for the pupils' performance, expectations that result from prior experiences with similar kinds of students or from hearsay about specific students.

Presumed Impact on Other Students

Observed differences in teachers' willingness to assume responsibility for teaching students with disabilities are often a function of the teachers' beliefs about the extent to which inclusion of a student in classes will interfere with the performance of others. Teachers tell us that they are willing to assume responsibility for teaching individual students who are handicapped as long as they do not have to take time away from other "normal" students or as long as the exceptional students do not interfere with the ability of "normal" students to profit from instruction.

Severity of the Condition

The willingness of teachers to teach students with disabilities is also a function of the severity of the handicap. Some teachers prefer to instruct students with severe handicaps, others to teach students with mild handicaps. We have learned that teachers are most resistant to teaching students who are very difficult to teach, who simply do not profit from very intense instruction.

The Demand for Quick, Simple Solutions

Assumption of responsibility for instructing students is clearly the critical issue in teaching students with disabilities, but a close second place goes to the demand among educators for instant, simple, easy-to-implement solutions to incredibly complex instructional problems. The demand for instant solutions has spawned an interesting marketing enterprise around special and remedial education. Workshops and inservice training programs promise step-by-step directives, and publishers and developers claim to have *the* intervention to assist students who are handicapped or failing in school. Educators have demanded, and have been provided with, *the* treatment or intervention that works and have given it widespread use without examining assumptions and/or requiring evidence of the safety or efficacy of the intervention. The professional literature in special and remedial education also publishes examples of instant, easy solutions to problems in the education of students who are handicapped. A perusal of several of the most recent issues of the major professional publications in this field was revealing.

Table 8.3 lists the claims made for special and remedial education products. These are verbatim extracts from advertisements for specific instructional programs. The claims made illustrate vividly the Madison Avenue approach that has come to characterize the products developed for this profession: claims are repeatedly made for a program as *the* answer, *the* solution to complex problems.

TABLE 8.3　Claims for specific tests and instructional programs found in professional journal advertisements

"Widely field tested and found to be effective when implemented with normal as well as handicapped and gifted students."

"_____ is the one program that works. It works for *you!* It works for pupils of *every age!*"

"_____ is the one program so thoroughly researched and concisely planned that it gives you every element you need to help pupils achieve a level of reading success never before attained."

"All the instruments you'll ever need for evaluation and testing."

"Need an individual test which *quickly* provides a stable and reliable estimate of intelligence in 4 or 5 minutes per form? Has three forms?"

"For the special child you can now diagnose specific Language and Auditory Processing problems— and then prescribe the correct materials for remediation—A great help when making IEPs."

"You can teach the obese mentally retarded person to lose weight—and keep it off—in just 19 weeks."

"Our products and services help you detect the handicapped, identify their particular difficulties, and provide remedial action."

"Can your students become confident spellers in only 15 minutes per day? YES, when you fill the time with lessons from _____ ."

"With this text, your students will be able to identify appropriate and effective methods for helping children with emotional and behavioral problems."

Do We Know What Works?

Appropriate intervention is the "bottom line" in the delivery of services to students with disabilities. Students are assessed for purposes of planning appropriate interventions, they are placed in settings where they will be taught appropriately, and the extent to which they are receiving appropriate instructional interventions is evaluated. Funds are made available for special education so that students may receive appropriate instruction, and laws are enacted to ensure appropriate instruction. Indeed, educators, related-services personnel, and policy makers have spent more time, effort, and energy trying to ensure appropriate assignment to settings and programs than teaching students.

Even though the profession does know which factors enhance the effectiveness of instruction, no one can say with assurance that specific instructional practices will work with all students. Because intervention effectiveness depends on the complex interaction of numerous variables, only a few of which are under the control of the teacher, education is necessarily experimental: educators must form hypotheses for what will work with students, must teach in accordance with those hypotheses, and then must continually evaluate the effectiveness of the interventions.

Research data on the characteristics of effective reading programs help to identify those factors that interact to determine the effectiveness of any instructional intervention. After an extensive review of the characteristics of successful reading programs, Samuels noted that the difference was greater in administrative arrangements than in curricular methodology and that successful programs differed from unsuccessful ones in their underlying assumptions. Successful programs assumed that "the school *can* have a significant impact on the academic achievement of its students" and that "most children are capable of mastering the basic skills" (1981, p. 2). These assumptions placed the responsibility for student failure on the school. This is not the prevailing mood of the day.

In terms of personnel characteristics, successful programs had strong administrative leaders who provided "time for planning and carrying out decisions, securing financial support, and running interference against counterforces" (p. 4). They also employed teacher aides in direct instruction and reading specialists who worked with teachers and aides to assist them in planning instruction. According to Samuels, the teacher's attitude was critical to success. He found that successful programs were consistently staffed by teachers who, because they were committed, dedicated, and supportive of project goals, devoted considerable time and energy to achieving project goals. They believed that student success and failure depended on what happened in the classroom.

Furthermore, successful reading programs were characterized by practical training and supervision in which regular staff meetings focused on actual problems. Teachers were given the opportunity to observe and model other successful teachers and programs, and they participated in decision making.

Samuels reported that successful reading programs had clearly stated and specific goals and objectives and that the most successful programs used a task analysis (direct instruction) approach as well as creating a warm, friendly classroom atmosphere. These programs emphasized teaching of skills, gave students opportunities to practice those skills, and used instruction and instructional materials relevant to the attainment of the objectives.

Successful programs also provided ample time for instruction, and that time was used efficiently. Instruction was kept at a low level of complexity. Classes were fairly structured. Teachers frequently and directly measured their pupils' progress.

Unsuccessful instructional programs, according to Samuels, were based on the bandwagon effect. The programs were developed more in response to the availability of federal funding or to parental pressure than to demonstrated need. They lacked systemwide commitment, either because they were based on "bottom-up" motivation (teachers were committed to the program, but administrators were not) or "top-down" motivation (the administrators required implementation of programs to which the teachers were not committed). Samuels felt that unsuccessful programs consistently failed to allow enough start-up and development time; had narrow, piecemeal approaches; and used time inefficiently.

One of the arguments we have repeatedly heard at major national conferences is that instruction for students with disabilities is difficult because no one knows what works with those students. This simply is not the case. From an extensive review of literature in psychology and education (Christenson, Thurlow, & Ysseldyke, 1987; Christenson, Ysseldyke, & Thurlow, 1987; Thurlow, Christenson,

& Ysseldyke, 1987; Thurlow, Ysseldyke, & Christenson, 1987; Ysseldyke, Thurlow, & Christenson, 1987), we have drawn several conclusions about instructional effectiveness for students with mild handicaps.

> First, there is not one kind of instruction that works best in general education and another kind that works best in special education. And, there are certain instructional factors that must be present and are appropriate for individual students' needs, regardless of setting. A second conclusion is that the literature is replete with academic correlates. It is not very hard to generate a laundry list of factors related to student achievement. . . . A list of factors related to achievement is not very helpful unless it is organized into something that can be implemented by the educator. Third, student achievement is a result of interacting and mutually influencing factors, specifically student, teacher, classroom, instructional, school district, and home characteristics (Ysseldyke & Christenson, 1987). (Christenson, Ysseldyke, & Thurlow, 1989)

Christenson, Ysseldyke and Thurlow (1989) identified nine factors that are critical for student achievement. Instructional outcomes for students are enhanced when:

1. Classrooms are managed effectively.
2. There is a sense of positiveness in the school environment.
3. There is an appropriate instructional match.
4. Goals are clear, expectations are explicitly communicated, and lessons are presented clearly.
5. Students receive good instructional support.
6. Sufficient time is allocated to instruction.
7. Opportunity to respond is high.
8. Teachers actively monitor student progress and understanding.
9. Student performance is evaluated appropriately and frequently.

Issues Regarding Whether Instruction Occurred

Fidelity of Treatment

Educators are often faced with the task of demonstrating that students with disabilities profit from a specific form of remedial or compensatory instruction. Or they are asked to demonstrate that a specific intervention works better than another. Or they are supposed to demonstrate that a specific intervention works with one kind of pupil but not with another kind. To demonstrate that an intervention has actually occurred in a way in which it was intended to occur (fidelity of treatment) is problematic at best, and in response researchers are increasingly documenting fidelity of treatment (Fuchs, in press).

Accountability

Another issue in instruction of students with disabilities is accountability. Educators are being held accountable for demonstrating that the interventions they employ actually do students some good. (We described earlier the shift nationally to outcomes-based education.) Teachers now have to specify their intended outcomes and provide data on the outcomes they actually achieved for students with disabilities. Conversely, students have begun to take legal action against schools, contending that they have not been taught. Or parents have taken action against schools alleging that the schools have breached their duty to educate, that they have passed students from grade to grade without teaching basic skills, or that they have graduated students before the students achieved competency.

Elliott, Witt, and Kratochwill (1991) noted the difficulty of evaluating the extent to which treatments or services have been effective. They recommended the use of case study and single case designs in making decisions about treatment outcomes. Such designs have been used extensively in research but less often in practice. We anticipate that demands for accountability and evidence of effectiveness will increase markedly in the next decade, as can already be seen in calls for national tests.

Competency Versus Time in Grade

School personnel teach content to students who are exceptional. Sometimes they modify their instructional objectives, and sometimes they modify their instructional techniques. Invariably, however, decisions must be made about whether to move students to new educational levels: to new grades, to junior high school, to high school, and so on. At issue are the criteria that should be used to make such transition decisions. Some believe the decisions should be competency based, with students moving only after they demonstrate mastery of the content of the curriculum. Others believe in "social promotion"— that is, progress through the grades and through levels of education should be a function of getting older.

Discussion Questions

1. It has been shown that prereferral intervention results in placement of fewer students in special education pullout programs. Recently, in some districts, this has been used to reduce the number of special education teachers. Teachers have begun to oppose prereferral intervention efforts because they stand to lose their jobs. How might special education teachers be used in ways other than staffing self-contained special education classrooms? How might special educators argue new roles with school boards?

2. Should schools prescribe interventions for which there is limited empirical evidence that the interventions work?

3. School personnel complain often about curriculum overload. What is realistic for a school to teach? On what basis should schools make decisions about what to teach?

CHAPTER 9

School Outcomes and Special Education

Desired Educational Outcomes
General Education Outcomes
Special Education Outcomes
Outcomes-Based Education

Issues Regarding Identifying and Collecting Data on Outcomes
Critical Outcome Domains
Outcome Information Needed at Different Levels
The Heterogeneity of the Student Population
Measurement of Outcomes

Effects of Policies Related to Educational Outcomes
Graduation Requirements
Minimal Competency Testing
Retention in Grade
Grading Practices
A National Test?
Documenting Special Education Outcomes

Learning is like rowing upstream; not to advance is to drop back.

—*Chinese proverb*

Along with the increased emphasis in the early 1990s on school reform (see Chapter 6) came questions about the results of education. As the nation set goals for education, it also began to think more specifically than before about the expected outcomes of education. Chester Finn, former secretary of education, described the shift as one away from the *process* of education (who teaches, how many students per teacher, etc.) and toward the *results* of education (Finn, 1990a). As might be expected, the stress on educational outcomes first emerged in general education with little or no regard for special education. In fact, the emphasis on

234

academic excellence was frequently translated into outcomes that placed students in special education even more at risk in the educational system.

Interest in school outcomes came first from general education's struggle with repeated evidence that education was not effective for large numbers of students. The American business community likewise began to emphasize the outcomes of schooling and their importance for the nation's future in a complex and competitive world: "In an earlier industrial era, the economy did not need to ensure that every child was well educated, partly because the available labor pool was large enough and partly because unskilled manual labor and low-skilled manufacturing jobs were sufficiently plentiful and well-paid to absorb those without higher level skills. This is no longer the case" (Committee for Economic Development, 1991, p. 2). Interest in outcomes was given even more impetus when specific outcomes and outcome indicators for each of the national goals set at the beginning of 1990 had to be identified (see Chapter 6).

In this chapter, we examine some issues regarding the outcomes that were identified in general education and in special education and their relationship to the notion of outcomes-based education. We then identify the many issues that arise from the emphasis on identifying and collecting data on outcomes; these issues range from the identification of critical outcome domains and the development of appropriate indicators of desired outcomes to how information is used. Finally, we examine several of the effects of educational policies based on outcomes (e.g., graduation requirements, minimal competency tests, retention, grades, and grading), and the additional issues they raise.

Desired Educational Outcomes

The national goals that were formulated and accepted by President Bush and the governors were worded to reflect a strong interest in outcomes (White House, 1990). In late 1990, the governors were suggesting that

> the learning outcomes required for all students, regardless of their destination after high school, must focus on thinking, reasoning, problem solving, and integration of knowledge. Students need to be able to apply what they learn in creative and imaginative ways, in novel contexts, and in collaboration with others. Learning outcomes should reflect the skills, knowledge, and attitudes students need to prepare them for employment, further education, and responsible citizenship. (National Governors' Association, 1990a, p. 17)

General Education Outcomes

But what kinds of outcomes are expected for students from the educational system in general? Viewed from the 1990 national education goals, the outcomes of interest are graduation from high school; literacy; mastery of specific subject matter material, particularly science and mathematics; and competency in using mind and knowledge to foster responsible citizenship, further learning, and productive employment. Specific goals include, for example; improving student achievement, reducing the dropout rate, increasing the high school graduation rate, and increasing the number of students ready for college-level work.

The national goals served as a springboard for other groups to think about educational goals. For example, in late 1990 the Council of Urban Boards of Education proposed six goals for improving urban schools that complemented the national goals (Bradley, 1990) but that addressed the critical educational needs of urban communities. Yet even before the national goals were announced by President Bush and the governors, many policy makers had suggested what they considered to be the important outcomes of education. Many of these are summarized in Table 9.1. Note, however, that the outcome categories in this table are broad. For example, the achievement outcome represents reading and mathematics achievement for CBE; reading, writing, computation, and communication for DLETA; achievement (subject knowledge, basic and higher-order thinking skills) for PSA; and so on. Despite such differences in types of desired outcomes, almost all groups agreed on the importance of attainment (or graduation from high school) and achievement.

Not everyone suggested outcomes that fell within the types of outcomes shown in Table 9.1, however. For example, Seiger-Ehrenberg (1985) identified two critical educational outcomes: intelligent and ethical action to accomplish tasks that society legitimately expects of all its members and the establishment and pursuit of worthwhile personal goals. Wang (1985) proposed outcomes that were applicable during public school education as well as at its completion: mastery of subject matter content, acquisition of a variety of learning and adjustment skills, development of positive attitudes toward learning, and development of positive self-perceptions.

At the same time that national groups and others were talking about the expected outcomes of education, many states were identifying on their own the outcomes that were to be produced by their educational systems. The results of a study conducted by Inman, Prebish, and Salganik (1990) make clear that the types of outcomes identified by most states were in the domains of student participation (e.g., attendance or absenteeism; mobility; academic course enrollment; rates of suspension, expulsion, and dropouts; participation in vocational education; participation in special services), attainment and progression (retention rates, grade point average, graduation rate, percentages taking ACT or SAT), and student achievement (test data, language proficiency). Nearly all states collected student test data at some point in the student's education. But the specific nature of these data (e.g., criterion or norm referenced) and who participated in them varied considerably both within states and across states.

The extent to which outcome data were used and organized also varied considerably from one state to the next. In most states, outcome data were used only to describe district performance. Some states, however, used data to make decisions about funding. For example, New Jersey used outcome data to award

TABLE 9.1   Desired outcomes proposed by general education groups

Outcome[b]	Group[a]						
	CBE	CCSSO	DLETA	NESAC	PSA	SSPEI	RAND
Achievement	X	X	X	X	X	X	X
Affective status/self-esteem	X	X	X	X	X		X
Aspirations							X
Attainment (graduation)	X	X		X	X	X	X
Attitudes							X
Career and beyond school			X	X		X	
Citizenship					X		
Creative thinking/problem solving			X				
Interpersonal/organization skills			X				
Participation (attendance)	X	X		X			X
Postsecondary experiences		X		X	X	X	
Progression (nonretention)	X			X			

[a] Groups (and years for references) are as follows:
CBE = Chicago Board of Education (Kirst, 1990)
CCSSO = Council of Chief State School Officers (Selden, 1990)
DLETA = Department of Labor, Employment, and Training Administration (Carnevale, Gainer, & Meltzer, 1988)
NESAC = National Education Statistics Agenda Committee, National Center on Education Statistics (NESAC, 1990)
PSA = Policy Studies Associates (McCollum & Turnbull, 1989)
SSPEI = Special Study Panel on Educational Indicators (Indicators Panel, 1990)
RAND = Rand Corporation (Shavelson, McDonnell, & Oakes, 1989)
[b] The grouping of outcomes for this table sometimes required broad interpretation of the specific outcomes listed. In addition, different outcomes were sometimes grouped together in the original lists. If the reader is interested in the specific outcomes identified by a particular group, it is advisable to examine the original document from which this summary was developed.

district certification. Kentucky began in 1989 to develop an outcomes indicator system to use in determining whether individual schools receive funding. Although the organization of data in most states was simply a listing of descriptive data for each of the indicators in use, in California an indicator much like the gross national product or the Dow-Jones Industrial Average was being used. Called CAI (California Accountability Index), this indicator included fifteen measures of outcomes in four clusters (achievement, college bound, dropout, and placement). Each indicator measured the percent of students who meet or exceed a set criterion on that variable (e.g., a standardized test score). The CAI had a mean of 1000 and a standard deviation of 100, and it assessed the "percent above" certain levels on the indicators. It allowed for comparisons to be made at school, district, and state levels.

Thus, in the realm of general education, there has been a move toward greater accountability about the outcomes of education and the desire to use indicators of educational outcomes to make policy and funding decisions. Major policy-making bodies (e.g., National Governors' Association, Council of Chief State School Officers) have called for data to provide either a national report card or a means for state-by-state comparisons. And there has been a shift from an educational wall chart approach (which includes only students taking the ACT or SAT) to national report cards (reflected in data collected by the National Assessment of Educational Progress, with voluntary participation of states increasing yearly) and even to national tests.

All these trends regarding the identification of educational outcomes in general education raise questions about whom to measure, what to measure, when to measure, and how to measure educational outcomes. These issues, some of which are summarized in Table 9.2, exist even without consideration of those students in special education.

A quick look through the general education outcomes suggests that the primary focus is on students bound for postsecondary education, particularly college. Yet only half of America's students proceed to college. Few of the outcomes seem to be directed toward students who hope to go on to full-time jobs following high school. In addition, many of the identified outcomes call for information that is defined variously by the states. For example, a common measure of the attainment outcome indicator is the high school graduation rate. But in some states only those who obtain a diploma through regular coursework within the traditional amount of time are counted as graduates. In other states, the high school graduation rate includes those who have obtained a General Educational Development (GED) certificate, those who have obtained a certificate of attendance (often used for students in special education), and those who have obtained a traditional diploma. Definitional issues abound (MacMillan, Balow, Widaman, Borthwick-Duffy, & Hendrick, 1990; Rumberger, 1987). Indeed, because of these and other issues, considerable effort has gone into improving indicators of educational outcomes. Some of these efforts were described in 1990 by the Southern Regional Education Board (Creech, 1990):

TABLE 9.2   Some issues regarding selected general education outcomes

Outcome Area	Selected Issues
Achievement	*Who* • Is too much emphasis placed on those who will go on to college? • Is most interest in the achievement of those in secondary grades? *What* • Is interest only in academic content areas? • What are the critical academic areas to assess? *When* • At what grades should achievement be assessed? *How* • Should achievement be assessed exclusively through standardized multiple-choice tests? • Is portfolio assessment a viable procedure for measuring achievement?
Attainment, participation, and progression	*Who* • Are only those who are at the proper age for graduation to be included in graduation rates? • Are those who receive GEDs to be counted in graduation rates? *What* • What criteria determine successful attainment for graduation? *When* • When is the graduation rate determined? • Should attainment be measured at several points during the school years? *How* • What is the base number for graduation rate: the number entering grade 12, the number entering grade 9, or some other number? • How are dropouts defined?
Postsecondary experiences	*Who* • Do educators look at only those attending some type of college program? • Should those who attend technical schools or training provided by employers be included in estimations of postsecondary experiences? *What* • Is enrollment in postsecondary education the only variable of interest? *When* • Should educators depend on reports from postsecondary institutions or from postschool follow-up studies?

• Twenty-seven states are participating in a dropout statistics field test conducted by the National Center for Education Statistics in which a set of definitions agreed to by the states is being used to collect comparable information.

• Thirty-seven states are participating in the NAEP trial state assessment of eighth grade mathematics in 1990.

• The Council of Chief State School Officers is conducting a science and math indicators project.

• The Education Data Improvement Project of the Council of Chief State School Officers is looking at data needed on public schools, definitions for comparable data, and how the data should be reported.

• The National Forum on Educational Statistics has made a series of recommendations for improving data on educational resources, staffing, student progression, postsecondary activities of students, and student achievement.

These and other activities reflect the whirlwind of events surrounding the interest in measuring educational progress by identifying outcomes and indicators of the outcomes within the sphere of general education. What is noteworthy in the midst of all this turmoil is the lack of reference to those students within special education. They seem to be viewed as irrelevant to the discussion at hand and as part of a different and separate system about which someone else needs to worry.

Special Education Outcomes

Limited attention was given to the special learning and adjustment needs of students with disabilities as educational goals were developed and outcome indicators identified in the late 1980s and early 1990s. For example, according to the assessment guidelines for the NAEP system, "some students sampled for participation in NAEP are excluded from the sample according to carefully defined criteria" (Mullis, 1990, p. 35). Among those who "may be incapable of participating meaningfully in the assessment" (p. 35) are many students on IEPs. These students may be excluded if "the student is mainstreamed less than 50 percent of the time in academic subjects and is judged to be incapable of taking part in the assessment, or the IEP team has determined that the student is incapable of taking part meaningfully in the assessment" (p. 36). In reality, despite the NAEP admonition to include a student if there is doubt, schools are probably excluding these students whenever possible, in part to spare the student the stress of this testing experience and in part to raise the district's average score.

There has been some attention to the importance of documenting the outcomes of special education, mostly at the state level. But much national concern has developed about documenting that special education can be held accountable for outcomes. Some of the concerned groups have identified outcomes for special education (see Table 9.3). For example, the National Council on Disability argued

TABLE 9.3   Desired outcomes proposed by special education groups

Outcome[b]	Group[a] MSRRC	NCD	SRI
Achievement/performance	X	X	
Employment	X	X	X
Independent living			X
Participation	X	X	
Postsecondary status	X		X
Quality of life—internal		X	
Quality of life—external		X	
Satisfaction	X		
Work readiness		X	

[a] Groups (and years for references) are as follows:
  MSRRC = Mid-South Regional Resource Center (1986)
  NCD = National Council on Disability (1989)
  SRI = Science Research Associates (Wagner, 1989)
[b] The grouping of outcomes for this table sometimes required broad interpretation of the specific outcomes listed. In addition, different outcomes were sometimes grouped together in the original lists. If the reader is interested in the specific outcomes identified by a particular group, it is advisable to examine the original document from which this information was taken.

that "the time has come to ask the same questions for students with disabilities that we have been asking about students without disabilities" (1989, p. 2). Included among the questions that the council suggested were ones related to student achievement and participation while in school (Are they achieving? Are they staying in school?) and questions about their readiness to move to new activities (Are they prepared to enter the work force when they finish school? Are they going to participate in postsecondary education and training? Are they prepared for adult life?).

As Table 9.3 reveals, there are differences between the outcomes generally identified for special education and those for general education (see Table 9.1). Even though many areas overlap (e.g., achievement, participation, postsecondary experiences/status), some of those identified in special education are not identified in general education (e.g., external quality of life, work readiness), and some of those identified in general education are not included in special education (e.g., creative thinking/problem solving, interpersonal/organizational skills). It can be argued, however, that the differences are more in the words than in the basic outcome areas.

Attention at the state level to the issue of special education outcomes and their indicators has taken different approaches. In some cases, states are attempting to mesh their outcome indicator systems with those of general education. In others, outcome indicators applicable only to special education are being identified. One approach has been to identify some common core outcomes to be achieved by all students. This is reflected in the work of the Connecticut Department of Education (1988). Making the assumption that outcome measures for special education should be essentially the same as for general education, Connecticut developed a common core of learning (CCL) that identified outcomes for all children. The CCL has three overall groups of outcomes (attitudes and attributes, skills and competencies, and understanding and application of competencies) organized into four categories for special education (student participation, academic competencies, attitudes and attributes, and graduate follow-up data— independent living skills). Another approach, to identify specific outcomes for individuals with specific categories of disability, was taken by the Michigan Department of Education through the Center for Quality Special Education, which identified lists of outcomes for students with autism, educable mental impairment, emotional impairment, hearing impairment, learning disabilities, physical and other health impairments, preprimary impairment, severe multiple impairments, speech and language impairments, trainable mental impairment, and visual impairment.

States vary on the specific domains assessed with outcome indicators. Some emphasize academic outcomes, and others stress postschool experiences such as employment and living arrangements. States also differ on the purposes for which outcome indicators are developed. All these factors interact to create various outcome indicators for special education, if such indicators are being identified at all. Furthermore, that something is being done to address the issue of outcomes in special education says nothing about the extent to which these activities are recognized by the general education community.

In addition to the general issues that arise, special education is faced with the issue of documenting the educational goals and objectives for an individual student: should the IEP be used to identify outcomes, and should the outcomes be different for each student? If the IEP objectives are used to define the desired outcomes of education for an individual child, then the concern becomes how to determine whether the student is successful in reaching these outcomes. Such an approach, however, does nothing toward bringing general education and special education together, not unless general education adopts the notion of individualized learning plans (ILPs) for all students. If this were to occur, the next step would be to integrate these IEPs and ILPs with a system for measuring progress using a common metric.

Outcomes-Based Education

Outcomes-based education reflects the belief that desired educational outcomes should direct the content of education. The basic notion is that curriculum development should be based on identified outcomes, rather than on a listing of subject matter to be covered. Thus, specific outcomes are identified as the basis for curriculum development. Spady identified two features of outcomes-based education: "*Clarity of focus*—the instructional organization, components, and practices of schools should be designed around the clearly defined outcomes all students must demonstrate; and *expanded opportunity*—schools must deliberately provide all students with the time and instruction they need to reach essential outcome goals" (1988, p. 5).

In Minnesota, one of the first states to institute statewide outcomes-based education, the State Board of Education adopted broad learner goals and program level learner outcomes. The board specified that a variance would be granted to all curriculum rules for every district that demonstrated specified course- and grade-level outcomes that were in alignment with those of the Board and that implemented an assessment process that provided data to all decision makers regarding student progress. Four assumptions underlying outcomes-based education identified as critical by the Minnesota Department of Education (1989) were:

• All students can learn and have success, success breeds success, and schools control the conditions for success.

• Content is prescribed in terms of learner outcomes (what is to be learned), rather than in terms of course syllabus (what is to be taught).

• Criterion-referenced assessment procedures are specifically developed to measure student progress on the predetermined outcomes (as opposed to using norm-referenced tests that may or may not measure achievement on the predetermined outcomes).

• Instructional design is based on a model in which learning is the constant and time the variable, rather than time being the constant and learning the variable.

When stated this way, outcomes-based education sounds much like the intent of the IEP. Given that the Minnesota assumptions indicate that "all students can learn" and that "learning is the constant and time is the variable," students in special education should fit right in with general education as long as the stated outcomes are appropriate. The extent to which this will occur in practice is unknown.

Issues Regarding Identifying and Collecting Data on Outcomes

Many issues arise in identifying outcomes that are appropriate for students in special education (outcomes that, it is hoped, mesh with general education outcomes) and in collecting data on these outcomes. Four of these issues merit consideration here: What are the critical outcome domains? Is different outcome information needed at different levels? How do educators accommodate the heterogeneity of the student population? How do educators measure outcomes?

Critical Outcome Domains

Whether the domains of outcomes for students with disabilities should be different from those for students without disabilities is a fundamental question in the consideration of critical outcome domains. Although most efforts in outcomes assessment have focused on developing measures of achievement, other areas have been identified as being important (e.g., see Burstein, 1989; Creech, 1990). Among these other domains are student participation and access, student status after completion of secondary school, and student attitudes, expectations, and aspirations. Even within general education, there is concern about the lack of tools for measuring cognitive and conative aspects of learning. Snow (1989) claimed that learners should be able to develop conceptual structures, procedural skills, learning strategies, self-regulatory functions, and motivational orientations. The recognition of these aspects of learning means a new consensus must be reached concerning the domains that should be emphasized in schools and the educational indicators that will be used to monitor and evaluate the outcomes.

Outcome Information Needed at Different Levels

Information on educational outcomes is important to the teacher in the classroom, to the school district trying to document the success of its educational programs, to the state being compared, and to the nation involved in international comparisons. The multiple levels at which outcome information can be used has created much confusion about identifying outcomes and collecting data on them. The teacher in the classroom needs information on outcomes for individual students so that programs and learning time can be adjusted for each student; at this level outcomes have to be fairly specific. At the district level, desired outcomes can be broader, even though they must still be specific enough to identify schools where problems may exist. At the state level, outcomes can be even broader and often system-level. The same is true at the national level. The international level requires that outcomes be broad enough to span the "gulfs of nationality, language, and culture" (Barrett, 1990).

The differences among possible outcomes identified at three different levels (international, national, and state) are shown in Table 9.4. As the table illustrates, information from each level could feed into the next higher level, and not all information at one level would have to be used at the next level. Likewise, tests could vary as a function of individual needs, not just grade. For example, a typical third grade student might be required to complete a standardized reading test, a student with severe visual impairments might be required to read from a large-print book, and a student with severe mental retardation might be required to point out the sign that would be by the men's, rather than the women's, restroom.

The Heterogeneity of the Student Population

Questions must be raised about how the heterogeneity of the student population will be taken into account in a system of outcome indicators. The issue of making fair comparisons among states, schools, or students when the make-up of the student population differs also must be addressed. At the broadest level, these issues involve determining how to integrate general education indicators with special education indicators. As educators move from outcome domains to sub-domains of outcomes and to indicators of outcomes, the issue of differences in students will have to be addressed. Students with severe mental disabilities may have to complete different kinds of tasks than students with sensory disabilities. Perhaps different weights will have to be applied to different kinds of tasks, or perhaps scores will have to be adjusted as a function of the numbers of students with disabilities who have been included in an indicator. These are difficult issues that educators are certain to face again and again as the nation continues to push for educational accountability.

Measurement of Outcomes

Many argue that there is a need for better assessment measures and particularly that tests should not be the only means of assessing student outcomes (e.g., Cronbach et al., 1980; Glaser, 1988; Shepard, 1989b). Among the questions that should be raised are:

What are the most appropriate assessment tools?

How should new dimensions of learning be measured?

Who should make decisions about appropriate tools and their role in monitoring the system?

What are the desired technical characteristics of outcomes indicators?

What level of construct validity must be attained for an indicator to be useful?

Should measurement approaches used in general education outcomes assessment influence measurement approaches in special education outcomes assessment?

Effects of Policies Related to Educational Outcomes

Outcomes-related policies have been enacted at many different levels. At the local and state levels, policies in the late 1980s and early 1990s focused primarily on graduation requirements, minimal competency testing, retention in grade, and grading practices. For example, graduation requirements were made stiffer so that America could be sure that those graduating really had gained some meaningful

TABLE 9.4 Possible outcomes at different administrative levels

Level	Outcome Domain	Outcome Indicator	Comments
International (information from nations)	Achievement	Percent meeting competency standard in math in grade 8 Percent meeting competency standard in reading in grade 8	Competency requirement might vary for individual students. A specific grade would be selected at which education was comparable across nations (before some students might be excluded from schools).
	Satisfaction	Percent parents happy with education of student in grade 8	
National (information from states or a national sampling plan)	Achievement	Percent meeting competency standard in math in grades 4, 8, and 12 Percent meeting competency standard in communication (reading, writing) in grades 4, 8, and 12 Percent meeting competency standard in leisure area (physical, artistic, etc.) in grades 4, 8, 12	Competency requirement might vary for individual students. Three grades would be selected to have better indication of education across grades.
	Satisfaction	Percent parents happy with education of student in grades 4, 8, and 12 Percent happy with education in grades 4, 8, and 12	
	Participation	Percent receiving certificate, GED, or diploma for successful school completion Percent dropping out of school at ages 16 and 17	Outcomes beyond achievement and satisfaction would be added but still at a system level (percent with certain characteristics).
	Transition readiness	Percent rated as having skills needed for next role (postsecondary education or work)	
State (information from districts or a state sampling plan)	Achievement	Percent meeting competency standard in math in grades 1–12 Average score of students on appropriate math exam in grades 1–12 Percent meeting competency standard in reading in grades 1–12	

TABLE 9.4   **(cont.)**

Level	Outcome Domain	Outcome Indicator	Comments
State (information from districts or a state sampling plan)	Achievement	Average score of students on appropriate reading exam in grades 1–12	
		Percent meeting competency standard in writing in grades 1–12	
		Average score of students on appropriate writing exam in grades 1–12	
		Percent meeting competency standard in leisure area in grades 1–12	
		Average score of students on appropriate leisure exam in grades 1–12	
		Percent meeting competency standard in social studies/social skills in grades 1–12	
	Satisfaction	Percent parents happy with education of student in grades 1–12	
		Percent happy with education in grades 1–12	
	Participation	Percent receiving certificate for successful school completion	
		Percent receiving GED for successful school completion	
		Percent receiving diploma for successful school completion	
		Percent dropping out of school at ages 14, 15, 16, and 17	
		Percent attending postsecondary education institution one year after high school	
		Percent in employment one year after high school	
	Transition readiness	Percent rated as having skills needed for next role (postsecondary education or work)	
		Percent retained in grade	

U.S.-Japan Comparisons Called Misleading

Those calling for the reform of U.S. schools frequently make glib comparisons between American and Japanese education. Japan, after all, has a high literacy rate, student achievement levels among the best in the world, and a booming economy. Nonetheless, trying to replicate the Japanese education system would be misguided, because education is tied so closely to cultural values and beliefs, argues Frank Betts, director of ASCD's Curriculum/Technology Resource Center.

Betts recently studied similarities and differences between the two systems and made a 3-week school visit to Japan in fall 1989. He says that sociological factors—universally high expectations, family structure and roles, homogeneity of the population (racially, culturally, and economically), obedience to authority, and group behavioral norms—are key reasons that Japanese students attain high academic levels. These factors help to minimize disruptive classroom behavior, students' coming to class unprepared, and wide variations in academic performance.

The U.S. might be able to replicate some of the structural elements of the Japanese system, but it is unlikely to duplicate such sociological factors, nor should it necessarily want to, says Betts. In order to match the Japanese model, "we would have to restructure a whole system of beliefs we hold about the values of independence, the rights of individuals, and the virtues of competition."

What elements of the Japanese system are worth considering? Betts says the Japanese experience confirms research on effective schools—they strongly support a safe environment, high expectations, effective time on task, continuity, collaborative learning, and the importance of parent involvement. A more continuous school year, a shorter school day, and more attention to building healthy group norms and developing each child's self-esteem through group success also are worth looking at.

"America's strengths, as well as its greatest vulnerabilities, can be found in our diversity, our sense of rugged individualism, and our com-

---

skills. Minimal competency testing had the goal of making sure that students could show some minimal levels of mastery before moving ahead in school. Retention in grade and the determination of course grades were woven into the fabric of outcome policies in the schools. Each of these policies had particular effects or the potential for effects on students in special education. At the national level, policy makers began to talk about a national test that would go beyond the NAEP. In mid-1991, President Bush endorsed an educational policy that called for voluntary tests for *every* student in grades four, eight, and twelve in math, English, and science.

petitive spirit," says Betts. "Since the attainment of real understanding—authentic learning as opposed to rote memory—is essentially an individual process, we potentially have a natural advantage over Japan when it comes to the kind of learning that affects the quality of life over time."

Japanese Schools: A Snapshot

• Japanese schools are organized in a 6-3-3 system; only grades 1–9 are compulsory.

• The school year is divided into three terms: two of 16–17 weeks and one of 9–10 weeks. Summer vacation is 5–6 weeks long. Students attend school Monday through Friday and part of the day Saturday, for a total of approximately 243 days per year (U.S. students average 180 days annually).

• Kindergarten is available but not compulsory. About half of the kindergartens are supported with public funds; the rest with private.

• U.S. and Japanese students receive about the same amount of classroom instructional time in grades 1–9, but in the last three years of schooling, Japanese students receive almost four years of American instructional time.

• Japanese students must pass exams to enroll in secondary school and college. About 93 percent enroll in upper secondary school (grades 10–12) and 33 percent enroll in higher education. The importance of the exams means many students seeking college admission spend as many as 20–30 extra hours each week in private cram schools costing up to $15,000 per year.

• All teachers must pass a standard national exam to be certified.

SOURCE: O'Neil, J., ed. (1991). "U.S.-Japan Comparisons Called Misleading: Japanese Schools—A Snapshot." *ASCD Update* 33(3) (March): 5. Reprinted with permission of the Association for Supervision and Curriculum Development. Copyright © 1991 by ASCD. All rights reserved.

Graduation Requirements

Graduation from high school has been tied for more than eighty years to the Carnegie unit, defined as five hours of related work per week or five periods of forty to sixty minutes for at least thirty-six weeks (Shaw & Walker, 1981). The Carnegie unit was established to define the requirements that had to be met by students entering an institution of higher education for the institution to qualify for Carnegie Pension funds for retired professors. Despite its initial purpose, the unit was quickly adopted as a way to define high school graduation requirements; typically this is done in terms of both a minimum number of units and a distri-

FIGURE 9.1   State high school graduation requirements

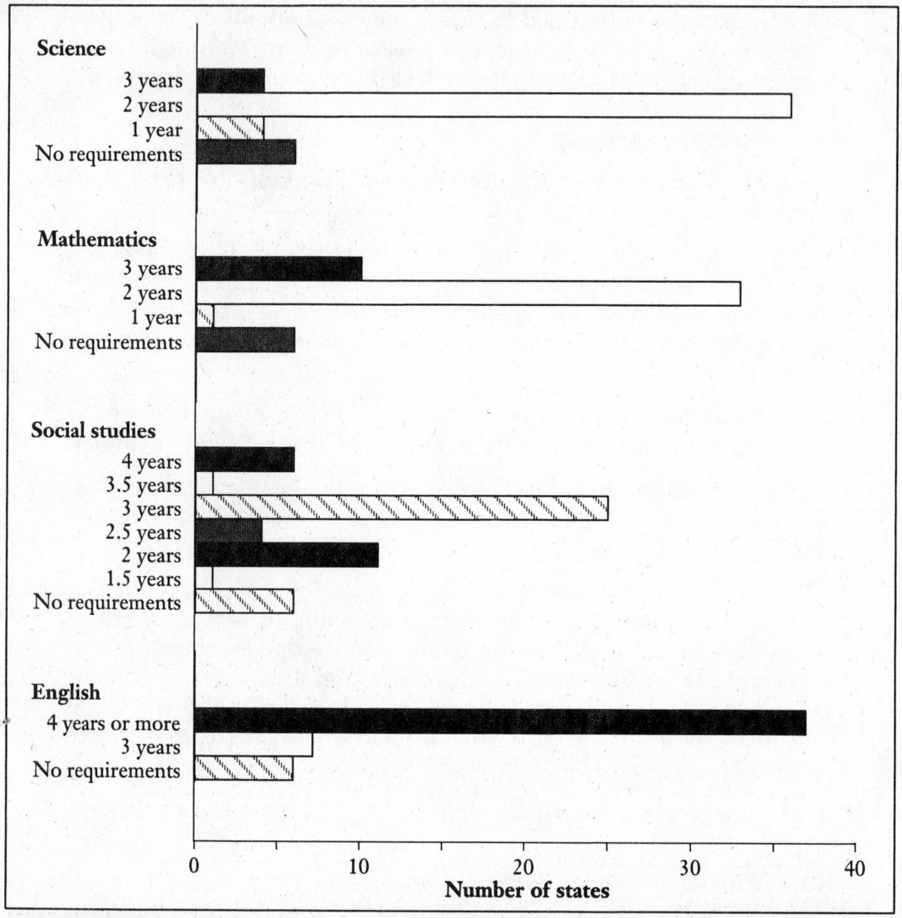

SOURCE: Adapted from the *Policy information report: The education reform decade*. Princeton, N.J.: ETS, 1991. Used with permission of Educational Testing Service, the copyright owner.

butional scheme of the content areas in which units had to be obtained. As noted by Hall and Gerber (1985), the reform movement led many states to increase the number of Carnegie units required for graduation as a way of stiffening graduation requirements. By the late 1980s, all but three states had policies regulating the minimum number of units for graduation, and thirty-six had raised the academic unit requirements (Bodner, Clark, & Mellard, 1987) (see Figure 9.1).

Students with disabilities, particularly those with mild disabilities, are required to fit into graduation requirements in different ways. Oftentimes these adaptations are established informally by schools or districts. In some cases, students with disabilities have to meet the same requirements as all other students.

In other cases, they are allowed to take special courses to fulfill credit requirements for Carnegie units; alternatively, for credit to be awarded, students have to be taught by a teacher certified in the subject matter (a special education course could count if the teacher was certified in the content area as well as in special education). In still other cases, credits for participation in a special program are counted, but are applied only toward an alternate document, such as a certificate of completion; this method seriously limits those students considering postsecondary education and even some of those hoping to obtain a job following completion of school. In further cases, each local education agency determines its own policy.

Hall and Gerber (1985) found that of thirty-six states responding to a survey, most (42 percent) awarded regular diplomas earned through special courses. Next in frequency (28 percent) came states that allowed local education agencies to make their own policies and then states that did not alter requirements in any way for students with disabilities (25 percent). More recently, Bodner et al. (1987) found that of the fifty states and the District of Columbia, thirty-six made specific allowances for students in special education. Of these thirty-six, all (100 percent) indicated that support services were provided in regular classes with no modifications, and thirty-five (97 percent) reported allowing classes with the same subject title but modified instruction. (In this survey, because respondents were allowed to select as many responses as applied, different policies might have applied to students with disabilities, perhaps determined on a categorical basis.) Thirty states (83 percent) also indicated that they allowed classes with the same subject title but modified content. Only nineteen states (53 percent) reported that they allowed classes with the same subject title but different content and modified instruction.

None of the suggested options for relating special education graduation to general education graduation has addressed the possible need for a completely different system for determining graduation—something other than the eighty-plus-year-old Carnegie unit. One possibility is a system based on attainment of specific outcomes.

Hall and Gerber (1985) nicely summarized many of the issues surrounding the alternative approaches to graduation requirements for students with disabilities. These issues include: the need to recognize the "stick-with-it-ness" of students who remain in school, even though taking alternative coursework; possible violations of equal protection rights; feasibility; and the need to protect the integrity of the regular graduation diploma. Bodner et al. also discussed several issues:

> When special education students in some states complete an instructional sequence based on their assessed strengths and weaknesses as detailed on their Individual Educational Plans (IEPs), they may also be differentiated from the norm group by their exit document. These students frequently receive a special education or modified diploma or certificate, rather than a regular diploma. There are two issues involved. First, while regular education students may complete a variety of education curricula (e.g., college preparatory, vocational education, basic education), their exit document follows one standard form, the regular diploma. Second, and more importantly, in spite of the differences among these curricula in content and rigor, there are no explicit or implicit value judgments attached to

these differences, while special education students in some states *are* treated differentially—sometimes regardless of the categorical area or level of severity of disability. As a consequence, differential diplomas or certificates awarded to special education students preclude or negatively affect some postsecondary education or employment opportunities. Thus, the value of individualized, appropriate education is diminished and may segregate students from successful transition and full participation opportunities. (1987, pp. 1–2)

Although there has been much discussion of the issues surrounding stiffer graduation requirements and the potential effects of alternative school completion documents, researchers have not directly assessed the effects of these. This lack may be due, in part, to the variability in definitions and criteria for the alternative approaches.

Minimal Competency Testing

The notion that students must meet certain minimal standards before continuing on with their education, or graduating, gained popularity in the 1970s. Approximately half of the states had some type of minimal competency testing program by the end of the 1980s (see Bodner et al., 1987; "State Education Statistics," 1988). By 1990, testing programs for monitoring, gatekeeping, remediation, or funds allocation were in existence in forty-seven states (ETS Policy Information Center, 1991) (see Figure 9.2). Nevertheless, there has been relatively little research data on the number of students with disabilities taking such tests or on the effects of minimal competency tests. Kreitzer, Madaus, and Haney (1989), along with many others, suggested that there might be a connection between minimal competency tests and dropout rates. With a greater tone of alarm, DeYoung, Huffman, and Turner suggested that "high school students already performing poorly might decide to forego the embarrassment of failing a statewide exit exam and leave school early, regardless of the concern shown by local educators" (1989, p. 73). Following their review of several different sources of information, Kreitzer et al. concluded that there were "several indications that MCT [minimal competency testing] may give students at risk of dropping out an extra push out the school door" (1989, p. 146).

Bodner et al. (1987) also looked at minimal competency testing with regard to students with disabilities. They found that nearly all the states with minimal competency testing had a specific policy or practice for students with disabilities. Most allowed for accommodations for these students, including extended time periods for testing or administration by the special education teacher. In some states, students with mild disabilities were specifically excluded from state norms and published results. Vitello (1988) reported that most states waived the requirement of minimal competency testing for students with disabilities. He also noted the paradoxical relationship between minimal competency testing and individualized educational planning.

FIGURE 9.2   State testing programs and purposes, 1990

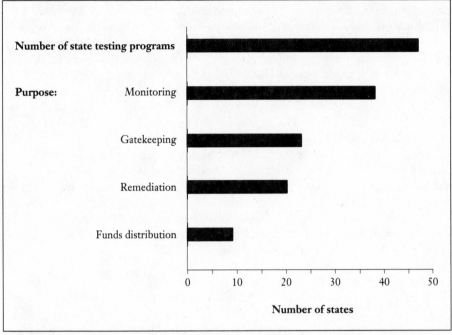

SOURCE: Adapted from the *Policy information report: The education reform decade*. Princeton, N.J.: ETS, 1991. Used with permission of Educational Testing Service, the copyright owner.

To the extent that minimal competency tests are actually used to end social promotion of students from one grade to the next, the implications for students with disabilities are great. There is evidence that the use of minimal competency testing does result in an increased rate of grade retention (Kreitzer et al., 1989).

Retention in Grade

One strategy for dealing with school failure is to have students repeat a grade. Many students in special education programs are older than their classmates because they have repeated a grade. The notion of retaining students at one grade level for a second time (more commonly known by students as "flunking") is consistent with the notions of school reform and the striving for educational excellence. Students should not be promoted for social reasons or for maintenance of self-esteem but rather only when the basic skills required for starting the next grade have been mastered. Of course, these viewpoints create considerable difficulty for students in special education programs, who often must have demonstrated below-grade performance to qualify for special education services.

In a comprehensive book on grade retention edited by Shepard and Smith (1989), the effects of grade retention are highlighted, along with popular beliefs about the effects of retention. Shepard and Smith (1989) concluded on the basis of multiple methods, operations, and perspectives about retention that retention in grade has no benefits for either school achievement or personal attainment; retention is strongly related to later dropping out of school; two years of kindergarten, even when one year is labeled a "transition program," fail to enhance achievement or solve the problem of inadequate school readiness; and from the students' perspective, retention is conflict laden and hurtful. Despite all this, an "abiding faith in the merits of retention" exists among teachers, parents, and educational reformers.

What are the alternatives to grade retention when the country is striving for educational excellence and stiffer educational standards? One alternative is to assume an outcomes-based education approach in which students are to reach certain goals regardless of how long it takes. Grades would no longer be a needed organizational structure for the school. Nevertheless, not all students in a school would progress unless outcomes and goals were carefully defined and criteria varied according to individual characteristics.

Grading Practices

Report card grades cause considerable difficulty for teachers in general education who have students with disabilities in their classes. Carpenter and his associates (Carpenter, 1985; Carpenter, Grantham, & Hardister, 1983) described many of the pertinent issues that arose in grading students with disabilities. In reviewing the recommendations for grading practice made by numerous professionals, they found that these recommendations could be divided into those promoting different standards (e.g., lowered grading standards, contract with students), those identifying different grading vehicles (e.g., pass-fail system, multiple marking system), and those suggesting different logistics (e.g., daily grading, individualized grading plan in the IEP).

The limited research on grades has found that students with learning disabilities tend to receive lower grades than low-achieving students (Donahoe & Zigmond, 1990) and that mainstream teachers tend to give D grades to students with learning disabilities simply for showing up for class or for appearing interested (Zigmond, Levin, & Laurie, 1985). Educators tend to prefer grading students with disabilities on the basis of effort, attitude, level of ability, and participation, rather than on the basis of performance, preparedness, attendance, and completion of assignments (Carpenter & Grantham, 1985). These practices raise the issue of grading policies and what students are learning in mainstream classes. Is it fair to place students where they do not learn and then allow them to pass to the next grade? How can educators ensure that students learn in the mainstream classroom and receive an earned passing grade?

A second issue is the use of the same or of a different grading system for students with disabilities. Unfortunately, it appears that grading policies for mainstreamed youth with disabilities are usually unwritten, even if they exist, and more often are individual teacher, rather than school, policies (Carpenter & Grantham, 1985).

A third issue is the purpose of grades (to determine successful completion of a course, to indicate standing relative to all others in the class) and the basis for grade assignments (competence, effort, relative standing to others). Chandler identified grades as one of the main sources of friction between the special education teacher and the regular class teacher. He argued that grades are sacrosanct in the general education system, with the argument being something like "If the child should be taught differently, why isn't he in a special classroom?; if he is in a regular classroom, then why can't he take a test like everyone else?; if he is graded differently, isn't that debasing the grades?" (1983, p. 242).

A National Test?

Discussion of a national test started in early 1991 and received increasing attention as major funding was received by the National Center on Education and the Economy, in conjunction with the Learning Research and Development Center at the University of Pittsburgh, to explore and develop a national examination system for students. This attention was escalated even more as President Bush announced that among his plans for education was the development of voluntary national tests. As initially conceived, the national test would be geared toward higher-level skills and the application of knowledge to real-world problems. The test might include performance examinations, portfolios, and projects that students would complete over time. But even before this prototype system was developed, a Senate subcommittee was sampling views of the need for a national achievement test (Harp, 1991). In April 1991, President Bush announced an education agenda that called for voluntary testing of *all* students in grades four, eight, and twelve and for the first test, fourth grade mathematics, to be ready for all students to take by 1993. Who would develop the national tests and what they would be like remained to be seen. But issues of whether they really would include *all* students and how they would be adjusted to meet the needs of students with special characteristics continued to be critical. Perhaps this would provide the opportunity for special educators and others recognizing the needs of students with disabilities to participate in a national assessment undertaking from the beginning.

Documenting Special Education Outcomes

The drive toward identifying outcomes and assessing those outcomes clearly has many implications for students with disabilities and raises many issues. General education has taken the approach that outcomes must be identified and that

---

Creating Better and More Accountable Schools for Today's Students

The president called on all Americans to help create better and more accountable schools based on world class standards and the principle of accountability. He encouraged all elements of our communities—families, businesses, unions, places of worship, neighborhood organizations and other voluntary associations—to work together with our schools to help the nation achieve educational excellence. . . .

A System of Voluntary National Examinations

Through the efforts of the National Education Goals Panel, a system of voluntary examinations will be developed and made available for all fourth, eighth, and twelfth grade students in the five core subjects.

• These American Achievement Tests will challenge all students to strive to meet the world class standards and ensure that, when they leave school, students are prepared for further study and the work force. The tests will measure higher order skills (i.e., they will not be strictly multiple choice tests).

• The president, working with the nation's governors, will seek congressional authorization for state-level National Assessment of Educational Progress assessments and for optional use of these assessments at district and school levels.

• Students who distinguish themselves on the American Achievement Tests will receive a Presidential Citation for Educational Excellence in recognition of their outstanding achievement.

• The president will seek authorization for Presidential Achievement Scholarships to reward academic excellence among low-income students pursuing postsecondary education opportunities. These financial awards will be based on superior high school and college performance.

SOURCE: U.S. Department of Education. (1991). *America 2000: An education strategy (Sourcebook)*. Washington, DC: Author.

---

education must be held accountable for students reaching these outcomes. In taking this approach, these educators have ignored students served in special education programs. In many cases, even those students in vocational track programs seem to have been left behind.

If special educators ignore the outcomes movement in general education, they are contributors to the separation of general education and special education. An alternative approach, however, is to look carefully at outcomes and decide how best to define them so that they are acceptable to general educators and yet are attainable by all students, including those with disabilities.

The need to do something about documenting the outcomes of education for students receiving special education services remains critical, regardless of the national agenda. Fifteen years after the initial enactment of the Education of Handicapped Children Act, and with a reauthorization and a new name (IDEA), concerns were being expressed about the effectiveness of special education. Some attempts to answer these questions referred to early childhood special education efficacy studies (see Chapter 10) and the positive results demonstrated in them. Other attempts to answer these questions referred to postschool follow-up studies (see Chapter 11) and the often negative findings associated with them. America's special educators have reached the point where desired educational outcomes have to be specified clearly for students before, during, and after school and their progress toward these outcomes measured.

Discussion Questions

1. How would you describe a set of outcome domains that would apply to all students?

2. To what extent and why should students with disabilities be excluded from standardized testing?

3. One approach to a common system for measuring attainment of outcomes is to develop a national test or a set of national tests. How would you do this in such a way as to allow all students to participate?

4. What alternative strategies to grades can be used to keep track of students' progress in school? Is there a way to merge the IEP with general education indicators of progress toward outcomes?

Issues in Early Intervention

The foundations of a better tomorrow must be laid today.

—Anonymous

Fetal alcohol syndrome and alcohol-related birth defects are on the rise. Babies born with AIDS are increasing in number each year. So are babies born addicted to cocaine. Medically fragile infants are surviving through extraordinary medical

FIGURE 10.1 Births to single women, 1950 to 1988

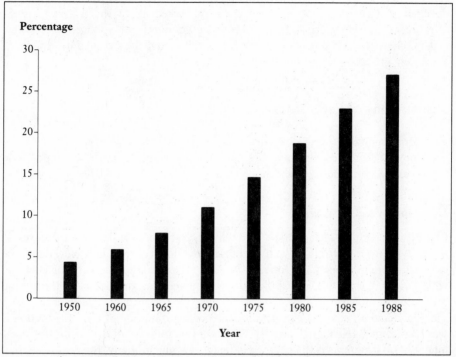

SOURCE: Committee for Economic Development. *The unfinished agenda: A new vision for child development and education*. New York: Research and Policy Committee, Committee for Economic Development, p. 9. (Original data for graph prepared by Ounce of Prevention Fund in Chicago using data from the National Center on Health Statistics, U.S. Department of Health and Human Services. Used with permission.

interventions to face life with significant mental and physical impairments. Even children born healthy face the possibility to a greater extent than ever before of poverty, homelessness, or physical abuse. The "Leave It to Beaver" family is gone: more than half of new marriages end in divorce; one-quarter of children are born outside of marriage (see Figure 10.1); approximately fifteen million children live with one parent, most often the mother; and two million children live with neither parent (Hodgkinson, 1989).

The needs of these youngsters are tremendous even before they reach the age of school attendance. For this reason, many educators and policy makers see early intervention as a critical component of meeting the educational goals of this country. Recognition of early intervention's importance is implicit in the first of the national goals identified by President Bush and the governors in 1990: "By the year 2000, all children will start school ready to learn."

Issues in early intervention have been prevalent for some time, but they have not been as urgent as they are now. In this chapter we describe some fundamental assumptions and trace the history of early intervention, including the downward escalation of services. Issues of assessment and identification are discussed as they relate to young children with disabilities and young children who are at risk for developing disabilities. Several questions are raised about the nature of early interventions, particularly as they apply to younger and younger ages. New constituencies for early intervention are identified, and the tremendous impact of these new groups on intervention are explored.

Assumptions of Early Intervention

Two fundamental assumptions—developmental plasticity and cost effectiveness—underlie early intervention for young children. Without these, there would be no reason to intervene before the school-age years.

Developmental Plasticity

From the beginning of his study of intelligence, Binet saw intelligence as something that resulted from an active transaction between the individual and the external stimuli (Sarason & Doris, 1979). He viewed intelligence as educable and wrote in 1911 that the educability of intelligence was the basis for pioneering early intervention work. Early interventionists believed that "we can ameliorate, that we can alter, that we can prevent further deterioration of mental function if we start young" (Kirk, 1977, p. 4). At the foundation of all discussions of early intervention programs is the nagging issue of how much, if any, the developmental progress of a child can be changed. To the extent that development is viewed as determined by nature, the individual's behavioral and learning capacities are assumed to be inherited and unchangeable. To the extent that development is viewed as determined by nurture, the individual's behavioral and learning capacities are assumed to be malleable and changeable. When behavior is viewed as changeable, intervention for the young child makes sense. This notion of developmental plasticity is the justification for an array of early intervention programs for children with and without identified disabilities. And the assumption of developmental plasticity directs assessment of young children and the goals of intervention.

Cost Effectiveness

In addition to the belief that lifelong outcomes can be changed through early intervention with high-risk youngsters, there is a belief in "the sooner, the better." According to this view, through early enough intervention the difficulties a child may build up can be avoided, which thereby reduces the number and intensity of interventions that will be needed. This view has implications for the overall costs of providing educational and posteducational services to students. Hirshoren and Umansky stated these views in relation to students with disabilities:

Early education for children with handicaps offers a number of benefits that warrant serious consideration by school systems. Early intervention with children who have some handicaps may alleviate many of the manifestations of the handicaps that could inhibit development and learning. Furthermore, provision of services in the early years could substantially reduce costs of later education. (1977, p. 191)

Policy reports have regularly noted the cost-effectiveness and cost benefits derived from early intervention. For example, in 1991 the Committee for Economic Development stated:

Quality preschool programs clearly provide one of the most cost-effective strategies for lowering the dropout rate and helping at-risk children to become more effective learners and productive citizens. It has been shown that for every $1 spent on a comprehensive and intensive preschool program for the disadvantaged, society saves up to $6 in the long-term costs of welfare, remedial education, teen pregnancy, and crime. (p. 28)

Such statements are especially interesting in light of professional articles that question the long-term beneficial outcomes of all but model early childhood programs. For example, Haskins wrote:

Research has shown that both model programs and Head Start have immediate positive impacts on tests of intellectual performance and social competence but that this impact declines over the first few years of public schooling. The evidence of improvement on long-term measures of school performance such as special education placement is substantial for model programs but thin and inconsistent for Head Start. There is limited but provocative evidence that model programs may have positive effects on life success measures such as teen pregnancy, delinquency, welfare use, and employment, but there is virtually no evidence linking Head Start attendance with any of these variables. Benefit-cost studies show that model programs can produce long-term benefits that exceed the value of the original program investment, but it would be premature to argue that Head Start is cost-beneficial. (1989, p. 274)

The resolution of this issue might be hard to achieve. Longitudinal research that is much more comprehensive than any conducted to date is needed to explore the long-term benefits of the array of typical early intervention programs that are now available nationwide. Such research is difficult to conduct and often subject to variable or discontinued funding. Besides, the results cannot be expected for nearly 20 years after the research starts.

Historical Background

In the early days of American education, compulsory attendance was thought to be the solution to the problems presented by parents who were "indifferent to the public good" and who refused to send their children to school. Nearly one-hundred years later, with compulsory education for children and youths aged six to sixteen well established, the need for something special for likely-to-be-failing

TABLE 10.1   Early education programs for children with disabilities

Year	Program	Comment
1964	Head Start	Designed to compensate for negative effects of poverty
1968	PL 90-538	Handicapped Children's Early Education Program, including assistance to develop demonstration models for serving all preschool children with handicaps and their families
1968	PL 93-380	Required states to submit plans and timetables for serving all children and youths with handicaps from birth to twenty-one years; also mandated *child find*
1972	Head Start (PL 92-424)	Provided that not less than 10 percent of national enrollment opportunities be designated for children with disabilities
1975	Head Start (PL 92-424)	Changed 10 percent base from national enrollment to state enrollment opportunities
1975	PL 94-142	Provided funding for children with handicaps, aged 3–5, who were served; also gave incentive grants for approved plans to serve these children
1986	PL 99-457, Part H—Handicapped Infants and Toddlers Program	Provided incentive money for states to serve infants and toddlers; programs to be phased in over a five-year period, 1987–1991
1991	IDEA (PL 101-476)	For Early Education for Handicapped Children, added priority areas for demonstration and outreach programs and directed the national technical assistance program toward specific groups; for Part H, added social work services to intervention services and specified requirements related to dissemination and training

youngsters was still on the minds of American leaders. The 1960s marked a turning point in the public and governmental response to these issues: with evidence of the scope and effects of poverty (Harrington, 1962; Hurley, 1989), and the pleas of civil rights leaders for quality education for all Americans, educators began designing educational programs for children not yet in school. These educators hoped that compensatory education could begin to counterbalance the negative effects of poverty on the development of young children. These educational efforts were the precursors of early education for students with disabilities (see Table 10.1), and the emergence of early childhood education in the 1960s was called a "rediscovery" by Frost (1968) and a "renaissance" by Shane (1969).

Head Start

In 1964, the Economic Opportunity Act provided massive funding for educational programs for preschool children. During the summer of 1965, 550,000 youngsters (about 10 percent of all children in preschool programs) were enrolled in school programs that were set up as part of Project Head Start. More than 40,000 teachers (many with no experience with preschool children) were hired, and a total of 100,000 adults participated in the programs to "compensate" for the negative effects of poverty likely to hamper some of America's youths. The curriculum in many programs was intense and was based on the assumption that the best way to overcome economic, cultural, and social disadvantage was to start school early. Copperman noted that prior to Head Start, "the primary goal of preschool child care was the normal and healthy psychosocial development of young children, to be achieved through peer-group play and other guided play activities" (1978, p. 57). To counteract the likely effects of social and economic disadvantages, early childhood education specialists recommended that accelerated academic development be adopted as the primary goal of preschool programs. The major effect of this early instruction seemed to be increases in readiness abilities. Nevertheless,

> the preponderance of recent research indicates that most of the gains experienced by preschool children in group educational programs disappear by the end of first or second grade. . . . Early intervention produces substantial gains in IQ as long as the program lasts. But the experimental groups do not continue to make gains when intervention continues beyond one year, and, what is more critical, the effects tend to "wash out" after intervention is terminated. The longer the follow-up, the more obvious the latter trend becomes. (pp. 58–59)

When the effects of Head Start seemed to "wash out," a logical follow-up was to provide additional compensatory education programs. In 1969, Congress established the Follow Through program to try compensating for the failings of the compensatory Head Start efforts. Copperman reported that the effects of this program were similar to those of its predecessor; indeed, some evidence indicated that Follow Through produced more negative than positive effects (Stebbins, St. Pierre, Proper, Anderson, & Cerva, 1977). Since the time of these reports, however, gains attributable to the Head Start program have been noted (Lee, Schnur, & Brooks-Gunn, 1988). These latter investigators controlled for initial differences in Head Start and comparison groups and found that Head Start children made larger gains than comparison group children who either were from other programs or had no preschool experience. Yet the greater gains still left the Head Start children behind their peers.

HCEEP

With the passage of PL 90-538 (Handicapped Children's Early Education Assistance Act) in 1968, Congress set the stage for the Handicapped Children's Early Education Program (HCEEP). The purpose of the program was to assist in the development of demonstration models for the provision of comprehensive services to all preschool-aged (birth to eight years) children with handicaps and their families (DeWeerd & Cole, 1976; Swan, 1980). The HCEEP was originally funded in 1969–1970 with an appropriation of $1 million, which supported 25 grants. The program grew in its first ten years, and in 1978–1979 the HCEEP received an appropriation of $22 million, which supported 214 grants and contracts.

Initial evaluation results of the program's effectiveness were favorable (DeWeerd & Cole, 1976; Stock et al., 1976; Swan, 1980). Furthermore, seven years after the completion of their "seed" grants, 86 percent of the 21 projects studied had received continuation funding and were still operating (Swan, 1980).

Head Start for Children with Disabilities

In 1972, the Head Start program was expanded by PL 92-424, which provided that not less than 10 percent of the national enrollment opportunities available through Head Start were to be designated for children with disabilities (LaVor, 1972; LaVor & Harvey, 1976). Legislation in 1975 (Head Start, Economic Opportunity, Community Partnership Act of 1974) altered the initial 10 percent enrollment opportunities from a national base to state bases. The change had the "net effect of forcing each state to focus on and meet the needs of children with disabilities within the state" and guaranteed that states would "no longer be able to disregard the minimum 10% requirement by averaging their totals with overall national or regional enrollments" (LaVor & Harvey, 1976, p. 227).

Education for preschool children with handicaps had arrived. And since its arrival, early education for young children with disabilities has continued to grow.

The Downward Escalation of Educational Services

The first major legislative support for early education for youngsters with disabilities came from PL 90-538 in 1968 and the establishment of model demonstration programs. PL 93-380 required that the state plans submitted to the Bureau of Education for the Handicapped include timetables and plans for providing services to all children and youths with handicaps from birth through age twenty-one. Similarly, the law mandated states to "establish and maintain efforts to *find* all handicapped children from birth through age 21" (see Cohen, Semmes, & Guralnick, 1979). PL 94-142 provided two sources of funds for preschool programs: states were entitled to funding according to the numbers of children with handicaps in their populations, which could include the number of children in the three to five-year-old range, and incentive grants were made available to states that provided approved plans to serve children in this age range (Cohen, 1976).

In 1977, Hirshoren and Umansky reported that twelve states offered certification for teachers of preschool children with handicaps. In 1980, Rose found that seven of forty-five states that responded to a survey indicated that their states had specific definitions for preschool children who had handicaps. In the same year, the Office of Special Education reported that sixteen states had mandated services for children aged three to five. By 1987, approximately 261,000 children

Preprimary Enrollment

Enrollment in preprimary education has risen substantially during the 1970s and 1980s, the National Center for Education Statistics has found.

Enrollment of 3- to 5-year-olds rose 19 percent between 1970 and 1980, the center found, and an additional 24 percent between 1980 and 1989. In contrast, public-school enrollment declined between 1971 and 1985.

It also found that enrollment in full-day preschool programs has risen even more sharply. In 1989, it found, 37 percent of the 3- to 5-year-olds enrolled in preschool programs attended school all day, compared with 32 percent in 1980, the data found.

Preprimary enrollment of 3- to 5-year olds, October 1970 to October 1989

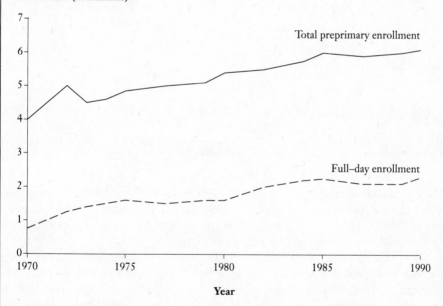

SOURCE: Preprimary enrollment. (1991). *Education Week, 10*(29) (April 10), p. 7. Reprinted with permission from *Education Week*. From data in National Center for Education Statistics, *Digest of Education Statistics: 1990* (Washington, D.C.: U.S. Government Printing Office, 1991).

FIGURE 10.2 Children served in preschool programs for students with disabilities

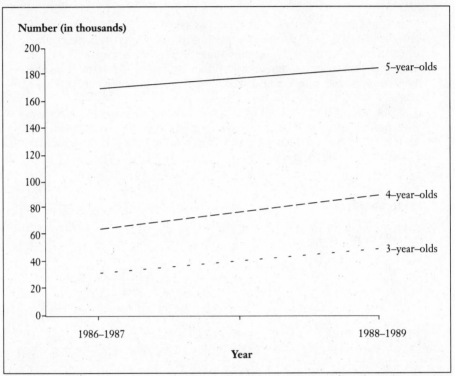

SOURCE: U.S. Department of Education. (1990b). *To assure the free appropriate education of all handicapped children: Twelfth annual report to Congress on the implementation of the Education of the Handicapped Act.* Washington, DC: Author.

in that age range were receiving early childhood special education and related services, a 33 percent increase from 1976–1977. In 1988–1989, this number increased to 362,443, primarily because of increases in the percentage of three- and four-year-olds being served (see Figure 10.2).

The rise of preschool education for children with disabilities did not occur without problems. Karnes and Zehrbach (1977) discussed many of the problems, including difficulties in identifying those who should be served, service models, and staffing patterns. Others expressed concerns about labeling children so young and about specific guidelines for early intervention. These issues have not gone away. Effective strategies for identifying and developing working interagency agreements continue to be a topic of concern (McNulty, 1989; Tingey & Stimell, 1989), as does staff development (Bailey, 1989; Hurley, 1989, Killoran & Tingey, 1989). Labeling and the appropriateness of a label such as "learning disabled" for children who have not yet reached school age have received renewed interest as well (National Joint Committee on Learning Disabilities, 1987; Peterson, 1987).

This issue has tremendous repercussions, as reflected in the following comments of a parent:

> I'm very concerned in my daughter's case, with the labeling being put on at the age of seven months. She was labeled with a mental disability at seven months. Never should of happened. Perhaps a number system rather than words. You know, this child needs 4 for physical development, but only a 2 on speech. Label the service, not the child." (Administration on Developmental Disabilities, 1988, p. 2)

Services for Infants and Toddlers with Disabilities

In 1986, PL 94-142 was amended by PL 99-457. This law reauthorized assistance for demonstration projects, training, and research and provided greater incentives to states to serve children aged three to five who were not yet being served (the law also extended to these children the rights and protections of PL 94-142 by 1990–1991). In a new Part H, the law provided states with new grant moneys to provide programs for infants and toddlers (i.e., from birth to two years). Along with this money came the requirement that the focus shift toward coordinated interagency planning (made explicit in the IFSP), thereby shifting planning away from a single agency concentrating on the child alone. With the enactment of the Handicapped Infants and Toddlers Program arose questions not only about the services needed by children with disabilities who were this young but about how to begin and then continue effective and meaningful interagency communication about these children (McNulty, 1989; Tingey & Stimell, 1989). Attention was quickly given to such considerations as the role of maternal and child health organizations (e.g., Bishop, 1988), the involvement of occupational therapy (e.g., Hanft, 1988), and the relevance of mental health agencies (e.g., Berman & Lourie, 1988).

During the first two years of the Handicapped Infants and Toddlers Program, all states participated. They were required only to (1) provide assurances that funds would be used to assist in planning, developing, and implementing a statewide system of early intervention services; (2) designate a lead agency responsible for the administration of funds; and (3) establish an interagency coordinating council. During the third year of the program, however, states were required to demonstrate that they had adopted a policy that incorporated all the components of a statewide system (see Table 10.2) or had obtained a waiver from the secretary of education. The U.S. Department of Education (1990b) reported that by January 1990, forty-eight applications had been received from states and territories; thirty-two had provided the necessary assurances, and sixteen had requested waivers. Many of the states requesting waivers had done so not because they did not have a plan but because they were awaiting state legislation mandating services to infants and toddlers or final agreements across state agencies or branches of state government. By March 1990, it was becoming clear that many

TABLE 10.2   Components of statewide early intervention services for infants and toddlers with handicaps

1. Definition of developmental delay
2. Timetable for serving all in need in the state
3. Comprehensive multidisciplinary evaluation of needs of children and families
4. IFSP and case management activities
5. Child find and referral system
6. Public awareness
7. Central directory of services, resources, experts, research, and demonstration projects
8. Comprehensive system of personnel development
9. Single line of authority in a lead agency designated or established by the governor for implementation of:
   a. General administration and supervision
   b. Identification and coordination of all available resources
   c. Assignment of financial responsibility to the appropriate agency
   d. Procedures to ensure the provision of services and to resolve intra- and interagency disputes
   e. Entry into formal interagency agreements
10. Policy pertaining to contracting or making arrangements with local services providers
11. Procedure for timely reimbursement of funds
12. Procedural safeguards
13. Policies and procedures for personnel standards
14. System for compiling data on the early intervention programs

SOURCE: U.S. Department of Education. (1990b). *To assure the free appropriate education of all handicapped children: Twelfth annual report to Congress on the implementation of the Education of the Handicapped Act.* Washington, DC: Author.

states needed more time to establish programs for infants and toddlers with disabilities (Viadero, 1991).

Many issues were identified as states began to work on providing services to very young children. For example, as states began to define the types of children to be served by the program, they had to consider how many children they would be capable of serving. These issues were summarized succinctly by the Administration on Developmental Disabilities:

> In considering the categories of disabilities, delay, and risk to use in defining eligibility, the overall decision relates to whether to cast a wide net or a narrow one: whether to bear the expense of broad inclusion and providing services to children who may not greatly benefit from them, or casting a narrow net with more stringent criteria and missing some children who could have benefited from services. (1988, pp. 9–10)

Commonly referred to as Part H, the program for infants and toddlers born with disabilities or at risk for developing them required significant interagency coordination. When the national economy shows signs of recession, it is likely that this requirement will cause much frustration. Agencies may find themselves wanting other agencies to assume financial responsibility for these young children in need.

Prebirth Services?

The mandating of services to children with disabilities from the time of birth leads to the question of whether something should or could be done before that time. In the realm of medicine, children who will be born with Down's syndrome can be identified in utero and in some cases surgery can be conducted on fetuses to prevent developmental disabilities. Some have argued that virtually certain predictions can be made that a child born to a parent with certain characteristics (e.g., drug abuser) will end up needing special education services. It has been estimated that of the children currently receiving special education services, one-third would have a more minor handicap or no handicap at all if adequate medical care had been provided during pregnancy and the first year of life (Hodgkinson, 1989). To what extent are Americans willing to mandate services at birth or before for all children who may need services at some point in their lives? And does this approach provide us with cost savings beyond imagination? Many of these issues arise with greater clarity as professionals talk about the changing population of children in the nation.

Issues Regarding Early Assessment

In Chapter 7 we discussed many issues regarding special education assessment. These included influences on assessment, bias in assessment, who conducts assessment, and the relevance of assessment to intervention. These issues are all relevant to early childhood intervention as well, and many are magnified in the assessment of children who are very young.

Are Neonatal Testing and Preschool Screening Enough?

For most children, the major assessment before school entrance has been the medical assessment conducted at the child's birth. Typically, this assessment includes an Apgar scale rating, measures of weight and length, a phenylketonuria (PKU) exam, and sensory observations. The Apgar scale includes ratings of the infant's color, heart rate, reflex, muscle tone, and breathing. The ratings are made by a hospital staff member (usually a nurse) at one minute and then at five minutes after birth. The PKU exam checks for the PKU metabolic disease, which can be curbed through dietary modification if detected early. Sensory observations confirm that the infant responds to visual and auditory stimuli.

After the initial assessment at the hospital, only those children with regularly scheduled physical examinations and those children participating in preschool screening are assessed for possible developmental disabilities or other conditions putting them at risk for adequate progress in school. Is this enough? Or is a more systematic approach, perhaps a screening program, necessary for infants and toddlers at some point after they leave the hospital?

The aspect of assessment of young children that we know most about (both in terms of having practiced it for the longest time and having conducted research on it) is preschool screening. Screening is a procedure designed to limit the number of children exposed to comprehensive assessments and to help in identifying those who may be in need of special help and should therefore be exposed to comprehensive assessment procedures. The definitions floating around as preschool screening became the subject of study were basically consistent with each other:

• Barnes indicated that the purpose of screening is "to identify those children in the general population who may be at-risk for a specific disability, or who may otherwise need special services or programs in order to develop to their maximum potential" (1982, p. 11).

• Meisels defined early childhood developmental screening as a "brief assessment procedure designed to identify children who, because of the risk of a possible learning problem or handicapping condition, should proceed to a more intensive level of diagnostic assessment" (1985, p. 1).

• Peterson maintained that the purpose of screening is to "identify children who are not within normal ranges of development and need further evaluation and who may be candidates for early intervention programs" (1987, p. 285).

Although the use of preschool screening programs to identify students with disabilities is no longer considered an issue (the demonstrated cost-efficiency of preschool programs implies benefits; see Casto & Mastropieri, 1986; White & Greenspan, 1986), how to go about running an efficient, quick, and accurate program remains an important overall issue.

In an extensive study of preschool screening programs, Thurlow, Ysseldyke, and O'Sullivan (1985) found considerable variability in procedures even within the state that in 1977 was the first to mandate preschool screening. Even though the state mandated only six screening components (vision, hearing, height, weight, health history, and developmental assessment, which included speech/language, cognitive, gross and fine motor, and social-emotional development), some programs opted to add dental inspections, nutritional screening, and laboratory tests of urine and blood. Some programs screened everyone in a district, others systematically eliminated certain children (such as those in Day Activity Centers), and others nonsystematically eliminated some children (such as those were not on census tract lists, and therefore probably had moved a lot or were homeless). Thurlow et al. also found that the goals of screening programs differed significantly, which in turn affected the number of children likely to be picked up in preschool screening. For example, one program might try to identify only those children with very significant developmental delays. Another program might try to identify all children who could benefit in any way from early childhood educational experiences.

Who Should Be Assessed?

A basic question in preschool screening is who should be identified. Should only those young children who are obviously handicapped be assessed, or should assessment encompass those young children who are at risk of evidencing a handicap later on if nothing is done? On one side of this issue are those who argue that the potential hazards of labeling are too great to justify identifying individual children who may be considered at risk (Stixrud, 1982). On the other side are those who promote the benefits of identifying all at-risk children (Meisels, 1985).

The debate continues. In some states, attempts have been made to use general labels for the young children in preschool programs (e.g., child with learning difficulties) rather than defining categorical labels (e.g., mental retardation, emotional disturbance), but the young children are still labeled as different even in this approach. And children who are attending special education programs for preschoolers (which tend to be separate from other early childhood programs) are labeled simply by their assignment to these programs.

Who Should Conduct Assessments?

As the age of those assessed becomes younger, the "who" of assessment becomes more important. Complications arise when the assessor is an "unfamiliar" individual (see Fuchs, Featherstone, Garwick, & Fuchs, 1984; Fuchs & Fuchs, 1986; Fuchs, Fuchs, Dailey, & Power, 1985; Fuchs, Fuchs, Garwick, & Featherstone, 1983; Fuchs, Zern, & Fuchs, 1983) or an individual with a style and language different from those of the child (Nuttall, Landurand, & Goldman, 1984). In most preschool screening programs, there appears to be differentiation of personnel according to area of assessment (see Table 10.3). Nevertheless, the professionals involved in the nonphysical areas of assessment are special education personnel and teachers (Ysseldyke, Thurlow, O'Sullivan, & Bursaw, 1986) who may not have adequate training for conducting these assessments.

The role of the parent(s) in assessments of very young children also merits consideration. It has been suggested that parents not be involved in the assessment of preschool children, whereas for younger children (including infants and toddlers) parent facilitation of the assessment is preferable (Salvia & Ysseldyke, 1991).

The participation of volunteers in the assessment process, particularly screening, also produces issues that must be addressed. For example, in a study of preschool screening programs with very high and very low referral rates (Ysseldyke, Thurlow, Weiss, Lehr, & Bursaw, 1985), coordinators indicated that the

TABLE 10.3   Preschool screening personnel

Screening Area	Professional
Physical health	MD Nurse
Hearing	MD Audiologist Nurse
Vision	MD Nurse Optometrist
Speech/language	Speech clinician Special educator/teacher
Motor	Special educator/teacher Occupational therapist
Social-emotional	Special educator/teacher Psychologist
Cognitive	Special educator/teacher

NOTE: Table includes only those roles listed by more than one-hundred programs.
SOURCE: Ysseldyke, J. E., Thurlow, M. L., O'Sullivan, P., & Bursaw, R. A. (1986). Current screening and diagnostic practices in a state offering free preschool screening since 1977: Implications for the field. *Journal of Psychoeducational Assessment*, *4*, 191–203, pp. 191–203. Used with permission.

use of volunteers influenced the frequency with which problems were identified and the eventual referral rates. If this variation is so, how are volunteers trained to identify children needing further evaluation?

What Should Be Assessed and How?

Assessment procedures constitute the largest category of assessment issues. In a survey of model early childhood programs, Lehr, Ysseldyke, and Thurlow (1987) found that the most frequently used procedure for screening was "other" (which included record reviews, observations, and some forms of parent involvement) but that family needs assessments and home visits were considerably less frequent than other procedures.

Assessment instruments are the primary topic of concern, especially in regard to validity, reliability, and representativeness of the standardization population of norm-referenced devices. For example, commonly used readiness tests have been shown to lack the needed levels of reliability for placement decisions (Meisels, 1987). And the instability of performance of young children and the lack of relationship between early measures of intelligence or achievement and later school performance lead to further questions about what to assess.

Where and When Should Assessment Occur?

The location and timing of preschool screening come with their own set of problems and questions. Although the optimal assessment environment is one with low anxiety and minimal confusion, screening is sometimes done in hallways, with young children moving from one noisy station to the next. Sometimes the same person moves along the stations with the child; sometimes a new assessor greets the child at each station. In some programs, care is taken to assure quiet testing conditions and sufficient preassessment time for getting acquainted with the assessor, but scheduling also has to be taken into account because the schedules of young children include naps and important mealtimes. Of equal importance are the length of the assessment—Peterson (1987) recommended a series of short testing sessions for young children—and the extent to which the timing of assessment is coordinated with further assessment and/or actual initiation of an intervention program (Lichtenstein & Ireton, 1984).

Nature of Intervention

The issue of what interventions should be provided is as complex as those regarding who needs early intervention. For young children birth to age three, an established IFSP guides the delivery of services, in part by establishing goals and identifying a case manager. For children between ages three and five, the IEP typically guides intervention efforts.

Where Should Intervention Occur?

An important aspect of providing early intervention for young children with disabilities is determining where services will be located. Of particular importance are the least restrictive environment for very young children, the flexibility and consistency of services, and the nature of related services incorporated into early childhood services (Administration on Developmental Disabilities, 1988). Should services for the very young be provided at home, in a clinic, or in a school? Should the location vary according to the age of the child or according to some other variable, such as the nature of the disability or its severity? To what extent can the LRE concept be applied to services for very young children with disabilities? This last issue is especially relevant because of the rapid growth in preprimary enrollment of three- to five-year-olds and the existence of preschool programs into which preschool children with disabilities can be mainstreamed.

Who Should Receive Services?

That assessors determine intervention is needed does not automatically mean that the child should be the focus of the intervention. Services can be targeted on the

---

The Gallup Poll on the Issue of Promotion Policy

Public opinion continues to oppose promotion from one grade to the next unless the student can pass examinations—presumably grade- and curriculum-appropriate examinations. Opinion seems not to have changed on the issue since the question was first asked in 1978. But it is probably accurate to say that a majority of educators hold a different opinion. Although few teachers approve of strictly "social" promotion, most believe that considerations other than passing an exam must be taken into account when decisions about promotion are made. There is much research evidence to support their belief. Certainly, making a child repeat a grade without taking other steps to help him or her learn is often counterproductive. This is an area in which the profession needs to educate the general public. (p. 45)

SOURCE: Elam, S. M. (1990). The 22nd annual Gallup poll of the public's attitude toward the public schools. *Phi Delta Kappan, 72*(1), 41–55.

---

child, the family unit, or both. It is important to determine whether the target of intervention efforts changes as a function of the age of the child, the nature of the disability, and/or its severity.

Part H essentially requires that the intervention be family focused. But exactly what this means is not clear. A survey of seven states that had written IFSP guidelines by 1988 reported that "all seven required a written plan, a case management system, and identified an IFSP planning process that included family input" (U.S. Dept. of Education, 1990b, p. 57). The extent to which including family input is the same as making the intervention family focused is questionable. As the U.S. Department of Education reported, "Few or none of the policies addressed such issues as the procedure by which the case manager was to be selected or changed; the definition of family; practices that protect the rights of the family; resolution of disputes for payments or services; or resolution of individual or systemic complaints" (p. 57).

Other issues, some of them very emotional, also remain to be resolved. For example, who decides, and how, that developmental delays in an infant are due to inadequate parenting, rather than to a physical condition, and that parent education is required to remedy the infant's delay? Or who determines, and how, that the only intervention for a toddler at a certain age beyond what the parents are already doing is physical therapy?

Who Should Provide Services?

Personnel needs are sure to be an issue as services are provided to younger and younger children. Although an elementary-level teacher can adequately serve a five-year-old, or perhaps even a four-year-old, teachers serving children younger than four are likely to need different skills. The U.S. Department of Education recognized this issue and cited research indicating that "skills required to work with infants and toddlers differ from those required to work with three through five year olds (Bricker & Slentz, 1989; McCollum, 1987)" (1990b, p. 58). An insufficient number of trained personnel to work with preschoolers was already an issue before states began to think about personnel for infants and toddlers with disabilities. The 1990 U.S. Department of Education report to Congress summarized the matter as follows:

> The implementation of Part H will result in an increased need for personnel to provide early intervention services. The number of personnel who will be available to work with infants and toddlers depends on several factors such as number of qualified personnel currently available, the professional standards that determine who is qualified, attrition rates, and the number currently in training who will make up the future work force. Part H requires that States develop policy and procedures for personnel standards and establish a comprehensive system of personnel development. (p. 58)

Furthermore, just as we expect greater involvement of the school nurse as students with more severe disabilities are served in their home schools (National Association of State School Nurse Consultants, 1990), we expect a greater need for nurses able to work interactively with educational personnel in meeting the needs of youngsters involved in early childhood special education.

What Should Be the Focus of Intervention?

Several issues arise regarding the focus of intervention: the sequence in which motor development, social, and academic objectives should be identified; the length and frequency of services; the maximal amount of services; and the variables affecting this amount. In looking at focus issues, White and Casto (1989), for instance, organized them into seven areas: setting of program, instructional grouping, duration/intensity of services, staffing, type of services, family involvement, and philosophical orientation. They suggested that philosophical orientation underlies all other issues and can vary along such dimensions as teacher-oriented versus child-oriented programming, extrinsic versus intrinsic motivation and reward system, and individualized teaching versus teaching to groups. Bricker (1989) concluded that the three most essential features of early intervention programs in the 1990s are the linking of assessment, intervention, and evaluation; mainstreaming or integration; and program evaluation.

New Constituencies for Early Special Education Intervention

At the same time that medical advances are enabling America to save increasing numbers of medically fragile infants each year, social problems are increasing the numbers of infants born with significant health problems and with hidden disabilities.

Drug- and Alcohol-Exposed Infants

It was the late 1980s before America really began to look at the potential impact of its drug problem. This occurred about the time that *Education Week* (Viadero, 1989) reported that an estimated 375,000 children were born each year exposed to cocaine. In a report released in June 1990 (cited in "Crack babies in preschool," 1990), the U.S. General Accounting Office (GAO) indicated that current estimates of the number of drug-exposed infants being born in the United States were probably much too low. In its study of ten hospitals, the GAO's figures indicated one drug-exposed baby in every eleven births. Researchers generally agree that the eventual costs of dealing with and helping these children will be very significant:

> Whatever the numbers may be, the GAO report agrees that the financial costs of drug-exposed births will be very high, down the line.
>
> For example, the per capita cost in the Los Angeles pilot preschool program for mildly impaired prenatally exposed children is estimated to be $17,000 a year. For those drug-exposed children who show significant physiologic or neurologic impairment, the Florida Department of Health and Rehabilitative Services estimates that total service costs to age 18 could be as high as $750,000 per child. ("Crack babies in preschool," p. 7)

A study conducted by the National Institute on Drug Abuse followed three hundred Chicago-area infants whose mothers used cocaine and possibly other drugs during pregnancy. With the caution that the infants in the Chicago area might be better off than similar children in the general population because their mothers had been motivated enough to seek drug treatment, the researchers found problems as late as age three. They confirmed the findings of several studies that cocaine babies were born smaller and weighed less than their drug-free peers. In addition, they found that cocaine babies spent most of their early weeks crying or sleeping and had a harder time than their peers maintaining a "quiet alert state" during which they could learn about their environment (Viadero, 1990). Although the cocaine youngsters appeared to catch up physically with their peers by age two, they "still tended to score lower than drug-free toddlers on tests measuring their ability to concentrate, interact with others in groups, and cope with an unstructured environment" (p. 15). Early examinations of limited numbers of three-year-old children who were cocaine babies indicated that many were easily distracted and exhibited language and/or behavior problems.

Other possible outcomes of the in utero exposure of infants to alcohol and drugs (and AIDS) were discussed in an action seminar held with the National Association of State Directors of Special Education in September 1989. A report containing recommendations for state directors of special education (NASDSE,

1989) indicated that research had documented the following effects of abuse of drugs by the mother during and after pregnancy:

Heroin: poor fetal growth, microcephality, neonatal withdrawal, seizures

Alcohol: fetal alcohol syndrome, malformation of microcephality, poor growth, developmental delay

Nicotine: poor fetal growth (four-hundred grams less for birth rate), increased mortality (135 percent more mortality than nonsmoking)

Cocaine: prematurity, low birth weight, placenta separation, genital abnormalities, developmental delays, central nervous system involvement (all resulting from the release of "emergency" chemicals such as adrenalin into the fetus's body; the shutting down of the fetus's "housekeeping" functions, thereby generating hypertension, rapid heart rate, strokes, and triggered labor; and the diminishing of the fetus's blood and nutrition supply)

Low-Birth-Weight Survivors

Low-birth-weight infants received attention in a study conducted by Sparling of the Frank Porter Graham Child Development Center at the University of North Carolina. In this largest study ever conducted on low-birth-weight children, 985 infants weighing five and a half pounds or less at birth were followed. As reported in *Education Week*:

> Some of the infants were given only traditional pediatric follow-up care. The rest received such care as well as intensive educational services at home, and later on, in special day-care programs. . . .
> By age 3, the researchers report, the children receiving special-educational services had significantly higher I.Q. scores and fewer behavior problems than did the toddlers receiving only health care. (Viadero, 1990, p. 15)

At the same time that the tremendous needs of low-birth-weight infants were being recognized, Congress was calling for funds to fight infant mortality (Pitsch, 1991a). This initiative called for improving access to prenatal care, reducing the number of low-birth-weight babies and birth defects, decreasing substance abuse among mothers, and cutting down the number of teenage pregnancies.

AIDS Babies

Tremendous implications for education accompany the growing number of babies born with the HIV infection that causes AIDS. These children are presumed to be at risk for developing AIDS within seven to ten years, their elementary school years. These children almost certainly will fall within the other health impairment category of special education. The extent to which schools will be able to deal with these youngsters, who may be expected to die regardless of educational

---

80,000 Women of Child-Bearing Age May Have AIDS Virus, Study Says

As many as 80,000 women of child-bearing age in the United States may be infected with the virus that causes AIDS, a new study concludes.

The study, which was published in last week's issue of the *Journal of the American Medical Association*, also estimates that about 1,800 babies born to these women each year will have the human immunodeficiency virus that causes the disease.

The report is based on the results of anonymous blood tests on more than 1.8 million infants born between 1988 and 1990 in 38 states and the District of Columbia. Since the antibodies that are measured in a newborn come mostly from the mother, the test is a better measure of the mother's H.I.V. status than the child's. But health officials believe about one-third of the babies who are born H.I.V.-positive eventually will develop AIDS.

Women in New York, New Jersey, and Florida had the highest rates of H.I.V. infection, the study found. And depending on the state, black women were 5 to 15 times more likely to be H.I.V.-positive than were white women, the study found.

SOURCE: 80,000 women of child-bearing age may have AIDS virus, study says. (1991, April 10). *Education Week*, p. 2.

---

treatment and its expenses, is unknown. The number of young children with HIV who will soon be in the schools is not insignificant.

Response to the New Constituencies

Despite the increasing recognition of needs among new constituencies of very young children, responses to these needs have been slow to emerge. For example, although an office of fetal alcohol syndrome was established by Congress in 1988, as of December 1990 staff for the office still had not been hired (Karaim, 1990). In response to drug-exposed infants, as 1990 came to a close some states were contemplating laws to allow prosecution of mothers of these infants for child abuse (Behrmann, 1990). In a commentary in *Exceptional Children*, Greer wrote, "Already in our schools is the advance guard of what will surely swell into an epidemic in a few short years: the drug babies. The question for today is, what preparation are we making (1990, p. 382)?

The answer to Greer's question is ambiguous. Most people are standing in awe of the problem, with a sense of dread. At a time when it is still possible to be proactive, or at least to engage in strategic planning for these new constituencies, little is happening. America's primary response seems to be to argue for changing the system so that no more of these constituencies will occur. Unfortunately, given the speed with which systemic changes are implemented and have an effect, Americans will probably be faced with addressing the issue of what to do with these new constituencies for the next twenty years at least.

Discussion Questions

1. Do assumptions of developmental plasticity and cost-effectiveness really guide early childhood special education? Are there other assumptions in play as well? If so, which ones?

2. Would there be significant benefits in providing special education services to children at risk of needing services later on?

3. Is there a way to link assessment to intervention for infants, toddlers, and preschoolers?

4. How should services to infants, toddlers, and preschoolers be provided if there is not enough trained and certified personnel? Can educators with alternative certifications be used?

5. What should America's response be to its potential new constituencies?

Transition Issues

Progress begins with getting a clear view of the obstacles.

—*Anonymous*

Life is a series of transitions. People make the transition from one class to another while in school and survive the transition period between childhood and adulthood known as adolescence. People also move from one place to another, from one type of relationship to another, or from student life to work life. These transitions, though often stressful, are made without too much difficulty by most persons. In the 1980s, however, professionals joined parents in realizing that not all individuals make transitions so easily. This realization led to an emphasis on the transition process and the difficulties many individuals with disabilities had in successfully accomplishing transitions. Special efforts were deemed necessary to successfully "transition" the individual with special needs.

Although the transition to adulthood has received considerable attention in the special education literature, it is not the only critical transition that youngsters with disabilities are required to make. For example, they must accomplish the transition into school in the first place and then negotiate numerous transitions within school. Not only are there the typical transitions from one grade level or type of school to the next, but there are unique special education transitions, such as from one type of placement to another or one school to another and between general education and special education settings. The transition from school to some "adult" endeavor, such as postsecondary training, work, or other form of activity, is another transition that has to be made. In this chapter, we discuss the issues that surround each of the types of transition that youngsters with disabilities face.

Transition into School

The first school-related transition required of a young child who has been identified as disabled is the transition from the preschool program into the formal K–12 educational system. At least two issues arise with this transition. First, should the child's handicap be made known to the school in which the child will be enrolled? This question, which is most relevant for children with mild disabilities, is highly related to the issue of early labeling. Second, to what extent should alternatives to traditional school placements be used for students with disabilities? Alternative school options, such as Montessori schools and private schools, and within-school options, such as transitional kindergartens and junior first grades, are possible choices.

Early Labeling

Although children in preschool special education programs need not be given a specific label of handicap, participation in the program itself is a type of label. In a detailed case study analysis of what happened to children as they left their preschool special education programs to move into elementary schools, Thurlow, et al. (1986) found extreme variability in the process. In some districts, program staff visited with staff of the elementary program to which the student was going, discussing in detail the child's strengths and weaknesses and recommending instructional techniques for the child. In one district, all information related to the child's participation in the early childhood special education program was deleted from the child's records, and the child was sent on to the elementary school without any indication of previous special education service. Unfortunately, follow-up of children in early childhood special education programs was a rare event. Informal input from the program in which no information followed the child indicated that nearly 60 percent of the children continued for another year without referral for evaluation for possible special education placement.

We do not have good data on what happens to students for whom extensive preparations are made for entry into the elementary school setting in addition to providing information on the students' special education status. Is it better to label, then drop the label? Is it better to make preparations for a smooth transition when the special education participation will be revealed? Or is it better not to prepare a transition in this way?

Alternatives to Traditional School Placements

Instead of having their children enter public school programs, some parents of young children with disabilities opt to send them to private schools or to schools with special programs, such as Montessori programs. No research has been conducted on either the extent to which this occurs or on the effects of this alternative. Another alternative is to hold the child out of school for a year so that when the child does enter, there is little likelihood of problems arising from immaturity. Some school districts encourage this practice.

Recently, Shepard and Smith (1989) published a book on the effects of retention in grade, more commonly known as flunking. Special grades, such as transitional kindergartens (to which a child goes after unsuccessfully completing a year in kindergarten), or junior first grades (to which a child goes because he or she is not quite ready for first grade), are a form of retention. Special words (transitional, junior) are used to deflate the negative aura that typically accompanies failure.

Some have likened these programs (particularly the practice of holding the child out of school for a year) to the practice of "redshirting" in college sports: a student is kept from playing a varsity sport until sophomore year so that the student's four years of eligibility do not start until then. In the conclusion to their book, Smith and Shepard argued that

> transition programs, which provide an extra year of school between kindergarten and first grade, are no different—in spite of their different philosophies—from simply retaining children for a second year in kindergarten. Although they are predicated on the idea that immature children should be given an extra year to grow or to repeat the pre-first grade experience, controlled studies show that children so treated do no better than their counterparts who are promoted directly into first grade. The findings of no difference or no benefit hold whether the children were selected for retention on the basis of immaturity or low achievement. (1989, pp. 215–216)

From a comprehensive review of the research literature on kindergarten retention, Shepard also noted that

> self-concept or attitude measures, only rarely included in research studies, showed no difference or negative effects from the extra-year placements. In this respect retention, whether it is called by a special name (transition), occurs for special reason (immaturity), or takes place in kindergarten rather than later, is still retention—and still ineffective. (1989a, p. 76)

With this kind of evidence, opposition to such programs has increased. In 1991, the National Association of Elementary School Principals (NAESP) passed a resolution opposing the practice (Cohen, 1991). Those who voted against the resolution noted the need for this transition program for developmentally immature children, despite the arguments of Shepard and Smith and more recent evidence presented by Ferguson of the noneffectiveness of the practice (Early Years, 1991). Ferguson's work is of interest because he looked specifically at children considered to be developmentally slow and included a control group. He found that teachers' ratings of the students revealed no differences in social skills, self-esteem, or rate of placement in special education. The students who went through the transitional program, however, were rated as more aggressive.

When NAESP passed its resolution, it noted the need to seek alternatives to the practice of retaining children through transitional kindergartens or junior first grades. The chairperson of the panel that drafted the resolution, Lillian Brinkley, suggested some possibilities (Cohen, 1991):

• Providing the child with a support system and tutors (peers, adult volunteers, older students)

• Encouraging consultation between teachers

• Pairing slower pupils with higher achievers

• Making classes smaller

• Providing more schooling (summer school or extended-year programs)

• Instituting midyear promotions

Transitions During School

Many of the transitions children and youths make are introduced as they mature, such as movement from smaller classrooms to larger classrooms, from smaller buildings to larger buildings, and from a single teacher all day to seven or eight different teachers during one day. Perhaps because of the ease with which these transitions are made by most students, there has been little research conducted on them. Nevertheless, it is not unreasonable to assume that these transitions are made more easily by children without disabilities than by children with them. Yet no special provisions are usually made to train students with disabilities in these transitions.

Transitions Between General and Special Education

Transitions seem to be required far more often of students with disabilities than of students without them. While the typical elementary school child is in a single room with a single teacher all day, students receiving special education services often leave the special education setting to go to the mainstream or leave the general classroom setting to go to a special classroom to meet with a specialist (most commonly the special education teacher). Sometimes they must go at more than one time to meet with more than one other teacher (e.g., they may see an occupational therapist in the morning and a special education teacher in the afternoon; or they may see two different special educators, one who specializes in academics and one who specializes in behavior). Students leaving the regular classroom to meet with these individuals not only have to adjust to dealing with more than one teacher; they also have to adjust to entering and leaving curriculum materials when other students do not and to explaining to other students why they leave the classroom and for what purpose.

Students who do not leave the classroom but who find themselves with the special education teacher inside the regular classroom may not have to make quite as many transition adjustments as other students with disabilities do, but the adjustments may still be considerable. When this type of integrated service is used by the special education teacher as simply a different location to carry on typical special education activities (e.g., use different materials, drill basic facts, etc.), the student must also learn to concentrate when other students in the same classroom are engaged in completely different tasks, perhaps even listening to a teacher lecturing to the class.

We have already indicated to some extent the difficulties that surround the student for whom special education is separate from general education. We have spoken of the disjointedness of curricula and of the student's having to work with many more adults than the typical student must. We wish to point out here that students who must travel from one classroom to another while classmates continue on with the work of the classroom are deprived of a significant amount of time during which they could be learning.

Dropping Out of School

Perhaps the most significant transition that students may make is to move out of school before completing it, an activity more commonly known as dropping out. Concern about dropouts was high in the 1960s just before the first wave of educational reform (during which academic excellence concerns were given greater emphasis). Concern about dropouts rose again during the third wave of reform as it became apparent that a large number of America's students were placed at risk by many of the reform activities.

Dropping out is, perhaps, the most negative of possible school outcomes. Schooling is compulsory by law, and schools are expected to serve all children and youths. When students drop out of a system that is supposed to be compulsory and that is supposed to meet their needs, it becomes an issue, particularly because the impact of school dropouts on the rest of society appears to be great (see, for example, Table 11.1).

The number of youths dropping out of school was identified as a major problem in the second half of the 1980s. By the mid-1980s, research had shown that nearly 25 percent of all youths in America were dropping out of school (School Dropouts, 1986). It also demonstrated that dropping out of school resulted in negative personal outcomes, such as unemployment, low income and lifetime

TABLE 11.1   Relationship between graduation rates and prisoner rates

Ten States with the Best Graduation Rates, 1987	Percent Graduated	Prisoners per 100,000 Population	1987 Rank
Minnesota	90.6	60	49th
Wyoming	89.3	195	28th
North Dakota	88.4	57	50th
Nebraska	86.7	123	40th
Montana	86.4	147	33rd
Iowa	86.2	101	43rd
Wisconsin	84.4	124	39th
Ohio	82.8	224	24th
Kansas	82.1	237	22nd
Utah	80.6	111	41st

SOURCE: Hodgkinson, H. L. (1989). *The same client: The demographics of education and service delivery systems*. Washington, DC: Institute for Educational Leadership, Center for Demographic Leadership, p. 15. Used with permission.

earnings, limited cognitive growth, and limited scholastic achievement gains (see Catterall, 1988; Ekstrom, Goertz, Pollack, & Rock, 1986; Grossnickle, 1986; Pallas, 1987; Rumberger, 1987). The damaging implications for society included billions of dollars in lost tax revenues, welfare and unemployment expenditures, and crime prevention funds expended for dropout youths (see Catterall, 1988; Hahn, Danzberger, & Lefkowitz, 1987).

For some time, the characteristics of those youths dropping out of school were studied and discussed. Factors commonly included within the lists of characteristics were attendance, number of school transfers, participation in free/reduced lunch programs, grade point average, educational level of parents, reading and math scores, ethnic/gender distinctions, language spoken at home, participation in extracurricular activities, pregnancy, and family status (Wells, Bechard, & Hamby, 1989). Characteristics of schools that seemed to produce more dropouts than the norm included overcrowding, low amounts of time that teachers engaged in instruction, weak leadership from the principal, low degree of order and discipline, retention policies, and changes associated with the reform movement in secondary schools (see Fine, 1986; Hess, 1987; Mann, 1986; Massachusetts Advocacy Center, 1986; School Dropouts, 1986).

Of particular note in the literature on dropouts was that policies that frequently affected students in special education programs (such as being held back in grade a second time or being suspended) often encouraged students to leave school permanently (Berlin & Duhl, 1984; Mann, 1986; Massachusetts Advocacy Center, 1986). Another factor associated with students in special education, race or ethnicity, was reported extensively in the literature: minority students (exclud-

TABLE 11.2   OSEP data on students' exit status, 1987–1988

Exit Category	Number	Percentage
Graduated with diploma	100,195	42.0
Graduated with certificate	26,832	11.3
Reached maximum age	5,971	2.5
Dropped out	65,395	27.4
Other/unknown	40,186	16.8

SOURCE: U.S. Department of Education. (1990b). *To assure the free appropriate public education of all handicapped children: Twelfth annual report to Congress on the implementation of the Education of the Handicapped Act.* Washington, DC: Author.

ing Asian Americans) more frequently left school than did nonminority students (California Dropouts, 1986; Ekstrom et al., 1986; Hess & Lauber, 1985; Stephenson, 1985). Particularly at risk were Hispanic students (Pitsch, 1991b).

The dropout literature has been plagued by definitional issues that continue, even though dropping out is acknowledged as a major national problem for American education. Different criteria are often used to define who is a dropout, and different procedures may be used to count dropouts. Variations in criteria can be a function of which students are actually included, the number of days a student must be absent from school to be considered a dropout, the age at which a student can be classified as a dropout, and the grade levels included. For example, some schools do not count students younger than sixteen as dropouts because the law mandates their attendance; this practice seriously underestimates the number of school leavers. Various rationales for exiting school also serve as criteria for defining a school dropout: often students pursuing a GED are counted as dropouts, whereas teenage mothers are not (Cipollone, 1986). In some cases, students in special education are entirely excluded from the calculation of dropout rates. Some researchers make distinctions among school leavers, age outs, push outs, and dropouts; others do not. Because of these differences, the National Center on Education Statistics obtained agreement from twenty-seven states to use the following definition: a student is a dropout if he or she was enrolled in school during the previous school year but was not enrolled at the beginning of the current year; has not graduated from high school or completed a state- or district-approved program; has not transferred to another public school district, private school, or state- or district-approved education program; has been suspended, expelled, or excused from school because of illness; or has died.

But even with these consistent criteria across states, it is not clear where students in special education programs will be counted. Currently, the Office of Special Education Programs is reviewing its school exit categories, shown in Table 11.2, because of the high percentage of students appearing in the other/unknown category.

Studies that compared special education dropout rates with control group dropout rates or normative data consistently showed that students with mild to moderate disabilities left school more often than students without handicaps (Bernoff, 1981; Bruininks, Thurlow, Lewis, & Larson, 1988; Hess & Lauber, 1985; Levin, Zigmond, & Birch, 1985; Owings & Stocking, 1986; Stephenson, 1985; White, Schumaker, Warner, Alley, & Deshler, 1980; Zigmond & Thornton, 1985). Studies that did not have a comparative dropout group showed that students in special education dropped out of school at very high rates. For example, Hasazi, Gordon, and Roe (1985) found that from a group of students in special education who had been mostly in resource rooms, 59 percent graduated from school, 13 percent left school at eighteen or older without graduating, and 28 percent "dropped" prior to age eighteen without graduating (i.e., 41 percent did not finish high school). Fardig, Algozzine, Schwartz, Hensel, and Westling (1985) found that the majority of a sample of rural students with mild disabilities (69 percent) finished the twelfth grade, a result implying that about 31 percent of these students dropped out of school.

An additional group of investigations reported and analyzed dropout information for different categories of disabilities. These studies indicated that two groups of students with handicaps abandoned school more often than other groups: students with learning disabilities and students with emotional disturbances. The annual reports to Congress (U.S. Dept. of Education, 1987, 1988b) showed that during 1984–1985 students with emotional disturbances dropped out of school more often than students with other disabilities; during the 1985–1986 school year students with learning disabilities left school more often than other students. The High School and Beyond studies (Lichtenstein, 1987; Owings & Stocking, 1986), which reported national data, indicated that students who identified themselves as having a specific learning disability dropped out of school at higher rates than students who identified themselves as having other disabilities.

In studies conducted in specific school districts or types of communities, the dropout trend was similar to the national trend. Edgar (1987) found that students with learning or emotional disabilities in Washington school districts dropped out of school at higher rates (42 percent) than students with other types of disabilities. In a study conducted in a suburban school district in Minnesota (Bruininks et al., 1988), students with severe emotional disabilities dropped out of school significantly more often (73 percent) than students with other disabilities, who dropped at rates ranging from 12 percent (students with speech impairments) to 28 percent (students with learning disabilities). These rates were in a district where approximately 3 percent of students without disabilities dropped out of school. The National Longitudinal Transition Study (Wagner, 1991) reported a national dropout rate of 32.5 percent over a two-year period.

Examination of the effects of dropping out of school for students with disabilities has been done primarily by looking at their employment status and adjustment. The results clearly indicate that dropping out of school has detrimental effects on the employment attainment of students with mild disabilities.

Dropout special education students demonstrate lower employment rates (Edgar, 1987; Hasazi et al., 1985; Hewitt, 1981; Porter, 1982; Zigmond & Thornton, 1985). Furthermore, a lower percentage of time after leaving high school is spent in employment by students who drop out compared to students who graduate.

There is a second type of dropout in schools, but this dropout has received little recognition and even less research. This is the student who attends school but is a functional dropout. Solomon described this type of student as one who remains in school but disengages from the pursuit of academic credentials. He saw this group of dropouts with the same outcomes as traditional dropouts: "They fail to acquire the competencies and credentials necessary for social and economic advancement in adult life" (1989, p. 79). Payne described this phenomenon as well:

> By the time they are of junior high age, if not sooner, many inner-city youngsters behave in ways that seem to unambiguously proclaim their lack of interest in schooling. Teachers are literally bombarded with these signals. Those teachers who hope to work successfully with such youngsters have to convince themselves that what we see of their day-to-day behavior may only be a reflection of more fundamental problems. (1989, p. 113)

The functional dropout is as great a problem as, if not more of a problem than, the student who no longer attends school. The functional dropout continues to sit in the classroom and use taxpayers dollars for instructors and materials, yet he or she may leave school in the same predicament as the actual dropout; both have a lower likelihood of obtaining and keeping a job after high school. Whether the functional dropout somehow benefits from obtaining a graduation diploma (if that happens) and the extent to which students in special education can be considered functional dropouts are unknown. Clearly, additional research is needed in this area.

Many different attempts have been made to prevent high-risk students from dropping out and to reengage students who have already dropped out. These have focused almost exclusively on students in general education, and most have not been investigated adequately or systematically. Programs designed explicitly for dropout-prone students in special education are few in number. Zigmond (1987) suggested that many of the strategies in general education dropout intervention programs already are part of special education programs, such as early identification, individualized approaches, smaller size classes, lower pupil-teacher ratio, vocational education, employment preparation and job training, and counseling. Therefore, existing dropout interventions in general education may be necessary but not sufficient to prevent students with handicapping conditions from dropping out of school.

New perspectives and approaches must be generated to overcome the dropout problem in special education. Edgar (1991) described a comprehensive approach to programming that may keep students with special needs engaged in schools. His approach includes such programs as academic support (tutors, Saturday school, resource teachers) and personal support (case manager, health services, counseling and treatment, prosocial recreation, mentors/benefactors) for students pursuing the academic track in high school. There would also be an alternative track designed specifically to develop work skills and to place students in jobs paying above-poverty-level wages.

Zigmond (1990) proposed four essential components to more effective secondary school programming for students with learning disabilities. First, the program should provide intensive instruction in the basic skills, particularly reading and math. Second, the program should provide instruction in such survival skills as behavior control, behaviors that please teachers, and study and test-taking skills. Third, the program should enable the student to complete successfully those courses required for high school graduation by, for instance, changing graduation requirements or using a consulting teacher to help mainstream teachers adjust mainstream demands to special education students. Fourth, the program should include explicit planning for life after high school; the implementation of this component can vary considerably. According to Zigmond, "The challenge for schools is to construct an efficient and affordable service delivery model with the appropriate combination of special and mainstream education experiences to address these components, and at the same time to develop an appealing and motivating educational program that holds students in school" (pp. 15–66). Zigmond proposed two models that can do this, one that emphasizes preparation for work and one that emphasizes preparation for some type of postsecondary training.

The models proposed by both Zigmond (1990) and Edgar (1991) suggest the use of tracks that accord with the eventual goal of the student's education. This leaves unaddressed, however, the question of when, how, and by whom the goal is to be determined. Clearly, many issues must be addressed as educators attempt to keep high-risk special education students in school and prepare them for life after school.

Postschool Transitions

The impetus for focusing attention on the transition from school to postschool activities (usually employment) was the 1983 amendments to the Education of the Handicapped Act Amendments of 1973. In Section 626 of PL 98-199, financial support was provided to an array of demonstration efforts to both stimulate improved programs for secondary special education and provide coordinated education, training, and related services to help in transitions to employment, vocational training, continuing education, and adult services. Madeleine Will, then assistant secretary for the Office of Special Education and Rehabilitative Services, spoke repeatedly about the need for building a bridge between school and adult experiences. In 1985, an institute devoted to the evaluation and extension of the federal initiative was established at the University of Illinois, Urbana-Champaign.

In 1987, a major national longitudinal transition study was funded to collect comprehensive transition data on students with disabilities (Wagner, 1991).

With the enactment of the amendments of PL 94-142 came even more emphasis on transition. A new explicit definition of transition services was provided:

> A coordinated set of activities for a student, designed within an outcome-oriented process, which promotes movement from school to post-school activities, including post-secondary education, vocational training, integrated employment (including supported employment), continuing and adult education, adult services, independent living, or community participation. The coordinated set of activities shall be based upon the individual student's needs, taking into account the student's preferences and interests, and shall include instruction, community experiences, the development of employment and other post-school adult living objectives, and, when appropriate acquisition of daily living skills and functional vocational evaluation.

This new law (PL 101-476) also required that the IEP include a statement of needed transition services beginning no later than age sixteen.

Why was all this attention devoted to postschool transition? For the most part, the efforts on behalf of students with disabilities grew out of a body of follow-up literature that indicated that students with disabilities were leaving school unprepared to work. Halloran succinctly summarized some of the issues when he wrote:

> Some students reach the end of their public school experience poorly prepared for competitive employment or independent living. As students approach the end of their formal schooling we frequently ask what they will be doing after school ends. Unfortunately, when we look back to determine what preparations have been made for students to live and work in our communities we often see a series of disjointed efforts lacking a focus on the skills necessary to confront the new expectations and demands of adult life. (1989, p. xiii)

A number of follow-up studies also indicated that former students who had received special education services did not necessarily fare very well after they left school. Most information obtained after the enactment of PL 94-142 focused primarily on employment, and most studies involved students with mild mental retardation or other mild disabilities (e.g., Fardig et al., 1985; Hasazi et al., 1985; Mithaug, Horiuchi, & Fanning, 1985; Semmel, Cosden, & Konopak, 1985; Wehman, Kregel, & Seyfarth, 1985). Follow-up studies of former students with moderate to severe mental disabilities (e.g., Edgar, 1987; Hasazi et al., 1985; Hawkins, 1984; Thurlow, Bruininks, & Lange, 1989; Wehman et al., 1985) indicated similar variability in employment rates and other adjustment indicators. The variability was, however, quite consistently on the low end of the scale (e.g., from 21 percent to 45 percent were employed) for students with moderate to severe disabilities.

The time was right for renewed emphasis on the postschool transition of youths with disabilities. Within two years of the enactment of PL 101-476 in 1991, major changes were to be in place as a result of other landmark legislation,

ADA Summary

The ADA eliminates discrimination in the areas of employment, public accommodations, public services, transportation, and telecommunications for the hearing impaired.

Employment: Effective July 26, 1992, all employers with twenty-five or more employees (dropping to fifteen or more on July 26, 1994) may not discriminate against qualified individuals with disabilities in hiring and promotion activities. In addition, employers must make reasonable accommodations to qualified applicants or employees with disabilities, including modifying work stations and equipment, unless undue hardship would result.

Transportation: Beginning after August 25, 1990, all new public buses and public rail vehicles for fixed route systems must be accessible. New vehicles for demand response service must be accessible unless the system provides individuals with disabilities a level of service equivalent to that provided to the general public. By January 26, 1992, comparable paratransit must be provided to individuals who cannot use fixed route bus service to the extent that an undue financial burden is not imposed.

Public Accommodations: By January 26, 1992, all areas of public accommodations, including restaurants, hotels, and theaters, stores, and day care centers, must be made accessible and cannot otherwise discriminate against persons with disabilities. Physical barriers in existing buildings must be removed if readily achievable. All new construction of public accommodations must be accessible.

Telecommunications: Telephone companies must provide relay services for individuals with hearing impairment and speech impairment.

SOURCE: "Senator Dave Durenberger Reports to Minnesotans on Disability Policy." (December 1990). *Legislative Update*.

specifically the Americans with Disabilities Act. The passage of ADA provided basic civil rights protections to people with disabilities, which would allow them to participate on an equal footing with others.

Appropriate Postschool Transition Services

Views on the nature of appropriate transition services vary from one person to the next. For example, some professionals view appropriate transition services as being part of a lifelong career development approach that includes preparation in daily living and personal-social skills and occupational guidance and preparation (see Brolin & Schatzman, 1989). Others view transition as more of a challenge to interagency cooperation (see Johnson, Bruininks, & Thurlow, 1987). Some see vocational training as the only need, whereas others identify significant personal adjustment needs. Some believe that the transition program should be different for students with learning disabilities or physical handicaps and students with mental retardation. Some argue that personal behavior skills are the most important information in a transition training program, whereas others view an introduction to community services, such as the Division of Rehabilitation Services and Supplemental Security Income, as more critical. These many different approaches raise questions. Should transition programs concentrate on transportation issues (drivers' licenses and special transportation services)? Should they include a focus on housing? Should the only focus be on getting a job? Should self-advocacy be included in all transition programs?

Transition programs are relatively new; there is little consistency in them and little in the way of research or evaluation results on their effectiveness. Rusch and DeStefano (1989), for example, created a list of "transition indicators" that could be used to evaluate transition programs:

- Early planning

- Interagency coordination

- Individualized transition plans

- Emphasis on integration

- Community-relevant curriculum

- Community-based training

- Business linkages

- Job placement

- Ongoing staff development

- Program evaluation

This list, of course, emphasized what its developers considered important. Halloran (1989) contended that effective transition programs have three essential components:

- Families of youths with disabilities are included as partners in developing and implementing purposeful activities that maximize independence.

- The program is community based, providing opportunities to experience and succeed in employment and other aspects of community life.

- Working partnerships exist with employers so that school efforts are consistent with employers' needs.

Berkell and Gaylord-Ross (1989) cited the transition program goals suggested by McDonnell, Sheehan, and Wilcox (1983):

• To provide opportunities and services that support quality adult living

• To maintain community integration in all living and work environments with people without disabilities

• To maximize the productivity and independence of those leaving school

These dimensions, however, do not really describe what transition programs must look like (see Table 11.3). Nor do they address the suggestion made by other researchers that successful programs take into consideration local differences (Halloran, 1989). Thus, the extent to which any specific program may transfer from one location to another is questionable.

Berkell and Gaylord-Ross (1989) suggested that transition programs should focus not on traditional diagnostic labels but on a functional analysis of disabilities (see Figure 11.1). They argued that this approach allows programs to focus on individual ability levels and learner needs. Essentially, they were arguing for a noncategorical approach to transition programming.

The Beginning of Postschool Services

For some time, thoughts about postschool transition were restricted to the year in which, or maybe the year before the one in which, the student was expected to leave school. It soon became evident, however, that this was too late, and schools began to address the transition needs of students several years before they were actually scheduled to leave school. The enactment of PL 101-476 indicated that transition services needed by a student should be included on the IEP beginning no later than age sixteen. But this does not say when transition services should begin. Perhaps they should begin at age fourteen or earlier for the student already on the pathway to dropping out. Perhaps they are not needed until age seventeen for the student with a mild hearing impairment and no associated difficulties. How soon before leaving school can educators be sure that students will maintain, rather than lose, critical skills? How long does it take to present all the transition skills that a student will need when the time comes to leave school? Should not the goals of transition programs actually be the goals of education, if those are critical for a student to have when leaving school?

Graduation Requirements

Today a high school diploma is a critical part of a student's transition from school to work. This has been found to be true for special education students (Thornton & Zigmond, 1986) just as for other students (see Wolman, Bruininks, & Thurlow, 1989). Yet states, and even districts within states, do not have consistent policies regarding the awarding of graduation diplomas to students in special education

TABLE 11.3 Sample transition planning process

Team Goals	Activities	Responsible Person	Time Line
To establish an individual transition team	1. Contact rehabilitation services to identify counselor 2. Contact developmental disabilities to identify a case manager 3. Identify ancillary staff (speech pathologist, occupational therapist, etc.) for team participation 4. Contact student's parents	Student's special education teacher	Sept. 1, 1985
To write an individual transition plan identifying long- and short-term transition objectives	1. Conduct a transition team meeting as part of the IEP process 2. Identify possible short-term and long-term employment and residential objectives 3. Assign responsibilities for implementation	Individual transition team members: • Special education teacher • Vocational education teacher • Developmental disabilities case manager • Rehabilitation counselor • Parents • Students	Oct. 1, 1985

To identify goals and procedures to assure student is provided with community-based vocational training	1. Identify job training sites for student:
	  (a) food services
	  (b) janitorial
	  (c) micrographics
	2. Utilize the supported work model for training
	3. Train at least four hours per school day, four days a week, at the job site
	4. Monitor and evaluate each position
		• Special education teacher
		• Vocational education teacher
		• Rehabilitation counselor
		• Developmental disabilities case manager
		• Occupational and physical therapists
		• Student
			Completed by Sept. 30, 1986

TABLE 11.3   Sample transition planning process (cont.)

Team Goals	Activities	Responsible Person	Time Line
To identify a job for student to begin her or his last year of school	1. Survey job market based on findings of job training 2. Establish employer interviews 3. Identify additional skills that require training, i.e., transportation, communication 4. Conduct job placement and training following the supported employment model	• Special education teacher • Vocational education teacher • Developmental disabilities case manager • Parents • Employer	Completed by Sept. 1, 1987
To provide supported employment services as needed after graduation	1. Determine a plan for a shift of responsibilities from the school system to adult service agencies 2. Assign responsibilities for job placement and follow-along services 3. Determine a plan for communication among team members and cooperating agencies throughout the transition years	• Developmental disabilities case manager • Rehabilitation counselor • Parents • Employer • Special education teacher • Vocational education teacher	June 1, 1988

SOURCE: Wehman, P., Moon, M., Everson, J., Wood, W., & Barcus, J. *Transition from school to work: New challenges for youth with severe disabilities*. Paul H. Brookes Publishing Co., P.O. Box 10624, Baltimore, MD 21285-0624. Copyright © 1988. Used with permission.

FIGURE 11.1   Functional Analysis Suggested by Berkell and Gaylord-Ross

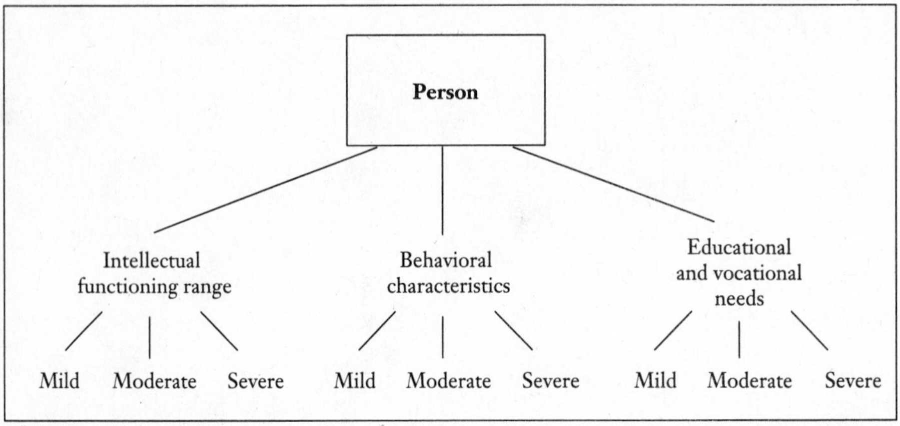

SOURCE: Berkell, D., & Gaylord-Ross, R. (1989). The concept of transition: Historical and current developments. In D. E. Berkell & J. M. Brown (Eds.), *Transition from school to work for persons with disabilities* (pp. 1–21). New York: Longman. Copyright © 1989 by Longman Publishing Group. Reprinted with permission from Longman Publishing Group.

programs. In addition to some students who receive regular graduation diplomas (by meeting regular school requirements, adjusted school requirements, or regular school requirements through modified classes), many students in special education leave schools with a certificate of completion, or they leave because they have reached the maximum age for which services are provided (aging out). Dropping out of school is not included in the discussion here, although it is another way students in special education frequently leave school. In the 1990 annual report to Congress, the U.S. Department of Education reported that approximately 42 percent of students with disabilities received a graduation diploma, 11 percent received a certificate, and 2.5 percent reached the maximum age allowed by the state for special education services (27 percent dropped out).

Clarification is needed about what states require for a student to receive an official diploma, rather than a certification of completion. In a comprehensive study conducted in 1987, Bodner, Clark, and Mellard found that thirty-six states had *increased* graduation requirements since implementation of PL 94-142 and that another set of thirty-six states had made some allowance for students in special education. At the time of their survey, Bodner and his associates found that thirty-one states had state policies determining exit documents, while the remaining states allowed local districts to make these determinations. Seventeen states required that different exit documents be awarded to students in regular and special education. Data from 1989 collected by the Council of Chief State School Officers (1990) indicated that twenty-six of the fifty-four states and territories had different graduation requirements for "IEP Completers," but the exact nature of these requirements was not provided.

The practice of allowing students to leave the regular school setting to earn a high school equivalency diploma by taking GED (General Educational Development) tests generates several questions for special educators. Is this a viable alternative route for students with disabilities? Or is this route simply one that achieves the goal (approved avenue for graduation), is achievable through intensive tutoring, but provides the student with few useable skills for entry into either work or some type of postsecondary education?

Kortering, Julnes, and Edgar attempted to address the graduation issue by looking at pertinent components of the U.S. Constitution, the Rehabilitation Act, PL 94-142, and their legal interpretations in case law. Kortering et al. noted that "courts have limited their reviews of cases pertaining to special education students and graduation to procedural concerns. . . . The result has been a set of judicial reviews that are limited in scope, yet they do provide specific guidelines to the local district" (1990, p. 12). Kortering et al. went on to delineate four guidelines that they believed could be drawn from the courts:

> First, the local district has the discretion to restrict the awarding of standard diplomas. . . . A second guideline is that procedures resulting in the differentiation of special education students should be based on standards that are both fair and have been articulated to the student and his or her parents. . . . A third guideline is that the local district keep in mind the courts' inclination to leave the responsibility of substantive academic matters to the expertise of professional educators. . . . A fourth guideline is that the goals and objectives stated on the IEP provide a proper means for evaluating whether a student can be graduated. (pp. 12–13)

The authors concluded their discussion by stating, "We have the opportunity, if not absolute duty, to define, in practice and outcome, what constitutes the graduation of special education students. A necessary first step is to establish, at the local level, how and when to graduate special education students" (p. 13). Until we are able to do as Kortering et al. suggested, it is not possible even to obtain a good assessment of the suggested differential effects of varying exit documents (e.g., Higgins, 1979).

Anticipated Services

With the enactment of PL 98-199, states were required by the Office of Special Education Programs to report on the types of services children and youths with disabilities who were exiting the educational system would need. In response to this requirement, states indicated that the most frequently needed service for youths with disabilities leaving the special education system was vocation/training services (U.S. Dept. of Education, 1990b). Next most frequently needed services were counseling and guidance. Much concern was expressed about the validity of these data, however; it was suggested that teachers and others submitting the information to states were not familiar enough with adult service agencies to be able to identify those a student might need. States reported to the federal agency the difficulty of collecting anticipated services data. In response, in 1990 funding

High School Diploma Alternatives

Each year more than 235,000 students with handicaps exit the secondary school system. Of this number, 27.4% drop-out before they obtain a diploma or certificate. At the same time, however, more than 350,000 adults annually earn alternative high school diplomas, either for personal satisfaction or as a means of qualifying for postsecondary study. Adults with or without a disability seeking a high school diploma (whether or not they have ever worked) may be eligible to participate on one of the three programs widely available for adults to earn a high school diploma.

General Educational Development—GED Program
The most common method of obtaining a high school equivalency diploma for people, including those with disabilities, is by passing the Tests of General Educational Development (GED). The GED Tests are designed to measure general knowledge and thinking skills, not specific facts, in the areas of writing, social studies, science, literature and the arts, and mathematics. Although these are skills usually learned in high school, the examinee may have obtained them through life or work experience, reading, and informal education. Alternatively, the GED candidate may learn the skills by attending GED classes available in various community settings.

Special editions of the GED Tests are available in braille, audiocassette, and large print formats for people who are visually impaired or who do not read standard print. For an examinee with a physical or cognitive disability that prevents being fairly tested under standard conditions, modifications of standard testing conditions may be used. For example, an examinee may be allowed additional time, the use of special adaptive devices, a scribe to record answers, or an individualized location. Special arrangements for testing candidates with disabilities can be made by the GED Chief Examiner with the approval of the state or province GED Administrator. For an Adult with specific learning disabilities, special testing must be approved by the GED Testing Service (GEDTS) as described in the booklet GED Test Accommodations for Candidates with Specific Learning Disabilities. Not all individuals with disabilities are entitled to special testing. Only examinees who can document the fact that the disability interferes with the ability to be tested fairly will be granted such accommodations by the GED Chief Examiner at the facility.

Earning a high school diploma by passing the GED Tests is not easy. Passing scores are established so that approximately 30% of graduating high school seniors cannot pass. Special editions of the test are no easier than regular print editions.

External Diploma Program—EDP
The External Diploma Program (EDP), another national adult high school completion program, designed to increase the number of high school

High School Diploma Alternatives (cont.)

graduates, was established in New York state in 1973. In 1979, the US Department of Education validated the program through the Joint Dissemination Review Process and eleven states have adopted the program. The program enrolls about 4,000 adults each year. In March 1990, the American Council on Education's Center for Adult Learning and Educational Credentials, which also sponsors the GED Testing Service, assumed the leadership responsibility of the program.

EDP offers adults who did not graduate from high school an opportunity to earn a high school diploma by demonstrating that they have competencies and skills generally expected of a high school graduate. Like the GED, the EDP is an assessment program. Reading comprehension skills, mathematical problem solving, and writing ability, as well as self-awareness, social awareness, consumer awareness, scientific awareness, and occupational preparedness must be demonstrated at a mastery level. In addition one individual competency must be demonstrated in an academic, occupational, or special talent area.

The process of the External Diploma Program begins with an evaluation of the basic academic skills. A candidate who needs to review skills is referred to educational resources within the community. With this procedure, the EDP builds on existing resources rather than requiring new ones.

The individual assessment approach appeals especially to mid-life and mid-career adults. Most adults completing the EDP are between 35 and 45 years old, are persons employed or returning to the workforce and wish to continue in some sort of postsecondary education or desire to qualify for additional occupational advancement. The EDP provides an individual the opportunity to qualify for credit based on previous career or volunteer service.

After the initial diagnostic phase, individuals enter the actual assessment, during which adults are required to demonstrate to a trained EDP evaluator 64 generalized competencies in life skills simulations. Since each assessment is individualized, it proceeds at the pace of the individual. Most adults complete the process within 6–9 months.

Adult High School Diploma

Adult High School Diploma (Carnegie Credits) is a program in which credit is given for courses, work experience, and life experiences. Students may earn credit by participating in time-based courses; completing independent study projects designed to demonstrate course proficiencies;

(continued)

High School Diploma Alternatives (cont.)

by demonstrating skills and knowledge through tests. A student's educational plan could include all three ways of earning credit. For example, basic military training, previous work experience, apprenticeship, or college credit may each be used to acknowledge necessary learning. The maximum number of credits which can be awarded in each category is set by the State Department of Education. The graduation requirements for adult students in a school system are the same as those for the students who are enrolled in the K–12 program. The Adult High School Diploma candidate should contact the local Board of Education for specific information.

The GED, EDP, and Adult High School Diploma are the most popular ways available for a person who left high school without a diploma. Additional routes to earning a high school diploma can be determined by contacting the Adult Education Department in each state or locality. At present the GED is the only high school equivalency option that specifically provides special accommodations for adults with disabilities, however, accommodations may be requested and provided in all options described.

SOURCE: National Clearinghouse on Postsecondary Education for Individuals with Disabilities, *Information from HEATH* 10(1) (January-February 1991). Reprinted by permission. For more information, contact GED Testing Service (Special Testing) and EDP, Center for Adult Learning and Educational Credentials, both at One Dupont Circle, Suite 20, Washington, DC 20036.

---

was awarded to the American Institute for Research (AIR) to develop and study student performance indicators of service needs. AIR planned to refine an instrument it had designed to collect data on anticipated services, which provided a list of services and definitions of them for the person completing the instrument.

Services for Transition to Postsecondary Training

Even though many individuals believe that vocational training is the key to transition for students with disabilities, a growing number of parents wondered why their children with normal intellectual capacities were not going to college or being encouraged to do so. Indeed, most students with mild disabilities apparently were not being encouraged to pursue any type of postsecondary training. This view was supported by data from the National Longitudinal Transition Study, which showed that only 15 percent of students in special education proceeded on to any type of postsecondary education following completion of high school (Butler-Nalin, Marder, & Shaver, 1989). The 15 percent included approximately 10 percent in a vocational or trade school, less than 5 percent in a two-year college, and less than 2 percent in a four-year college. In each of these situations, the percentages reflected only students who took at least one course, not students enrolled in a program to completion.

Much of the impetus for college services for students who had been in special education in high school came from parents of students with learning disabilities—that is, students who had normal intellectual capabilities but whose academic achievement was below the expected level. During the 1980s, universities and colleges across the United States found themselves pressured into providing programs for students with disabilities, particularly students with learning disabilities. One source of pressure, already noted, was the parents of young adults with learning disabilities. The other source was Section 504 of the Rehabilitation Act of 1973, which required that institutions of higher education receiving federal grants make accommodations to the physical or mental limitations of applicants. Accommodations viewed as reasonable under this mandate included changing schedules, relocating program components, and modifying equipment.

Surveys of postsecondary programs have typically focused on services provided to students with learning disabilities. In one study (Beirne-Smith & Deck, 1989), four-year colleges and universities offering services for students with learning disabilities were found most often to provide basic tutoring, then a reader for the student, then note-taking assistance. Recognition of nonacademic needs was also evident in the 108 responding institutions. Included here were referrals to other campus programs, community services, consultation with faculty, and individual counseling. Another study, conducted by Woods, Sedlacek, and Boyer (1990), found similar services in a survey of thirteen large state universities identified by the Disabled Student Service National Data Bank as providing comprehensive services to at least twenty students with learning disabilities. Primary support services provided by all included tutoring, test administration service, and consultation to faculty on classroom accommodations. These were followed closely by reader service, which was provided by 92 percent. Woods et al. also looked at accommodations and found that all responding institutions allowed students to have extra time for exams; 85 percent also arranged for testing in an alternate format. The extent to which these services and other accommodations for students with learning disabilities, and other disabilities as well, make a difference is not well documented at this time.

Adult Illiteracy

Literacy became a big issue in the late 1980s when the nation's first lady identified it as her priority. Literacy became one of the nation's educational goals in 1990 following the historic summit meeting of the president and the nation's governors. In the process of giving renewed emphasis to literacy, various reports indicated

FIGURE 11.2 Number of States Providing Special Education Services up
to Maximum Ages between 17 and 25

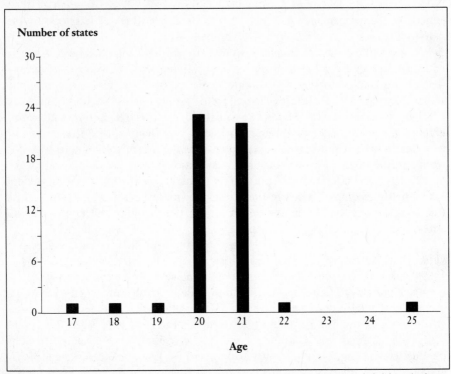

NOTE: One state that provides services for thirteen years, beginning in kindergarten, is excluded from the figure.
SOURCE: U.S. Department of Education. (1990b). *To assure the free appropriate public education of all handicapped children: Twelfth annual report to Congress on the implementation of the Education of the Handicapped Act.* Washington, DC: Author.

that functional illiteracy characterized 13 percent of seventeen-year-olds and 40 percent of minority youths, that only 16 percent of seventeen-year-olds had adequate reading skills, that only 5 percent of seventeen-year-olds had advanced reading skills, and that at all grade levels students were unable to express themselves well enough to ensure that their writing would accomplish its purpose.

Literacy issues have become identified to a large extent with disadvantaged, often minority populations. Illiteracy has many times been associated with dropouts and with the tremendous costs of these former students to society. The meaning of literacy, because it is a socially defined term, has been expanded beyond the traditional academic scope to encompass quantitative literacy (e.g., Rivera-Batiz, 1990) and workplace literacy (see Gadsden, Wagner, & Hirschhorn, 1990).

Common approaches to attacking the problem of illiteracy are directed at reducing the number of dropouts and changing the repetitive pattern of illiteracy within families. Programs have been directed not only at the adult level, where the effects of illiteracy are most evident and pronounced, but also at the primary and secondary school levels (Stacey, Alsalam, Gilmore, & To, 1988). Chapter I programs are often cited as a school intervention for illiteracy, and dramatic proposals have even emphasized early childhood reading development programs (National Governors' Association, 1986).

The most notable aspect of the literacy issue is the lack of attention to individuals with disabilities. Indeed, an extensive adult literacy survey being conducted by the National Center on Education Statistics appears to be excluding individuals with disabilities from the sample. Nevertheless, educators must ask how many students in special education end up as part of America's illiterate; if the numbers are significant, perhaps exceptional students should be included in the educational system for more years than is now the case. Some states provide special education services until only age seventeen, whereas others provide services through age twenty-five (see Figure 11.2). Does providing services later in life make a difference? Is it worth the investment? Much is unknown and has to be addressed.

Discussion Questions

1. Is there a need to be concerned about transitions for students with disabilities other than those transitions occurring when the student leaves school?

2. What is the best way to ensure a smooth transition from a preschool special education program to an elementary school program?

3. Is it more important for a student in special education to stay in school (being helped to do so by whatever means needed) or to master basic skills?

4. Are there other essential components of effective programs for keeping students in special education engaged in school beyond those suggested by Edgar (1991) and Zigmond (1990)?

5. What is the best solution to the graduation requirement dilemma? Are reform agendas for general education and the needs of students in special education at the time of leaving school completely at odds?

6. How should adult literacy be defined for students who have been in special education programs? Is this definition different from that for the general population?

CHAPTER 12

Legal Issues

The Roles of Legislatures and Courts in American Education
Where Do Laws and Rules Come From?
Definitional Issues
Categorization, Classification, and Eligibility Issues
Assessment Issues
The Magnitude and Validity of Testing
Instruction Issues
School Outcomes Issues
Early Intervention
Transition Issues
Economic Issues
Home-School Collaboration Issues
Unresolved Issues

'Tis easier to make certain things legal than to make them legitimate.

—*Nicholas Chamfort*

Students who are handicapped have the legal right to a free appropriate public education. But this leaves unresolved that matter of who may be considered handicapped, who decides that students are handicapped, and who decides they need to be tested. Likewise, it does not address the extent to which parents have the right to disagree with decisions the schools make about their children, to refuse to have their children evaluated, and to turn elsewhere, if possible, for help when they disagree with school decisions. Who pays for the very extensive extra services required by some students who are handicapped? Should students who are handicapped receive the same high school diploma as students who are not handicapped? Do students who are gifted have the right to special education services (gifted students are not listed in federal legislation)? These and other legal issues permeate special education.

Consider this scenario: Harold is considered emotionally disturbed and suicidal. His parents want to place him in a private residential facility where he can receive round-the-clock supervision and care. The cost for this facility is $50,000 per year. Who pays the cost?

Or consider this scenario: Roberto is a seven-year-old child with AIDS. Is he eligible for special education services, and if so, under what category? And under what circumstances may he be suspended or excluded from school?

The field of special education is loaded with legal questions such as these. Indeed, educators today are as much concerned with matters of litigation and legislation as of education. Since the beginning of the 1970s, the courts and the federal and state legislatures have become deeply involved in the process of schooling, and educators, especially special educators, have been compelled year by year to comply with an ever-larger number of court mandates and laws. Litigation regarding special education has focused on the extent to which the schools, by virtue of administrative arrangements and decisions, deny the equal protection of the law to many students. Earlier litigation concentrated on the right to treatment (education) and due process, but more recently, litigation has addressed the assessment of students and accompanying decision-making practices. Since the late 1970s, many of the methods by which educators assign students to instructional alternatives have been challenged, school assessment practices have been cited as discriminatory, and schools have been charged with failing to provide appropriate education to minority students and/or students with handicaps.

These students always have been with us; it is the attention they receive from the courts and legislatures that makes them more important now. School systems that fail to comply with the mandates of federal legislation are threatened with losing funds appropriated by Congress.

Contemporary litigation and legislation are based on efforts to clarify and in some cases to redefine the fundamental purposes of schooling. Earlier we observed that three ideas directed the development of American education: democracy, nationalism, and individualism. We described the four basic values and ideals of democracy: the worth of the individual, the equality of all individuals, the equality of opportunity, and faith in reason. Two of these ideals—equality of all individuals and equality of opportunity—are rights guaranteed by the equal protection clause (the Fourteenth Amendment) of the U.S. Constitution. It is the Fourteenth Amendment that has been cited as being violated most often when the actions of schools have been tested in the courts. (For a comprehensive treatment of legal issues in special education, see Rothstein [1990].)

The Roles of Legislatures and Courts in American Education

The idea of public schooling initiated the legislative action that enabled the Commonwealth of Massachusetts to tax its citizens for the purpose of establishing schools and providing children with free education. But until recently, the courts have had a hands-off policy toward the affairs of schools. As Bersoff noted, "There was a time when the behavior of school officials went virtually unexamined by the courts. Pleading lack of expert knowledge, judges were wary of interfering with the discretion of administrators to educate their students" (1979, p. 31). In

Selected, Key Federal Statutes Affecting the Education and Civil Rights of Children and Youth with Disabilities

P.L. 99-372, The Handicapped Children's Protection Act of 1986.
This law provides for reasonable attorneys' fees and costs to parents and guardians who prevail in administrative hearings or court when there is a dispute with a school system concerning their child's right to a free appropriate special education and related services.

P.L. 99-457, The Education of the Handicapped Act Amendments of 1986.
This law mandates services for preschoolers with disabilities and established the Part H program to assist states in the development of a comprehensive, multidisciplinary, and statewide system of early intervention services for infants and toddlers (birth to age 3). This law also reauthorized the discretionary programs and expanded transition programs.

P.L. 100-407, The Technology-Related Assistance for Individuals with Disabilities Act of 1988.
The primary purpose of this law is to assist states in developing comprehensive, consumer-responsive programs of technology-related assistance and to extend the availability of technology to individuals with disabilities and their families. Assistive technology device is broadly defined in the law to give the states flexibility in the programs to be developed. Assistive technology services under this law include 8 activities related to developing consumer-responsive services with federal funds.

P.L. 101-127, The Children with Disabilities Temporary Care Reauthorization Act of 1989.
This law is actually a part of a larger federal law, the Children's Justice Act, P.L. 99-401. Title II of this law includes provisions to fund temporary child care (e.g., respite care) for children who have a disability or chronic illness and crisis nurseries for children at risk of abuse or neglect. In 1989, P.L. 101-127 extended and expanded this program for two years and included an increase in funding for these programs from $5 million to $20 million in 1990 and 1991. By July, 1990, 87 grants were awarded to states to develop and establish respite care programs and crisis nurseries.

Selected, Key Federal Statutes Affecting the Education and Civil Rights of Children and Youth with Disabilities (cont.)

P.L. 101-336, The Americans with Disabilities Act of 1990.
This law, based on the concepts of the Rehabilitation Act of 1973, guarantees equal opportunity for individuals with disabilities in employment, public accommodation, transportation, State and local government services, and telecommunications. The ADA is the most significant federal law assuring the full civil rights of all individuals with disabilities.

P.L. 101-392, The Carl D. Perkins Vocational and Applied Technology Education Act of 1990.
This law amended P.L. 98-524 for the purpose of making the United States more competitive in the world economy. This law is closely interwoven with the Education of the Handicapped Act (P.L. 94-142) toward guaranteeing full vocational education opportunity for youth with disabilities.

P.L. 101-476, The Education of the Handicapped Act Amendments of 1990.
This law changed the name of EHA to the Individuals with Disabilities Education Act (IDEA). This law reauthorized and expanded the discretionary programs, mandated transition services and assistive technology services to be included in a child's or youth's IEP, and added autism and traumatic brain injury to the list of categories of children and youth eligible for special education and related services.

P.L. 101-496, The Developmental Disabilities Assistance and Bill of Rights Act of 1990.
This law authorizes grants to support the planning, coordination, and delivery of specialized services to persons with developmental disabilities. In addition, this law provides funding for the operation of state protection and advocacy systems for persons with developmental disabilities. The original law was enacted in 1963 by P.L. 88-164. In 1987, P.L. 100-146 significantly expanded the Act to include persons with mental retardation, autism, cerebral palsy, and epilepsy.

SOURCE: Home, R. L. (1991). Selected key federal statutes affecting the education and civil rights of children and youth with disabilities. *News Digest,* 1(1), p. 13. Used with permission. For a free copy or subscription, contact National Information Center for Children and Youth with Disabilities, 1-800-999-5599.

amplifying his remarks, Bersoff cited a portion of the record in an 1893 case, *Watson* v. *City of Cambridge,* in which the court stated:

> The management of schools involves many details, and it is important that a board of public officers . . . having jurisdiction to regulate the internal affairs of the schools should not be interfered with or have their conduct called into question before another tribunal. . . . A jury composed of men of no special fitness to decide educational questions should not be permitted to say that their answer is wrong. (p. 864)

Bersoff also reported that as recently as 1968 the courts maintained a hands-off policy on intervention into the affairs of the school, as evidenced in *Epperson* v. *Arkansas:* "Courts do not and cannot intervene in the resolution of conflicts which arise in the daily operation of school systems and which do not directly and sharply implicate basic constitutional values" (p. 104).

The courts' hands-off policy can be said to have ended with the U.S. Supreme Court's declaration in *Tinker* v. *Des Moines Independent Community School District* (1969) that "students in school as well as out of schools are persons under our Constitution . . . possessed of fundamental rights which the State must respect" (p. 515). Since 1969, according to Bersoff,

> [the Supreme Court] . . . has decided such issues as the reach of compulsory education laws, the requirements of due process prior to infliction of disciplinary and academic sanctions, the immunity of school officials from money damage liability for violations of students' civil rights, the allocation of financial resources to pupils in poor school districts, the education of non-English speaking children, the permissibility of sex-separate high schools, the legality of special admissions programs for minorities, the obligation of colleges and universities to admit handicapped students, and most recently, the validity of system-wide remedies to reduce school segregation. (1979, p. 33)

Over time, special education has undergone radical changes as a result of judicial and legislative actions (see box). But the situation produced by these changes is a dynamic one because the law is always changing. Practices that were followed yesterday may be illegal today, and procedures that are required today may be replaced by others tomorrow. Laws, rules, and regulations change as society's social and economic priorities change. Nevertheless, despite the evolutionary nature of the process, at any time the specific laws, practices, and procedures that govern education are expected to reflect the broad principles of freedom and equality that society through the Constitution has agreed on. As we write this text—even as you read it—Congress, state legislatures, and the courts are shaping public policy in special education by making and interpreting laws that affect how students are treated in the schools.

Where Do Laws and Rules Come From?

Practices in special education today have been shaped in good part by national and state constitutions and laws, administrative regulations and guidelines, court

FIGURE 12.1   The legal basis for special education

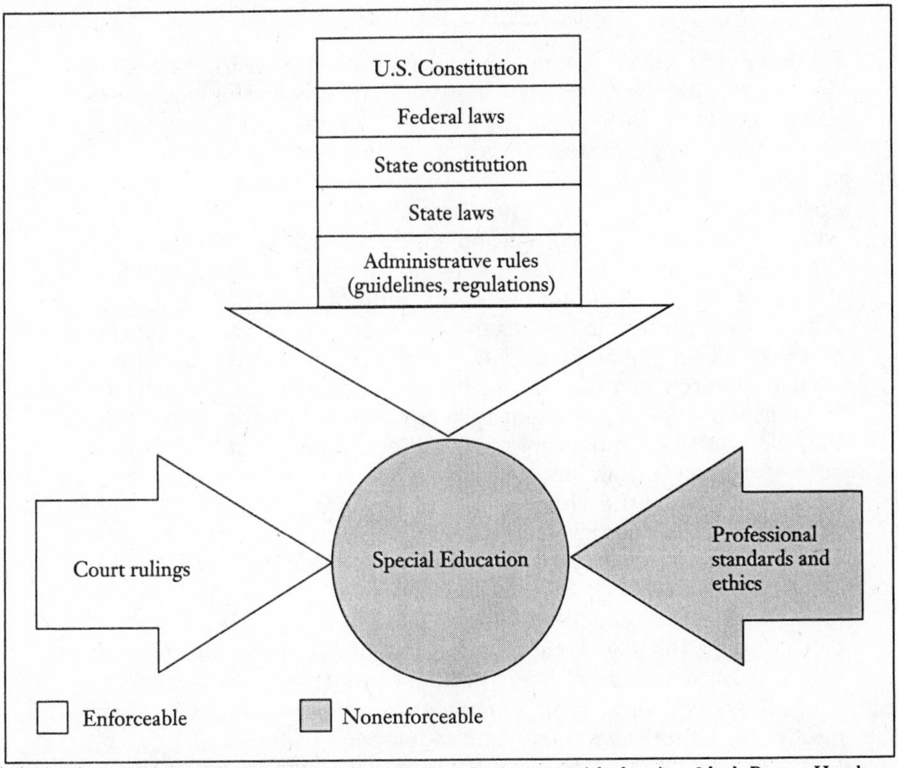

U.S. Constitution

Federal laws

State constitution

State laws

Administrative rules
(guidelines, regulations)

Court rulings

Special Education

Professional
standards and
ethics

☐ Enforceable   ▨ Nonenforceable

SOURCE: Ysseldyke, J. E., & Algozzine, B. (1990). Introduction to special education. 2d ed. Boston: Houghton Mifflin, p. 41. Used with permission.

rulings, and the standards and ethics of the profession. The relationship among these elements is shown in Figure 12.1

Federal and state constitutions set forth broad political principles that guide the lawmaking process at both national and state levels, which defines certain elements of education (see box). Administrative rules and regulations are usually written to clarify laws and have the force of law.

The courts interpret these laws, regulations, and guidelines in light of the Constitution and precedent (earlier related judicial decisions, especially those in the same jurisdiction as that held by the court). Although in theory the courts are not lawmaking bodies, their rulings can change existing law, a situation that by implication gives courts the power to make new laws. As a result, courts regulate who receives special education and what type is provided (Ysseldyke & Algozzine, 1990).

Professional standards and codes of ethics have indirect influence on the practice of special education. The standards that bear most directly on that practice are

---

How Federal Laws and Regulations are Determined

It is helpful to know how laws are named or referred to. Whenever an Act is passed by the Congress and signed into law by the President, it is given a number, such as P.L. 94-142. "P.L." stands for **Public Law**. The first set of numbers means the session of Congress during which the law was passed. For example, the 94 means the 94th session of the U.S. Congress. The second set of numbers identifies what number the law was in the sequence of passage and enactment during that session. Thus, the 142 means that this was the 142nd law that Congress passed and the President signed during the 94th session of Congress.

It is also important to understand that federal laws are often changed, or amended, regularly. Public Law 94-142, the Education for All Handicapped Children Act, has had several amendments since its passage in 1975. Therefore, it is important to keep up-to-date on these changes, as they often affect the delivery of special education, related services, and other programs in your state.

Laws passed by the Congress provide a general framework of policy related to a particular issue. Once a law is passed, Congress delegates to an administrative agency within the Executive Branch the task of developing detailed regulations to guide the law's implementation. Federal regulations are detailed in the *Code of Federal Regulations* (*CFR*). The *CFR* interprets the law, discusses each point of a law, and further explains it. Copies of most federal regulations are available in the public library. The *CFR* is readable and helpful in understanding the laws. State agencies must comply with federal laws and regulations.

At the federal level, special education is an area in which elaborate sets of regulations exist. The regulations for the Education of the Handicapped Act, for example, spell out the procedures and programming that must be provided to children and youth with disabilities in order for states to receive federal funds. States may go beyond what is required in the regulations. For example, some states have broader definitions of which children are entitled to special education and, thus, may include gifted children in their special education programming.

SOURCE: Home, R. L. (1991). How federal laws and regulations are determined. *News Digest*, 1(1), 2. Used with permission. For a free copy or subscription, contact National Information Center for Children and Youth with Disabilities, 1-800-999-5599.

---

the Standards for Professional Practice published by the Council for Exceptional Children (CEC). These standards identify instructional responsibilities, behavioral management techniques, the amount of instruction and supervision required to perform support services, responsibilities to parents, and advocacy standards. They also define criteria for professional employment, professional development, and intra- and inter-professional behavior. The CEC Code of Ethics defines broad principles that special educators are responsible for upholding and advancing.

. . . For the most part, in special education as in general education, professional standards and ethical codes are not enforceable; they do not have the power of law. But this does not mean that they are not important. Although a school district would not take legal action against a teacher for unethical conduct, it probably would take formal action to dismiss the teacher. (pp. 44–45)

Courts, legislatures, and administrative agencies act as checks on one another in the lawmaking and rule-making process. To illustrate this interaction, Rothstein (1990) cited activities regarding who pays attorneys' fees. In 1975, Congress passed PL 94-142, which did not specify responsibility for paying attorneys' fees incurred as part of due process hearings. In 1984, the Supreme Court decided in *Smith* v. *Robinson* that parents could not recover the money they spent on attorneys' fees. In 1986, Congress responded to that decision by passing the Handicapped Children's Protection Act, which said that in some situations attorneys' fees could be paid by school districts. The issue is now being argued in the lower courts, and there is pressure on personnel in the U.S. Department of Education to develop guidelines to aid school districts and parents in deciding when attorneys' fees can be reimbursed. The issue may again rise to the Supreme Court level.

It is hard to identify the extent to which specific court rulings affect individual school districts and even specific states because there are actually fifty-one separate court systems in the United States. There are three levels of federal courts: the U.S. Supreme Court, the appeals courts, and the federal district courts. Each state has a supreme court, a court of appeals, and trials courts (see Fisher and Sorenson [1985] for a picture of the various levels and alternative paths a judicial controversy can take). The rulings of the courts are applicable only in their specific jurisdiction. Supreme Court rulings apply everywhere. The rulings of a U.S. appeals court apply only in the region served by that court. The rulings of a state trial court are applicable only in the area in that state served by the court.

There are many ways in which we could share with you the critical legal issues confronting the fields of special and remedial education. The most comprehensive treatment of legal issues in special education to date is a 1990 text by Laura Rothstein entitled *Special Education Law*. Rothstein's text is an issues-oriented text, and legal cases are organized by specific issues. The text is must reading for those concerned about legal issues in special education. We deal with essentially the same issues as does Rothstein, but we have organized them in the same way in which our textbook is organized. We have relied heavily on Rothstein's work in clarifying our own thinking on the issues. Those who want more specifics and details regarding these issues are encouraged to read Rothstein.

Definitional Issues

When provisions for education are specified in law, they are not necessarily accompanied by corresponding definitions. Thus, a law can declare that students be educated in the least restrictive environment but leave the definition of LRE to the courts and to local education agencies. As a result, several complex definitional issues have been debated in the courts, and the outcomes have directly affected the life opportunities of many students.

The Definition of a Handicap   One of these issues is what constitutes a handicap. The Education for all Handicapped Children Act lists eleven categories of handicapping conditions eligible for services. Some groups (for example, students who are gifted) are not covered by the legislation, and students who need related services but do not require special education may be excluded. There are major questions regarding the extent to which students who have chronic infectious diseases (hemophilia, AIDS, tuberculosis) are eligible for special education. The courts have taken positions on such issues. For example, in *Espino* v. *Besteiro* (1981), a district court in Texas required that the school air-condition a classroom for a single student who could not regulate his body temperature. In *Antkowiak* v. *Ambach* (1986), a district court in New York ruled that a gifted student who had anorexia was eligible for placement in the Devereaux Treatment Center at no cost to her parents because her anorexia was due to underlying emotional disturbance. In *Roe* v. *Commonwealth of Pennsylvania* (1986), a Pennsylvania district court ruled that a student with an IQ lower than 130 was not entitled to special education for gifted students. In *School District of Nassau County* v. *Arline* (1987), the U.S. Supreme Court ruled that a student with tuberculosis could be considered a handicapped person under Section 504 of the Rehabilitation Act.

The Definition of Right to Education   An important court decision that set the stage for later litigation, including that in *Arline*, was *Tinker* v. *Des Moines Independent Community School District* (1969). The issue it addressed was the right of students to wear black armbands to protest the Vietnam War. The Supreme Court ruled that children and youths were "persons" under the Constitution and had First Amendment rights independent of their parents, and it reaffirmed that children and youths did not lose their civil rights when they attended school. The establishment of the principle that children and youths are persons who have rights was later cited in many judicial rulings relating to special education.

The courts have also tried to define the concept of the right to education. In *Mills* v. *Board of Education* (1972), the district court in Washington, DC, ruled that all students with mental retardation had the right to a free appropriate education and that denial of due process to such students constituted violation of the Fourteenth Amendment. In *PARC* v. *Commonwealth of Pennsylvania* (1972), the court required the Pennsylvania Department of Education to engage in extensive efforts to locate and evaluate all students who were mentally retarded and who were not enrolled in school. In *City of Cleburne* v. *Cleburne Living Center* (1985), the U.S. Supreme Court ruled that students with handicaps did not have the special protection of the law and that people with handicaps should be treated like everyone else. In *Plyler* v. *Doe* (1982), the court said that even though individuals who were mentally retarded would not be given special treatment under the law, education would.

The Definition of Provision of Services   Another issue taken up by the courts is where to draw the line in providing education and services to students—are there some students who are so handicapped that it does not make sense to involve them in an instructional program? In *Timothy* v. *Rochester School District* (1988), the district court in New Hampshire addressed the meaning of the term *uneducable* by ruling that Timothy was too handicapped to profit from learning experiences. Following *Hendrick Hudson District Board of Education* v. *Rowley* (1982), some school districts began taking the stand that prior to qualifying for placement in special education, a child had to be shown to be capable of benefiting from the service. The courts have been slow to accept this argument, however.

The Definition of Appropriate Education   For much of the 1970s and early 1980s, the substantive issues in court cases were eligibility, access to special education, and bias in assessment. Recently, however, courts have been addressing the issue of the appropriateness of services students receive and in the process have been faced with defining "free and appropriate." In 1977, the U.S. Department of Health, Education, and Welfare defined appropriate education as "the provision of regular or special education and related aids and services that . . . are designed to meet individual educational needs of handicapped persons as adequately as the needs of nonhandicapped persons." In the *Rowley* case, the Supreme Court further defined appropriate education as "educational instruction specially designed to meet the unique needs of the handicapped child, supported by such services as are necessary to permit the child to 'benefit' from the instruction" (1982, p. 19). As might be imagined, the courts are still struggling with the question of when students are in a position to benefit from their educational experiences.

Unfortunately, however, these two definitions of appropriate education do not help in identifying the actual or intended meaning of the term *appropriate*. Is an adequate education appropriate, and if so, what is adequate? This dilemma is complicated by the fact that an operational definition of appropriate education would require a statement of the goals of education, which raises a host of other questions. What are the goals of education? How do they differ for students with handicaps and their nondisabled peers? To what extent are these goals even attainable?

Categorization, Classification, and Eligibility Issues

The courts regularly intervene in classification, placement, fee payment, categorization, labeling, and eligibility matters. Because students must be declared eligible for special education services before these can be provided and in most states students must be formally labeled or categorized to receive services, the courts have addressed the extent to which specific students are members of categories and the extent to which students ought to be categorized. In many cases, the substantive issue has been bias in assessment that has resulted in assignment of students to stigmatized categorical groups.

Classification   Classification has been repeatedly addressed by the courts. In 1967, Judge Wright rendered an important decision in the case of *Hansen* v. *Hobson*, which brought suit on behalf of black students who were assigned in disproportionate numbers to lower ability groups or lower tracks in the Washington, DC, schools. The chief argument was against the practice of using pupil performance on standardized aptitude and achievement tests to make grouping or placement decisions. Judge Wright ruled:

> The evidence shows that the method by which track assignments are made depends essentially on standardized aptitude tests which, although given on a system-wide basis, are completely inappropriate for use with a large segment of the student body. Because these tests are standardized primarily on and are relevant to a white middle class group of students, they produce inaccurate and misleading test scores when given to lower class and Negro students. (p. 514)

The courts have been able to demonstrate again and again that educational placements based on pupil performance on ability or achievement tests result in the disproportionate placement in lower tracks of minority students and of those from lower socioeconomic backgrounds. The courts have ruled that these readily observable instances constitute a denial of equal protection of the law.

Placement   Educators today advocate a continuum of placements for students who are handicapped, with the placements varying in degree of restrictiveness. Within such a model, placement in a residential facility is seen as very restrictive. According to Rothstein, *Kruelle* v. *New Castle County School District* (1981) was the earliest major decision on residential placements, and it is "still cited as a standard on the issue" (1990, p. 150). Paul Kruelle was a child with profound retardation for whom the district court recommended full-time residential placement. The U.S. circuit court of appeals upheld the district court recommendation. Both courts ruled that the child required continuous and consistent supervision and that such supervision was not available in the six-hour school program.

The courts can go so far as to mandate placement out of state, as a circuit court did in *Antkowiak* v. *Ambach* when it ruled that the school district had to pay for the child to be enrolled at the Devereaux Treatment Center in Pennsylvania. One category of students for whom placement arguments have been especially prevalent is deaf students. Educators and parents regularly debate whether students who are deaf should attend regular schools or separate facilities. In *Lachman* v. *Illinois State Board of Education* (1988), the circuit court upheld a district court ruling that the child could be educated in a regular school where his educational needs could be met in an appropriate manner.

In debating placement issues such as mainstreaming and least restrictive environment, the courts have also considered the extent to which students have the right to placement with their age-appropriate peers. The issue becomes whether the students have the right to attend not only regular classes but which regular classes. The issue is unsettled. The Supreme Court in *Hendrick-Hudson District Board of Education* v. *Rowley* noted that an appropriate placement must approximate the grade levels used in the state's regular education system.

Payment of Fees   The courts have addressed the payment of fees by school districts for students to attend private schools. In *Burlington School Committee* v. *Department of Education* (1985), the lower courts asked the Supreme Court for a ruling on the meaning of appropriate education. Michael Panaco, a first grader with a specific learning disability, was enrolled in a private school because his parents contended that he was not receiving an education that met his unique needs in the local public school. The Court noted that "where a court determines that a private placement desired by the parents was proper under the Act and that an IEP calling for placement in a public school was inappropriate, it seems clear beyond cavil that appropriate relief includes . . . placing the child in a private school" (p. 231). The Court ruled that the most important element of PL 94-142 was an appropriate educational program, wherever it took place.

Categorization   In addition to debating specific placements, the courts get into the categorization argument. They may, for example, rule in individual cases whether a specific student meets the criteria for being classified mentally retarded, learning disabled, or some other condition. Many court cases have focused on the other health impaired category and have asked whether students who have chronic illnesses are eligible for services under this category. For example, in *School Board of Nassau County* v. *Arline,* the court ruled that a student with tuberculosis could be considered handicapped and a member of the other health impaired category.

Assessment Issues

The courts have regularly entered disputes between parents and schools over whether students should be assessed and how. Courts have gotten involved most often when the issue has been the use of test results in making decisions to place students in allegedly inferior educational environments. In a consent decree reached as part of *Diana* v. *State Board of Education* (1970), the state of California agreed to test all children whose primary language was not English in both their primary language and English, eliminate "unfair verbal items" from tests, re-evaluate all Mexican American and Chinese students enrolled in EMR classes by using only nonverbal items and testing them in their primary language, and develop IQ tests that would reflect Mexican American culture and would be standardized only on Mexican Americans. *Diana* arose when the parents of Mexican American students entered into a class-action suit against the state, arguing that the assignment of Mexican American students to EMR classes on the basis of their performances on standardized intelligence tests was discriminatory. In *Covarubias* v. *San Diego Unified School District* (1971), a consent decree established the right of the plaintiffs and only those plaintiffs to monetary damages as a result of their misclassification as handicapped.

Schools and state education agencies have been charged with discriminatory intent when their assessment practices resulted in the disproportionate assignment of blacks and minority students to special education classes. Although educators and psychologists have been unable to reach a consensus on the meaning of nondiscriminatory assessment, PL 94-142 mandated schools to select and administer assessment devices in racially and culturally nondiscriminatory ways. As early as 1967, the court had ruled in *Hansen* v. *Hobson* that the standardized tests employed by the Washington, DC, schools for making tracking decisions were inappropriate for use with black students because the tests were developed and standardized on white middle-class students. In *Lora* v. *New York City Board of Education* (1978), the assessment procedures of the school district were cited as inadequate and discriminatory. But contrast the decisions in the *Larry P.* and *PASE* cases: whereas in *Larry P.* v. *Riles* (1979) the California State Supreme Court declared discriminatory the IQ tests that were used to place black students in EMR classes, in *PASE* v. *Hannon* (1980) the Illinois district court ruled that two standard intelligence tests were not biased against black children. Without a clear definition of terms such as biased, discriminatory, and nondiscriminatory, decisions on whether tests exhibit these characteristics are at best problematic. As a result, several questions regarding the recent litigation and legislation are still unanswered:

1. How big a difference may (or must) be observed in the test performance of blacks and whites before the test is considered biased?

2. If intelligence tests are banned, how will MR placement be determined?

3. What is race?

4. To what extent are classes for students with handicaps a dead end?

5. Does recent litigation mean the end of EMR classes?

The Magnitude and Validity of Testing

Recent court cases have mandated that testing be limited (*Larry P.* v. *Riles*) and expanded (*Frederick L.* v. *Thomas* [1978]; *Lora* v. *New York City Board of Education*). What, then, should educators do? Should intellectual assessment be discontinued, or should more and better intelligence tests be administered to identify the increasing number of students with handicaps? What are the standards for better tests of intelligence?

According to PL 94-142, tests must be validated for the purposes for which they are used. In *Larry P.* v. *Riles,* Judge Peckham ruled that school personnel could use intelligence tests to make EMR placement decisions regarding black students only if before doing so they could demonstrate that the tests they planned to use were valid for making EMR placement decisions for black students. Sarason and Doris pointed out, however, that

> anyone who sets for himself the task of collecting, describing, and criticizing intelligence tests either currently in use or advertised for use has staked out at least half a career. In the face of such a bewildering array of tests, conceptions, and criticisms, it is understandable if one concludes that far from being naked the emperor not only has a surfeit of clothes but he is wearing them all at the same time. This is said to suggest that as one gets overwhelmed pursuing test after test and tries to organize the various underlying conceptions into some coherent framework, one may well conclude that the concept of intelligence has all the characteristics of an inkblot onto which people have projected meanings on the basis of which they wish to urge other people to see what they see, to "measure" it in the same way they do. (1979, p. 30)

Courts and legislatures have ordered that tests be validated for the purposes for which they are used. Yet examination of some of the purposes for which tests are employed in special and remedial education reveals that educators cannot achieve compliance with the mandate. Tests are used to differentiate individuals; to identify those who are mentally retarded, learning disabled, and emotionally disturbed; and to spot those who have incipient learning disabilities. They are used to identify children who have limited intelligence, body image problems, auditory sequential memory deficits, or figure-ground pathology or who suffer from hysteria, hypochondriasis, and depression. But educators are not certain what these terms mean and what these conditions are and have no idea of what to do (with any degree of validity) when they find them. Sarason and Doris observed that definitions of such conditions as mental retardation, learning disabilities, and emotional disturbance are constantly shifting because they reflect changing societal values and attitudes:

> Why define intelligence and mental retardation? Why measure them? We can now formulate an answer: in the realm of human behavior and actions, the need to define and measure always reflects dominant social needs as the society at the time perceives them, and these perceptions are inevitably colored by moral or value judgments. Neither the substance of definitions nor the types of measuring devices to which they give rise are neutral, dispassionate affairs, although the effectiveness with which the culture transmits these dominant perceptions to us ordinarily obscures how rooted in the culture we and the definitions are. What we take to be "natural" and objective is not free from the influences of social time and place. (1979, p. 36)

How can educators demonstrate the validity of tests for measuring things that are neither defined nor conceptualized? Current measures of traits, aptitudes, and abilities do not provide empirical evidence for their validity as measures of those traits, aptitudes, and abilities.

The courts have also entered into the debate about appropriate assessment by ruling on the meaning of informed consent for evaluations, payment for evaluations, and specific evaluation procedures and limitations. For example, in *Seals* v. *Loftus* (1985), the court ruled that the school had to pay for extensive out-of-school neurological and psychological evaluations. In *Matty T.* v. *Mississippi Department of Education* (1981) and in *Luke S.* v. *Louisiana Department of Education* (1983), the issue was the timeliness and appropriateness of assessment procedures used with black students. The district courts ordered the state departments of education to develop procedures whereby school personnel could and would engage in prereferral interventions before referring students for evaluations. The court also ruled that such evaluations had to be completed quickly following formal referral. Recently, states have begun to require that student promotion and graduation be based on satisfactory performance on minimum competency tests. In *Debra P.* v. *Turlington* (1984), the court ruled that students who were handicapped could be required to take such minimum competency tests as long as it could be shown that the tests covered the content of the curriculum to which the students were exposed. In *Brookhart* v. *Illinois State Board of Education* (1984), the court ruled that minimum competency tests were valid when used with students who were handicapped.

Instruction Issues

Given that under PL 94-142 students who are handicapped are granted the right to a free appropriate education, it should come as no surprise that the courts have been heavily involved in litigation regarding instruction, specifically appropriate instruction. As we noted earlier, the courts have tried to define appropriate education. They have also addressed extended services, right to psychological services and counseling as part of instruction, delivery of health services, provision of "extra" services, and parental participation in the development of IEPs. In *Hendrick-Hudson Board of Education* v. *Rowley* (1982), the Court overturned a lower court ruling that had required a school to provide an interpreter for a deaf student. The case began when Amy Rowley's parents asked the school to provide a sign language interpreter in their deaf daughter's class on a full-time basis. The school was providing speech therapy, use of a hearing aid, and a tutor for one hour a day and had offered sign language instruction to those of Amy's teachers who wanted it. But the school refused to put an interpreter in Amy's classroom. The Supreme Court ruled that the school was acting within its rights. In writing the decision for the Court, Justice Rehnquist stated that schools did not have to develop the maximum potential of students with handicaps; they just had to give students access to educational opportunities.

In *Irving Independent School District* v. *Tatro* (1984), the issue was the responsibility of a school to provide a medical procedure, in this case catheterization, to a student with a handicap. Chief Justice Burger writing for the majority reasoned that a service that enables a handicapped child to remain at school during the day is an important means of providing the child with the meaningful access to education that Congress envisioned. Services like CIC [clean intermittent catheterization, which involves washing a small metal tube called a catheter, inserting the catheter in the bladder to allow urine to drain, pulling the catheter out, and wiping the bladder region] that permit a child to remain at school during the day are not less related to the effort to educate than are services that enable the child to reach, enter, or exist in the school. (p. 104)

Burger went on to say that catheterization, because it could be carried out by a school nurse, was a related, not a medical, service. Schools are not required to provide medical services that have to be administered by a physician (with the exception of some assessment and diagnostic services); but they must provide services that can be carried out by a school nurse.

In *Frederick L.* the issue was provision of "appropriate" educational services to students who were learning disabled, whereas, in *Lora* the issue was delivery of "appropriate educational services" to students who were emotionally disturbed. A number of services are specifically listed in PL 94-142 as related services that are to be available to the child; included are psychological services and counseling. In *Max M.* v. *Illinois State Board of Education* (1986), the Illinois court ruled that parents could be reimbursed for psychological and psychiatric services the child received out of school, but the Court also put some limitations on the amount of reimbursement.

Another issue addressed by the courts is precisely with whom the school should communicate. Given the relatively high divorce rate, schools are faced with making decisions about which parent they should contact. In *Fay* v. *South Colonie Central School District* (1986), the Second Circuit Court of Appeals indicated that schools did not have to communicate routine announcements to both parents with legal custody but that parents with legal custody had access to students' records.

School Outcome Issues

The recent move to outcomes-based education and to specification of outcomes for students has not been tested by the courts. Yet in a real sense the courts have been concerned with outcomes for some time. We see court intervention in outcomes in several "malpractice suits." In *Meiner* v. *Missouri* (1982), the U.S. circuit court held that damages were never available as a remedy for alleged educational malpractice. In *Manecke* v. *School Board* (1985), the circuit court ruled that damages might be available as a remedy for malpractice, but it did not specify the conditions in which such damages might be awarded. And there is considerable variation in court decisions on whether states are immune from damages.

Early Intervention

In 1986 Congress amended PL 94-142 and extended all rights and protections of the law to preschoolers with handicaps. Effective in the 1990–1991 academic year, all states that applied for funds under PL 94-142 had to provide free appropriate education to all children with handicaps aged three through five.

At the same time, as part of PL 99-457, Congress established a new state grant program for infants and toddlers with handicaps. Eligible for early intervention are children from birth through age two who are delayed in development or at risk of substantial delay in development. The states have the authority to specify the criteria for deciding whom to serve.

To receive the federal funds that are available as part of PL 99-457, states must have an agency that administers the services and an interagency coordinating council to help develop programs and services. By the 1990–1991 academic year, statewide early intervention systems had to be in place, providing all eligible infants and toddlers with multidisciplinary assessments, individualized programs, and case management services.

PL 99-457 specified that each school district use a multidisciplinary assessment to develop an individualized family service plan (IFSP) for each student. The IFSP must include:

• A statement of the student's present level of cognitive, social, speech and language, and self-help development

• A statement of the family's strengths and needs related to enhancing the student's development

• A statement of the major outcomes expected for the student and family

• Criteria, procedures, and time lines for measuring progress

• A statement of the specific early intervention services necessary to meet the unique needs of the student and family, including methods, frequency, and intensity of service

• Projected dates for initiation and expected duration of services

• The name of the person who will manage the case

• Procedures for transition from early intervention into a preschool program

Transition Issues

With enactment of PL 101-476, transition services became a right. Congress defined transition services as

> a coordinated set of activities for a student, designed within an outcome-oriented process, which promotes movement from school to post-school activities, including post-secondary education, vocational training, integrated employment (including supported employment), continuing and adult education, adult services, independent living, or community participation. The coordinated set of activities shall be based upon the individual student's needs, taking into account the student's preferences and interests, and shall include instruction, community experiences, the development of employment and other post-school adult living ob-

jectives, and, when appropriate, acquisition of daily living skills and functional vocational evaluation.

The courts have addressed a number of what we call "transition issues." They have addressed suspension, graduation requirements, and dropout.

Suspension   In *Honig* v. *Doe* (1988), the Supreme Court reaffirmed the decision of a lower court that schools could not exclude students with handicaps, particularly emotional handicaps, because of their behavior. The case involved the suspension of two students who were receiving special education services in the San Francisco school district. The students (called John Doe and Jack Smith in the decision) had been expelled for different reasons.

Student Doe had been placed in a developmental center for students with handicaps. While attending school, he assaulted another student and broke a window. When he admitted these offenses to the principal, he was suspended for five days. The principal referred the matter to the school's student placement committee with the recommendation that Doe be expelled. The suspension was continued indefinitely as permitted by California state law, which allowed suspensions to extend beyond five days while expulsion proceedings were being held.

Student Smith's IEP stated that he was to be placed in a special education program in a regular school setting on a trial basis. Following several incidences of misbehavior, the school unilaterally reduced his program to half-day. Although his grandparents agreed to the reduction, the school district did not notify them of their right to appeal. A month later Smith was suspended for five days when he made inappropriate sexual comments to female students. In accordance with California law Smith's suspension also was continued indefinitely while expulsion proceedings were initiated by the school placement committee (Yell, in press).

The case went through several levels of courts, eventually ending up in the Supreme Court. Justice Brennan writing for the majority stated that schools could not unilaterally exclude students with disabilities. When placement was being debated, the child had to remain in the current educational setting unless school officials and parents agreed otherwise. The decision left a number of questions unanswered (Yell, in press): In what ways can these students be disciplined? How should the schools deal with students who are a danger to themselves or others but whose parents do not consent to removal?

Graduation Requirements   According to Rothstein, "The issue of graduation requirements involves two different questions of obligation by educational agencies. The first is whether diploma requirements may be imposed on handicapped students. The second is whether there is any obligation to a handicapped student once the diploma has been awarded" (1990, p. 174).

In *Brookhart* v. *Illinois State Board of Education*, a suit was brought on behalf of fourteen elementary and secondary students who were handicapped and were required to pass a minimum competency test to receive a high school diploma.

The district court ruled that the plaintiffs did not have to pass the minimum competency test because the test did not assess the content of their curriculum. Rather than receiving the standard high school curriculum, the object of the test, the students had received unique instruction as specified in their IEPs. The court ruled that if the students had been given notice early enough of the requirement to pass the minimum competency test, their IEPs could have been adjusted to include the content of the tests. Because the test did not include the content of the curriculum for the students (as ruled earlier in *Debra P*. v. *Turlington*), the students did not have to pass the tests to graduate. They did, however, have to meet two other graduation requirements: completion of seventeen course credits and fulfillment of the state's graduation requirements. We are not aware of a court case in which the court has taken action on whether the school may issue different diplomas to students who are handicapped.

Dropout   In what conditions can a student who is handicapped drop out of school? Rothstein raised a number of issues regarding dropout but stated clearly that these issues have not really been addressed by the courts. She described the dilemmas as follows:

> In many states, students are not required to attend school beyond a certain age, usually around 14 to 16. This raises an interesting question as to whether a student who is receiving special education may elect to stop attending school. For example, a student who has reached 16 in a state where 16 is the cutoff for mandatory attendance may wish to stop attending school. If that student is receiving some programming for a learning disability, for example, what is the obligation of the school to try to keep that student in school? Is there any greater obligation for that student than there is for a student who is not receiving special education? What happens if the parents do not care? Is there any greater obligation to try to persuade the parents to "force" the child to attend because the student is receiving special education? Once the student becomes 18, the parents no longer have the legal power to force the student to attend anyway. (1990, pp. 178–179)

Economic Issues

Provision of special education services costs school districts extra money. Specialized equipment, additional resources, and specially designed transportation equipment are all part of the picture. School districts are reimbursed by state departments of education for portions of the salaries of special education teachers. The courts have intervened in disputes over who pays for special education, the extent to which cost is the responsibility of local education agencies (LEA) versus state education agencies (SEA), and the extent to which parents may be reimbursed for the fees they pay to attorneys who assist them in achieving an appropriate educational program for their children.

When local school districts fail to provide services for students, courts sometimes have to decide whether the state is then responsible for providing services.

Although several circuit courts have ruled that the state is responsible, the U.S. Supreme Court has not ruled on the issue. States and local education agencies also get into disputes about who is responsible for paying for the educational programs of specific children. Such cases usually arise when the student is a resident of one district but the services are provided in a neighboring district or state or when the student requires very expensive educational interventions. The courts' rulings have typically been different for each case.

In *Burlington School Committee* v. *Department of Education* the U.S. Supreme Court ruled that reimbursement for private school tuition was an appropriate form of relief for a court to grant. In *Smith* v. *Robinson* (1984), the school district had agreed to place Thomas Smith, a youngster with cerebral palsy and physical and emotional handicaps, in a day treatment program at a hospital in Rhode Island. After a period of time, the school district informed the parents that the Rhode Island Department of Mental Health, Retardation, and Hospitals would have to take over the expense of the program. The state supreme court ruled that the duty of funding the educational program rested with the local school, not the state. The parents appealed the case to a federal district court and in addition asked for payment of attorney's fees. The district court agreed with the parents, but the court of appeals did not. The U.S. Supreme Court ruled that parents were responsible for paying the attorney's fees.

So the Supreme Court had ruled that parents could be reimbursed for private school tuition but not for attorneys' fees. In 1986, Congress settled the issue by passing the Handicapped Children's Protection Act, an amendment to PL 94-142. The amendment specified that courts could award attorney's fees to parents who won in current proceedings or in cases that began after July 4, 1984. Parents now have the right to collect for attorney's fees, but they must work in good faith to try settling their case. Also, there are specific conditions in which parents are not entitled to recover attorneys' fees.

Schools encounter excess costs in provision of services to students who are handicapped. The courts regularly get involved in disputes about who pays the excess costs. In *Bevin* v. *Wright* (1987), a district court in Pennsylvania ruled on the extent to which the Pittsburgh school district was responsible for paying the costs of home nursing services that enabled a seven-year-old girl with severe physical and mental handicaps to attend school. The court ruled that the costs were clearly beyond those intended by the law and would have to be born by the parents. The court cited the Supreme Court ruling in *Rowley*, arguing that although "all handicapped children are entitled to some form of education tailored to their individual needs and abilities, it does not require school districts to provide the best possible education without regard to expense."

Home-School Collaboration Issues

The courts have dealt with the definition of "parents" for purposes of legislation relevant to students who are handicapped. The law specifies that the term *parents* is intended to include grandparents, stepparents, surrogate parents, or guardians who have legal responsibility for children. As noted above in our discussion of *Fay* v. *South Colonie School District*, schools should communicate important information (anticipated changes in enrollment, solicitation of informed consent for testing) to both parents if the parents are separated or divorced and have legal custody.

Unresolved Issues

The courts have not resolved all the major legal issues about delivery of special education services to students who are handicapped. There are many unresolved issues. In the following list, we provide a sample of unresolved issues to spur your thinking and discussion (also see Rothstein, 1990):

• Where should the line be drawn in the provision of services? How many students should be served in special education?

• How can the regular class be thought of as the least restrictive environment if in it teachers are supposed to deliver individualized instruction for students with disabilities?

• If a seventeen-year-old student who is receiving special education services wants to drop out of school, may she or he?

• To what extent are specific tests (or items on tests) biased?

• If a nineteen-year-old student accepts a high school diploma, is he or she still eligible to receive special education services? The law says such services are available until age twenty-one.

• Should scarce resources be used to upgrade the teaching of "average" students or to provide special education services to students who are handicapped?

• Does a student who is specifically categorized have the right to be taught by an instructor who is specifically certified to teach in that category?

• When students who require extensive services change districts, who pays for the cost of educating the students?

• What remedy do parents have when schools do not comply with procedural requirements?

• In what conditions may a student who is handicapped be expelled from school?

• If a student who is handicapped can survive in a regular classroom with supports, is the student automatically entitled to the supports? Who pays for the supports?

• Who is responsible for paying for the educational services received in a juvenile detention center by students who are handicapped?

• What happens if a student needs a particular service and the district does not have the money to pay for it?

• What relief (in terms of respite care) is available to parents of students who are handicapped? Who pays for it?

• What happens if placement in a separate facility is clearly the least restrictive placement for a student, but there is no certified special education teacher in the facility?

• Should schools be required to give notice to both parents if they are divorced? In what conditions can one parent prohibit the other from access to a student's records or notification regarding school events?

• Is a student who needs only related services but not special education considered handicapped?

• Does least restrictive placement require placement with age-appropriate peers?

• Is it permissible to have separate scout troops for students who are handicapped?

• Do students who are handicapped and attend parochial schools have the same rights as those who attend public schools?

• Are students with AIDS eligible for special education under the category other health impaired?

Discussion Questions

1. Why do you suppose it has taken so much legal activity to get school districts to allow students with disabilities to attend school and to provide appropriate services for those students?

2. Discuss any of the unresolved issues cited at the end of this chapter.

CHAPTER 13

Working with Parents, Families, and Community Agencies

The Nature of Parent Involvement
Assigning Responsibility
Parent Involvement and Improved Achievement
The Home Environment's Influence on Schooling
Parent Control of Children
Effects of Disabilities on Families

Home-School Collaboration and Cooperation
Barriers to Collaboration
Communication Between Parents and School Personnel
Empowerment
Home Alone: Latchkey Children
Foster Care
Homelessness

Interagency Interface

If we could succeed in establishing rather different and closer relations between home and school, such as are aimed at by parent-teacher associations, much might be accomplished.

—*Lillian Lincoln, Everyday Pedagogy (1915)*

In the first edition of this textbook (published in 1982) we did not include a separate chapter on issues in working with families, parents, and community agencies. Does this mean that educators have only recently discovered the importance of working with parents, families, and agencies? Or does it mean that issues in doing so have arisen only recently? The answer to both is probably no.

Professionals' views about parents and willingness to work collaboratively with parents in the education and socialization of children have changed since the beginning of the 1980s. Educators and parents alike now recognize that early intervention, especially intervention with the families of children who have disabilities, is crucial and effective. Parents have become stronger advocates for the rights of their children, and there are legal mandates for parent involvement in the educational programs of their children. Indeed, PL 99-457 specified that schools develop for very young children an individual family service plan. There is movement away from the child as the sole focus of intervention to the family as the unit of intervention.

There is also a new emphasis on parent-professional partnerships. Educators see parents as colleagues in intervention rather than as passive recipients of treatments. Much of the new focus on families and parents is rooted in the work of Bronfenbrenner. He argued that professionals cannot understand adequately the behavior of the individual student without understanding the influences that the family has on that behavior.

The problems students bring to school are becoming increasingly complex. Solution of those problems requires the planning, organization, and management of interventions by multiple sources and varied disciplines. Increasingly, schools are collaborating with community agencies and organizations in delivering interventions. In this chapter we describe the issues school personnel confront as they endeavor to work well with families, parents, and community agencies. Involvement, collaboration, cooperation, and interface are terms we hear repeatedly these days. Let us examine some of the issues surrounding these terms and concepts.

The Nature of Parent Involvement

It is very popular these days to talk about parent involvement. The authors of this text regularly attend conferences where we listen to keynote speakers calling for increased parent involvement and home-school collaboration as essential to solving the problems that schools, children, and families face. Teachers tell us of the need to involve parents in their children's education. Parents sometimes talk about their desire to participate in the education of their children. But what does parent involvement mean, and do professionals and parents really want this meaningful involvement? And even if they do, what improvement does parent involvement contribute to the educational performance of students with disabilities?

To address these issues means investigating the nature of parent involvement. Henderson, Marburger, and Ooms (1986), for instance, differentiated five kinds of parent involvement: parents as partners, collaborators and problem solvers (helping school personnel resolve problems), audience, supporters, and advisers and co-decision makers. Schools involve parents all along the continuum from active involvement to passive reception. Henderson et al. advocated the involvement of parents as partners in the educational enterprise and indicated what schools must do to enable effective family-school partnerships. First, parents are more likely to become involved in their children's educational programs if the school climate is open, helpful, and friendly, which can be accomplished by

The Kentucky Education Reform Act (KERA)
and Special Education

As school districts begin responding to the Kentucky Education Reform Act passed by the 1990 General Assembly, parents of children with special needs must *stay involved* to make certain that special education services do not become—or remain—a low priority. Some important things that parents can do include:

• Keep letting your Superintendent and your School Board members know of your interest in special education programs.

• Attend School Board meetings. Your School Board must develop its policy for school-based decision making by January 1, 1991; offer your input into this policy development whenever the opportunity is available to do so.

• Be involved in the PTA, PTO, or other major parent organization of your child's school; parent members of the school's "school-based decision making" team will be selected by the PTA, PTO, or—in the absence of either—by the large parent group formed for this purpose. You must be a member of the group in order to be a candidate for the school-based decision making team.

• Under the KERA, school districts will be receiving significantly more money for students with special needs; ask your Superintendent and School Board members how they intend to spend these monies. (The fiscal year budget approved by the School Board is public information; you have a right to examine it at the Superintendent's Office.)

• Remember also: Part B funds are provided by the Federal Government to help school districts provide related services (occupational therapy, physical therapy, etc.). Your special education coordinator will be developing your district's Part B budget early this Fall and you have the right to be involved in developing this budget. Contact your special education coordinator and ask how you can help

SOURCE: Kentucky Coalition for Persons with Handicaps.

putting parent lounges into schools and having set times when parents and teachers have lunch together, among other things.

Second, parents are more likely to become involved in the educational program when there is frequent, clear, two-way communication. They are also more likely to communicate when they are encouraged to comment on school policies and issues and to share in making decisions about programs.

Third, parents are more likely to become involved when they are treated as collaborators, rather than recipients of advice from experts. Active efforts must be made to involve parents, especially those who are considered very hard to reach. Schools in which administrators actively express and promote a philosophy of partnership are likely to have high levels of parental involvement, as are schools in which parents are expected to work as volunteers, even after their children finish school. Parental involvement is greater when school personnel make extensive efforts to reach parents who are unavailable.

Henderson et al. are not the only writers who have described degrees or types of parent involvement. Epstein (Brandt, 1989) identified five types of parent involvement, which range from parent fulfillment of basic obligations (like providing for health and safety, getting the child ready for school, and building the kind of home environment that supports learning) to parent involvement in governance of schools. But how parents should be involved in schools and what approach to involvement is best are still unanswered questions, though most educators have strong opinions about them.

Williams and Chavkin (1989) identified essentials for a strong parent involvement program. These include the presence of written policies on how parents and teachers are to work together, administrative support, training, two-way communication, networking, and evaluation. Unfortunately, few parent involvement efforts have been adequately evaluated.

Assigning Responsibility

If schools and parents are to work together, identifying who is responsible for what aspects of the education and socialization of children is essential. Where do the responsibilities of parents end and those of the school begin? Since the early 1980s, society has thrust on schools and school personnel an increased set of demands for child rearing, socialization, and the elimination of social problems. Epstein (1990) described parent involvement from the perspective of responsibility for children, child rearing, instruction, and child development. She identified and defined three perspectives on responsibility: separate responsibility, shared responsibility, and sequential responsibility. Separate responsibility stresses the "inherent incompatibility, competition, and conflict between families and schools" (p. 121). "This perspective," according to Epstein "assumes that school bureaucracies and family organizations are directed, respectively, by educators and parents whose different goals, roles and responsibilities are best fulfilled independently" (p. 121). Shared responsibility, which focuses on coordination, cooperation, and complementarity, assumes that families and schools bear joint responsibility for the socialization and education of children together. Sequential responsibility assumes that parents and teachers have primary responsibility for the education and socialization of children at different points in children's lives. It is common from this perspective to presuppose that parents are responsible for child rearing and socialization for the first five or six years of the child's life and that the school takes over once formal schooling starts. The particular perspective a professional or a parent holds on parent involvement influences the extent to which and the method by which parents become involved in their children's educational program.

Just as perspectives vary from one person to another, so do they change from one era to another. In the early nineteenth century, for example, schools were controlled by parents or at least by the community of parents. Lines of demarcation between parent and school responsibility were clear. Schools taught a common curriculum; families taught ethics, values, religion, and ethnicity. Now parents clearly are more involved in making curricular decisions. This involvement derives from several factors. More mothers are highly educated; indeed, many have degrees in teaching but choose not to teach. More parents are knowledgeable about child development and are more engaged in educating infants and toddlers. The federal government has promoted parent involvement by insisting that parents take part in planning IEPs for their children with disabilities (Epstein, 1990).

Parent Involvement and Improved Achievement

There is much rhetoric about parent involvement, so much that it seems logical to suppose that involving parents in students' educational programs will lead to improved educational performance for students. But although the correlation between parent involvement in education and student achievement is well documented, there is little evidence of any direct, causal link.

Enhanced pupil performance and achievement are not the only benefits assumed to derive from increased parental involvement. Rich (1987) identified a number of reasons for family involvement in students' schooling: increased student achievement, promotion of home learning, improved student behavior, family acceptance of children, benefits to parents, teacher acceptance of students, and benefits to the community resulting from increased family involvement. Yet there is no research evidence to indicate that these benefits actually do take place.

The Home Environment's Influence on Schooling

Much is written on how dysfunctional families produce dysfunctional children, who in turn experience much difficulty in school. Yet this is not always the case. Two of our colleagues at the University of Minnesota, Garmezy and Masten, conducted extensive research on factors related to the development of competence in children and observed that some children, in spite of incredibly adverse circumstances, did end up competent (Masten, Garmezy, Tellegen, Pellegrini, Larkin & Larsen, 1988). Garmezy and Masten also identified factors that contributed to resilience and development of competence.

Christenson (1990) used a home rating scale to examine differences in educationally relevant home factors among students who were learning disabled, emotionally disturbed, mentally retarded, and nonhandicapped. She looked at routine, organization, lack of stress, security, responsibility, expectations, valuing education, support for academics, and support for school. She summed these to produce an index of quality of the home environment and reported that the home environment for students with learning disabilities and students with no handicaps was rated significantly higher than the home environment for students who were emotionally disturbed. (Remember, however, that not every student from a stressed, aversive environment has problems.)

Parent Control of Children

The August 1, 1990, issue of *Education Week* included a report on enactment of get-tough policies in certain states and localities; these penalized parents for failure to control their children. But where does the responsibility of parents end? In Los Angeles 150 parents have been arrested because their children joined gangs. Wisconsin has adopted policies allowing cuts in welfare payments to parents whose children do not attend school. In Arkansas, Maryland, Mississippi, and Texas, there are threats of fine or jail for parents who refuse to attend parent-teacher conferences. Should schools and society in general police the involvement of parents in children's education? Should parents be punished when the actions they take are deemed to be not in the best educational interest of their children? Who decides?

The Effects of Disabilities on Families

Are families adversely affected by the presence of children with disabilities? Most people believe they are. Yet the research on this issue is pretty mixed. It is very risky to say anything about how students with disabilities affect their families. Gartner, Lipsky, and Turnbull argued that the family is the central social institution affecting the life of the child with disabilities, yet they also stated that "to recognize that families are important in the life of a child with disabilities, and vice versa, is to say no more—and no less–than what is true of all families and all children" (1991, p. 57).

Methodological problems abound in studying the effects of (any kind of) children on their families. Effects differ according to condition and severity (Seligman & Darling, 1989). Effects also differ according to parents' perceptions of whether their children measure up to cultural standards (Epstein, 1990). The interrelationships among factors that affect outcomes are complex. Differing disabilities affect families in varying ways, and the same kind of disability may have radically different effects from one family to the next.

The effects children with handicaps have on their families have also changed significantly with the times. In the not too distant past, medical personnel and laypersons advised parents to avoid raising their children with disabilities and to seek assistance in the form of institutional placement. Parents who chose to keep their children at home were subject to stigma (as children with disabilities were labeled, so, too, were their parents. Those who put their children in institutions often had to meet the burden of major costs and had to look the other way when their sons and daughters received shoddy care. Significant changes in social values since the early 1970s have led to a situation in which institutionalization is the exception, not the rule. Families are expected to assume responsibility for their children with disabilities and to assume responsibilities associated with raising those children. As a result, families with children who are disabled have become very visible.

Families of children with disabilities are perfectly capable of coping with their children. Beavers observed that

> in any family with an identifiably "different" characteristic (e.g., ethnic, extremely rich or poor, military) or member (e.g., schizophrenic, homosexual, celebrity), effective family coping is taken for granted or not noticed, while problematic family interaction is spotlighted. In our study, we discovered very early that families with a handicapped child are usually likable, always interesting, and not stereotypical; they have distinctive family personalities. Subjectively, we learned to appreciate their resourcefulness and their many strengths. (1989, p. 196)

Parents of children who are handicapped do go through a predictable set of stages in reacting to the news that their children have disabilities. The stages are the same as those people go through when they learn that they have a serious (terminal) illness: denial, bargaining, anger, depression, acceptance, and stigma.

Students with disabilities do confront their families with challenges when providing care: care for their everyday needs as well as for their disabilities. Different disabilities confront parents with different care needs. Students with disabilities are often stigmatized, and when they are their families can be similarly stigmatized. Differing conditions carry with them different stigmas. Ysseldyke and Algozzine (1990) indicated that stigma differ as a function of condition and of the beholder's perceptions of the causes of the conditions.

Home-School Collaboration and Cooperation

Home-school collaboration is advocated by most educators as one way to address the problems students experience in school. Professionals and parents readily support the notion that it is important to get schools and parents working more closely together. Yet home-school collaboration is not easy, and it does not always work.

Barriers to Collaboration

As might be expected, there has been considerable discussion and disagreement in the professional literature about the factors that serve as barriers to effective home-school collaboration. And there are differing perspectives on how to overcome some of the barriers.

Table 13.1   Barriers to effective home-school collaboration

1. Parents feel anxious about surrendering their children to strangers who may have values different from their own and may inculcate in the children those values.
2. Teachers worry that parent involvement in decision making removes teacher independence and autonomy.
3. Sometimes teachers and parents will accede to their required responsibilities (as articulated by principals to diminish conflict and confusion); sometimes they will not.
4. Parents and teachers have inaccurate, often negative stereotypes of each other.
5. Because parents and teachers are busy, the pressure of having to get many things done in short periods of time interferes with effective collaboration.
6. Because many families have very low incomes, the financial pressures of making ends meet become primary to worrying about how their children are doing in school.
7. Parents are sometimes afraid to come to school because they do not view schools as safe environments.
8. Parents cannot always come to school because they cannot afford or have no access to child care for younger siblings.
9. School policies sometimes discourage home-school collaboration–for instance, in some schools union contracts specify that volunteers cannot be used for teaching functions.
10. Teachers and parents hold different views on who ought to be in charge of major decisions.
11. Parents and teachers sometimes attribute student failure or poor performance to different, mutually exclusive factors, which sometimes means they blame each other.
12. Many homes are socially stressed, and many students who experience difficulties in school are from socially stressed homes. The stresses may be such that they contribute to or exacerbate the difficulties students experience in school or take precedence over any difficulties students experience in school.

SOURCE: Henderson, A. T. Marburger, C. L., & Ooms, T. (1986). *Beyond the bake sale: An educator's guide to working with parents.* Washington, DC: National Committee for Citizens in Education; Imber-Black, E. (1988). *Families and larger systems.* New York: Guilford.

Henderson, Marburger, and Ooms (1986) identified twelve barriers to effective home-school collaboration. Some of these same barriers were identified by Imber-Black (1988). These are shown in Table 13.1.

Note that one of these barriers is the negative stereotypes parents and teachers hold about each other. According to Henderson et al., parents believe that teachers teach too much by rote, that parent-teacher conferences are routine and unproductive, that teachers send home only bad news, that teachers do not follow through on what they say they will do, that they do not welcome interactions with parents, and that they care more about discipline than about teaching. Teachers believe that parents are not interested in school, that they do not show up when asked, that they promise but do not follow through, that they only pretend to understand what teachers are trying to accomplish, that they do children's homework for them, and that they worry too much about how other kids are doing. (Imber-Black also identified negative stereotypes as a barrier.)

Leitch and Tangri (1988) identified two categories of barriers to home-school collaboration. First, teachers and parents lack knowledge about how they can use each other more effectively. When Leitch and Tangri asked about barriers to collaboration, nearly 50 percent of teachers attributed barriers to parents. Parents saw themselves as primary barriers, whereas teachers said parents, the system, and themselves were the barriers.

Second, mutual understanding and planning are lacking. "It isn't misperceptions of each other that are the root of home-school problems, it is the lack of specific planning, or, at a more basic level, the lack of knowledge about how each can use the other person more effectively that is the major barrier" (p. 74).

Nevertheless, there is much to support the contention that collaboration between teachers and parents of students with disabilities is greater than that between teachers and students who are not disabled. Recent legislation requires relatively heavy involvement of parents in the assessment of students, in the development of an IEP, in the planning of transition services, and in the setting of career goals and exploration of career options.

Communication Between Parents and School Personnel

Nearly every major report on schooling stresses the role of parents in making education work, and nearly every one of those reports calls attention to "the need for effective communication between parents and school personnel." It is thought that maximum education will occur where families and schools are brought into working relationships and where they communicate.

Epstein (1990) reported that large numbers of parents were excluded from communication with schools. She surveyed parents in six hundred Maryland elementary schools and found that more than 30 percent had no conference with a teacher during the year, 60 percent had never talked with a teacher by phone, and most had never engaged in deep or frequent discussions with teachers. At the same time, in the 1987 Metropolitan Life Survey of the American Teacher, most parents (85 percent) and teachers (78 percent) expressed satisfaction with the frequency of contacts between parents and schools. More than 50 percent of the teachers *and* of the parents said they were uneasy or reluctant about approaching the other to talk about the child (Leitch & Tangri, 1988).

A specific issue arises in communication between school personnel and parents of students with disabilities. Students do not receive special education services without first going through a due process hearing. Usually due process hearings are congenial events. Sometimes, however, they are antagonistic, pitting parents against school personnel. When such is the case, it is not an easy matter to resume communication following a hearing.

Empowerment

PL 99-457 specified that school personnel work with families to develop an IFSP. Each state develops rules, regulations, and guidelines for doing so, and each state has a bureaucracy to implement the law. Implementation takes two forms, which Dunst, Trivette & Deal (1988) called a child-focused model or a family-centered model. In a child-focused model the interventions are expert driven, and the services provided are prescriptive and designed to correct weaknesses. In a family-centered model the interventions are consumer driven and designed to link needs to available services, rather than to create new ones; the services are responsive in nature and are designed to strengthen informal support networks.

School personnel can operate as partners with parents in serving and assisting children, or they can treat parents and children as clients (or patients) who are the recipients of the services to be delivered. In choosing a way in which to operate, they create either empowerment outcomes or dependency outcomes. Professionals can work with parents in an effort to strengthen natural support systems, or they can create new systems. Suppose we want to put in place a system of respite care in which parents of children with disabilities can get relief by having someone serve as a foster parent for a few days or for a weekend. There are two ways to put such a program into effect. We can create a new support system, establishing and training individuals to work as foster parents and provide respite care. Or we can find people with whom the parents already feel comfortable and train those individuals to care for children with disabilities. We can look to create new social services for students or make an effort to use those that are now in place. The more we can rely on natural structures or arrangements, the more we empower parents. When parents have to rely on social service agencies to provide services and make arrangements for them, they may become dependent.

Home Alone: Latchkey Children

The spring 1991 issue of *Teaching Exceptional Children* included a special focus on latchkey children. Why? What is the relationship between children and youths home alone and special education? To what extent is lack of child care and supervision a problem for students with disabilities? Rowland and Robinson (1991) reported on some of these issues: they reported the case of a fourteen-year-old student with mental retardation who was unable to receive day care after school because the center that provided such care did not take children older than twelve, and they reported that students with disabilities were dependent on supervision well into adolescence, long after nondisabled peers had become self-sufficient, a problem compounded by the lack of services for students during the summer.

Coleman and Apts (1991) identified the risks to students who are home alone. Such children may not have the cognitive capability and social maturity to fend for themselves. They may lack the physical skills necessary to enter a house and remain at home alone. They may be unable to attend to their basic self-help and self-care needs. They may not know how to protect a house key, get from home to school and vice versa on their own, use a telephone, prepare snacks, manage their time, and apply first aid in dealing with emergencies. Decisions to leave children home alone are usually last resort decisions, but parents do often choose to do so. As a result, schools increasingly have to look into after-school programs

Home Alone

Some 14 percent of 8th graders surveyed in 1988 said they usually were home after school without adult supervision for more than three hours, according to data from the National Education Longitudinal Study of 1988.

According to the survey, 13 percent of the students said they were never at home after school without an adult present; 32 percent were home without adult supervision less than one hour each day; 28 percent reported one to two hours alone; and 13 percent reported two to three hours alone. Over all, 60 percent spent anywhere from less than an hour to two hours alone after school.

Hispanic students in the survey were more likely than most other groups to say they were never home without an adult after school. Whites were less likely to be home without an adult for more than three hours. Blacks and American Indians were more likely to be without an adult for more than three hours.

According to the data, students from the lowest socioeconomic quartile were more likely to say they were never home without a parent after school. Yet that group also had a higher percentage who said they were home without an adult for more than three hours a day.

Length of Time 8th Graders Spend After School Each Day Without an Adult Present

Characteristics	None, Never Happens	Less than 1 Hour	1–2 Hours	2–3 Hours	More than 3 Hours
Total	13.3%	32.4%	27.8%	12.9%	13.6%
Race					
Asian and Pacific Islander	16.7	29.0	25.8	12.6	15.9
Hispanic	20.7	29.0	22.8	11.2	16.3
Black	16.2	28.1	23.2	12.8	19.5
White	11.6	33.8	29.5	13.1	12.0
American Indian/ Native Alaskan	16.0	30.8	21.1	13.3	18.8
School Type					
Public	13.0	32.1	27.9	13.0	14.0
Catholic	13.4	34.0	26.4	13.9	12.3
Independent	15.3	36.7	30.5	9.7	7.9
Other private	20.1	34.6	27.8	8.7	8.8

SOURCE: Home alone. (1991, March 6). *Education Week*, p. 3. Used with permission. The *NELS:88* study includes data gathered from nearly 25,000 students nationwide. Copies of the report—*A Profile of the American 8th Grader*—are available from the Superintendent of Documents, U.S. Government Printing Office, Washington, D.C. 20402.

for students with disabilities and develop instructional programs to enable students to care for themselves.

Foster Care

Foster care has become the care of choice when children with disabilities cannot stay with their families. Since the mid-1970s, there have been increased community integration of students with disabilities and increased effort to care for these students in familylike structures. Thus, there is more and more foster care for children with disabilities. Hill, Lakin, Novak, and White (1987) reported that 20.5 percent of the children and youths in foster care were homeless children.

Educators face incredible difficulties finding suitable foster care settings for students with disabilities. New challenges are coming in the form of children with medical illnesses (children with AIDS, crack babies, babies who have experienced drug exposure in utero, and children and youths who have multiple health or emotional problems).

Homelessness

Homelessness has become a potent issue for special education. Many students with disabilities spend their evenings in homeless shelters and receive their meals from food shelves, some sleep in their cars and do their homework on the steps of a shopping mall, and others live in motels. With no home to return to they find it difficult to do their homework. And for many the doors to a different life, one involving extensive education, are closed.

When is a student homeless? A "homeless" individual is defined in the Stewart B. McKinney Homeless Assistance Act of 1987 as one who lacks a fixed, regular, adequate nighttime residence or has a primary nighttime residence in a supervised publicly or privately operated shelter for temporary accommodation.

Until the early 1980s, the American homeless population consisted primarily of men. Each year since then, however, increasing numbers of younger and younger people have become homeless. Consider the change in the population of homeless individuals from 1987 to 1990. In 1987, the U.S. Conference of Mayors found that families with children were the fastest growing segment of the homeless population. That year, it was estimated that there were 220,000 homeless school-age children and youths, about one-third of whom did not attend school on a regular basis. At that same time, the National Coalition for the Homeless estimated that there were at least two times as many (about 400,000) homeless children. In 1990, the National Law Center on Homelessness and Poverty estimated that 450,000 children and youths were homeless and that another 2 million were "precariously housed" (Wells, 1989). There are also large numbers of students who have been thrown out of their homes by their parent(s) or guardian.

As we were completing this text, considerable debate was raging about the number of homeless people. Communities were debating the number of individuals identified as homeless in the census data. It was argued that census takers had failed to visit difficult-to-reach and unsafe places, precisely the places often frequented by the homeless.

What are the effects of homelessness on pupil academic achievement and behavior in schools? Most students who are homeless also live in large urban environments. These children and youths experience constant moves and frequent changes in schools. They see life as temporary, have little structure in their lives, lack continuity, do not have opportunities to establish strong friendships, have no sense of their own space and possessions, and experience repeated shifts in classmates, schools, and curricula. It should not be surprising, then, to see students who leave projects half-finished, get depressed over leaving familiar places and friends, withdraw, act aggressively, do not complete their homework, fall behind academically, are restless, fight with other students for control of things, have difficulty with transitions, have poor attention span, and demonstrate developmental delays. Students who are homeless can be expected to have major academic deficits and developmental delays and to evidence behavior problems. If they stay in one place long enough to be assessed, it can be expected that large numbers of these students will be declared eligible for special education services. How can schools and the personnel who work in schools move to combat the effects of homelessness?

Interagency Interface

Professionals talk often about interagency collaboration, but few know what it means or what it comprises. Interagency collaboration has been defined as

> a process which: encourages and facilitates an open and honest exchange of ideas, plans, approaches, and resources across disciplines, programs and agencies; enables all participants jointly to define their separate interests and mutually identify needed changes in order to best achieve common purposes; and utilizes formal procedures to help clarify issues, define problems, and make decisions. (Midwest Regional Resource Center Task Force, 1979, p. 6)

Why all the excitement about this topic? McLaughlin and Christensen (1980) identified several reasons for the push for interagency collaboration. Among these are increased federal initiatives; economic pressures; pressure from clients, parents, and advocates; the need to reduce duplication of services; development of improved treatments; the need for additional comprehensive services; and overlap in service definitions. Also affecting increased interagency collaboration are the pressure for professionals to work together, the fragmented service delivery system, and the multiple funding bases for services. So is interagency collaboration needed? We think so, especially to ensure appropriate placement of students in services, avoid duplication of effort, manage cases across agencies, and promote resource sharing. Collaboration is also needed to facilitate transitions from community or institutional placement to school, prevent disrupted adoptions, and assist individuals in planning their careers.

Interagency collaboration involves hard work. Many professionals are now actively working on models for interagency collaboration. In doing so they focus on matters such as the need for individuals and individual agencies to take on leadership and the importance of organizations having shared goals.

Discussion Questions

1. What steps might a school take to facilitate home-school collaboration and to overcome barriers to involvement of parents?

2. Think about your own educational experience. To what extent were your parents involved in your educational program? How were the parents of others in your school involved? How has parent involvement changed over time?

CHAPTER 14

Economic Issues in Special Education

The Role of Government in Education

Financial Issues
  The Cost of Special Education
  Payment for Special Education Services
  Funding Formulas
  Funding Incentives and Disincentives
  The Influence of Funding Patterns on Research
  Escalating Costs
  Cost of Transportation
  Cost of Teacher Salaries

Efficiency Issues
  What Should Be Considered as "Benefits"?
  Equity Versus Efficiency
  No Matter the Cost?
  The Cost Versus the Benefit of Prevention

As a nation, we now invest more in education than in defense. But the results have not improved, and we're not coming close to our potential or what is needed.

—*George Bush, in* America 2000

Special education is supported by federal and state tax dollars, and these moneys are allocated on the basis of child counts by categories. Because special education in its present form has evolved in response to how money is allotted to education, it can be argued that funding drives the direction of special education.

When educators and other school personnel are asked to describe the economic issues in special education, they point to measures of productivity, how districts fund special education, who pays for what, and when costs become more important considerations than benefits. They want to know if and how the costs of education will rise in the 1990s, whether the cost of educating a student in a self-contained classroom is greater, and if students with disabilities who graduate from high school can expect to enjoy greater earnings than those who drop out of school before graduation.

Yet not all these are economic, or strictly economic, issues. Indeed, discussion of economic or cost issues can never be considered independent from matters of social value, appropriateness, and effectiveness. And there are trade-offs among these considerations. Suppose administrators in the Jefferson county schools decide that they must reduce their expenditures for provision of special education services and that the way to accomplish this is to reduce the number of salaried special education teachers by combining small classes of students in various parts of the district. Costs for salaried personnel will decrease, while transportation costs will increase.

In other circumstances, however, "cost issues are often secondary in relationship to policy directives or important social values" (Lewis, Bruininks, & Thurlow, 1989, p. 483). Society may decide, through court action or legislation, that certain students are entitled to a free appropriate education and that the cost of providing this service may be secondary. Or a court may rule that a school district is negligent in the inappropriate assessment of and placement of minority students in special education classes and that the school district must reeducate its psychological services personnel regardless of the cost of doing so.

In this chapter we discuss two kinds of economic issues—issues of finance, such as the cost of delivering services and allocating resources to students with special needs, and issues of efficiency, such as the relationship between costs and outputs, cost-effectiveness, and productivity. This classification of the issues is not as distinct as it at first seems because the economic issues presented here have social and political dimensions or ramifications. We begin by examining the role of government in the provision of education so we can differentiate the regulatory, financial, and administrative role of government in education.

The Role of Government in Education

In Chapter 2 we observed that governments establish schools to prepare the young to assume society's responsibilities. (Yet parents operating independently of government intervention can and do establish schools.) Governments intervene in education, and specifically in special education, for several reasons:

1. Governments intervene to protect minors because, as common thinking goes, they are unable to stand up for their own rights, and parents and society will not necessarily do so.

2. Government agencies intervene because the benefits of education to society (rather than to the individual) are large and therefore must be protected. Such benefits include the establishment of a strong national defense, the provision of an educated citizenry, the inculcation of common values, the belief in and practice

of democracy, social cost reductions (in the form of decreased crime, increased health, and decreased unemployment), and equality of opportunity.

3. Government agencies intervene to ensure freedom and prevent the creation of monopolies: because provision of education is a state, rather than a federal, responsibility, this prevents monopolistic control of education.

4. Governments intervene to facilitate the efficiency of operation that is thought to result from central control of resources.

5. Governments intervene to ensure equity of access for all children and youths, regardless of handicapping condition, race, or gender.

Government intervention is of three types: regulation, finance, and administration. Government regulation takes the form of requirements, such as those specifying that all students must attend school and that schools must provide services to all students. Government finance of education varies according to how high in the system the student is. Because at higher levels the student derives more individual benefits from education, he or she is expected to pay more of the costs. At lower levels, education is subsidized by state and local agencies. Government administration occurs through state and federal agencies, which regularly send teams of personnel to monitor compliance with corresponding rules and regulations.

Financial Issues

As a social service, education in general and special education in particular must compete for dollars with highways, sanitation, and other services. To the extent that members of society value special education more than other services, special education is financed more heavily. Government spending patterns influence public policy on the education of students with disabilities (though the converse is also true). Policy makers also decide which education programs to emphasize: preschool programs, basic primary education for young children, programs to keep adolescents from dropping out of school, or vocational programs for illiterate adults.

The Cost of Special Education

Estimating the cost of providing special education services is difficult. The best we can do is cite national averages. In nearly all instances, the largest cost component for educating students with handicaps is personnel costs. About 80 percent of the funds for special education are used to pay teachers and other direct-services personnel. Remaining costs comprise transportation, food, health, and rehabilitation services.

The cost of providing services varies as a function of the nature of the handicapping condition. It costs more to provide educational and related services to students with severe handicaps than to students with milder handicaps. Shell reported that

> it is not uncommon for one child to require a traveling chair, a stand-in table, a tilt table, and a wheelchair desk built or modified to the chair's specifications. The cost of this equipment can easily exceed $7,000 per child. Many kinds of equipment must be replaced as the child's functional ability changes or as the child's size increases. Special equipment to use in teaching self-feeding skills or for communication with children having limited oral language can also push the equipment cost per child into the thousands. (1981, p. 8)

A tenuous balance exists between society's willingness to provide special education and related services to students who are handicapped and society's ability to pay for these services. In times of financial prosperity, attempts to limit services or the number of students declared eligible for services are few. When school districts have plenty of money to spend on educating students with disabilities, diagnostic personnel are encouraged to locate and identify as many students with handicaps as possible. When funds are limited, however, concerns grow about the large number of students being declared handicapped.

Payment for Special Education Services

In a few instances, parents, private industry, or private organizations pay for the provision of special education services. This is especially true when services are provided in private schools or in private residential facilities. More generally, however, the public—through federal, state, and local tax dollars—pays the cost of educating exceptional students.

Dollars for education in general and for special education in particular come from federal, state, and local governments. It is difficult to estimate the proportion available from each source because the amount of money spent on education varies from state to state. In the 1970–1971 academic year, for example, about 53 percent of funding for all education came from local sources, 39 percent came from state governments, and 8 percent came from the federal government. In the 1978–1979 school year, the state share of revenues rose above the local share for the first time. Table 14.1 and Figure 14.1 illustrate trends in revenue receipts of public elementary and secondary schools from federal, state, and local sources. These data indicate that state and local governments are the primary source of revenues for public schools. In areas where state and local support is low, however, federal sources may provide as much as 20 to 30 percent of the moneys spent on education. According to information presented in the annual report to Congress (U.S. Dept. of Education, 1988b), federal contribution through state grant programs to support education of students who were handicapped increased from $251,770,000 in fiscal year 1977 to $1,338,000,000 in fiscal year 1987. Thus, the per child allocation increased from $72 per student to $315 per student during that same period. But

TABLE 14.1   Revenue receipts of public elementary and secondary schools from federal, state, and local sources, 1919–1920 to 1984–1985

| | Percentage Distribution[a] | | |
School Year	Federal	State	Local (including intermediate)[b]
1919–1920	0.3	16.5	83.2
1929–1930	0.4	16.9	82.7
1939–1940	1.8	30.3	68.0
1941–1942	1.4	31.4	67.1
1943–1944	1.4	33.0	65.6
1945–1946	1.4	34.7	63.9
1947–1948	2.8	38.9	58.3
1949–1950	2.9	39.8	57.3
1951–1952	3.5	38.6	57.9
1953–1954	4.5	37.4	58.1
1955–1956	4.6	39.5	55.9
1957–1958	4.0	39.4	56.6
1959–1960	4.4	39.1	56.5
1961–1962	4.3	38.7	56.9
1963–1964	4.4	39.3	56.3
1965–1966	7.9	39.1	53.0
1967–1968	8.8	38.5	52.7
1969–1970	8.0	39.9	52.1
1970–1971	8.4	39.1	52.5
1971–1972	8.9	38.3	52.8
1972–1973	8.7	40.0	51.3
1973–1974	8.5	41.4	50.1
1974–1975	9.0	42.2	48.8
1975–1976	8.9	44.6	46.5
1976–1977	8.8	43.4	47.8
1977–1978	9.4	43.0	47.6
1978–1979	9.8	45.6	44.6
1979–1980	9.8	46.8	43.4
1980–1981	9.2	47.4	43.4
1981–1982	7.4	47.6	45.0
1982–1983[c]	7.1	47.9	45.0
1983–1984[c]	6.8	47.8	45.4
1984–1985[d]	6.5	48.8	44.7

[a]Because of rounding, details may not add to 100 percent.
[b]Includes a relatively small amount from nongovernmental sources (gifts and tuition and transportation fees from patrons). These sources accounted for 0.4 percent of total revenue receipts in 1967–1968.
[c]Revised from previously published figures.
[d]Preliminary data.
SOURCE: U.S. Department of Education. (1986a). *Statistics of state school systems: Revenues and expenditures for public elementary and secondary education.* Washington, DC: U.S. Department of Education, National Center for Education Statistics; and Center for Education Statistics, *Common core of data* survey.

FIGURE 14.1   Sources of revenue for public elementary and secondary schools, 1920 to 1985

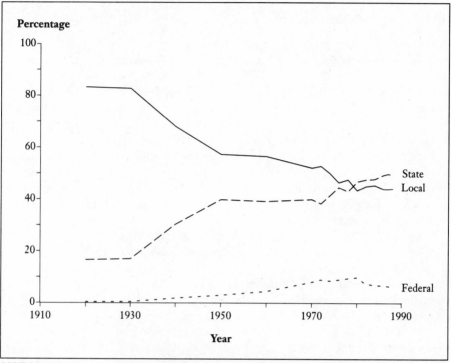

SOURCE: U.S. Department of Education (1986a). *Statistics of state school systems: Revenues and expenditures for public elementary and secondary education.* Washington, DC: U.S. Department of Education, National Center for Education Statistics; and Center for Education Statistics, *Common core of data* survey.

despite this increase, the relative percentage of federal support remained around 12 percent of the total cost of educating students with handicaps.

The question of who is responsible for funding programs is actively debated among and within the different levels of government. Debate is especially intense when federal laws mandate services that state or local education agencies are expected to pay for. Ultimately, the schools are responsible for providing all services that students need, including related services. They must work with local agencies to determine who pays for which service. What happens if the schools cannot raise needed money? They have to pay for related services themselves. This process has serious implications. When funds are limited, administrative personnel may discourage teachers and others from recommending needed related services.

Even when funds are not limited, special education competes with regular education for financial resources. From all the funds provided for education, moneys must be allocated between general and special education. When a state increases the percentage of moneys allocated to special education, moneys allocated to general education typically go down.

Funding Formulas

Most of the funding for special education comes from state and local treasuries. Considerable variation exists both among and within states in the ways special education funds are distributed. Bilken pointed out that the "standard state funding mechanisms for special services include one of the following: direct subsidy for special services (e.g., transportation, counseling, resource room programs); funding of types of personnel (e.g., special teachers, itinerant teachers); or per capita student funding" (1989, p. 8).

One approach to funding, called *special program reimbursement*, allocates moneys to districts on the basis of the kinds of students served and the kinds of services provided. Those who support this method contend that it is more expensive to serve some categories of students than others and that within any one category, the intensity of service for certain students varies.

In some states, moneys are allocated to special education according to the number of full-time special education personnel employed by individual districts, a practice known as *teacher unit funding*. State education department personnel make a decision to provide funding for a certain proportion of the salaries of special education personnel. For example, the state may fund 30, 60, or even 90 percent of the salary of each faculty member teaching special students.

In other instances, funding for special education is based on the numbers of students served, a method called *pupil unit funding*. Because it costs more to educate students with handicaps than students without them, this method determines funds distributed by using a calculation factor based on these excess costs. For example, state departments of education typically pay districts a per pupil expenditure; they multiply this amount by the calculation factor (such as 1.25 or 4.0) to pay the costs of educating students with disabilities.

In some states, funding patterns recognize that it is more costly to educate some kinds of handicapped students than others. Funding procedures are similar to pupil unit funding, but different multipliers are used for different categories; this method is known as *weighted funding*. The state education department may decide, for instance, that it costs twice as much to educate students who are blind than it does to educate students who are learning disabled. If schools receive 2.3 times the regular per pupil allocation for each student with a learning disability, they receive 4.6 times the regular allocation for each student who is blind.

Funding Incentives and Disincentives

The federal dollars that support the implementation of public laws on the education of students with handicaps are distributed as formula grants based on the number of students being served. Different funding mechanisms give districts lots of opportunities to manipulate the identification of students. Biklen put it this way:

> It is not hard to imagine the programmatic imperatives that can derive from such funding mechanisms. If state reimbursement rates provide more funding for learning disabilities than for "slow learners" or underachievers, for example, the ranks of students labeled "learning disabled" can be expected to expand. Similarly, if a state provides near total funding for certain types of services (e.g., for private or state residential schools), and a far less substantial allotment for serving students in their home districts, local school boards might be tempted to "place" more students outside the district. These effects of fiscal incentives have been well documented. (1989, p. 9)

Thus, when funds are allocated differently to different categories of students, there is a financial incentive to identify students as members of the better reimbursed category.

In those states in which teacher unit funding is used, there is a disincentive for identification of students as disabled because schools that identify large numbers of students end up with larger classes, not necessarily with more money for their programs. The only time schools receive more money is when they employ more personnel. This becomes a critical issue when teachers' unions do battle with local school districts over class sizes and cost issues. School districts then look to state departments of education to change allocation rules and funding formulas.

The Influence of Funding Patterns on Research

The research priorities established by the U.S. Department of Education usually determine the direction of research activities in special education. During the 1950s and 1960s, the federal government made mental retardation a research priority, and centers for research on mental retardation were established across the country. As funding priorities changed, new centers were established and old ones changed their names and expanded their missions. During the mid- and late 1970s, institutes were funded to conduct research on learning disabilities and on early intervention. In the 1980s, there was less federal support for research on learning disabilities; instead, support shifted to research on students with severe handicaps and transition services for older students with disabilities. In the 1990s, emphasis will be on early childhood education. Decisions to shift research efforts are often motivated by economics: researchers go "where the money is."

Escalating Costs

Special education is an expensive business. It is estimated that about 10 percent of a district's costs go to provision of special education services. Lewis, Bruininks, and Thurlow (1989) reported that from 1980 to 1988, per pupil costs for regular instruction increased about 7 percent annually, while annual increases for special education exceeded 12 percent. The amount of money appropriated for state and local grants for the education of children with handicaps, for example, was $1,475,449 in fiscal year 1989 and $1,564,017 in 1990. In addition to appropriations for educating children with handicaps, moneys appropriated for vocational education services, rehabilitation services, and a variety of other services, such as Head Start, also increased. Not all the moneys in these other areas went to educating students with handicaps.

Cost of Transportation

School districts incur extra costs in the provision of transportation to students who are disabled. Such students often must be transported long distances to receive appropriate educational services, and they must often be transported using special equipment (buses designed for wheelchairs, equipped with oxygen, etc.). Lewis et al. noted that

> transportation costs within special education have always been recognized as a necessary component for the delivery of such educational services; however the magnitude of such costs has not always been appreciated. For example, it is important to note that in almost every case of special education service by an external agency in this study there were significant concurrent transportation costs to the district beyond just tuition charges. Although daily transportation costs for special education students being served by external agencies averaged only $6, as compared to average daily tuition rates of $12, in almost half of the individual student cases daily transportation costs exceeded or almost equaled the average daily tuition rate being charged by the external agency to which the student was being transported. In this study, transportation costs represented almost one-half of all costs to the district in sending students out to external agencies. (1989, p. 481)

Cost of Teacher Salaries

Teacher salaries become an issue because it is thought by general education teachers (and sometimes the general public) that the provision of special education means hiring additional personnel who have specialized training and who are paid at rates higher than those of general education teachers. This is not always the case, however. Lewis et al. reported that

> contrary to conventional wisdom, the average salaries of teachers in special education within the district under study were less than those of regular teachers by over 11 percent—i.e., $25,335 versus $28,500. It is typically assumed that because teachers in special education necessarily must have additional training and licensure in their respective service areas (generally after initial certification as regular teachers), and with salary schedules closely aligned with such training and experience, the average salaries in special education will necessarily exceed those of regular teachers. Consequently, it often is assumed that the average cost of instructional staff in special education will inherently always be more expensive than regular instruction. This case study indicates that these assumptions and

results are not necessarily always true. The teaching staff of regular classes in this school district apparently also had considerable advanced training and experience and/or the special education personnel in this district were, on average, younger than the staff of regular instruction. (1989, p. 481)

When there are disparities in salary between regular and special education teachers, several issues arise. For example, a disparity in salaries will have an effect on self-esteem: teachers who are paid less may view themselves as worth less. Disparities may also affect expectations: an administrator may expect more of teachers who are paid more, less of those who are paid less. Differences in self-esteem and expectation may in turn translate into differences in teacher performance, with those who are paid less performing in accord with their perceptions of the "low regard" with which they are held. Finally, salary disparities may have an impact on peer relations: teachers' relations with one another may be negatively affected when there are salary disparities.

Efficiency Issues

For the most part, the efficiency and productivity of special education have received only minimal attention in both the research and policy literature because special educators have been concerned with matters of finance, specifically with the cost of providing special education services. The examination of the relationships between costs and outcomes is quite new to special education.

What Should Be Considered as "Benefits"?

If educators are to look at the extent to which students with disabilities profit from special education, what factors should be considered as benefits? There are no "typically used" indicators of benefits: sometimes educators talk about academic outcomes as benefits (improved academic skills, usually as evidenced through an achievement test), yet such an indicator is hardly useful when it comes to students with disabilities. In this case, educators consider the extent to which provision of services to such students results in increased output (earnings, contributions to the tax base), reduced use of alternative programs (institutional environments), reduced program costs, and improved quality of life. Indicators of benefits from schooling are measured in terms of employment status (competitive paid employment, sheltered paid employment, no employment), earned income, participation in the work force (hours worked per week), financial independence (receipt of Social Security benefits, receipt of Medicaid, possession of an independent checking account), community adjustment, and degree of independence in living arrangements (group home, foster care, independent living). Those who study the benefits of education for students with disabilities, especially those who want to know whether education is efficient, must make tough choices in selecting outcomes indicators. At issue is whether to select academic indicators, personal/

social/affective indicators, or quality of life indicators. Also at issue is whether indicators should differ as a function of the severity of an individual's disability.

Equity Versus Efficiency

The most efficient provision of services to students is not always the most equitable. Take, for instance, the provision of vouchers to parents so that they can send their children to any school they choose. This practice is widely advocated as well as widely abhorred, and there are financial and efficiency arguments for and against such open enrollment.

Advocates of open enrollment argue that provision of vouchers and choice will result in a market-driven school system in which schools become competitive (to attract or retain students) and improve their quality. They argue that structural change in schools will come only through the withholding of resources. They point out that schools that lose students will either cut back, close, or get better and that this will result in improved efficiency.

Those who argue against choice say that the practice of providing parents with vouchers will result in the use of those vouchers primarily by parents of upper- and upper-middle-class students, parents who can afford to pick up some of the costs of transporting students and who are aware enough of their options to take advantage of them. Opponents argue that provision of vouchers will result in increased social stratification.

No Matter the Cost?

When individuals or groups believe they have been abused or shortchanged by the educational system, they sometimes take it on themselves to redress wrongs through litigation. Parents of children who were mentally retarded sued the Pennsylvania Department of Education for alleged exclusion of their children from the educational system. Parents of students with learning disabilities in Philadelphia sued the school district for failure to provide their children with an "appropriate" education. The courts sometimes mandate that educators take action, no matter the cost, to redress wrongs.

When instances of alleged abuse become very frequent, or when there are repeated court cases on the same or similar issues, legislatures take remedial action. In the late 1960s and early 1970s, there were many instances in which professional associations, advocacy groups, or individuals sued school districts for failure to provide access to educational services for students with disabilities, for exclusion of services (or changes in placement without due process), for alleged bias in assessment, and for inappropriate placement. In 1975, President Gerald Ford signed the Education for all Handicapped Children Act into law. That law included provisions that mandated access, fair assessment, due process, and placement in least restrictive environments. Cost was not an issue. The social value of the ideals outweighed funding considerations.

It Is Cheaper, Easier, and More Effective to:

1. Keep people from falling into poverty in the first place rather than to get them out later.

2. Keep all kinds of families intact rather than arrange adoption and foster care facilities later.

3. Keep students performing at grade level by "front loading" resources toward those most at risk, rather than telling them at the *end* of third grade that they failed when no effort was made to provide the resources that could have meant success.

4. Keep people out of prisons rather than trying to rehabilitate them later.

5. Keep low-income people in an expanding supply of affordable housing rather than increasing the number of homeless families, often with children and one or more full-time workers.

6. Keep mass transit so that low-income workers can continue to have jobs, housing, and some freedom.

7. Keep kids from getting sick (or hungry) rather than providing massive programs for curing (or feeding) them after the damage has been done.

Although these points are obvious, it is estimated by the author that we spend in general 15 percent of our money on prevention programs and *85 percent* on rather ineffective "cures" in all social service areas.

SOURCE: Hodgkinson, H. L. (1989). *The same client: The demographics of education and service delivery systems* (p. 27). Washington, DC: Institute for Educational Leadership, Center for Demographic Policy. Used with permission.

The Cost Versus the Benefit of Prevention

Many educational programs have been developed for the purpose of preventing later school difficulties and then providing costly educational interventions (see box). One example of such a program is Project Head Start. Instituted as part of President Lyndon Johnson's War on Poverty, Head Start has been funded for more than twenty years. The program was started in an effort to close the experiential gap between children who were disadvantaged by virtue of their family's social and economic status and those who were not. The children were given preschool experiences that would enable them to be on an even footing with nondisadvantaged children when they entered school. Has the program worked?

The High Cost of Failure

Business people know that it is less expensive to prevent failure than to try to correct it later. Early intervention for poor children from conception to age five has been shown to be a highly cost-effective strategy for reducing later expenditures on a wide variety of health, developmental, and educational problems that often interfere with learning. Long-term studies of the benefits of preschool education have demonstrated returns on investment ranging from $3 to $6 for every $1 spent. Prenatal care has been shown to yield over $3.38 in savings on the costs of care for low-birthweight babies. Early immunization for a variety of childhood diseases saves $10 in later medical costs. Supplementing nutrition for poor women, infants, and children yields a $3 payback in savings on later health care costs.

At the same time, the costs of not intervening early can be astronomical.

• Every "class" of dropouts earns about $237 billion less than an equivalent class of high school graduates during their lifetimes. As a result, the government receives about $70 billion less in tax revenues.

• Each year, taxpayers spend $16.6 billion to support the children of teenage parents.

• About 82 percent of all Americans in prison are high school dropouts, and it costs an average of $20,000 to maintain each prisoner annually. In comparison, a year of high-quality preschool costs about $4,800 and has been shown to decrease the rate of arrest in the teenage years by 40 percent.

SOURCE: Research and Policy Committee of the Committee on Economic Development. (1991). *The unfinished agenda: A new vision for child development and education.* New York: Committee on Economic Development. Used with permission.

Has participation in preschool intervention put the children on an even footing, has it reduced or eliminated later academic difficulty, has it saved society money in the long run? Lee, Brooks-Gunn, and Schnur recently addressed these questions by comparing disadvantaged children who attended Head Start, other preschool programs, and no preschool. They reported that

Large initial group differences were observed between Head Start children and both comparison groups, with those in Head Start at a disadvantage on nearly every demographic and cognitive measure. Adjusting for initial background and cognitive differences, Head Start children showed significantly larger gains on the Preschool Inventory and Motor Inhibition tests than either comparison group, with Black children in Head Start (especially those of below-average initial ability) gaining the most. However, despite substantial gains, Head Start children were still behind their peers in terms of absolute cognitive levels after a year in the program. Head Start proved an impressive instrument of short-term change, even compared with other preschool experience. Gains in behaviors other than intelligence suggest that the effects may not be limited to the cognitive domain. (1988, p. 210)

The Committee on Economic Development has called for full funding of Head Start three times in the past three years, and it has maintained that

> education is an investment, not an expense. If we can ensure that all children are born healthy and develop the skills and knowledge they need to be productive, self-supporting adults, whatever is spent on their development and education will be returned many times over in higher productivity, incomes, and taxes and in lower costs for welfare, health care, crime, and myriad other economic and social problems. (1991, p. 15)

Full funding of Head Start and other preventive programs designed to ensure adequate development and early education of poor children would cost about $9 billion more than is currently spent. At issue is whether funds should be spent on such preventive and developmental programs or on other national priorities, such as defense, transportation, and housing.

Discussion Questions

1. Identify some of the ways in which the federal government and the state in which you live regulate, finance, and administer special education services.

2. Identify at least three financial incentives for identifying students in your state as disabled and in need of special education services.

3. Currently, in most states, delivery of special education services is tied to funding, and funding to categorical identification of students. What are some alternatives to that practice, and what are some merits and limitations of the various alternatives?

CHAPTER 15

Competing Perspectives on Special Education in the Next Century

The Future of Special Education
Training People Versus Training Professionals
Reform Versus Resignation
Assessing Students Versus Assessing Outcomes
Continuing Choices Versus Historical Challenges
Performance Versus Postulates
Self-Determination Versus Societal Responsibility

Special Education in the Future
Reform Versus Renewal
An Ounce of Prevention Is Worth a Pound of Cure
An Ounce of Pretention Is Worth a Pound of Manure
An Ounce of Intervention Is Worth a Pound of Assure

We find that whole communities suddenly fix their minds upon one object, and go mad in its pursuit; that millions of people become simultaneously impressed with one delusion, and run after it, till their attention is caught by some new folly more captivating than the first.

—*Charles Mackay*

Special education is a subsystem of regular education, but whether this will always be the case we do not know. Nor can we say whether special education will continue to be organized categorically, how assessment practices will evolve, what conditions special education teachers will encounter, and how school reform will affect special education. In short, we do not believe that we can predict the future of special education because the direction of special education has been shaped by a mixture of social, legal, political, philosophical, and financial realities and will continue to be so influenced. Who would have anticipated the degree of progress that has been made in the past two decades?

Nevertheless, we do have some thoughts on where special education is going. We hope you will recognize the precarious nature of making statements about the future. And we hope that those who read this text in 2010 will not rub in our faces the extent to which we were wrong.

The Future of Special Education

Views of the future are typically presented differently by the optimist and by the pessimist. To the optimist, the glass is always half full; to the pessimist, it is half empty. And just as nobody "really knows what time it is," nobody really knows if the glass is empty or full. Perceptions control much of human behavior, and the perceptions people have about training, educational reform, assessment, human responsibility, educational choice, and performance measurement will control the destiny of these matters for the future of special education. The competing perspectives that characterize contemporary opinions about these and other areas of professional practice will drive efforts to improve special education in the next century.

Training People Versus Training Professionals

The issues that will shape the direction of personnel training efforts in special education for the next century will be grounded in past and current practices and in the views people hold about the nature of teaching (see box) and its professional development. Some of these issues center on the differences between special education and regular teachers, between trained and untrained teachers, and among special education teachers. Other issues address what public expectations of special education teachers are, whether these teachers are the only ones who can deliver services to exceptional children, and if not, what expectations attach to other professionals providing services. Still other issues look at who is training teachers of exceptional students and what expertise the teachers need or possess.

In regard to the last set of issues, Pugach and Lilly argued that "teacher education programs tend to follow rather than lead the field of practice" (1984, p. 48). This is largely due to the simple fact that universities prepare students to work in schools that are controlled by regulations and requirements originating in state departments of education:

> Universities prepare students to compete for real jobs in real schools and must therefore be sensitive to professional conditions, as well as hiring practices and criteria, in K–12 schools.
> Universities offer teacher education programs through a maze of state regulations for program approval and teacher certification that are nearly always reflective of current and past practice in education, not future trends or directions. (Lilly, 1989, p. 144)

In the years following the passage of PL 94-142, the demand for special education personnel grew at unprecedented rates as school districts delivered more and varied services to broader numbers and wider age ranges of students with

Issues Reflected in Contemporary Practices

I am certain that you are aware of the many changes occurring in our state educational system today. Many of these issues and components can be facilitated by a cooperative endeavor among the many levels of exceptional children's services personnel. Please bear with me as I point out a few of the more salient elements of these changes and current concerns.

The traditionally limited funding available for special education services is being effectively reduced through actual reductions, or limited inflationary measures. Many of the major funding resources are looking toward programs and agencies involved in, or proposing to develop, cooperative relationships.

Projections of future demands indicate that we will not be able to adequately train sufficient numbers of special education professionals needed. Local Education Agencies will be developing pedagogical training programs for local certification of quality personnel who are at present filling these positions with emergency or provisional certification.

The Regular Education Initiative, least restrictive environment principles of PL 94-142, and resource limitation are factors involved in the placement of more exceptional children in regular education classrooms with teachers unprepared to teach them. Local parent and advocacy groups are voicing concern over what they perceive as a reduction in services.

New mandates of federal and state laws require expansion of services and programs to meet the needs of exceptional persons (i.e., transition programs for the mildly handicapped; pre-school assessment; and, programs for at-risk children), yet no resources are forthcoming for the development or maintenance of these new requirements.

Current discussions at the national and state level are focusing on radical shifts in the manner in which we prepare teachers. Schools of education are experimenting with alternate models of pre-service teacher preparation programs; and, local education agencies are developing mentor training programs for initially certified personnel.

The literature indicates that special education practitioners are not using results of current research to improve educational programs for exceptional children. Conversely, many special educational professionals are developing and implementing innovative and effective programs and models, but are unable to disseminate this information to their colleagues.

SOURCE: Excerpted from a letter from T. J. Wasileski to special education chairpersons in North Carolina, January 15, 1991. Used by permission of the author.

What Makes Teaching Difficult?

1. Students are seldom cooperative participants in instruction, and many are highly resistant to it.

2. Teachers are often blamed for failure they believe they cannot control and are powerless to change.

3. Teachers perceive their pay as grossly inadequate.

4. Teachers do not receive additional compensation for particularly effective lessons or for doing a really good job; in fact, there is often no relationship between how effectively a teacher teaches and the pay received for doing it.

5. Teachers often do not have strong social and cultural support for what they do; teaching and "book learning" are not highly valued in this culture.

6. Teachers are expected to control and coerce students more than they are expected to stimulate their creativity and natural talents.

7. Parents often view teaching as inexpensive (and not particularly effective) child care.

8. Students view much of what goes on in schools as stifling their natural interests and destroying their natural motivation.

disabilities and handicaps (U.S. Dept. of Education, 1990a). The need for qualified personnel to work with students with special learning needs will probably continue into the next century. Because special education populations have been steadily growing, there is no reason to believe that this growth will subside; in fact, new groups of children and youths with special learning needs (e.g., children with AIDS, crack babies, minority students with learning problems) are increasingly appearing as "hot topics" in professional journals (Barnes, 1986; Cantwell & Baker, 1991; Centers for Disease Control, 1987a, 1987b; Fradd & Correa, 1989; Jason et al., 1990; Shaywitz & Shaywitz, 1991). At the same time, teacher attrition rates in special education are increasing, and enrollments in and graduations from personnel preparation programs are declining (U.S. Dept. of Education, 1990b).

The decline in recruitment, the growth in reported personnel shortages, the projections of teacher retirements, the expansion of services, and the increase in the number of students receiving special education make personnel preparation concerns central and critical. Although the status of these current conditions "signal an impending crisis" in the provision of services to students with disabilities, they also represent only a portion of the problems related to meeting

TABLE 15.1   Personnel needed to serve students with special needs

Type of Personnel	Personnel Needed	Percentage of Total Needed
Teachers		
Learning disabilities	7,759	29.1
Speech and language impairment	3,598	13.5
Mental retardation	3,999	15.0
Emotional disturbance	4,388	16.5
Hardness of hearing and deafness	610	2.3
Multiple handicaps	776	2.9
Orthopedic impairment	365	1.4
Other health impairment	316	1.2
Visual handicaps	394	1.5
Deafness, blindness	50	0.2
Cross-categorical programs	4,398	16.5
Total teachers	26,653	100.0
Other personnel		
Psychologists	1,326	8.5
School social workers	728	4.7
Occupational therapists	713	4.6
Audiologists	190	1.2
Paraprofessionals	6,625	42.5
Vocational education teachers	593	3.8
Work-study coordinators	291	1.9
Physical education coordinators	403	2.6
Recreational therapists	67	0.4
Diagnostic staff	680	4.4
Supervisors	700	4.5
Physical therapists	755	4.8
Counselors	763	4.9
State education agency supervisors	109	0.7
Other noninstructional staff[a]	1,628	10.5
Total other personnel	15,571	100.0

[a]Includes staff needed in health services (nurses, psychiatrists, etc.), food services, maintenance, and pupil transportation.
SOURCE: U.S. Department of Education. (1990b). *To assure the free appropriate public education of all handicapped children: Twelfth annual report to Congress on the implementation of the Education of the Handicapped Act* (Tables 1.14 and 1.15, pp. 37–38). Washington, DC: Author.

personnel needs in special education (U.S. Dept. of Education, 1990b, p. 39247). Local school districts also report high levels of need for staff other than teachers (see Table 15.1), and problems go beyond simple concerns for meeting supply and demand.

Current practices allow some local school district administrators and state education agency personnel to waive training requirements so that people with emergency or restricted certification can fill positions on a temporary or permanent basis (Goodlad, 1990). Alternative certification is a "generic term applied to any non-traditional route to certification which permits an individual who does not hold an appropriate certificate to begin teaching while pursuing the appropriate certificate through a supervised program of academic study and 'on the job' training" (Olson, 1990, p. 1). The extent of these practices has been estimated to be high (e.g., virtually all states make some provision for alternative certification), and their impact on special education remains a topic of future research. There is concern that the impact will not be positive because by definition these "professionals" are not fully qualified to teach students in special education. A serious issue will surface if efforts to compare "qualified and unqualified" teachers produce inconsequential differences in terms of outcomes that matter to students. Indeed, there is some evidence that categorical certification has little to do with teacher effectiveness.

Observing that teacher certification and training programs typically adhere to the same categorical delineations as student-based identification systems, Marston (1988) examined academic achievement of students taught by teachers prepared in the same or different categorical certification programs. His results were less than complimentary for categorical training perspectives:

> LD students taught by LD teachers do not improve more than LD students taught by EMR teachers. Likewise, EMR pupils instructed by EMR licensed teachers do not improve more than EMR students taught by teachers with LD certification. Rather, both LD and EMR pupils make similar gains when taught by teachers with varying certification. (Marston, 1987, p. 427)

Concerns about the quality and quantity of special education teachers have also led to the development of alternative preparation programs. Traditional university-based training programs are being replaced or supplemented with school district–based offices designed to provide continuing and entry-level teachers with courses and information necessary to practice in public schools. The perspectives of these programs vary greatly in terms of the academic preparation and field experiences needed for completion (U.S. Dept. of Education, 1990b), and concern for their effects on alternative certification practices is evident in most states (Olson, 1990). The range of these provisions includes programs that limit professional studies (e.g., education courses) and stress essential content knowledge (e.g., English, math, and science courses) to those that stress traditional professional studies coupled with alternative professional experiences as the basis for certification. For years, private schools have been staffed with a pool of people with strong content knowledge but little professional preparation. Many public school teachers, "desperate for better education experiences for their own children, are strapping themselves financially to send their children to private schools, which they believe are doing a better job of quality education" (Glasser, 1990, p. 6). As the search for better schools continues, comparisons of the teaching styles provided by people trained and entering education along different paths will very likely become very common.

How will the training of teachers change as a result of concern for current practices and the future? Nobody knows, but professionals have prepared predictive platforms and proposed plenty of postulates as planks in the bridge that must be built to move from the present state of affairs to a more desirable one. For example, Lilly predicted that

> separate systems of teacher preparation in special education [would] go the way of separate systems of education for children [and that for] programs for preparing teachers of students labeled "mildly handicapped" (or "learning disabled," "behaviorally disordered," or "educable or mildly mentally retarded") special education as a separate entity in teacher education [would] disappear. (1989, p. 146)

He based his prediction on observations of interest in a system of national teacher certification (Carnegie Forum, 1986) and on increasing incentives for continuing education and advancement for practicing teachers.

Concerned by persistent patterns of neglect in professional preparation efforts, Goodlad presented 19 "essential presuppositions—as postulates—to guide our journey through the teacher education landscape and, ultimately to shape our evaluation of it" (1990, p. 191). The postulates that he believed would shape the future of teacher education follow (pp. 191–192):

> *Postulate 1.* Programs for the education of the nation's educators must be viewed by institutions offering them as a major responsibility to society and be adequately supported and promoted and vigorously advanced by the institution's top leadership.
> *Postulate 2.* Programs for the education of educators must enjoy parity with other campus programs as a legitimate college or university commitment and field of study and service, worthy of rewards for faculty geared to the nature of the field.
> *Postulate 3.* Programs for the education of educators must be autonomous and secure in their borders, with clear organizational identity, constancy of budget and personnel, and decision-making authority similar to that enjoyed by the major professional schools.
> *Postulate 4.* There must exist a clearly identifiable group of academic and clinical faculty members for whom teacher education is the top priority; the group must be responsible and accountable for selecting students and monitoring their progress, planning, and maintaining the full scope and sequence of the curriculum, continuously evaluating and improving programs, and facilitating the entry of graduates into teaching careers.
> *Postulate 5.* The responsible group of academic and clinical faculty members described above must have a comprehensive understanding of the aims of education and the role of schools in society and be fully committed to selecting and preparing teachers to assume the full range of educational responsibilities required.
> *Postulate 6.* The responsible group of academic and clinical faculty members must seek out and select for a predetermined number of student places in the program those candidates who reveal an initial commitment to the moral, ethical, and enculturating responsibilities to be assumed.

Postulate 7. Programs for the education of educators, whether elementary or secondary, must carry the responsibility to ensure that all candidates progressing through them possess or acquire the literacy and critical-thinking abilities associated with the concept of an educated person.

Postulate 8. Programs for the education of educators must provide extensive opportunities for future teachers to move beyond being students of organized knowledge to become teachers who inquire into both knowledge and its teaching.

Postulate 9. Programs for the education of educators must be characterized by a socialization process through which candidates transcend their self-oriented student preoccupations to become more other-oriented in identifying with a culture of teaching.

Postulate 10. Programs for the education of educators must be characterized in all respects by the conditions for learning that future teachers are to establish in their own schools and classrooms.

Postulate 11. Programs for the education of educators must be conducted in such a way that future teachers inquire into the nature of teaching and schooling and assume that they will do so as a natural aspect of their careers.

Postulate 12. Programs for the education of educators must involve future teachers in the issues and dilemmas that emerge out of the never-ending tension between the rights and interests of individual parents and special-interest groups, on one hand, and the role of schools in transcending parochialism, on the other.

Postulate 13. Programs for the education of educators must be infused with understanding of and commitment to the moral obligation of teachers to ensure equitable access to and engagement in the best possible K–12 education for all children and youths.

Postulate 14. Programs for the education of educators must involve future teachers not only in understanding schools as they are but in alternatives, and how to effect needed changes in school organization, pupil grouping, curriculum, and more.

Postulate 15. Programs for the education of educators must assure for each candidate the availability of a wide array of laboratory settings for observation, hands-on experiences, and exemplary schools for internships and residencies; they must admit no more students to their programs than can be assured these quality experiences.

Postulate 16. Programs for the education of educators must engage future teachers in the problems and dilemmas arising out of the inevitable conflicts and incongruities between what works or is accepted in practice and the research and theory supporting other options.

Postulate 17. Programs for educating educators must establish linkages with graduates for purposes of both evaluating and revising these programs and easing the critical early years of transition into teaching.

Postulate 18. Programs for the education of educators, in order to be vital and renewing, must be free from curricular specifications by licensing agencies and restrained only by enlightened, professionally driven requirements for accreditation.

Postulate 19. Programs for the education of educators must be protected from the vagaries of supply and demand by state policies that allow neither back door "emergency" programs nor temporary teaching licenses.

Clearly strong emotion has emerged from efforts to postulate "what ought to be" if teacher education is to make substantive gains in improving what has passed as professional practice for quite some time (Johnson, 1990; Lilly, 1989; Wise, 1990). The education of special educators will surely profit from similar soul-searching, and the benefits that will accrue if these postulates are put into practice will serve special educators well.

Reform Versus Resignation

The 1980s will probably be seen as the decade of school reform. Many different initiatives designed to improve education can be grouped under the rubric of school reform. Approaches ranging from simple administrative practices such as lengthening the school day or setting higher expectations for students to full-scale restructuring of educational systems (e.g., providing open enrollment options) have been proposed in efforts to change education (Goens & Clover, 1990). Interest in school reform has generated considerable local, state, and national activity. Beginning with identification of the sad state of affairs characterized as an educational system and ending with articulated goals and questions related to how to achieve them, efforts to improve education moved rapidly during the 1980s.

But not everybody believes education can be reformed, at least not in its present state. Sarason painted a particularly bleak picture:

> When I say that schools have been intractable to reform, I mean that for the large majority of students, including most from nonpoverty backgrounds, the declared aims of schooling are empty rhetoric that bears little relationship to their social experience. Further, I mean that failure of educational reform derives from a most superficial conception of how complicated settings are organized: their structure, their dynamics, their power relationships, and their underlying values and axioms. Schools today are not what they were twenty or thirty years ago. They have changed but in the spirit of the popular song containing the line "I am true to you in *my* fashion," which means that the changes are cosmetic and not fundamental. Schools will remain intractable to desired reform as long as we avoid confronting (among other things) their existing power relationships. (1990, p. 5)

He argued that a fundamental error in conceptualizing how to change the system is the traditional misplacement of blame for school failure onto a litany of inappropriate villains (e.g., inadequate teachers; irresponsible parents; irrelevant or inadequate curricula; unmotivated students from whom too little is expected, demanded, or obtained; improvement-defeating bureaucracies; inadequate or inappropriate promotion and graduation standards; and lack of the competitiveness that goads organizations to progress in other arenas). He saw the alteration of power relationships in classrooms and schools as a first step in improving educational systems.

Alternative perspectives on power are also at the base of other proposals to radically alter educational systems. Building on the principles postulated by Deming that transformed Japan into the "world's richest country," Glasser (1990, p. 3) called for movement from boss management to lead management as the only way to really achieve quality schools. Under boss management, the power rests with the boss, and the needs of the boss are more important than those of the workers:

1. The boss sets the jobs and without consulting the workers and establishes the standards for what workers are to do. Bosses do not compromise or consult; workers adjust to the job as the boss defines it.

2. The boss usually tells, rather than shows, the workers how the work is to be done and rarely asks for input as to how a job might be done better.

3. The boss (or a designated representative) inspects the work. Because workers are not involved in this process, they often settle for just enough quality to get by the evaluation of the boss.

4. When workers resist, the boss uses punishment, power, and coercion to obtain compliance and in doing so creates a workplace in which workers and managers are constant adversaries.

By substituting teacher for boss and student for worker, the parallels to educational workplaces become transparent and serve as sufficient basis for considering lead management as an alternative for improving educational systems. As Deming put it, "The goal is clear. The productivity of our systems must be increased. The key to change is the understanding of our managers, and the people to whom they report, about what it means to be a good manager" (quoted in Glasser, 1990, p. 31). The principles of lead management illustrate what this means:

1. The leader engages the workers in a discussion of the quality of the work to be done and the time needed to do it so that they have a chance to add their input. The leader makes a constant effort to fit the job to the skills and the needs of the workers.

2. The leader (or a worker designated by the leader) shows or models the job so that the worker who is to perform the job sees exactly what the manager expects. At the same time, the workers are continually asked for their input as to what they believe may be a better way.

3. The leader asks the workers to inspect or evaluate their own work for quality, with the understanding that the leader accepts that they know a great deal about how to produce high-quality work and will therefore listen to what they say.

4. The leader is a facilitator in that he shows the workers that he has done everything possible to provide them with the best tools and workplace as well as a noncoercive, nonadversarial atmosphere in which to do the job. (Glasser, 1990, pp. 31–32)

Clearly much of what passes as instruction in contemporary classrooms bears strong resemblance to boss management and little resemblance to lead management (see Table 15.2). And even though we see the principles of lead management as truly promising alternatives for reforming education, we believe the likelihood of significant changes happening is very small—not because people do not want to change but because they are resigned to ineffective reform strategies that address

TABLE 15.2   Comparison of competing instructional management styles

Boss Management	Lead Management
Boss teacher sets the learning agenda, and students are expected to comply because it is right to do so. Students have little or no say in the process.	Lead teacher discusses content, defining critical aspects and explaining why specific topics are taught and how students can use them in their daily lives.
Boss teacher tells students to work independently and sets specific dates for assignments and tests. Students are seldom asked for input on instructional goals or methods. Preset curriculum targets control instructional time.	Lead teacher answers immediate questions and uses small cooperative groups as primary work structures. Teacher uses student input as to when test should be given. Competency and quality are the rule. Amount of time needed to master a task does not control instruction.
Boss teacher grades students using preset standards. Students pass if they meet minimum standards (e.g., D or better), and plenty of students are failing.	Lead teacher involves students, as individuals and as members of groups, in evaluating the quality of their classwork, homework, and test performances.
Boss teacher gives students little authority. Control and compliance with rules for behavior are hallmarks of the management style, and plenty of time is spent "disciplining" students.	Lead teacher continually facilitates by talking to students and listening to their input on how to keep the classroom a good place to learn.

the wrong problems and ask the wrong questions. This is evident in efforts to explain the failure of school reform to adequately correct education's errant course (Glasser, 1990; Sarason, 1990) and in efforts to improve assessment and other important practices.

Assessing Students Versus Assessing Outcomes

States are mandating changes in their assessment practices. Some states are merging special education with regular education, breaking down barriers that required specific kinds of low-level performances on tests to permeate. School districts are enabling assessors to engage in new roles and new activities. School psychologists are now working as behavior management specialists and collaborative consultants, rather than as psychometric robots. University training programs, like the one at the University of Minnesota, are changing the way they train assessors. They are moving away from training professionals to administer the major intelligence tests and instead educating them in ecological appraisal, assessment of instructional environments, curriculum-based measurement, portfolio assessment, and collaborative problem solving. Indeed, the National Association of School Psychologists published an entire compendium of alternative educational delivery systems (Graden, Zins, & Curtis, 1988). Practitioners who spoke in the past of norm-referenced appraisal, technical adequacy, aptitude × treatment interactions, and bias in assessment now talk about performance-based assessment, neuropsychological appraisal, curriculum-based measurement, assessment of instructional environments, and assessment anchored to outcomes. It would be easy to conclude that a major revolution is taking place in assessment practices.

But the more we have read and the more we observe assessment practices in schools, the more we doubt that fundamental change is taking place. We get discouraged. We repeatedly ask ourselves questions such as "Will those who assess children really discontinue their heavy reliance on tests?" "What are the incentives for people to change their practices?" "Will training programs really adapt the way they train professionals?" "Will we ever see an end to the practice of describing child pathology as the focus of assessment?"

In fact, society has changed significantly over the past two decades, and students now enter school with significantly more problems (and individually with many more severe problems) than they did in the early 1970s. Schools are undergoing restructuring and reform. Yet assessment practices today look for the most part as they did in 1970, and there is little reason to believe they will change. Sure, the social, political, economic, and cultural happenings since 1970 have influenced assessment practices, but they have not led to fundamental change. Assessment practices in the future will probably look much like they look today. Some assessors will engage in curriculum-based measurement and prereferral intervention, monitor data on pupil progress, focus at the preschool level, and engage in multidisciplinary problem solving. Most, we believe, will continue to function as psychometric robots. Jack Bardon, in a recent keynote address to the North Carolina Association of School Psychologists (October 1990), pointed out that "Assessment practices are whatever professionals make of them. They are a function of the styles, knowledge base, characteristics, demeanor, professional biases, creativity, temperament, savvy, wisdom, energy, assertiveness, etc. of the individual assessor more so than they are a function of what the field is or somebody says it should be."

We hope we are wrong. Perhaps when all is said and done, change will come about by chaos. McGarry contended that enduring changes require the reformation of entire networks of interlocking elements, that chaos provides the most fertile source for new structures, and that attempts to change assessment practices by adjusting one factor at a time will fail. McGarry argued further that

> change can occur gradually, but only if major sections of the cultural network change incrementally, until an entirely new network has been created. An easier way to make incremental change, however, is to initiate it at a cusp in the organizational life—at a time when the former structure is collapsing in the face of a changed environment or from exhaustion of its own internal energies. (1990, p. 15)

Continuing Choices Versus Historical Challenges

What will the future look like if choice is fully implemented in more states? When we talk about choice we mean the perspective that grew in the 1980s regarding the potential for marketplace influences to work in education. According to this concept, if educational institutions were subjected to the laws of the marketplace, consumers would show their desire for quality products, and as a result, schools would begin to "clean up their act" so that they would not go out of business. The result would be increases in the number of good schools and decreases in the number of bad and not-so-good schools.

But even as the notion of educational choice picked up speed, questions were raised about what it meant for students with disabilities. Would students with disabilities or their parents participate in the opportunity for choice? Would it make a difference in a program that was so heavily influenced by federal funding? And did parents really know what programs were the best for their children with unique educational needs? These and many other questions will continue to face us if the nation moves toward increased educational choice.

Performance Versus Postulates

Will educators ever really be concerned about what difference special education makes, or will they continue to give lip service to propositions and postulates about what "ought to be" evaluated? Few states assess the educational outcomes of students with mild disabilities beyond what is required by federal mandates (e.g., dropout rate, anticipated need for services). And for the most part few states have the resources to do more in the area of outcomes assessment than what is required by law. If this is the case, how can educators expect to give more then lip service to the notion of evaluating the effectiveness of special education? Even if states did have the resources to evaluate special education, would they know what to collect for outcome data and how?

There are many basic questions related to outcomes assessment that have not yet been solved. For example:

• To what extent should effectiveness indicators for students with disabilities differ from effectiveness indicators for students without disabilities?

• Should desired outcomes for students with disabilities be noncategorical?

• Should desired outcomes differ as a function of severity of disability?

• Should desired outcomes differ as a function of developmental level?

• Should professionals be gathering data on outcomes at the level of the individual, the building, the district, or the state?

Even if states did know the answers to these and other questions, so what? If educators are not yet able to link outcomes back to programs, what difference does worrying about outcomes make that they know what the outcomes should be?

Self-Determination Versus Societal Responsibility

It was not that long ago that people in America, and other countries as well, thought that it was the responsibility of society to take care of those individuals who supposedly were not able to take care of themselves. At the beginning of the twentieth century, Americans were very concerned with promoting reproduction of only the most capable individuals. Individuals with disabilities, particularly those with mental impairments, were held in very low regard. Not until the middle of the century did Americans begin to recognize that they had been mistreating people with disabilities. Progress was slow, but the move was toward realizing that every individual could be valued. In 1985, Dybwad was quoted as saying, "Thirty-five years ago parents revolted and protested the neglect and exclusion of their children with mental retardation. The most significant progress since that time has been the emergence of individuals with mental retardation as persons in their own right. As fellow human beings claiming their place in our society" (Lovett, 1985, p. 89).

Since that time, individuals with disabilities and their advocates have begun to recognize that citizens have a right not just to be valued but also to make decisions for themselves. They have a right to self-determination. The notion was eloquently stated by Williams:

> In this final analysis, we are *all people first*. Isn't this what the Declaration of Independence tells us: that we are *all people first and foremost?* And, that as such we are endowed with certain inalienable rights and that among these are the right to life, liberty and the pursuit of happiness.
>   But, without being afforded the right and opportunity to make choices in our lives, we will never obtain full, first class American citizenship. This is why we are here today: to reassert these fundamental rights and lay claim to them as ours. (1989, p. 16)

But despite the apparent acceptance of this concept, the issue still remains: whether Americans with disabilities now enjoy the right to self-determination, and if so, what limits, if any, to self-determination obtain. Does society believe that even if an individual cannot make the best decisions for himself or herself, that individual still has the right to make those decisions, no matter what the individual's mental abilities or physical capabilities might be? For example, is society willing to allow the individual who graduates from high school under alternative graduation criteria for students who received special education services to make the decision to attend college, even though the individual has no possible chance of success there? Or is society willing to allow a young couple with mental retardation to make the decision to have children?

Or does our society believe that some individuals must be protected from their own decisions and that society must be protected as well? Is societal responsibility a cover-up for society's unwillingness to allow all individuals with disabilities the right to self-determination? Do we believe that in order to protect itself, society must assume greater responsibility for making decisions for others, particularly those with disabilities?

The ambivalence of society toward self-determination for all people can be seen in common special education practices. According to Taylor (1988), the concepts of least restrictive environment, cascade of services, and continuum of placements, although progressive when first proposed, do not provide necessary direction for the achievement of self-determination or independence and represent stumbling blocks to full inclusion of people with handicaps and disabilities in all aspects of life. Taylor identified the following flaws in the least restrictive environment principle:

• The LRE principle favors less restriction in placements but implies that more restrictive environments are appropriate for some people. Principles and practices are not well developed for deciding when a more (or less) restrictive placement is appropriate for a particular person.

• The LRE principle confuses intensity of service with service environments. There is little evidence to support the assumption that certain types of services can be provided only in more segregated, more restrictive environments.

• The LRE principle is based on a model in which students have to demonstrate that they are "ready" for less restrictive placements before they can be placed in them. There is little evidence supporting the belief that more restrictive environments prepare people for life in less restrictive settings.

• The LRE principle supports professional decision making and limits how individuals participate in their own placement decisions. Appropriateness of a placement is more often based on professional judgments than on individual choices or desires.

• The LRE principle sanctions infringements on people's rights by focusing on acceptable amounts of restriction. Deciding that no measure of restriction would be appropriate supports rights currently enjoyed by people without disabilities and handicaps.

• The LRE principle defines when movement should occur and ignores interpersonal relations of individuals. Friendships and a sense of community may be ignored if people must go to least restrictive environments simply because they are ready and the new settings are judged appropriate.

• The LRE principle directs attention to setting, rather than to services provided in programs. There is little evidence to support the equation of the restrictive nature of a program with the place in which it is provided.

These types of issues will continue to plague special education, education in general, and society as a whole. Americans must examine the extent to which they still limit the self-determination of others through legislation that excludes certain small businesses from the requirements for assuring accessibility to all, through policies that propose a national test for schools that systematically excludes most students served in special education, and through neighborhood restrictions on the presence of housing for individuals with various forms of disabilities. Americans will continue to struggle with issues surrounding the notions of social responsibility and the rights of all individuals to make choices for themselves.

Special Education in the Future

Will special education be different ten, twenty, or a hundred years from now? Nobody knows. Will national education goals and a continuing resurgence of interest in reform make a difference in how America's schools look in the future? Again, nobody knows. Based on historical analyses and the well-articulated views of some (cf. Glasser, 1990; Sarason, 1990), the answer is probably "not unless drastic reform changes how schools are structured and organized." Nevertheless, the future is not so bleak for professionals who believe that renewal should replace reform as the driving force in improving education.

Reform Versus Renewal

McPherson (1991, p. 17) provided the following illustrations of how reform and renewal differ:
- Reform is for institutions; renewal is for individuals.
- Reform adds something new; renewal recaptures what already exists.
- Reform assumes blame; renewal begins with faith.
- Reform is imposed, often by groups outside of education; renewal is contractual, an agreement between willing partners.
- Reform is for the many; renewal is for the one.
- Reform can be codified rather easily; renewal is difficult to describe.

For special education to prosper in the future, it is time for both reform and renewal to happen. Efforts at reform and renewal must be taken seriously, not swept aside as unnecessary or unprofessional. Whether reform or renewal captivates the ideals and actions of future special educators, there is plenty of hard work ahead, and the demand for quick, simple solutions that has captured the interest of many contemporary practitioners will probably be replaced by a sincere, realistic recognition that the forces of change move very slowly in education, one person at a time.

When we think about the future, we see the need for reform and renewal in several areas of practice. Clearly, conditions in regular education require restructuring for special education to avoid destruction by the sheer numbers of students believed to need special services. We also think that systems for classifying and funding special education programs require radical reform. Finally, instructional practices require renewed attention if children and youths with special learning needs are to continue profiting from special education services.

An Ounce of Prevention Is Worth a Pound of Cure

About 3–5 percent of the school population is referred for special education each year, and most of the students who are referred end up in special education programs (Algozzine, Christenson, & Ysseldyke, 1982). If special education is to improve, changes in referral practices are essential. We wish to see the following changes:

• Special and regular education teachers develop collaborative teaching models so students remain in regular classes.

• Special and regular education teachers develop prereferral intervention practices that work and use them so students remain in regular classes.

• Special and regular education teachers share responsibility for students with special learning needs.

In the best of all possible worlds, regular and special education teachers work with all students. There is no reason for the skills of special education teachers to be restrictively applied only to students with handicaps and disabilities. Similarly, the benefits of education with people without handicaps or disabilities for students with special learning needs are widely accepted. There is no reason special areas of instruction such as sign language or study skills should be taught only to some students. Any student needs to learn what any other student needs to learn to be better able to get along in the world of the future. Just as it was judged unfair to segregate students of color in separate but equal facilities because of the stigma attached to separation and because of the deprivation of interaction with students of other backgrounds, it should be judged unfair to separate and restrict learning experiences on the basis of perceived need (unless the need is judged universal) or learning characteristics. There is no reason special education and regular education have to be organized and have to function as they do today. The models for collaborative teaching have simply not been clearly articulated, proposed, and practiced.

Referring students for placement in special education programs takes time and costs money. The extensiveness of referral practices controls an important instructional variable; that is, time spent gathering assessment data, waiting for assessment information, and making decisions is too often time spent not teaching students with special learning needs. But time spent developing, implementing, and modifying classroom instructional practices prior to referral is time well spent teaching students with special learning needs. If teachers believe that more education should be provided in regular classrooms, the search for successful prereferral interventions will be more successful. Convincing them that this is how it should be will not be easy because for years they have been told that the right place for students with disabilities is outside the classroom in "special" environments.

Only by encouraging teachers to share responsibility for students with special learning needs will special education change from a separate but equal system to one that speaks for unitary interests and provides effective teaching in classrooms for all children. There is no reason special education teachers cannot have home-rooms just like those of regular teachers. There is no reason special education teachers have to teach only students with special learning needs. There is no reason special education should be provided only after a student has been referred by a regular classroom teacher.

An Ounce of Pretention Is Worth a Pound of Manure

There are more students classified as learning disabled than any other category of special education. The practice continues despite convincing evidence that there is no defensible system for doing it. Similar controversies are evident for most categories of special education. Typically, the practice of classifying and labeling students is justified as a method of providing funding for students in need of special education. We think it is time to start viewing classification differently. We wish to see special and regular educators call a moratorium on identification and classification practices and embrace alternative ways to fund special education and provide resources for students with special learning needs.

Considerable evidence exists to suggest that current identification and classification practices are biased. Students who meet criteria share many characteristics with students who do not meet criteria, just as students who are considered normal also share many of the same characteristics. The benefits of classifying students are generally valued more by the people who do the classifying than by the people who are classified. If professionals stop classifying students for at least a year, they may just find out that they can exist without doing it forever.

When the federal government develops a defense budget, it does so without regard for how many people have special learning needs. When universities develop budgets, they generally do so using past levels of funding and projected cost-of-living increases. It is not necessary to continue classifying students to justify special education funding. Using past levels of resource allocations and reasonable levels of yearly increases, administrators can develop reasonable federal, state, and local budgets that will include appropriate support for special education. In fact, when regular education budgets are developed, they are created without regard to the number of students who fit other categories (e.g., sex, race, geographic region). There is no reason special education should be funded *only after* a student has been classified.

An Ounce of Intervention Is Worth a Pound of Assure

A free appropriate education is guaranteed by federal law. Placing students in special education programs, however, in no way guarantees or assures that they receive free appropriate education. Receiving an individualized educational program does not either. Being placed in a special class does not guarantee that principles embodied in the least restrictive environment concept will be adhered to in the program that is provided there. We think it is time to start viewing intervention differently. We wish to see special and regular education teachers demonstrate effective techniques when working with all children and youths.

Teaching is systematic presentation of content assumed necessary for mastery within an area of instruction. Effective teachers plan their instructional presentations based on their knowledge of what their students currently know. They manage their instructional presentations and modify their teaching based on feedback from their students. Whether they teach students who are called gifted, nonhandicapped, mildly handicapped, or severely handicapped in preschool, elementary, secondary, or college programs, effective teachers plan, manage, deliver, and evaluate their instructional presentations. There is no magic here: good teaching is good teaching, and the best way to improve education is one person at a time.

Working together educators can identify problems and point to areas needing solutions. Working individually educators can make a difference. If every teacher changes the way students with special learning needs are treated, education will be improved. If one hundred teachers change the way students with special learning needs are treated, education will be improved. If one teacher changes the way students with special learning needs are treated, education will be improved. It is time to think globally but act locally in efforts to improve education in general and special education in particular.

We end this book as another book was ended:

> We are reminded of the story of two frogs who fell into a cream can. They swam around for a while discussing the fact that it would be nearly impossible to get out of the can. One frog, bemoaning this fact, finally gave up, sank to the bottom of the can, and drowned. The other frog worked vigorously, swimming around the can so fast and so hard that the cream turned to butter, thereby giving the frog a "platform" from which to escape. (Ysseldyke & Algozzine, 1984, pp. 430–431)

We encourage you to do whatever you can to improve the practice of special education.

Discussion Questions

1. Some people believe that teachers are born, not made. They see few problems in allowing people with nontraditional education backgrounds to enter the teaching profession. What do you think?

2. What are the major forces working against reform in education? To what extent do obstacles in regular education influence reform efforts in special education? Why do you think reform will succeed or fail?

3. What changes are occurring in how assessment information is being used in making decisions about students?

4. What models have characterized societal attitudes toward people with disabilities and handicaps? Do you think all people are capable of making their own decisions? Do you think everybody has a right to decide what she or he should or should not do? Do you think education should help people make their own decisions?

5. What do you think education will be like in the next century? Will special education be essentially as it is today, or will it be different? How will what happens in regular education influence what happens in special education?

Cases and Statutory Materials

Bevin, H. v. Wright, 666 F. Supp. 71 (W.D. Pa. 1987).

Board of Education of Hendrick Hudson School District v. Rowley, 458 U.S. 176 (1982).

Brookhart v. Illinois State Board of Education, 697 F.2d 179 (7th Cir. 1983).

Burlington School Committee v. Department of Education, 471 U.S. 359 (1985).

Covarubias v. San Diego Unified School District, Civ. No. 70-394-S (S.D. Cal., filed Feb. 1971) (settled by consent decree, July 31, 1972).

Debra v. Turlington, 635 F.2d 342 (5th Cir. 1981).

Diana v. State Board of Education, C.A. No. C-70-37 R.F.P. (N.D. Cal. filed Feb. 3, 1970).

Epperson v. Arkansas, 393 U.S. 97, 104 (1968).

Fay v. South Colonie Central School District, 802 F.2d 21 (2d Cir. 1986).

Frederick L. v. Thomas, 419 F. Supp. 960 (E.D. Pa. 1976), aff'd, 57 F.2d 373 (3d Cir. 1977).

Hansen v. Hobson, 269 F. Supp. 401 (D.D.C. 1967).

HEW Regulations, Supp. 42 Fed. Reg. No. 86, 22676 (1977).

Honig v. Doe, 108 S. Ct. 592 (1988).

Irving Independent School District v. Tatro, 468 U.S. 883 (1984).

Lachman v. Illinois State Board of Education, 852 F.2d 290 (7th Cir. 1988).

Larry P. v. Riles, 793 F.2d 969 (9th Cir. 1984).

Lora v. New York City Board of Education, 456 F. Supp. 1211, 1275 (E.D.N.Y. 1978).

Mannecke v. School Board, 762 F.2d 912 (11th Cir. 1985).

Max M. v. Illinois State Board of Education, 629 F. Supp. 1504 (N.D. Ill. 1986).

Miener v. Missouri, 673 F.2d 969 (8th Cir.), cert. denied, 459 U.S. 909 (1982).

Parents in Acton on Special Education (PASE) v. Hannon, 506 F. Supp. 831 (N.D. Ill. 1980).

Seals v. Loftus, 614 F. Supp. 302 (E.D. Tenn. 1985).

Tinker v. Des Moines Independent Community School District, 393 U.S. 503, 511 (1969).

Watson v. City of Cambridge, 157 Mass. 561, 563, 32 N.E. 864, 864–865 (1983).

References

Abeson, A., & Zettel, J. (1977). The end of the quiet revolution: The Education for All Handicapped Children Act of 1975. *Exceptional Children, 44*, 115–128.

Abikoff, H. (1991). Cognitive training in ADHD children: Less to it than meets the eye. *Journal of Learning Disabilities, 24*, 205–209.

Administration on Developmental Disabilities. (1988). *Mapping the future for children with special needs: P.L. 99-457.* Des Moines: University of Iowa.

Alberto, P. A., & Troutman, A. C. (1986). *Applied behavior analysis for teachers* (2nd ed.). Columbus, OH: Merrill.

Algozzine, B. (1991). Observations to accompany analyses of the tenth annual report to Congress. *Exceptional Children, 57*, 217–275.

Algozzine, B. (1992). *Behavior problem management: Educator's resource service–revised.* Gaithersburg, MD: Aspen Publishers.

Algozzine, B., & Algozzine, K. (1990). *Help identifying gifted and high-achieving students (HIGHS): Examiner's manual.* Charlotte, NC: Decision Products.

Algozzine, B., Christenson, S., & Ysseldyke, J. E. (1982). Probabilities associated with the referral to placement process. *Teacher Education and Special Education, 5*, 19–23.

Algozzine, B., Morsink, C. V., & Algozzine, K. M. (1988). What's happening in self-contained special education classrooms? *Exceptional Children, 55*, 259–265.

Algozzine, B., Salvia, J., & Ysseldyke, J. (1984). Who should teach the difficult-to-teach students? *Educators Forum, 6*, 4–5.

Algozzine, B., Schmid, R., & Mercer, C. D. (1981). *Childhood behavior disorders: Applied research and educational practice.* Rockville, MD: Aspen Systems.

Algozzine, B., & Ysseldyke, J. E. (1983). Learning disabilities as a subset of school failure: The oversophistication of a concept. *Exceptional Children, 50*, 242–246.

Algozzine, B., & Ysseldyke, J. E. (1986). The future of the LD field: Screening and diagnosis. *Journal of Learning Disabilities, 19*, 394–398.

Algozzine, B., & Ysseldyke, J. E. (1987). In defense of different numbers. *Remedial and Special Education, 8*(2), 53–56.

Allington, R. L., & McGill-Franzen, A. (1989). Different programs, indifferent instruction. In D. K. Lipsky & A. Gartner (Eds.), *Beyond separate education: Quality education for all* (pp. 75–97). Baltimore, MD: Brookes.

American Association of Colleges for Teacher Education. (1991). Teacher education programs eliminated in Oregon budget cuts. *AACTE Briefs, 12*(4), 1–2.

American Educational Research Association (AERA), American Psychological Association (APA), and National Council on Measurement in Education (NCME). (1985). *Standards for Educational and Psychological Testing*. Washington, DC: American Psychological Association.

American Psychiatric Association. (1979). *Diagnostic and statistical manual of mental disorders (DSM III)*. Washington, DC: Author.

American Psychiatric Association. (1982). *Diagnostic and statistical manual of mental disorders* (3rd ed.). Washington, DC: Author.

American Psychiatric Association. (1987). *Diagnostic and statistic manual of mental disorders, revised*. Washington, DC: Author.

Anastopoulos, A. D., DuPaul, G. J., & Barkley, R. A. (1991). Stimulant medication and parent training therapies for attention deficit–hyperactivity disorder. *Journal of Learning Disabilities, 24*, 210–218.

Angoff, W. H., & Ford, S. F. (1971). *Item-race interaction on a test of scholastic aptitude*. Princeton, NJ: Educational Testing Service.

Arter, J. A., & Jenkins, J. R. (1979). Differential diagnosis—prescriptive teaching: A critical appraisal. *Review of Educational Research, 49*, 517–556.

Asch, A. (1984). Personal reflections. *American Psychologist, 39*, 551–552.

Asch, A. (1989). Has the law made a difference? What some disabled students have to say. In D. K. Lipsky & A. Gartner (Eds.), *Beyond separate education: Quality education for all* (pp. 181–205). Baltimore, MD: Brookes.

Association for Persons with Severe Handicaps. (1981). Resolution on intrusive interventions. *TASH Newsletter, 7*, 1–2.

Atkins, M.S., & Pelham, W. E. (1991). School-based assessment of attention deficit–hyperactivity disorder. *Journal of Learning Disabilities, 23*, 197–204.

Atkins, M.A., Pelham, W. E., & White, K. J. (1990). Hyperactivity and attention deficit disorders. In M. Hersen & V. Van Hassett (Eds.), *Psychological aspects of developmental and physical disabilities: A casebook* (pp. 137–156). New York: Pergamon.

Baer, D., & Bushell, D. (1981) The future of behavior analysis in the school? Consider its recent past, and then ask a different question [Special issue]. *School Psychology Review, 10*(2).

Bailey, D. B. (1989). Issues and directions in preparing professionals to work with young handicapped children and their families. In J. J. Gallagher, P. L. Trohanis, & R. M. Clifford (Eds.), *Policy implementation & PL 99-457: Planning for young children with special needs* (pp. 97–132). Baltimore, MD: Brookes.

Bardon, J. (1982). The psychology of school psychology. In C. R. Reynolds & T. B. Gutkin (Eds.), *The handbook of school psychology* (pp. 3–14). New York: Wiley.

Bardon, J. (1991). Keynote Address at North Carolina Association of School Psychologists. Atlantic Beach, NC, October, 1991.

Barnes, D. M. (1986). Brain function decline in children with AIDS. *Science, 232*, 1196.

Barnes, K. E. (1982). *Preschool screening: The measurement and prediction of children at risk*. Springfield, IL: Thomas.

Baron, J. B. (1990, October). Use of alternative assessments in state assessment: The Connecticut experience. Paper presented at the OERI conference on *The promise and peril of alternative assessment*. Washington, DC: Office of Educational Research and Improvement.

Barrett, M. J. (1990, November). The case for more school days. *The Atlantic,* pp. 78–106.

Bayley, N. (1965). Consistency and variability in the growth of intelligence from birth to 18 years. *Journal of Genetic Psychology, 75,* 96.

Beavers, J. (1989). Physical and cognitive handicaps. In L. Combrinck-Graham (Ed.), *Children in family contexts: Perspectives on treatment.* New York: Guilford.

Becker, G., & Jauregui, J. (1985). The invisible isolation of deaf women: Its effect on social awareness. In M. Degan & N. Brooks (Eds.), *Women and disability: The double handicap* (pp. 23–26). New Brunswick, NJ: Transaction.

Behrmann, J. (1990). Caring for and educating the children of drug-using mothers: A challenge for society and schools in the 1990s. *Counterpoint, 11*(2), 15.

Beirne-Smith, M., & Deck, M. D. (1989). A survey of postsecondary programs for students with learning disabilities. *Journal of Learning Disabilities, 22,* 456–457.

Bennis, W. G., Benne, K. D., & Chin, R. (Eds.). (1969). *The planning of change* (2nd ed.). New York: Holt, Rinehart and Winston.

Bereiter, C. (1969). The future of individual differences. *Harvard Educational Review, 39,* 162–170.

Berkell, D., & Gaylord-Ross, R. (1989). The concept of transition: Historical and current developments. In D. E. Berkell & J. M. Brown (Eds.), *Transition from school to work for persons with disabilities* (pp. 1–21). New York: Longman.

Berlin, G., & Duhl, J. (1984). *Educational equity and economic excellence: The critical role of second chance and basic skills and job training programs.* New York: Ford Foundation.

Berman, C., & Lourie, I. S. (1988). Mental health issues in early intervention programs. *OSERS News in Print, 1*(4), 9.

Bernoff, L. (1981). *Early school leavers: High school students who left school before graduating, 1979–1980* (Publication No. 404). Los Angeles: Unified School District, Research and Evaluation Branch.

Berry, G. L., & Lopez, C. A. (1977). Testing programs and the Spanish-speaking child: Assessment guidelines for school counselors. *School Counselor, 24,* 261–269.

Bersoff, D. N. (1979). Regarding psychologists testily: Legal regulation of psychological assessment in the public schools. *Maryland Law Review, 39,* 27–120.

Bijou, S. W. (1971). Environment and intelligence: A behavioral analysis. In R. Cancro (Ed.), *Intelligence: Genetic and environmental contributions.* New York: Grune and Stratton.

Bilken, D. (1989). Redefining education. In D. Bilken, D. L. Ferguson, & A. Ford (Eds.), *Schooling and disability* (pp. 1–24). Chicago: National Society for the Study of Education.

Bilken, D., Ferguson, D. L., & Ford, A. (1989). *Schooling and disability: Eighty-eighth yearbook of the National Society for the Study of Education* (pp. 1–24). Chicago: University of Chicago Press.

Bilken, D., Ford, A., & Ferguson, D. L. (1989). Elements of integration. In D. Bilken, D. L. Ferguson, & A. Ford (Eds.), *Schooling and disability: Eighty-eighth yearbook of the National Society for the Study of Education* (pp. 256–272). Chicago: University of Chicago Press.

Binet, A., & Simon, T. (1916). *The development of intelligence in children.* Baltimore, MD: Williams and Wilkins.

Bishop, K. K. (1988). Maternal and child health activities for 0–5 year olds: An overview. *OSERS News in Print, 1*(4), 8.

Blackman, H. P. (1989). Special education placement: Is it what you know or where you live? *Exceptional Children, 55,* 459–462.

Bloom, B. (1964). *Stability and change in human characteristics.* New York: Wiley.

Bodner, J. R., Clark, G. M., & Mellard, D. F. (1987). *State graduation policies and program practices related to high school special education programs: A national study.* Lawrence: University of Kansas, Department of Special Education. (ERIC Document Reproduction Service No. ED 294 347)

Bogdan, R., & Kugelmass, J. (1984). Case studies of mainstreaming: A symbolic interactionist approach to special schooling. In L. Barton & S. Tomlinson (Eds.), *Special education and social interests* (pp. 83–97). London: Croom Helm.

Bogdan, R., & Taylor, S. (1976). The judged, not the judges: An insider's view of mental retardation. *American Psychologist, 31,* 47–52.

Bower, E. M. (1969). *Early identification of emotionally handicapped children in school (2nd ed.).* Springfield, IL: Charles C. Thomas.

Bower, E. M. (1982). *Early identification of emotionally handicapped children in school* (3rd ed.). Springfield, IL: Thomas.

Boyd, W. L., & Walberg, H. J. (Eds). (1990). *Choice in education: Potential and problems.* Berkeley, CA: McCutchan.

Boyer, E. L. (1983). *High school: A report on American secondary education.* Princeton, NJ: Carnegie Foundation for the Advancement of Teaching.

Braaten, S., Kauffman, J. M., Braaten, B., Polsgrove, L., & Nelson, C. M. (1988). The regular education initiative: Patent medicine for behavioral disorders. *Exceptional Children, 55,* 21–28.

Bradley, A. (1990, October 3). Goals for urban schools offered by boards group. *Education Week,* p. 10.

Brandt, R. (1989). On parents and schools: A conversation with Joyce Epstein. *Educational Leadership, 47*(2), 24–27.

Bricker, D. (1989). Essential features for early intervention programs in the 1990's. *Institute on Community Integration IMPACT, 2*(2), 4–5.

Bricker, D., & Slentz, K. (1989). Personnel preparation: Handicapped infants. In M. C. Wang, H. J. Walberg, & M. C. Reynolds (Eds.), *The handbook of special education research and practice* (Vol. 3, pp. 319–346). Oxford: Pergamon.

Brightman, A. J. (1984). *Ordinary moments: The disabled experience.* Baltimore, MD: University Park Press.

Brolin, D. E., & Schatzman, B. (1989). Lifelong career development. In D. E. Berkell & J. M. Brown (Eds.), *Transition from school to work for persons with disabilities* (pp. 22–41). New York: Longman.

Brookover. (1963).

Broudy, H. S. (1978). Conflicts in school programs. *Today's Education, 67,* 24–27.

Brown, D. T. (1979). Issues in accreditation, certification, and licensure. In G. Phye & D. Reschly (Eds.), *School psychology: Perspectives and issues* (pp. 88–116). New York: Academic.

Brown, L., & York, R. (1974). Developing programs for severely handicapped students: Teacher training and classroom instruction. In L. Brown, W. Williams, & T. Crowder (Eds.), *A collection of papers and programs related to public school services for severely handicapped students* (pp. 1–18). Madison, WI: Madison Public Schools.

Bruininks, R. H., Thurlow, M. L., Lewis, D. R., & Larson, N. W. (1988). Post school outcomes for students in special education and other students one to eight years after high school. In R. H. Bruininks, D. R. Lewis, & M. L. Thurlow (Eds.), *Assessing outcomes, costs and benefits of special education programs* (pp. 9–111). Minneapolis: University of Minnesota, University Affiliated Program.

Burstein, L. (1989). *NESAC outcomes subcommittee: Idea paper.* Washington, DC: National Forum on Educational Statistics Committee.

Butler-Nalin, P., Marder, C., & Shaver, D. M. (1989). *Making the transition: An explanatory model of special education students' participation in post-secondary education.* Menlo Park, CA: SRI.

Byers, J. (1989). AIDS in children: Effects on neurological development and implications for the future. *Journal of Special Education, 23,* 5–16.

California Dropouts. (1986). *A status report.* Sacramento: California State Department of Education.

Callahan, R. E. (1961). *An introduction to education in American society.* New York: Knopf.

Can Ivan read better than Johnny? (1961, May 27). *Saturday Evening Post,* pp. 30–33.

Cantwell, D. P., & Baker, L. (1991). Association between attention deficit–hyperactivity disorder and learning disorders. *Journal of Learning Disabilities, 24,* 88–95.

Carnegie Council on Adolescent Development. (1989). *Turning points: Preparing American youth for the 21st century.* New York: Carnegie.

Carnegie Forum on Education and the Economy. (1986). *A nation prepared: Teachers for the twenty-first century.* New York: Carnegie Corporation.

Carnevale, A. P., Gainer, L. J., & Meltzer, A. S. (1988). *Workplace basics: The skills employers want.* Alexandria, VA: American Society for Training and Development, U.S. Department of Labor, Employment, and Training Administration.

Carpenter, D. (1985). Grading handicapped pupils: Review and position statement. *Remedial and Special Education, 6*(4), 54–59.

Carpenter, D., & Grantham, L. B. (1985). A statewide investigation of grading practices and opinions concerning mainstreamed handicapped pupils. *Diagnostique, 11*(10), 31–39.

Carpenter, D., Grantham, L. B., & Hardister, M. P. (1983). Grading mainstreamed handicapped pupils: What are the issues? *Journal of Special Education, 17*(2), 183–188.

Carter, J., & Sugai, G. (1989). Survey on prereferral practices: Responses from state departments of education. *Exceptional Children, 55,* 298–302.

Casto, G., & Mastropieri, M. A. (1986). The efficacy of early intervention programs for handicapped children: A meta-analysis. *Exceptional Children, 52,* 417–424.

Catterall, J. S. (1988). *Dropping out of school in the north central region of the United States: Costs and consequences.* Los Angeles: North Central Regional Educational Laboratory.

Center, D. B. (1990). Social maladjustment: An interpretation. *Behavioral Disorders, 15*(3), 141–148.

Centers for Disease Control. (1987a). Classification system for human immunodeficiency virus (HIV) infection in children under 13 years of age. *Morbidity and Mortality Weekly Report, 36,* 225–230.

Centers for Disease Control. (1987b). Human immunodeficiency virus infection in the United States: A review of current knowledge. *Morbidity and Mortality Weekly Report, 36* (Suppl. S-6), 1–19.

Chandler, J. N. (1983). Making the grade. *Journal of Learning Disabilities, 16,* 241–242.

Children with Attention Deficit Disorders. (1988). *Attention deficit disorders: A guide for teachers.* Plantation, FL: Author.

Christenson, S. L. (1990). Differences in students' home environments: The need to work with families. *School Psychology Review, 19,* 505–517.

Christenson, S. L., Thurlow, M. L., & Ysseldyke, J. E. (1987). *Instructional effectiveness research: Implications for effective instruction of handicapped students* (Monograph No. 4). Minneapolis: University of Minnesota, Institute for Research on Learning Disabilities.

Christenson, S. L., & Ysseldyke, J. E. (1989). Assessing student performance: An important change is needed. *Journal of School Psychology, 27,* 409–426.

Christenson, S. L., Ysseldyke, J. E., & Thurlow, M. L. (1987). *Instructional psychology and models of school learning: Implications for effective instruction of handicapped students* (Monograph No. 2). Minneapolis: University of Minnesota, Institute for Research on Learning Disabilities.

Christenson, S. L., Ysseldyke, J. E., & Thurlow, M. L. (1989). Critical instructional factors for students with mild handicaps: An integrative review. *Remedial and Special Education, 10,* 21–31.

Cipollone, A. (1986). *The utility of school dropout literature for comprehensive high schools.* Unpublished manuscript.

Cline, D. H. (1990). A legal analysis of policy initiatives to exclude handicapped/disruptive students from special education. *Behavioral Disorders, 15*(3), 159–173.

Cohen, D. L. (1991, April 17). Expressing 'alarm' N.A.E.S.P. votes to oppose retaining pupils in grade. *Education Week,* p. 4.

Cohen, S. A. (1976). The fuzziness and the flab: Some solutions to research problems in learning disabilities. *Journal of Special Education, 10,* 129–136.

Cohen, S., Semmes, M., & Guralnick, M. J. (1979). Public Law 94-142 and the education of preschool children. *Exceptional Children, 45,* 279–285.

Cohn, S. J., Cohn, C. M., & Kanevsky, L. S. (1988). Giftedness and talent. In E. W. Lynch & R. B. Lewis (Eds.), *Exceptional children and adults: An introduction to special education* (pp. 456–501). Glenview, IL: Scott Foresman.

Coleman, M. (1986). *Behavior disorders: Theory and practice.* Englewood Cliffs, NJ: Prentice-Hall.

Coleman, M., & Apts, S. (1991). Home-alone risk factors. *Teaching Exceptional Children*, *23*, 36–38.

College Board. (1983). *Academic preparation for college: What students need to know and be able to do*. New York: Educational Equality Project.

Committee for Economic Development. (1985). *Investing in our children: Business and the public schools*. New York: Author.

Committee for Economic Development. (1987). *Children in need: Investment strategies for the educationally disadvantaged*. New York: Author.

Committee for Economic Development. (1991). *The unfinished agenda: A new vision for child development and education*. Washington, DC: Author.

Comptroller General. (1981). *Disparities still exist in who gets special education*. Washington, DC: General Accounting Office.

Congressional Budget Office. (1987). *Educational achievement: Explanations and implications of recent trends*. Washington, DC: Author.

Connecticut Department of Education. (1988). *Plan for statewide evaluation of special education programs*. Hartford, CT: Author.

Copperman, P. (1978). *The literacy hoax: The decline of reading, writing and learning in the public schools and what we can do about it*. New York: Morrow.

Council for Children with Behavior Disorders. (1990a). Position paper on the provision of service to children with conduct disorder. *Behavioral Disorders*, *15*(3), 180–189.

Council for Children with Behavior Disorders. (1990b). Position paper on the use of behavior reduction strategies with children with behavioral disorders. *Behavioral Disorders*, *15*, 225–260.

Council of Chief State School Officers. (1990). State education indicators: 1989. Washington, DC: Author.

Council for Exceptional Children. (1990). *Policy manual*, Sections 8.315 and 8.316. Reston, VA: Council for Exceptional Children.

Crack babies in preschool suggest problems ahead for schools. (1990). *Counterpoint*, *11*(1), 7.

Creech, J. D. (1990). *Educational benchmarks*. Atlanta: Southern Regional Education Board.

Criswell, E. (1981). Behavioral perspective of emotional disturbance. In B. Algozzine, R. Schmid, & C. D. Mercer (Eds.), *Childhood behavior disorders: Applied research and educational practice* (pp. 113–143). Rockville, MD: Aspen Systems.

Cromwell, R. L., Blashfield, R. K., & Strauss, J. S. (1975). Criteria for classification systems. In N. Hobbs (Ed.), *Issues in the classification of children* (Vol. 1, pp. 4–25). San Francisco: Jossey-Bass.

Cronbach, L. J., (1969). Heredity, environment, and educational policy. *Harvard Educational Review*, *39*, 190–199.

Cronbach, L. J., Ambron, S. R., Dornbusch, S. M., Hess, R. D., Hornik, R. C., Phillips, D. C., Walker, D. F., & Weiner, S. S. (1980). *Toward reform of program evaluation: Aims, methods, and institutional arrangements*. San Francisco, CA: Jossey-Bass.

Cronbach, L. J., & Furby, L. (1970). How should we measure "change"—or should we? *Psychological Bulletin, 74*, 68–80.

Cross, C. (1990, October). Paper presented at the OERI conference on the promise and peril of alternative assessment. Washington, DC: Office of Educational Research and Improvement.

Cuban, L. (1990). Four stories about national goals for American education. *Phi Delta Kappan, 72*, 265–271.

Cubberley, E. P. (1922). *A brief history of education.* Boston: Houghton Mifflin.

Cubberley, E. P. (1934). *Readings in public education in the United States.* Boston: Houghton Mifflin.

Danielson, L. C., & Bellamy, G. T. (1989). State variation in placement of children with handicaps in segregated environments. *Exceptional Children, 55*, 448–455.

Darling-Hammond, L. (1990). Achieving our goals: Superficial or structural reforms. *Phi Delta Kappan, 72*, 286–295.

Davies, S. P. (1976). The institution in relation to the school system. In M. Rosen, G. R. Clarke, & M. S. Kivitz (Eds.), *The history of mental retardation* (pp. 225–239). Baltimore, MD: University Park Press.

Davis, J. (1989). The regular education initiative: What professionals think. Unpublished doctoral dissertation, Michigan State University.

Davis, J. C., & Maheady, L. (1990). *The regular education initiative: What do three groups of educational professionals think?* Manuscript submitted for publication.

Degan, M., & Brooks, N. (1985). Introduction—Women and disability: The double handicap. In M. Degan & N. Brooks (Eds.), *Women and disability: The double handicap* (pp. 1–5). New Brunswick, NJ: Transaction.

Deming, W. E. (1982). *Out of the crisis.* Cambridge, MA: MIT, Center for Advanced Engineering.

Deno, E. (1970). Special education as developmental capital. *Exceptional Children, 37*, 229–240.

Deno, S. L. (1986). Formative evaluation of individual student programs: A new role for school psychologists. *School Psychology Review, 15*(3), 358–374.

Deno, S., & Mirkin, P. (1977). *Data-based program modification: A manual.* Reston, VA: Council for Exceptional Children.

Deshler, D. D., & Schumaker, J. B. (1988). An instructional model for teaching students how to learn. In J. L. Graden, J. E. Zins, & M. J. Curtis (Eds.), *Alternative educational delivery systems: Enhancing educational options for all students* (pp. 391–412). Silver Spring, MD: National Association of School Psychologists.

DeWeerd, J., & Cole, A. (1976). Handicapped children's early childhood program. *Exceptional Children, 43*, 155–157.

DeYoung, A. J., Huffman, K., & Turner, M. E. (1989). Dropout issues and problems in rural America, with a case study of one central Appalachian school district. In L. Weiss, E. Farrar, & H. G. Petrie (Eds.), *Dropouts from school: Issues, dilemmas, and solutions* (pp. 55–77). Albany: State University of New York Press.

Dix, D. (1976). Memorial to the legislature of Massachusetts. In M. Rosen, G. R. Clark, & M. S. Kivitz (Eds.), *The history of mental retardation* (Vol. 1, pp. 47–58). Baltimore, MD: University Park Press.

Doll, E. (1924). Current problems in mental diagnosis. *Journal of Psycho-Asthenics, 29,* 298–308.

Donahoe, K., & Zigmond, N. (1990). Academic grades of ninth-grade urban learning-disabled students and low-achieving peers. *Exceptionality, 1*(1), 17–27.

Donnellan, A. M., Negri-Shoultz, N., Fassbendes, L., & LaVigna, G. (1988). *Progress without punishment: Effective approaches for learners with behavior problems.* New York: Teachers College Press.

Don't expect me to be perfect. (1990, Special issue summer/fall). *Newsweek,* p. 62.

Dunkin, M. J. (1987). Teaching: Art or science? In M. J. Dunkin (Ed.), *The International Encyclopedia of Teaching and Teacher Education* (p. 19). New York: Pergamon.

Dunst, C. J., Trivette, C. M., & Deal, A. G. (1988). *Enabling and empowering families: Principles and guidelines for practice.* Cambridge, MA: Brookline Books.

Dwyer, C. A. (1976). Test content in mathematics and science: The consideration of sex. Paper presented at the annual meeting of the American Educational Research Association.

Early years. (1991, April 17). *Education Week,* p. 7.

Edgar, E. (1987). Secondary programs in special education: Are many of them justifiable? *Exceptional Children, 53,* 555–561.

Edgar E. (1991). Providing ongoing support and making appropriate placements: An alternative to transition planning for mildly handicapped students. *Preventing School Failure, 35*(2), 36–39.

Edgar, E. & Hayden, A. H. (1984–1985). Who are the children in special education and how many children are there? *Journal of Special Education, 18,* 523–539.

Edgerton, R. B. (1967). *The cloak of competence.* Berkeley: University of California Press.

Edmonds, R. R. (1982). Programs of school improvement: An overview. *Educational Leadership, 40,* 4–11.

Education Commission of the States, Task Force on Education for Economic Growth. (1983). *Action for excellence: A comprehensive plan to improve our nation's schools.* Denver: Author.

Educational Policies Commission. (1938). *The purposes of education in American democracy.* Washington, DC: National Education Association, American Association of School Administrators.

80,000 women of child-bearing age may have AIDS virus, study says. (1991, April 10). *Education Week,* p. 2.

Ekstrom, R. B., Goertz, M. E., Pollack, J. M., & Rock, D. A. (1986). Who drops out of high school and why? Findings from a national study. *Teachers College Record, 87*(3), 356–373.

Elam, S. M. (1990). The 22nd annual Gallup Poll of the public's attitude toward the public schools. *Phi Delta Kappan, 72*(1), 41–55.

Elkind, D. (1969). Piagetian and psychometric conceptions of intelligence. *Harvard Educational Review, 39,* 171–189.

Elliott, S. N., Witt, J. C., & Kratochwill, T. R. (1991). *Selecting, implementing and evaluating classroom interventions.* Silver Spring, MD: National Association of School Psychologists.

Engelmann, S., Granzin, A., & Severson, H. (1979). Diagnosing instruction. *Journal of Special Education, 13,* 355–365.

Epps, S., Ysseldyke, J. E., & McGue, M. (1984). Differentiating LD and non-LD students: I know one when I see one. *Learning Disability Quarterly, 7,* 89–101.

Epstein, J. (1990, April 4). Large numbers of parents are excluded from communication. *Education Week,* p. 8.

ETS Policy Information Center. (1990). *The education reform decade.* Princeton, NJ: Educational Testing Service.

Fairweather, J. S., & Shaver, D. M. (1991). Making the transition to postsecondary education and training. *Exceptional Children, 57,* 264–270.

Famous educator's plan for a school that will advance students according to ability. (1958, April 14). *Life,* pp. 120–121.

Fardig, D. B., Algozzine, R. F., Schwartz, S. E., Hensel, J. W., & Westling, D. L. (1985). Post-secondary vocational adjustment of rural, mildly handicapped students. *Exceptional Children, 52,* 115–121.

Farina, A., Thaw, J., Felner, R. D., & Hust, B. E. (1976). Some interpersonal consequences of being mentally ill or mentally retarded. *American Journal of Mental Deficiency, 80,* 414–422.

Farrell, E. E. (1908). Special classes in the New York City schools. *Journal of Psycho-Asthenics, 13,* 91–96.

Favell, J. E., Azrin, N. H., Baumeister, A. A., Carr, E. G., Dorsey, M. F., Forehand, R., Foxx, R. M., Lovaas, O. I., Risley, T. R., Romanczyk, R. G., Schroeder, S. R., & Solnick, J. V. (1982). The treatment of self-injurious behavior. *Behavior Therapy, 13,* 529–554.

Ferguson, D. L. (1989). Severity of need and educational excellence. In D. Bilken, D. L. Ferguson, & A. Ford (Eds.), *Schooling and disability: Eighty-eighth yearbook of the National Society for the Study of Education* (pp. 25–58). Chicago: University of Chicago Press.

Ferguson, D., & Asch, A. (1989). Lessons from life: Personal and parental perspectives on school, childhood, and disability. In D. Bilken, D. Ferguson, & A. Ford (Eds.), *Schooling and disbility: Eighty-eighth yearbook of the National Society for the Study of Education* (pp. 108–140). Chicago: University of Chicago Press.

Fessler, M. A., Rosenberg, M. S., & Rosenberg, L. A. (1991). Concomitant learning disabilities and learning problems among students with behavioral/emotional disorders. *Behavioral Disorders, 16,* 97–106.

Figueroa, R. A., Fradd, S. H., & Correa, V. I. (1989). Bilingual special education and this special issue. *Exceptional Children, 56,* 174–178.

Fine, M. (1986). Why urban adolescents drop into and out of public high school. *Teachers College Record, 87*(3), 393–409.

Fine, M., & Asch, A. (1988). Disability beyond stigma: Social interaction, discrimination, and activism. *Journal of Social Issues, 44*(1), 3–22.

Finn, C. E. (1990a). The biggest reform of all. *Phi Delta Kappan, 71,* 584–592.

Finn, C. E. (1990b). Why we need choice. In W. L. Boyd & H. J. Walberg (Eds.), *Choice in education: Potential and problems* (pp. 3–20). Berkeley, CA: McCutchan.

Fischer, L., & Sorenson, G. P. (1985). *School law for counselors, psychologists, and social workers.* New York: Longman.

Forest, M. (1987). Keys to integration: Common sense ideas and hard work. *Entourage, 2,* 16–20.

Fort, S. J. (1900). Special school for special children. *Journal of Psycho-Asthenics, 5,* 28–38.

Fradd, S. H., & Correa, V. I. (1989). Hispanic students at-risk: Do we abdicate or advocate? *Exceptional Children, 56,* 105–110.

Friedman. (1972). *Introduction to statistics.* New York: Random House.

Frost, J. L. (1968). *Early childhood education rediscovered.* New York: Holt, Rinehart and Winston.

Fuchs, D. (1991). Mainstream assistance teams: A prereferral intervention system for difficult-to-teach students. In G. Stoner, M. Shinn, & H. Walker (Eds.), *Interventions for achievement and behavior problems* (pp. 241–268). Silver Spring, MD: National Association of School Psychologists.

Fuchs, D., Featherstone, N., Garwick, D. R., & Fuchs, L. S. (1984). Effects of examiner familiarity and task characteristics on speech and language-impaired children's test performance. *Measurement and Evaluation in Guidance, 16*(4), 198–204.

Fuchs, D., & Fuchs, L. S. (1986). Test procedure bias: A meta-analysis of examiner familiarity effects. *Review of Educational Research, 56*(2), 243–262.

Fuchs, D., & Fuchs, L. (1988). Evaluation of the adaptive learning environment model. *Exceptional Children, 55,* 115–127.

Fuchs, D., & Fuchs, L. (1990). Making educational research more important. *Exceptional Children, 57,* 102–107.

Fuchs, D., & Fuchs, L. S. (in press). Framing the REI debate: Abolitionists vs. conservationists. In J. W. Lloyd, A. C. Repp, & N. N. Singh (Eds.), *Perspectives on the integration of atypical learners in regular educational settings.* Dekalb, IL: Sycamore.

Fuchs, D., Fuchs, L. S., Benowitz, S., & Barringer, K. (1987). Norm-referenced tests: Are they valid for use with handicapped students? *Exceptional Children, 54,* 263–272.

Fuchs, D., Fuchs, L. S., Dailey, A. M., & Power, M. H. (1985). The effect of examiners' personal familiarity and professional experience on handicapped children's test performance. *Journal of Educational Research, 78*(3), 141–146.

Fuchs, D., Fuchs, L. S., Garwick, D. R., & Featherstone, N. (1983). Test performance of language-handicapped children with familiar and unfamiliar examiners. *Journal of Psychology, 114,* 37–46.

Fuchs, D., Fuchs, L. S., Power, M. H., & Dailey, A. M. (1985). Bias in the assessment of handicapped children. *American Educational Research Journal, 22,* 185–198.

Fuchs, D., Zern, D. S., & Fuchs, L. S. (1983). Participants' verbal and nonverbal behavior in familiar and unfamiliar test conditions: An exploratory analysis. *Diagnostique, 8,* 159–169.

Fuchs, L., & Deno, S. L. (1991). Paradigmatic distinctions between instructionally relevant measurement models. *Exceptional Children, 57,* 488–500.

Fuchs, L., & Fuchs, D. (1986). Linking assessment to instructional interventions: An overview. *School Psychology Review, 15*(3), 318–324.

Furlong, M. J., & Yanagida, E. H. (1985). Psychometric factors affecting multidisciplinary team identification of learning disabled children. *Learning Disability Quarterly, 8*, 37–44.

Gadsden, V., Wagner, D., & Hirschhorn, L. (1990). Workplace literacy: Studying the workplace. *Literacy Research Newsletter, 6*(1), 1, 3.

Gage, N. L. (1978). The yield of research on teaching. *Phi Delta Kappan, 60*, 229–235.

Gage, N. L. (1990). Dealing with dropout problem. *Phi Delta Kappan, 72*, 280–285.

Gallagher, J. J. (1970). Three studies of the classroom. In J. J. Gallagher, G. A. Nuthall, & B. Rosenshine (Eds.), *Classroom observation* (pp. 74–108). Chicago: Rand McNally.

Gallagher, J. J. (1976). The sacred and profane uses of labeling. *Mental Retardation, 14*, 3–7.

Gallagher, J. J. (1988). National agenda for educating gifted students: Statement of priorities. *Exceptional Children, 55*, 107–114.

Gardner, H. (1983). *Frames of mind: The Theory of multiple intelligences.* New York: Basic Books.

Garrett, J. E., & Brazil, N. M. (1989). *Categories of exceptionality: A ten-year follow-up.* Unpublished manuscript.

Gartner, A., & Lipsky, D. K. (1987). Beyond special education: Toward a quality system for all students. *Harvard Educational Review, 57*, 367–395.

Gartner, A., Lipsky, D., & Turnbull, D. (1991). *Supporting families with a child with a disability.* Baltimore, MD: Brookes.

Gerber, M. M. (1984). The Department of Education's sixth annual report to Congress on PL 94-142: Is Congress getting the full story? *Exceptional Children, 51*, 209–224.

Gerber, M. M., & Levine-Donnerstein, D. (1989). Educating all children: Ten years later. *Exceptional Children, 56*, 17–27.

Gickling, E., & Havertape, J. (1981). Curriculum-based assessment. In J. Tucker (Ed.), *Non-test-based assessment: A training module* (pp. 189, 409). Minneapolis: National School Psychology Inservice Training Network.

Gilhool, T. K. (1989). The right to an effective education: From Brown to PL 94-142 and beyond. In D. K. Lipsky & A. Gartner (Eds.), *Beyond separate education: Quality education for all* (pp. 243–253). Baltimore, MD: Brookes.

Glaser, R. (1988). Cognitive and environmental perspectives on assessing achievement. In *Assessment in the service of learning: Proceedings of the 1987 ETS invitational conference* (pp. 71–83). Princeton, NJ: Educational Testing Service.

Glasser, W. (1990). *The quality school: Managing students without education.* New York: Harper and Row.

Goens, G. A., & Clover, S. I. R. (1990). *Mastering school reform.* Boston: Allyn and Bacon.

Goetz, L., & Sailor, W. (1990). Much ado about babies, murky bathwater, and trickle down politics: A reply to Kauffman. *Journal of Special Education, 24*, 334–339.

Goldman, R. D., & Hewitt, B. N. (1976). Predicting the success of black, Chicano, Oriental and white college students. *Journal of Educational Measurement, 13*, 107–117.

Goldstein, H., Arkell, C., Ashcroft, S., Hurley, O., & Lilly, S. (1975). Schools. In N. Hobbs (Ed.). *Issues in the classification of children* (Vol. 2, pp. 4–61). San Francisco: Jossey-Bass.

Good, T., & Brophy, J. (1986). The social and institutional context of teaching: School effects. In *Third hndbook of research on teaching* (pp. 161–193) New York: American Educational Research Association.

Goodlad, J. I. (1979a). Can our schools get better? *Phi Delta Kappan, 60*, 342–347.

Goodlad, J. I. (1979b). *What schools are for.* Bloomington, IN: Phi Delta Kappa Education Foundation.

Goodlad, J. I. (1983). *A place called school: Prospects for the future.* New York: McGraw-Hill.

Goodlad, J. I. (1990). Better teachers for our nation's schools. *Phi Delta Kappan, 72*, 184–194.

Gordon, E. W. (1971). Methodological problems and pseudo issues in the nature-nurture controversy. In R. Cancro (Ed.), *Intelligence: Genetic and Environmental Contributions* (pp. 240–251). New York: Grune and Stratton.

Gorham, K. A., Des Jardins, C., Page, R., Pettis, E., & Scherber, B. (1976). Effect on parents. In N. Hobbs (Ed.), *Issues in the classification of children* (Vol. 2, pp. 154–188). San Francisco: Jossey-Bass.

Gough, P. B. (1990). Moving beyond rhetoric. *Phi Delta Kappan, 72*, 259.

Graden, J. L., Casey, A., & Bonstrom, O. (1985). Implementing a prereferral intervention system: Part II. The data. *Exceptional Children, 51*, 487–496.

Graden, J. L., Casey, A., & Christenson, S. L. (1985). Implementing a prereferral intervention system: Part I: The model. *Exceptional Children, 51*, 377–384.

Graden, J. L., Zins, J., & Curtis, M. (1988). *Alternative educational delivery systems.* Washington, DC: National Association of School Psychologists.

Greenburg, D. (1984). The 1984 annual report to Congress: Are we better off? *Exceptional Children, 51*, 203–208.

Greenburg, D. E. (1989). The tenth annual report to Congress: One more ride on the merry-go-round. *Exceptional Children, 56*, 10–13.

Greer, J. V. (1990). The drug babies. *Exceptional Children, 56*, 382–384.

Grosenick, J. K., & Huntze, S. (1980). *National needs analysis in behavior disorders: A model for a comprehensive needs analysis in behavior disorders.* Columbia: University of Missouri, Columbia.

Grossman, H. (1973). *Manual on terminology and classification in mental retardation.* Baltimore, MD: Garamond/Pridemark.

Grossnickle, D. R. (1986). *High school dropouts: Causes, consequences, and cure* (Fastback 242). Bloomington, IN: Phi Delta Kappa Educational Foundation.

Guess, D. (1988). Problems and issues pertaining to the transmission of behavior management technologies from researchers to practitioners. In R. H. Horner (Ed.), *Behavior management and community integration for individuals with developmental disabilities and severe behavior problems.* Washington, D.C.: U.S. Office of Special Education and Rehabilitative Services.

Hagen, E. (1980). *Identification of the gifted.* New York: Teachers College Press.

Hahn, A., Danzberger, J., & Lefkowitz, B. (1987). *Dropouts in America. Enough is known for action.* Washington, DC: Institute for Educational Leadership.

Hall, J., & Gerber, P. (1985). The awarding of Carnegie units to learning disabled high school students: A policy study. *Educational Evaluation and Policy Analysis, 7*(3), 229–235.

Hall, V., Greenwood, C., & Delquadri, J. (1976). *The importance of opportunity to respond to childrens' academic success.* Kansas City, KS: Juniper Gardens Children's Center.

Hallahan, D. P., & Kauffman, J. M. (1977). Labels, categories, behaviors: ED, LD, and EMR reconsidered. *Journal of Special Education, 11,* 139–149.

Hallahan, D. P., & Kauffman, J. M. (1989). *Exceptional children* (4th ed.). Englewood Cliffs, NJ: Prentice-Hall.

Hallahan, D. P., Keller, C. E., & Ball, D. W. (1986). A comparison of prevalence rate variability from state to state for each of the categories of special education. *Remedial and Special Education, 7*(2), 8–14.

Halloran, W. (1989). Foreword. In D. E. Berkell & J. M. Brown (Eds.), *Transition from school to work for persons with disabilities* (pp. xiii–xvi). New York: Longman.

Hanft, B. (1988). Occupational therapy and early intervention. *OSERS News in Print, 1*(4), 11.

Harp, L. (1991, March 13). Senate subcommittee samples views on need for national achievement test. *Education Week,* p. 35.

Harrington, M. (1962). *The other America.* Baltimore, MD: Penguin.

Hasazi, S. B., Gordon, L. R., & Roe, C. A. (1985). Factors associated with the employment status of handicapped youth exiting high school from 1979 to 1983. *Exceptional Children, 51,* 455–469.

Haskins, R. (1989). Beyond metaphor: The efficiency of early childhood education. *American Psychologist, 44,* 274–282.

Hatlin, P. H., Hall, A. P., & Tuttle, D. (1980). Education of the visually handicapped. In L. Mann & D. A. Sabatino (Eds.), *Fourth review of special education.* New York: Grune and Stratton.

Hawkins, J. A. (1984). *Follow-up study of special education graduates: Class of 1983.* Rockville, MD: Department of Educational Accountability. (ERIC Document Reproduction Services No. ED 256-786)

Hawley, R. A. (1990). The bumpy road to drug-free schools. *Phi Delta Kappan, 72,* 310–314.

Haywood, H. C. (1979). What happened to mild and moderate mental retardation? *American Journal of Mental Deficiency, 83,* 429–431.

Heller, K. A., Holtzman, W., & Messick, S. (1982). *Placing children in special education: A strategy for equity.* Washington, DC: National Academy Press.

Henderson, A. T., Marburger, C. L., & Ooms, T. (1986). *Beyond the bake sale: An educator's guide to working with parents.* Washington, DC: National Committee for Citizens in Education.

Hendrick, I. G., & MacMillan, D. L. (1989). Selecting children for special education in New York City: William Maxwell, Elizabeth Farrell, and the development of ungraded classes, 1900–1920. *Journal of Special Education, 22*, 395–418.

Hennessy, J. J., & Merrifield, P. R. (1976). A comparison of the factor structures of mental abilities in four ethnic groups. *Journal of Educational Psychology, 68*(6), 754–759.

Hess, A. G., & Lauber, D. (1985). *Dropouts from the Chicago public schools: An analysis of the classes of 1982, 1983, 1984.* Chicago: Chicago Panel on Public School Finances.

Hess, F. (1987). *A comprehensive analysis of the dropout phenomenon in an urban school system.* Paper presented at the annual meeting of the American Educational Research Association.

Heward, W. L., & Orlansky, M. D. (1989). *Exceptional Children* (3rd ed.). Columbus, OH: Merrill.

Hewitt, S. K. N. (1981). *Learning disabilities among secondary in-school students, graduates, and dropouts.* Unpublished doctoral dissertation, University of Minnesota, Minneapolis.

Higgins, S. (1979). *Policy options regarding graduation and their impact on handicapped students.* Reston, VA: Council for Exceptional Children. (ERIC Document Reproduction Service No. ED 191 200)

Hirsch, J. (1971). Behavior-genetic analysis and its biosocial consequences. In R. Caucro (Ed.), *Intelligence: Genetic and environmental contributions* (pp. 88–106). New York: Grune and Stratton.

Hirshoren, A., & Umansky, W. (1977). Certification for teachers of preschool handicapped children. *Exceptional Children, 44*, 191–193.

Hobbs, N. (1975). *Issues in the classification of children.* San Francisco: Jossey-Bass.

Hodgkinson, H. L. (1985). *All one system: Demographics of education—Kindergarten through graduate school.* Washington, DC: Institute for Educational Leadership.

Hodgkinson, H. L. (1989). *The same client: The demographics of education and service delivery systems.* Washington, DC: Institute for Educational Leadership, Center for Demographic Leadership.

Home alone. (1991, March 6). *Education Week,* p. 3.

Horn, J. L. (1924). *The education of exceptional children: A consideration of public school problems and policies in the field of differentiated education.* New York: Century.

How federal laws and regulations are determined. (1991). *News Digest, 1*(1), 2.

Howe, S. G. (1848). *Report of commission to inquire into the conditions of idiots of the Commonwealth of Massachusetts* (Senate Document No. 51). Boston: State Department of Education.

Howell, K. W. (1986). Direct assessment of academic performance. *School Psychology Review, 15*(3), 324–335.

Hudson, F., Graham, S., & Warner, M. (1979). Mainstreaming: An examination of the attitudes and needs of regular classroom teachers. *Learning Disability Quarterly, 3*, 558–562.

Hurley, O. L. (1989). Implications of PL 99-457 for preparation of preschool personnel. In J. J. Gallagher, P. L. Trohanis, & R. M. Clifford (Eds.), *Policy implementation & PL 99-457: Planning for young children with special needs* (pp. 133–145). Baltimore, MD: Brookes.

Hurley, R. (1969). *Poverty and mental retardation: A causal relationship.* New York: Random House.

Hyman, I. A. (1979). Will the real school psychologist please stand up? III. A struggle of jurisdictional imperialism. *School Psychology Digest, 8*, 174–180.

Imber-Black, E. (1988). *Families and larger systems.* New York: Guilford.

Indicators Panel. (1990). *Three draft outlines of the final report of the Special Study Panel on Education Indicators, appendix* (Staff report). Washington, DC: National Center for Education Statistics.

Inman, D., Prebish, S. L., & Salganik, L. H. (1990). *Summary profiles: State education indicator systems.* Washington, DC: Pelavin.

Interagency Committee on Learning Disabilities. (1987). *Learning disabilities: A report to the U.S. Congress.* Washington, DC: U.S. Department of Health and Human Services,

Jacobs, J. (1986). *Educating students with severe handicaps in the regular education program, all day, every day.* Paper presented at the annual conference of the Association for Persons with Severe Handicaps. San Francisco.

Jason, L. A., Betts, D., Johnson, J. H. Weine, A. W., Warren-Sohlberg, M. L., Shinaver, C. S. I., Neuson, L., Filippelli, L., & Lardon, C. (1990). Prompting competencies in high-risk transfer children. *Special Services in the Schools, 1–2,* 21–36.

Jensen, A. (1967). *Estimation of the limits of heritability of traits by comparison of monozygotic and dizygotic twins.* Washington, DC: National Academy of Sciences.

Jensen, A. R. (1968a). Patterns of mental ability and socio-economic status. *Proceedings of the National Academy of Sciences. 60,* 1330–1337.

Jensen, A. R. (1968b). Social class, race, and genetics: Implications for education. *American Educational Research Journal, 5,* 1–42.

Jensen, A. R. (1969). How much can we boost IQ and scholastic achievement? *Harvard Educational Review, 39,* 1–123.

Jensen, A. R. (1976). Test bias and construct validity. *Phi Delta Kappan, 58,* 340–346.

Jensen, A. R. (1979). *Bias in mental testing.* New York: Free Press.

Johns, B. (1991). Highlights of the new IDEA. *DLD Times, 8*(2), 5.

Johnson, D. R., Bruininks, R. H., & Thurlow, M. L. (1987). Meeting the challenge of transition service planning through improved interagency cooperation. *Exceptional Children, 53,* 522–530.

Johnson, J. M., & Pennypacker, H. S. (1980). *Strategies and tactics of human behavioral research.* Hillsdale, NJ: Earlbaum.

Johnson, T. W. (1990). Taking a first step toward reform. *Phi Delta Kappan, 72,* 202–203.

Jones, R. L., Gottlieb, J., Guskin, S., & Yoshida, R. K. (1978). Evaluating mainstream programs: Models, caveats, considerations, and guidelines. *Exceptional Children, 44,* 588–601.

Joyce, B. (1990). *Changing school culture through staff development.* Alexandria, VA: Association for Supervision and Curriculum Development.

Joyce, B., & Weil, M. (1972). *Models of teaching.* Englewood Cliffs, NJ: Prentice-Hall.

Kagan, S. L. (1990). Readiness 2000: Rethinking rhetoric and responsibility. *Phi Delta Kappan, 72,* 272–279.

Kamin, L. J. (1975). Social and legal consequences of IQ tests as classification instruments: Some warnings from our past. *Journal of School Psychology, 13*, 317–323.

Kantrowitz, B. (1990, Summer/Fall special issue). Homeroom [Special issue]. *Newsweek*, pp. 50–54.

Karaim, R. (1990, December 11). High incidence of alcohol abuse causing defects, retardation in babies, experts say. *St. Paul Pioneer Press*, p. 3.

Karnes, M. B., & Zehrbach, R. R. (1977). Early education of the handicapped: Issues and alternatives. In B. Spodek & H. J. Walberg (Eds.), *Early childhood education*. Berkeley, CA: McCutchan.

Katz, I. (1981). *Stigma: A social psychological analysis*. Hillsdale, NJ: Erlbaum.

Kauffman, J. M. (1977). *Characteristics of children's behavior disorders* (2nd ed.). Columbus, OH: Merrill.

Kauffman, J. M. (1980). Where special education for disturbed children is going: A personal view. *Exceptional Children, 46*, 522–527.

Kauffman, J. M. (1985). *Characteristics of children's behavior disorders* (3rd ed.). Columbus, OH: Merrill.

Kauffman, J. M. (1989a). *Characteristics of children's behavior disorders* (4th ed.). Columbus, OH: Merrill.

Kauffman, J. M. (1989b). The regular education initiative as Reagan-Bush education policy: A trickle-down theory of education of the hard-to-teach. *Journal of Special Education, 23*, 256–278; *24*, 319–325.

Kauffman, J. M., Gerber, M. M., & Semmel, M. I. (1988). Arguable assumptions underlying the regular education initiative. *Journal of Learning Disabilities, 21*, 6–12.

Kauffman, J. M., & Hallahan, D. P. (1990). What we want for children: A rejoinder to REI proponents. *Journal of Special Education, 24*, 340–345.

Kauffman, J. M., Lloyd, J. W., & McKinney, J. D. (1988). [Special issue]. *Journal of Learning Disabilities, 21*(1).

Kaufman, M. J., Kameenui, E. J., Birman, B., & Danielson, L. (1990). Special education and the process of change: Victim or master of educational reform? *Exceptional Children, 57*, 109–115.

Kavale, K. A., & Forness, S. R. (1985). Learning disability and the history of science: Paradigm or paradox. *Remedial and Special Education, 6*(4), 12–24.

Keller, C. E., Ball, D. W., & Hallahan, D. P. (1987). Questioning the defense of different numbers: A reply to Algozzine and Ysseldyke. *Remedial and Special Education, 8*(2), 57–59.

Keogh, B. K. (1988). Improving services for problem learners: Rethinking and restructuring. *Journal of Learning Disabilities, 21*, 19–22.

Keogh, B. K., Major-Kingsley, S., Omori-Gordon, H., & Reid, H. P. (1982). *A system of marker variables for the field of learning disabilities*. Syracuse, NY: Syracuse University Press.

Killoran, J., & Tingey, C. (1989). Staff development in early intervention. In C. Tingey (Ed.), *Implementing early intervention* (pp. 79–94). Baltimore, MD: Brookes.

Kirk, S. A. (1977). General and historical rationale for early education of the handicapped. In N. E. Ellis & L. Cross (Eds.), *Planning programs for early education of the handicapped* (pp. 28–46). New York: Walker.

Kirk, S. A., & Gallagher, J. J. (1986). *Educating exceptional children* (5th ed.). Boston: Houghton Mifflin.

Kirk, S. A., & Gallagher, J. J. (1989). *Educating exceptional children* (6th ed.). Boston: Houghton Mifflin.

Kirst, M. W. (1990). *Accountability: Implications for state and local policy makers. Policy Perspectives.* Washington, DC: U. S. Department of Education, Information Services Office of Educational Research and Improvement.

Knoff, H. M. (1985). Attitudes toward mainstreaming: A status report and comparison of regular and special educators in New York and Massachusetts. *Psychology in the Schools, 22,* 411–418.

Kortering, L. J., Julnes, R., & Edgar, E. B. (1990). An instructive review of the law pertaining to the graduation of special education students. *Remedial and Special Education, 11*(4), 7–13.

Kreitzer, A. E., Madaus, G. F., & Haney, W. (1989). Competency testing and dropouts. In L. Weiss, E. Farrar, & H. G. Petrie (Eds.), *Dropouts from school: Issues, dilemmas, and solutions* (pp. 129–152). Albany: State University of New York Press.

Lambert, N. (1981). *Diagnostic and technical manual, AAMD adaptive behavior scale—school edition.* Monterey, CA: CTB/McGraw-Hill.

Lambert, N. (1981). School psychology training for the decades ahead. *School Psychology Review, 10,* 2.

LaVor, M. (1972). Economic opportunity amendments of 1972, Public Law 92-424. *Exceptional Children, 39,* 249–253.

LaVor, M. (1979). Federal legislation for exceptional persons: A history. In F. Weintraub, A. Abeson, J. Ballard, & M. LaVor (Eds.), *Public policy and the education of exceptional children.* Reston, VA: Council for Exceptional Children.

LaVor, M., & Harvey, J. (1976). Headstart, Economic Opportunity, Community Partnership Act of 1974. *Exceptional Children, 42,* 227–230.

Lee, V. E., Schnur, E., & Brooks-Gunn, J. (1988). Does Head Start work? A 1-year follow-up comparison of disadvantaged children attending Head Start, no preschool, and other preschool programs. *Developmental Psychology, 24*(2), 210–222.

Lehr, C. A., Ysseldyke, J. E., & Thurlow, M. L. (1987). Assessment practices in model early childhood education programs. *Psychology in the Schools, 24,* 390–399.

Leitch, M. L., & Tangri, S. S. (1988). Barriers to home-school collaboration. *Educational Horizons, 66,* 70–74.

Lentz, F. E., & Shapiro, E. S. (1986). Functional assessment of the academic environment. *School Psychology Review, 15*(3), 346–357.

Lerner, J. (1985). *Learning disabilities* (4th ed.). Boston: Houghton Mifflin.

Lessen, E. I., & Rose, T. L. (1980). State definitions of preschool handicapped populations. *Exceptional Children, 46,* 467–469.

Levin, E., Zigmond, N., & Birch, J. (1985). A follow-up study of 52 learning disabled students. *Journal of Learning Disabilities, 18,* 2–7.

Levy, L., & Rowitz, L. (1973). *The ecology of mental disorders.* New York: Behavioral Publications.

Lewis, A. C. (1990). The murky waters of monitoring achievement of the national goals. *Phi Delta Kappan, 72,* 260–261.

Lewis, D. R., Bruininks, R. H., & Thurlow, M. L. (1989). Cost analysis for district-level special education planning, budgeting, and administrating. *Journal of Education Finance, 14*(4), 466–484.

Lezotte, L. W. (1989). School improvement based on the effective schools research. In D. K. Lipsky & A. Gartner (Eds.), *Beyond separate education: Quality education for all* (pp. 25–37). Baltimore, MD: Brookes.

Lichtenstein, R., & Ireton, H. (1984). *Preschool screening: Identifying young children with developmental and educational problems.* Orlando, FL: Grune and Stratton.

Lichtenstein, S. J. (1987). *A study of selected post-school employment patterns of handicapped and nonhandicapped graduates and dropouts.* Unpublished doctoral dissertation, University of Illinois, Urbana-Champaign.

Lilly, M. S. (1989). Teacher preparation. In D. K. Lipsky & A. Gartner (Eds.), *Beyond separate education: Quality education for all.* Baltimore, MD: Paul H. Brookes.

Lincoln, D. F. (1903). Special classes for feeble-minded children in the Boston public schools. *Journal of Psycho-Asthenics, 7,* 83–93.

Linn, R. L. (1990, October). Discussant to paper by Resnick presented at the OERI Conference on the Promise and Peril of Alternative Assessment. Washington, DC.

Lipsky, D. K., & Gartner, A. (1987). Capable of achievement and worthy of respect: Education for the handicapped as if they were full-fledged human beings. *Exceptional Children, 54,* 69–74.

Lipsky, D. K., & Gartner, A. (1989a). *Beyond separate education: Quality education for all.* Baltimore, MD: Brookes.

Lipsky, D. K., & Gartner, A. (1989b). Building the future. In D. K. Lipsky & A. Gartner (Eds.), *Beyond separate education: Quality education for all* (pp. 255–290). Baltimore, MD: Brookes.

Lloyd, J. W., Crowley, E. P., Kohler, F. W., & Strain, P. S. (1988). Redefining the applied research agenda: Cooperative learning, prereferral, teacher consultation, and peer-mediated interventions. *Journal of Learning Disabilities, 21,* 43–52.

Lovett, H. (1985). *Cognitive counseling and the person with special needs: Adapting behavioral approaches to the social context.* New York: Praeger.

Lovitt, T. (1978). Reactions to planned research. Paper presented at the Roundtable Conference on Learning Disabilities. Minneapolis, MN: Institute for research on Learning Disabilities.

Ludlow, B. (1989). Shortage of qualified special education personnel declared national emergency. *American Association on Mental Retardation News and Notes, 2*(3), 1–5.

Lynn, L. (1983). The emerging system for educating handicapped children. *Policy Studies Review, 2,* 21–35.

Lynn, R. (1979). *Learning disabilities.* New York: Free Press.

Lyon, R. (1983). Subgroups of learning disabled readers: Clinical and empirical identification. In H. Myklebust (Ed.), *Progress in learning disabilities* (Vol. 5, pp. 67–94). New York: Grune and Stratton.

Lyon, R. (1985). Identification and remediation of learning disabilities subtypes: Preliminary findings. *Learning Disabilities Focus, 1*(1), 21–35.

Macchiarola, F. J. (1989). Foreword. In D. K. Lipsky & A. Gartner (Eds.), *Beyond separate education: Quality education for all* (pp. xi–xix). Baltimore, MD: Brookes.

Mack, J. (1985). An analysis of state definitions of severely emotionally disturbed children. In Council for Exceptional Children, *Policy options report.* Reston, VA: Author.

MacMillan, D. L. (1982). *Mental retardation in school and society* (2nd ed.). Boston: Little, Brown.

MacMillan, D. L., Balow, I. H., Widaman, K. F., Borthwick-Duffy, S., & Hendrick, I. G. (1990). Methodological problems in estimating dropout rates and the implications for studying dropouts from special education. *Exceptionality, 1*(1), 29–39.

Maheady, L., & Algozzine, B. (1991). The regular education initiative: Can we proceed in an orderly and scientific manner? *Teacher Education and Special Education, 14,* 66–73.

Mann, D. (1986). Can we help dropouts: Thinking about the undoable. *Teachers College Record, 87*(3), 307–323.

Mann, L. (1979). *On the trail of process.* New York: Grune & Stratton.

Marston, D. (1987). Does categorical teacher certification benefit the mildly handicapped child? *Exceptional Children, 53,* 423–431.

Marston, D. (1989). Measuring progress on IEPs: A comparison of graphing approaches. *Exceptional Children, 55,* 38–44.

Martin, R. (1975). *Legal challenges to behavior modification: Trends in schools, corrections, and mental health.* Champaign, IL: Research Press.

Massachusetts Advocacy Center. (1986). *The way out: Student exclusion practices in Boston middle schools.* Boston: Author.

Masten, A. S. (1989). Resilience in development: Implications of the study of successful adaptation for developmental psychopathology. In D. Cicchetti (Ed.), *The emergence of a discipline: Rochester Symposium on Developmental Psychopathology* (Vol. 1, pp. 261–294). New York: Cambridge University Press.

Masten, A. S., Garmezy, N., Tellegen, A., Pellegrini, D. S., Larkin, K., & Larsen, A. (1988). Competence and stress in school children: The moderating effects of individual and family qualities. *Journal of Child Psychology and Psychiatry, 29,* 745–764.

Matluck, J. H. & Mace, B. J. (1973). Language characteristics of Mexican American children: Implications for assessment. *Journal of School Psychology, 11,* 365–386.

Matuszek, P., & Oakland, T. (1972). *A factor analysis of several reading readiness measures for different socioeconomic and ethnic groups.* Paper presented at the annual meeting of the American Educational Research Association.

McBride, J. W., & Forgnone, C. (1985). Emphasis of instruction provided LD, EH, and EMR students in categorical and cross-categorical resource programs. *Journal of Research and Development in Education, 18*(4), 50–54.

McCollum, J. A. (1987). Early interventionists in infant and early childhood education programs. *Topics in Early Childhood Special Education, 7*(3), 24–25.

McCollum, H., & Turnbull, B. J. (1989). *Educational indicators.* Washington, DC: Policy Study Associates.

McDonnell, J., Sheehan, M., & Wilcox, B. (1983). *Effective transition from school to work and adult services: A procedural handbook for parents and teachers.* Lane County, OR: Lane County Education Service District.

McGill-Franzen, A. (1987). Failure to learn to read: Formulating a policy problem. *Reading Research Quarterly, 22,* 475–490.

McKinney, J. D. (1984). The search for subtypes of specific learning disabilities. *Journal of Learning Disabilities, 17,* 43–50.

McKinney, J. D. (1988). Research on conceptually and empirically derived subtypes of specific learning disabilities. In M. C. Wang, H. J. Walberg, & M. C. Reynolds (Eds.), *The handbook of special education: Research and practice* (pp. 253–282). Oxford: Pergamon.

McKinney, J. D. (1989). Longitudinal research on the behavioral characteristics of children with learning disabilities. *Journal of Learning Disabilities, 22,* 141–150, 165.

McKinney, J. D., & Hocutt, A. M. (1988). Policy issues in the evaluation of the regular education initiative. *Learning Disabilities Focus, 4,* 15–23.

McKinney, J., & Speece, D. (1986). Academic consequences and longitudinal stability of behavioral subtypes of learning disabled children. *Journal of Educational Psychology, 78,* 365–372.

McLaughlin, J. A. & Christensen, M. (1980). *A study of interagency collaborative agreements to discover training needs for special education administrators.* Washington, DC: Bureau of Education for the Handicapped.

McLeskey, J., Skiba, R., & Wilcox, B. (1990). Reform and special education: A mainstream perspective. *Journal of Special Education, 24,* 319–325.

McNulty, B. A. (1989). Leadership and policy strategies for interagency planning: Meeting the early childhood mandate. In J. J. Gallagher, P. L. Trohanis, & R. M. Clifford (Eds.), *Policy implementation & PL 99-457: Planning for young children with special needs* (pp. 147–167). Baltimore, MD: Brookes.

McPherson, R. B. (1991, April 10). Reform versus renewal. *Education Week,* p. 17.

Meisels, S. J. (1985). *Developmental screening in early childhood: A guide* (rev. ed.). Washington, DC: National Association for the Education of Young Children.

Meisels, S. J. (1987). Uses and abuses of developmental screening and school readiness testing. *Young Children, 42*(2), 4–6, 66–73.

Mercer, C. D., Forgnone, C., & Wolking, W. (1976). Definitions of learning disabilities used in the United States. *Journal of Learning Disabilities, 9,* 376–386.

Mercer, J. (1973). *Labeling the mentally retarded.* Berkeley: University of California Press.

Mercer, J., & Ysseldyke, J. E. (1977). Designing diagnostic-intervention programs. In T. Oakland (Ed.), *Psychological and educational assessment of minority children* (pp. 70–90). New York, NY: Brunner/Mazel.

Mid-South Regional Resource Center. (1986). *Effectiveness indicators for special education: A reference tool.* Lexington, KY: Author.

Mikulecky, L. (1990). National adult literacy and lifelong learning goals. *Phi Delta Kappan, 72,* 304–309.

Miles, B. S., & Simpson, R. L. (1989). Regular educators' modification preferences for mainstreaming mildly handicapped children. *Journal of Special Education, 22,* 479–491.

Minnesota Department of Education. (1989). *A progress report on the evolution of a Minnesota vision for outcome-based education.* St. Paul: Author, Instructional Effectiveness Division.

Mirkin, P. K. (1980). In J. E. Ysseldyke & M. L. Thurlow (Eds.), *The special education assessment and decision-making process: Seven case studies (Research report no. 44),* pp. 100–113. Minneapolis: University of Minnesota, Institute for Research on Learning Disabilities.

Mithaug, D. E., Horiuchi, C. N., & Fanning, P. N. (1985). A report on the Colorado statewide follow-up survey of special education students. *Exceptional Children, 55,* 230–239.

Moore, D. R., & Davenport, S. (1990). School choice: The new improved sorting machine. In W. L. Boyd & H. J. Walberg (Eds.), *Choice in education: Potential and problems* (pp. 187–224). Berkeley, CA: McCutchan.

Moores, D. F. (1978). *Educating the deaf: Psychology, principles, and practices.* Boston: Houghton Mifflin.

Moores, D. F. (1982). *Educating the deaf: Psychology, principles, and practices* (2nd ed.). Boston: Houghton Mifflin.

Morsink, C. V., Thomas, C. C., & Correa, V. I. (1990). *Interactive teaming.* Columbus, OH: Merrill.

Mullis, I. (1990). *The NAEP Guide: A description of the content and methods of the 1990–1992 assessments.* Washington, DC: NAEP.

Myers, P., & Hammil, D. C. (1990). *Learning disabilities.* Austin, TX: PRO-ED.

NASDSE. (1989). *NASDSE action seminar: Infants exposed in utero to AIDS, alcohol, drugs.* Washington, DC: Author.

Nash, E. D. (1901). Special schools for defective children. *Journal of Psycho-Asthenics, 6,* 42–48.

Nathan, J. (1990). *Public schools by choice: Expanding opportunities for parents, students, and teachers.* Minneapolis: Free Spirit Publishing Co.

National Association of State Directors of Special Education. (1990). *Education of the Handicapped Act Amendments of 1990 (PL 101-476): Summary of major changes in Parts A through H of the act.* Washington, DC: Author.

National Association of State School Nurse Consultants. (1990). *Delegation of nursing care in a school setting.* Washington, DC: Author.

National Center for Education Statistics. (1990). *The condition of education: Volume 1. Elementary and secondary education.* Washington, DC: Author.

National Coalition of Advocates for Students, National Association of School Psychologists. (1989). Position statement: Advocacy for appropriate educational services for all students. 235–236.

National Commission on Excellence in Education. (1983). *A nation at risk: The imperative for educational reform.* Washington, DC: U.S. Government Printing Office.

National Council on Disability. (1989). *The education of students with disabilities: Where do we stand?* Washington, DC: Author.

National Education Association, Department of Superintendence. (1922). *Ideals of public education.* Chicago: Author.

National Education Association, Instruction, N. C. o. t. P. o. (1963). *Deciding what to teach*. Washington, DC: Author.

National Education Association. (1979). Teacher opinion poll. *Today's Education, 68,* 10.

National Governors' Association. (1986). *Time for results: The governors' 1991 report on education*. Washington, DC: Author.

National Governors' Association. (1988). *Results in education: 1988*. Washington, DC: Author.

National Governors' Association. (1990a, July). *National goals for education* (Draft document). Washington, DC: Author.

National Governors' Association. (1990b). *State actions to restructure schools: First steps*. Washington, DC: Author.

National Joint Committee on Learning Disabilities. (1987). Learning disabilities and the preschool child. *DLD Times, 4*(3), 5–10.

National Law Center on Homelessness and Poverty. (1990). *Shut out: Denial of education to homeless children*. Washington, DC: Author.

National Society for the Prevention of Blindness. (1966). *Estimated statistics on blindness and vision problems*. New York: Author.

Neisser, U. (1967). *Cognitive psychology*. New York: Appleton-Century-Crofts.

Neisworth, J. T., & Greer, J. G. (1975). Functional similarities of learning disability and mild retardation. *Exceptional Children, 42,* 17–21.

Nelson, C. M., & Rutherford, R. (1990). Troubled youth in public schools. In P. Leone (Ed.), *Troubled and troubling youth: Multidisciplinary perspectives* (pp. 38–60). Newbury Park, CA: Sage.

NESAC. (1990). *A guide to improving the national education data system*. Washington, DC: U.S. Department of Education, National Center for Education Statistics.

Newland, T. E. (1969). *Blind learning aptitude test*. Champaign, IL: Author.

Newland, T. E. (1973). Assumptions underlying psychological testing. *Journal of School Psychology, 11,* 316–322.

Newland, T. E. (1980). Assessing the cognitive capability of exceptional children. In W. Cruickshank (Ed.), *Psychology of exceptional children and youth* (pp. 38–61). Englewood Cliffs, NJ: Prentice-Hall.

Norby, J., Thurlow, M. L., Christenson, S. L., & Ysseldyke, J. E. (1990). *The challenge of complex school problems*. Austin, TX: Pro-Ed.

Nuttall, E. V., Landurand, P. M., & Goldman, P. (1984). A critical look at testing and evaluation from a cross-cultural perspective. In P. C. Chinn (Ed.), *Education of culturally and linguistically different exceptional children* (pp. 42–62). Reston, VA: Council for Exceptional Children.

Office of Educational Research and Improvement. (1988). *Youth indicators, 1988: Trends in the well-being of American youth*. Washington, DC: U.S. Department of Education.

Olson, C. O. (1990). *Alternative certification guidelines*. Raleigh: North Carolina Department of Public Instruction.

Olson, L. (1989, January 9). Minnesota's education leadership: Leitmotif for policy issues looming. *Education Week*, pp. 1, 20.

"On cases of contagion." (1987, March 4). *New York Times*, p. A21.

Owings, J., & Stocking, C. (1986). *High school and beyond, a national longitudinal study for the 1980's: Characteristics of high school students who identify themselves as handicapped.* Washington, DC: National Center for Education Statistics. (ERIC Document Reproduction Service No. ED 260 546)

Pallas, A. (1987). *Center for Education Statistics: School dropouts in the United States.* Washington, DC: U.S. Department of Education, Office of Educational Research and Improvement.

Patton, J. P., Prillaman, D., & Van Tassal-Baska, J. (1990). The nature and extent of programs for the disadvantaged gifted in the United States and territories. *Gifted Child Quarterly, 34*(3), 94–96.

Payne, C. (1989). Urban teachers and dropout-prone students: The uneasy partners. In L. Weiss, E. Farrar, & H. G. Petrie (Eds.), *Dropouts from school: Issues, dilemmas, and solutions* (pp. 113–128). Albany: State University of New York Press.

Peterson, N. L. (1987). *Early intervention for handicapped and at-risk children: An introduction to early childhood special education.* Denver: Love.

Phillips, V., & McCullough, L. (1990). Consultation-based programming: Instituting the collaborative ethic in shcools. *Exceptional Children, 56*, 291–304.

Pitsch, M. (1991a, April 3). Congress provides funds to fight infant mortality. *Education Week*, p. 26.

Pitsch, M. (1991b, January 23). Hispanic graduation rates lags others', A.C.E. finds. *Education Week*, p. 4.

Porter, A. C. (1990). *Assessing national goals: Some measurement dilemmas.* Paper presented at the 1990 ETS Invitational Conference Proceedings: The assessment of National Educational Goals.

Porter, S. H. (1982). Employment characteristics of handicapped graduates and dropouts. *Adult Literacy and Basic Education, 6*(4), 238–244.

Preprimary enrollment. (1991). *Education Week, 10*(28), 7.

Pugach, M. (1987). The national reports and special education: Implications for teacher education. *Exceptional Children, 53*, 308–314.

Pugach, M. (1990). The moral cost of retrenchment in special education. *Journal of Special Education, 24*, 326–333.

Pugach, M., & Lillp, M. S. (1984). Reconceptualizing support services for classroom teachers: Implications for teacher education. *Journal of Teacher Education, 35*(5), 48–55.

Purkey, S., & Smith, M. (1985). School reform: The district policy implications of the effective schools literature. *Elementary School Journal, 85*(3).

Pyecha, J. (1980). *A national survey of individualized education programs (IEPs) for handicapped children.* Research Triangle Park, NC: Research Triangle Institute.

Quay, H. C. (1973). Special education: Assumptions, techniques, and evaluative criteria. *Exceptional Children, 40*, 165–170.

Ramsey, R., & Algozzine, B. (1990). Teacher competency testing: What are special education teachers expected to know? *Exceptional Children, 53*, 574–578.

Ramsey, R. S., & Algozzine, B. (1991). Teacher competency testing: What are special education teachers expected to know? *Exceptional Children, 57*, 339–344.

Ramsey, R. R., Algozzine, B., & Henley, M. (In press). *Characteristics of mildly handicapped students*. Boston: Allyn and Bacon.

Reddaway, J. L. (1990). Discussant to paper entitled *NAEP: A national report card for education and the public*. Paper presented at the 1990 ETS Invitational Conference Proceedings: The Assessment of National Educational Goals.

Reform plan for schools. (1957, September 2). *Life*, pp. 123–136.

Reinert, H. (1967). *Children in conflict*. St. Louis: Mosby.

Renzulli, J. (1979). *What makes giftedness?* Los Angeles: National and State Leadership Training Institute of the Gifted and Talented.

Resnick, L. (1990). *Assessment and educational standards*. Paper presented at the OERI conference on the Promise and Peril of Alternative Assessment. Washington, DC. October 29.

Reynolds, C. J. (1991, Winter). Viewpoint. *The Forum*, p. 1.

Reynolds, M. C. (1978). Final notes. In J. Grosenick & M. Reynolds (Eds.), *Teacher education*. Minneapolis: University of Minnesota, Leadership Training Institute/Special Education.

Reynolds, M. C., & Birch, J. W. (1982). *Teaching exceptional children in all America's schools*. Reston, VA: Council for Exceptional Children.

Reynolds, M. C., Wang, M. C., & Walberg, H. J. (1987). The necessary restructuring of special and regular education. *Exceptional Children, 53*, 391–398.

Rhodes, W. C. (1967). The disturbing child: A problem of ecological management. *Exceptional Children, 33*, 449–455.

Rhodes, W. C. (1970). A community participation analysis of emotional disturbance. *Exceptional Children, 37*, 309–314.

Rhodes, W. C., & Tracy, M. L. (1972). *A study of child variance: Conceptual models* (Vol. 1). Ann Arbor: University of Michigan.

Rich, D. (1987). *Schools and families*. Washington, DC: National Education Association.

Richert, S. E. (1987). Rampant problems and promising practices in the identification of disadvantaged gifted students. *Gifted Child Quarterly, 31*(4), 149–154.

Riese, W. (1959). *A history of neurology*. New York: M. D. Publications.

Rivera-Batiz, F. (1990). *Quantitative literacy and the likelihood of employment among young adults in the U.S.* Paper presented at the annual meeting of the American Educational Research Association, San Francisco.

Robinson, G. (1983). *Effective schools: A summary of research*. Arlington, VA: Educational Research Service.

Robinson, N., & Robinson, H. (1976). *The mentally retarded child*. New York: McGraw-Hill.

Rotberg, I. C. (1990). I never promised you first place. *Phi Delta Kappan, 72*, 296–303.

Rothstein, L. F. (1990). *Special education law*. New York: Longman.

Rourke, B. P. (1985). *Neuropsychology of learning disabilities: Essentials of subtype analysis*. New York: Guilford.

Rowland, B. H., & Robinson, B. E. (1991). Latchkey kids with special needs. *Teaching Exceptional Children, 23*, 34–35.

Rueda, R. (1989). Defining mild disabilities with language-minority students. *Exceptional Children, 56*, 121–128.

Rumberger, R. W. (1987). High school dropouts: A review of issues and evidence. *Review of Educational Research, 57*, 101–121.

Rusch, F., & DeStefano, L. (1989). Transition from school to work: Strategies for young adults with disabilities. *Interchange, 9*(3), 1–8.

Rusch, F. R. & Phelps, I. A. (1987). Secondary special education and transition from school to work: A national priority. *Exceptional Children, 53*, 487–492.

Rutter, M. (1978). Diagnosis and definition. In M. Rutter & E. Schopler (Eds.), *Autism: A reappraisal of concepts and treatment* (pp. 31–45). New York: Plenum Press.

Ruttiman, A., & Forest, M. (1986). With a little help from my friends: The integration facilitator at work. *Entourage, 1*, 24–33.

Sacks, O. (1985). *The man who mistook his wife for a hat and other clinical tales*. New York: Harper Collins.

Sailor, W. (1989). The educational, social, and vocational integration of students with the most severe disabilities. In D. K. Lipsky & A. Gartner (Eds.), *Beyond separate education: Quality education for all* (pp. 53–74). Baltimore, MD: Brookes.

Salvia, J., & Ysseldyke, J. E. (1981). *Assessment in special and remedial education* (2nd ed.). Boston: Houghton Mifflin.

Salvia, J., & Ysseldyke, J. E. (1991). *Assessment* (5th ed.). Boston: Houghton Mifflin.

Sameroff, A. J., & Zax, M. (1973). Schizotaxia revisited: Model issues in the etiology of schizophrenia. *American Journal of Orthopsychiatry, 43*, 744–754.

Samuels, S. J. (1981). Characteristics of exemplary reading programs. In J. Guthrie (Ed.), *Comprehension and teaching: Reviews of research*. Newark, DE: International Reading Association.

Samuels, S. J., & Miller, N. L. (1985). Failure to find attention differences between learning disabled and normal children on classroom and laboratory tasks. *Exceptional Children, 51*, 358–375.

Sapon-Shevin, M. (1988). Working towards merger together: Seeing beyond distrust and fear. *Teacher Education and Special Education, 11*, 103–110.

Sarason, S. B. (1990). *The predictable failure of educational reform*. San Francisco: Jossey-Bass.

Sarason, S. B., & Doris, J. (1979). *Educational handicap, public policy, and social history*. New York: Free Press.

Schenck, S. J. (1980). The diagnostic/instructional link in individualized education programs. *Journal of Special Education, 14*, 337–345.

Scheyneman. (1976). *Validating a procedure for assessing bias in test items in the absence of an outside criterion.* Paper presented at the annual conference of the American Educational Research Association.

School Dropouts. (1986). *Everybody's problem.* Washington, DC: Institute for Educational Leadership.

Schumaker, J. B., Deshler, D. D., & McKnight, P. (1989). *Teaching routines to enhance the mainstream performance of adolescents with learning disabilities* (Final Report). Lawrence, KS: University of Kansas.

Schumaker, J. B., Deshler, D. D., & McKnight, P. C. (1991). Teaching routines for content areas at the secondary level. In G. Stoner, M. Shinn, & H. Walker (Eds.), *Interventions for achievement and behavior problems* (pp. 473–494). Silver Spring, MD: National Association of School Psychologists.

Seiger-Ehrenberg, S. (1985). Educational outcomes for a K–12 curriculum. In A. L. Costa (Ed.), *Developing minds: A resource for teaching thinking* (pp. 7–10). Washington, DC: Association for Supervision and Curriculum Development.

Selden, R. W. (1990). *State indicator systems in education.* Washington, DC: Council of Chief State School Officers.

Selected, key federal statutes affecting the education and civil rights of children and youth with disabilities. *News Digest 1*(1), 13.

Seligmann, J. (1990, Special issue, summer/fall). Chance of a lifetime. *Newsweek*, pp. 68–72.

Seligman, M., & Darling, R. B. (1989). *Ordinary families, special children: A systems approach to childhood disability.* New York: Guilford.

Semmel, D. S., Cosden, M. A., & Konopak, B. (1985). *A comparative study of employment outcomes for special education students in a cooperative work placement program.* Paper presented at the annual convention of the Council for Exceptional Children.

Shane, H. (1969). Editorial: The renaissance of early childhood education. *Phi Delta Kappan, 50*, 369, 412–413.

Shavelson, R. J. (1990). *What alternative assessment looks like in science.* Paper presented at the OERI conference on the Promise and Peril of Alternative Assessment.

Shavelson, R., McDonnell, L., & Oakes, J. (1989). *Indicators for monitoring mathematics and science education.* Santa Monica, CA: RAND.

Shaw, R. C., & Walker, W. (1981). High school graduation requirements—from whence did they come? *NASSP Bulletin, 65*, 96–102.

Shaywitz, S. E., & Shaywitz, B. A. (1991). Introduction to the special series on attention deficit disorder. *Journal of Learning Disabilities, 24*, 68–71.

Shea, T. M. (1978). *Teaching children and youth with behavior problems.* St. Louis: Mosby.

Shell, P. (1981). Straining the system: Serving low-incidence handicapped students in an urban school system. *Exceptional Education Quarterly, 2*, 1–10.

Shepard, L. A. (1989a). A review of research on kindergarten retention. In L. A. Shepard & M. L. Smith (Eds.), *Flunking grades: Research and policies on retention* (pp. 64–78). London: Falmer.

Shepard, L. A. (1989b). Why we need better assessments. *Educational Leadership, 46*(7), 4–9.

Shepard, L. A., & Smith, M. L. (1989). *Flunking grades: Research and policies on retention.* London: Falmer.

Short, E. J., Feagans, L., McKinney, J. D., & Appelbaum, M. I. (1986). Longitudinal stability of LD subtypes based on age- and IQ-achievement discrepancies. *Learning Disability Quarterly, 9,* 214–225.

Shriner, J., Ysseldyke, J. E., Gorney, D., & Franklin, M. J. (1991). Alternative explanations for variability in prevalence of students who are gifted and talented. Minneapolis, MN: Unpublished.

Silberman, C. E. (1970). *Crisis in the classroom: The remaking of American education.* New York: Random House.

Silver, L. B. (1990). Attention deficit–hyperactivity disorder: Is it a learning disability or related disorder? *Journal of Learning Disabilities, 23,* 394–397.

Singer, J., & Butler, J. (1987). The Education for All Handicapped Children Act: Schools as agents of social reform. *Harvard Educational Review, 57,* 125–152.

Skiba, R., & Deno, S. (1991). Terminology and behavior reduction: The case against "punishment." *Exceptional Children, 57,* 298–313.

Sleeter, C. E. (1986). Learning disabilities: The social construction of a special education category. *Exceptional Children, 53,* 46–54.

Smith, M. L., & Shepard, L. A. (1989). Flunking grades: A recapitulation. In L. A. Shepard & M. L. Smith (Eds.), *Flunking grades: Research and policies on retention* (pp. 214–236). London: Falmer.

Smith, R. C., & Lincoln, C. A. (1988). *America's shame, America's hope: Twelve million youth at risk.* Chapel Hill, NC: MDC, (ERIC Document Reproduction Service No. ED 301 620).

Smith, S. W. (1990). Comparison of individualized education programs (IEPs) of students with behavioral disorders and learning disabilities. *Journal of Special Education, 24,* 85–100.

Smith, S. W., & Simpson, R. L. (1989). An analysis of individualized education programs (IEPs) for students with behavior disorders. *Behavioral Disorders, 14,* 107–116.

Smith, T. E. C., Price, B. J., & Marsh II, G. E. (1986). *Mildly handicapped children and adolescents.* St. Paul, MN: West.

Snow, R. E. (1989). Toward assessment of cognitive and conative structures in learning. *Educational Research, 18*(9), 8–14.

Solomon, R. P. (1989). Dropping out of academics: Black youth and the sports subculture in a cross-national perspective. In L. Weiss, E. Farrar, & H. G. Petrie (Eds.), *Dropouts from school: Issues, dilemmas, and solutions* (pp. 79–93). Albany: State University of New York Press.

Spady, W. G. (1988). Organizing for results: The basis of authentic restructuring and reform. *Educational Leadership, 46*(2), 4–8.

Speece, D. L., McKinney, J. D., & Appelbaum, M. I. (1985). Classification and validation of behavioral subtypes of learning disabled children. *Journal of Educational Psychology, 77,* 67–77.

Stacey, N., Alsalam, N., Gilmore, J., & To, D. (1988). *Education and training of 16- to 19-year-olds after compulsory schooling in the United States.* Washington, DC: U.S. Government Printing Office.

Stainback, S., & Stainback, W. (1985). *Integration of students with severe handicaps in the regular classroom.* Reston, VA: Council for Exceptional Children.

Stainback, S., & Stainback, W. (1989). Classroom organization for diversity among students. In D. Bilken, D. Ferguson, & A. Ford (Eds.), *Disability and society: Eighty-eighth yearbook of the National Society for the Study of Education* (pp. 195–207). Chicago: University of Chicago Press.

Stainback, S., Stainback, W., & Forest, M. (1989). *Educating all students in the mainstream of regular education.* Baltimore, MD: Brookes.

Stainback, W., & Stainback, S. (1984). A rationale for the merger of special and regular education. *Exceptional Children, 51,* 102–111.

Stainback, W., & Stainback, S. (1987). Integration versus cooperation: A commentary on "Educating children with learning problems: A shared responsibility." *Exceptional Children, 54,* 66–68.

State education statistics. (1988, March). *Education Week,* pp. 18–19.

Stebbins, L., St. Pierre, R., Proper, E., Anderson, R., & Cerva, T. (1977). *Education as experimentation: A planned variation model.* Cambridge, MA: ABT Associates.

Stephenson, R. S. (1985). *A study of the longitudinal dropout rate: 1980 eighth-grade cohort followed from June, 1980 through February, 1985.* Miami: Dade County Public Schools.

Sternberg, R. J. (1985). *Beyond IQ: A triarchic theory of human intelligence.* Cambridge: Cambridge University Press.

Stevens, L. J., & Price, M. (1991). *Special education for the 1990's: New and/or increasing populations.* Wayne, PA: Radnor Township School District.

Stixrud, W. R. (1982). *Plaintalk about early education and development.* Minneapolis, MN: University of Minnesota, College of Education, Center for Early Education and Development.

Stock, J. R., Newbord, J., Wnek, L. L., Schenck, E. A., Gabel, J. R., Spurgeon, M. S., & Ray, H. W. (1976). *Evaluation of Handicapped Children's Early Education Program (HCEEP): Final Report* (Contract No. EC-0-74-0402). North Columbus, OH: Battelle Center for Improved Education.

Strauss, A. A., & Lehtinen, L. E. (1947). *Psychopathology and education of the brain-injured child.* New York: Grune and Stratton.

Strully, J. (1986). *Our children and the regular classroom: Or why settle for anything less than the best?* Paper presented at the meeting of the Association for Persons with Severe Handicaps.

Swan, W. W. (1980). The Handicapped Children's Early Education Program. *Exceptional Children, 47,* 12–16.

Swart, E. (1990). So, you want to be a 'professional' *Phi Delta Kappan, 72,* 315–319.

Talbot, M. E. (1964). *Eduoard Seguin: A study of an educational approach to the treatment of mentally defective children.* New York: Teachers College Press.

Taylor, S. (1988). Caught in the continuum: A critical analysis of the principle of the least restrictive environment. *Journal of the Association for Persons with Severe Handicaps, 13*(1), 41–53.

Thondike, R. M., & Lohman, D. F. (1990). *A century of ability testing.* Chicago, IL: Riverside Publishing Company.

Thornton, H., & Zigmond, N. (1986). Follow-up of post-secondary age LD graduates and dropouts. *LD Research, 1*(1), 50–55.

Thurlow, M. L., Bruininks, R. H., & Lange, C. (1989). *Assessing post-school outcomes for students with moderate to severe mental retardation* (Project Report No. 89-1). Minneapolis: University of Minnesota, Department of Educational Psychology.

Thurlow, M. L., Christenson, S. L., & Ysseldyke, J. E. (1987). *School effectiveness research: Implications for effective instruction of handicapped students* (Monograph No. 3). Minneapolis: University of Minnesota, Institute for Research on Learning Disabilities.

Thurlow, M. L., Ysseldyke, J. E. (1979). Current assessment and decision-making practices in model LD programs. *Learning Disability Quarterly, 2,* 15–24.

Thurlow, M. L., Ysseldyke, J. E., & Christenson, S. L. (1987). *Student cognitions: Implications for effective instruction of handicapped students.* Minneapolis, MN: University of Minnesota Institute for Research on Learning Disabilities.

Thurlow, M. L., Ysseldyke, J. E., & O'Sullivan, P. (1985). *Preschool screening in Minnesota: 1982–83* (Research Report No. 1). Minneapolis: University of Minnesota, Early Childhood Assessment Project. (ERIC Document Reproduction Service No. ED 269 950)

Thurlow, M. L., Ysseldyke, J. E., Weiss, J. A., Lehr, C. A., O'Sullivan, P. J., & Nania, P. A. (1986). *Policy analysis of exit decisions and follow-up procedures in early childhood special education programs* (Research Report No. 14). Minneapolis: University of Minnesota, Early Childhood Assessment Project.

Tingey, C., & Stimell, F. (1989). Increasing services through interagency agreements, volunteers, and donations. In C. Tingey (Ed.), *Implementing early intervention* (pp. 63–78). Baltimore, MD: Brookes.

Tittle, C. K. (1973). Women and educational testing. *Phi Delta Kappan, 55,* 118–119.

Tolor, A., & Brannigan, G. C. (1975). Sex differences reappraised: A rebuttal. *Journal of Genetic Psychology, 127,* 319–321.

Trachtman, G. (1981). On such a full sea. *School Psychology Review, 10,* 138–181.

Tucker, J. A. (1980). Ethnic proportions in classes for the learning disabled: Issues in nonbiased assessment. *Journal of Special Education, 14,* 93–105.

Tucker, J. A. (1989). Less required energy: A response to Danielson and Bellamy. *Exceptional Children, 55,* 456–458.

Twentieth Century Fund, Task Force on Federal Elementary and Secondary Education. (1983). *Making the grade.* New York: Author.

Ullman, L. P., & Krasner, L. (1969). *A psychological approach to abnormal behavior.* Englewood Cliffs, NJ: Prentice-Hall.

Ullman, L., & Krasner, L. (1969). *A socio-psychological approach to abnormal behavior.* Englewood Cliffs, NJ: Prentice-Hall.

U.S. Department of Education. (1986a). *Statistics of state school systems: Revenues and expenditures for public elementary and secondary education.* Washington, DC: Author.

U.S. Department of Education. (1986b). *What works: Research about teaching and learning.* Washington, DC: Author.

U.S. Department of Education. (1987). *To assure the free appropriate public education of all handicapped children: Ninth annual report to Congress on the implementation of the Education of the Handicapped Act.* Washington, DC: Author.

U.S. Department of Education. (1988a). *Digest of educational statistics* (No. CS 88-600). Washington, DC: National Center for Education Statistics.

U.S. Department of Education. (1988b). *To assure the free appropriate public education of all handicapped children: Tenth annual report to Congress on the implementation of the Education of the Handicapped Act.* Washington, DC: Author.

U.S. Department of Education. (1989a) *Digest of education statistics.* Washington, DC: National Center for Education Statistics.

U.S. Department of Education. (1989b). *To assure the free appropriate public education of all handicapped children: Eleventh annual report to Congress on the implementation of the Education of the Handicapped Act.* Washington, DC: Author.

U.S. Department of Education. (1990a, September 25). Improving the retention of special education teachers. *Federal Register, 55*(186), 39247–39249.

U.S. Department of Education. (1990b). *To assure the free appropriate public education of all handicapped children: Twelfth annual report to Congress on the implementation of the Education of the Handicapped Act.* Washington, DC: Author.

U.S. Department of Justice, Civil Rights Division, Coordination and Review Section. (1990). *Americans with Disabilities Act requirement: Fact sheet.* Washington, DC: Author.

U.S. General Accounting Office. (1981). *Disparities still exist in who gets special education.* Washington, DC: U.S. Government Printing Office.

U.S. News and World Report. (1957, March 15). pp. 38–44.

U.S. News and World Report. (1961, September 4). p. 45.

U.S. Office of Education. (1977). Assistance to states for education of handicapped children: Procedures for evaluating specific learning disabilities. *Federal Register, 42*, 65082–65085.

U.S. Senate. (1975, June 2). *Education for All Handicapped Children Act* (No. 94-168).

Van Sickle, J. H. (1908–1909). Provision for exceptional children in the public schools. *Psychological Clinic, 2*, 102–111.

Van Tassel-Baska, J., Patton, J.,& Prillaman, D. (1989). Disadvantaged gifted learners at-risk for educational attention. *Focus on Exceptional Children, 22*(3), 1–16.

Vasquez, J. (1972). Measurement of intelligence and language differences. *Aztlan, 3*,155–163.

Viadero, D. (1988, March 30). Researchers' critique escalates the debate over "regular education" for all students. *Education Week*, p. 20.

Viadero, D. (1989, October 25). Drug-exposed children pose special problems. *Education Week*, pp. 1, 10–11.

Viadero, D. (1990, September 5). Study of drug-exposed infants finds problems in learning as late as age 3. *Education Week*, p. 15.

Viadero, D. (1991, March 27). Law to aid handicapped infants faces critical test. *Education Week*, pp. 1, 28–29.

Vitello, S. J. (1988). Handicapped students and competency testing. *Remedial and Special Education, 9*(5), 22–27.

Vogel, S. A. (1982). On developing LD college programs. *Journal of Learning Disabilities, 15*, 518–528.

Wagner, M. (1989). *National transition longitudinal study.* Palo Alto, CA: SRI.

Wagner, M. (1991). *School completion of students with disabilities: What do we know? What can we do?* Paper presented at the Annual Leadership Conference for State Directors of Special Education.

Walker, B. J. (1991). Convention highlights reading assessment changes. *Reading Today, 8*(4).

Walker, R. (1990, April 11). Lawmakers in Kentucky approve landmark school-reform bill. *Education Week*, pp. 1, 34–35.

Wallace, A. (1973). Schools in revolutionary and conservative societies. In F. Lanni & E. Story (Eds.), *Cultural relevance and education issues* (pp. 38–49). Boston: Little, Brown.

Wang, M. C. (1980). Adaptive instruction: Building on diversity. *Theory into Practice, 19*(2), 122–127.

Wang, M. C. (1981). Mainstreaming exceptional children: Some instructional design and implementation considerations. *Elementary School Journal, 81*, 194–221.

Wang, M. C. (1985). *Toward achieving excellence for all students.* Washington, DC: National Center for Educational Statistics. (ERIC Document Reproduction Service No. ED 272 572).

Wang, M. C. (1989). Adaptive instruction: An alternative for accommodating student diversity through the curriculum. In D. Lipsky & A. Gartner (Eds.), *Beyond separate education: Quality education for all* (pp. 99–119). Baltimore, MD: Brookes.

Wang, M. C., & Birch, J. (1984). Comparison of a full-time mainstreaming program and a resource room approach. *Exceptional Children, 51*, 33–40.

Wang, M. C., & Lindvall, C. M. (1984). Individual differences and school learning environments. In E. W. Gordon (Ed.), *Review of research in education* (pp. 161–225). Washington, DC: American Educational Research Association.

Wang, M. C., Reynolds, M. C., & Walberg, H. J. (1986). Rethinking special education. *Educational Leadership, 44*(1), 26–31.

Wang, M. C., Reynolds, M. C., & Walberg, H. J. (1987). *Repairing the second system for students with special needs.* Paper presented at the Wingspread Conference on the Education of Children with Special Needs.

Wang, M. C., & Walberg, H. J. (1988). Four fallacies of segregationism. *Exceptional Children, 55*, 128–137.

Wehman, P., Kregel, J., & Seyfarth, J. (1985). Transition from school to work for individuals with severe handicaps: A follow-up study. *Journal of the Association of the Severely Handicapped, 10*(3), 132–136.

Weinberg, L. A., & Weinberg, C. (1990). Seriously emotionally disturbed or socially maladjusted? A critique of interpretations. *Behavioral Disorders, 15*(3), 149–158.

Wells, A. S. (1989). Educating homeless children. *Digest* (ERIC Clearinghouse on Urban Education, Institute for Urban and Minority Education). New York: Teachers College.

Wells, S., Bechard, S., & Hamby, J. V. (1989). *How to identify at-risk students. Solutions and strategies.* Clemson, SC: Clemson University, National Dropout Prevention Center.

Werner, H., & Strauss, A. A. (1941). Pathology of figure-background relation in the child. *Journal of Abnormal and Social Psychology, 36,* 236–248.

White, K. R., & Casto, G. (1989). What is known about early intervention. In C. Tingey (Ed.), *Implementing early intervention* (pp. 3–20). Baltimore, MD: Brookes.

White, K. R., & Greenspan, S. P. (1986). An overview of effectiveness of preventive intervention programs. In I. R. Berlin & J. Noshpitz (Eds.), *Basic handbook of child psychiatry* (pp. 87–123). New York: Basic Books.

White, W. J., Schumaker, J. B., Warner, M. M., Alley, G. R., & Deshler, D. D. (1980). *The current status of young adults identified as learning disabled during their school career.* (Research Report No. 21). Lawrence: University of Kansas, Institute for Research in Learning Disabilities.

White House. (1990). *National goals for education* (Press release). Washington, DC: Author.

White House. (1991, February 4). *The national education goals: A second report to the nation's governors.* Washington, DC: Author.

Whiteman, M., & Deutsch, M. (1968). Social disadvantage as related to intellective and language development. In M. Deutsch, I. Katz, & A. Jensen (Eds.), *Social class, race, and psychological development.* New York: Holt, Rinehart and Winston.

Will, M. (1984). *OSERS program for the transition of youth with disabilities: Bridges from school to working life.* Washington, DC: U.S. Department of Education, Office of Special Education and Rehabilitative Services.

Will, M. (1986). *Educating children with learning problems: A shared responsibility.* Washington, DC: U.S. Department of Education, Office of Special Education.

William T. Grant Foundation, Commission on Work, Family, and Citizenship. (1988). *The forgotten half: Non-college youth in America.* Washington, DC: Author.

Williams, R. (1989, January 9–10). *Creating a new world of opportunity: Expanding choice and self-determination in lives of Americans with severe disability by 1992 and beyond.* Paper presented at the National Conference on Self-Determination, Arlington, VA.

Williams, R. J., & Algozzine, B. (1979). Teachers' attitudes toward mainstreaming. *Elementary School Journal, 80*(2), 63–67.

Williams, D. L., & Chavkin, N. F. (1989). Essential elements of strong parent involvement programs. *Educational Leadership, 47,* 18–20.

Willoughby, S. S. (1990). *Mathematics education for a changing world.* Alexandria, VA: Association for Supervision and Curriculum Development.

Wise, A. E. (1990). Policies for reforming teacher education. *Phi Delta Kappan, 72,* 200–202.

With goals in place, focus shifts to setting strategy. (1990, March 7). *Education Week,* pp. 1, 20.

Wolman, C., Bruininks, R. H., & Thurlow, M. L. (1989). Dropouts and dropout programs: Implications for special education. *Remedial and Special Education, 10*(5), 6–20, 50.

Wood, F. H. (1990). [Special issue]. *Behavioral Disorders, 15*(3), 139.

Woods, P. A., Sedlacek, W. E., & Boyer, S. P. (1990). Learning disability programs in large universities. *NASPA Journal, 27*(3), 248–256.

Wyche, L. G. (1989). The tenth annual report to Congress: Taking a significant step in the right direction. *Exceptional Children, 56,* 14–16.

Yates, A. J. (1954). The validity of some psychological tests of brain damage. *Psychological Bulletin, 51,* 359–379.

Yeager, R. C. (1990, September). The Reader's Digest home eye test. *Reader's Digest,* pp. 93–100.

Yell, M. L. (1989). *Honig* v. *Doe:* The suspension and expulsion of handicapped students. *Exceptional Children, 56,* 60–69.

Ysseldyke, J. E. (1973). Diagnostic-prescriptive teaching: The search for aptitude-treatment interactions. In L. Mann & D. A. Sabatino (Eds.), *The first review of special education* (pp. 1–37). New York: Grune and Stratton.

Ysseldyke, J. E. (1982). Remediation of ability deficits in adolescents: Some major questions. In L. Mann, L. Goodman, & L. Wiederholt (Eds.), *The Learning disabled adolescent* (pp. 37–61). Boston: Houghton Mifflin.

Ysseldyke, J. E. (1989). Editor's note. *Exceptional Children, 56,* 7.

Ysseldyke, J. E., & Algozzine, B. (1982). *Critical issues in special and remedial education.* Boston: Houghton Mifflin.

Ysseldyke, J. E., & Algozzine, B. (1983). LD or not LD: That's not the question! *Journal of Learning Disabilities, 16,* 29–31.

Ysseldyke, J. E., & Algozzine, B. (1984). *Introduction to special education.* Boston: Houghton Mifflin.

Ysseldyke, J. E., & Algozzine, B. (1990). *Introduction to special education* (2nd ed.). Boston: Houghton Mifflin.

Ysseldyke, J. E., Algozzine, B. A., & Mitchell, J. (1982). Special education team decision making: An analysis of current practice. *Personnel and Guidance Journal, 60,* 308–313.

Ysseldyke, J. E., Algozzine, B., Richey, L., & Graden, J. (1982). Declaring students eligible for learning disability services: Why bother with the data? *Learning Disability Quarterly, 5,* 37–44.

Ysseldyke, J. E., Algozzine, B., Shinn, M., & McGue, M. (1982). Similarities and differences between underachievers and students classified learning disabled. *Journal of Special Education, 16,* 73–85.

Ysseldyke, J. E., & Christenson, S. L. (1987). Evaluating students' instructional environments. *Remedial and Special Education, 8,* 17–24.

Ysseldyke, J. E., & Marston, D. (1990). The use of assessment information to plan instructional interventions. In T. Gutkin & C. Reynolds (Eds.), *The Handbook of School Psychology* (2nd ed., pp. 663–684). New York: Wiley.

Ysseldyke, J. E., Reynolds, M. C., & Weinberg, R. A. (1984). *School psychology: A blueprint for the future of training and practice*. Minneapolis: National School Psychology Inservice Training Network.

Ysseldyke, J. E., & Thurlow, M. L. (1980). *The psychoeducational assessment and decision-making process: Seven case studies* (Research Report No. 44). Minneapolis: University of Minnesota, Institute for Research on Learning Disabilities.

Ysseldyke, J. E., Thurlow, M. L., & Christenson, S. L. (1987). *Teacher effectiveness and teacher decision making: Implications for effective instruction of handicapped students*. Minneapolis: University of Minnesota, Institute for Research on Learning Disabilities.

Ysseldyke, J. E., Thurlow, M., Graden, J., Wesson, C., Algozzine, B., & Deno, S. (1983). Generalizations from five years of research on assessment and decision making: The University of Minnesota Institute. *Exceptional Education Quarterly, 4*(1), 75–93.

Ysseldyke, J. E., Thurlow, M. L., O'Sullivan, P., & Bursaw, R. A. (1986). Current screening and diagnostic practices in a state offering free preschool screening since 1977: Implications for the field. *Journal of Psychoeducational Assessment, 4*, 191–203.

Ysseldyke, J. E., Thurlow, M. L., Weiss, J. A., Lehr, C. A., & Bursaw, R. A. (1985). *An ecological study of school districts with high and low preschool screening referral rates* (Research Report No. 6). Minneapolis: University of Minnesota, Early Childhood Assessment Project. (ERIC Document Reproduction Service No. ED 269 955).

Zigmond, N. (1987). *Convergent studies of LD students at risk for dropping out of high school: An overview*. Paper presented at the annual convention of the American Educational Research Association, Washington, DC.

Zigmond, N. (1990). Rethinking secondary school programs for students with disabilities. *Focus on Exceptional Children, 23*(1), 1–22.

Zigmond, N., Levin, E., & Laurie, T. (1985). Managing the mainstream: An analysis of teacher attitudes and student performance in mainstreaming high school programs. *Journal of Learning Disabilities, 18*, 535–541.

Zigmond, N., & Thornton, H. (1985). Follow-up of postsecondary age learning disabled graduates and dropouts. *Learning Disabilities Research, 1*(1), 50–55.

Author/Source Index

Subject Index

out-of-school, 130–133
private, 315
pullout programs, 8, 20, 125
in regular class, 132
regular education initiative, 8–9, 125–128, 145
in residential facility, 132
in resource room, 132
in separate programs, 19, 132, 283–284
tests used for, 180–181, 182–184
variability across states in, 132–133
see also Mainstreaming
Pluralistic model, for intervention development, 215, 219
Plyler v. *Doe*, 312–313
Policy Studies Associates, outcomes proposed by, 237
Postschool transitions, 289–302
anticipated services for, 297, 300
appropriate services for, 291–293, 294–295, 296
beginning of, 293
college for learning disabled and, 300–301
emphasis on, 289–291
graduation requirements, 293, 296–297, 298–300
literacy and, 301–302, 303
PL 101–476 and, 293
sample planning process for, 294–295
states providing services for, 303
vocational training, 297, 300
Postsecondary Enrollment Options Program, 225
Postsecondary experiences, issues regarding, 239
Practical issues, 14–20
administrative arrangement versus instructional method, 14–15
core curriculum versus special curriculum, 17–19
educational service versus teacher relief, 16–17
service versus custodial care, 15–16
stay put placement versus pullout program, 19–20
Practice, issues reflected in, 20–28
full versus selective exclusion, 21–22
practices versus people, 22–24
profession versus practice, 25–28
special versus general responsibilities, 24–25
Practices, differentiating people from, 22–24
Prebirth services, 269
Prereferral Intervention, 209, 212–214, 216–217
Preschool enrollment, 46–47
Preschool screening programs, for early intervention, 270–273
Preschool special education programs, transition to elementary school setting, 281–282

Prevalence rates
for categories of exceptional students, 104, 105
identification practices and, 109
labeling and, 123–125
by state, 180–181, 182–184
Prevention
cost versus benefit of, 351–353
special education for, 10
Prisoner rates, graduation rates and, 285
Private placement, courts on payment for, 315, 323
Private school students, attitudes toward school of, 48
Process dysfunctions, disability caused by, 203–205
Program evaluation, tests for, 171, 172
Project Head Start, *see* Head Start
Projective assessment, 185
Promotion
courts on, 318
retention in grade versus, 248, 253–254, 282–283
"social," 274
Protection in evaluation procedures (PEP), 53, 59, 174–175, 188, 190–191
Psychoeducational process model, for intervention development, 215, 218, 219
Public laws, *see* Laws
Pullout programs, 8, 20, 125
Punishment, of handicapped students, 225–226
Pupil performance, assessment of, 186
Pupil unit funding, 346

Race, America segregated by, 35; *see also* Minorities
Radical mainstreaming, 22
Rand Corporation, outcomes proposed by, 237
Reader's Digest home eye test, 96–97
Readiness for school, as national goal, 42, 44, 145–146, 152
Reading programs, effective, 230–231
Reading skills
assessment, 194–196
progress in school based on, 45–46
Referral, need for changes in, 370–371
Reform, *see* School reform
Regular classrooms, placement in, 81, 82, 83, 125–126, 132
Regular education initiative, 8–9, 125–128, 145
Rehabilitation Act of 1973 (PL 93–112), 176, 297, 301
Reliability, of assessment instruments, 189–190
Relief, special education as, 16–17
Remediation, special education as, 9
Renewal, school reform versus, 369
Reports, three waves of educational reform and, 141–144

Reader Response Form

We would like your reactions to the material presented in the second edition of *Critical Issues in Special Education*. We will use the information you provide to improve subsequent editions of this book. Please take a few minutes and complete the items below. When you have finished, mail the form to College Marketing, Houghton Mifflin Company, One Beacon Street, Boston, MA 02108. Thanks.

1. Do you think there are chapters that we could have included to provide more complete coverage of the "issues"? If so, what are they?

2. Do you think any of the present chapters are unnecessary? If so, what are they?

3. Do you think the coverage in any chapter was insufficient? If so, indicate the chapter and material that should be added.

4. Do you think the coverage in any chapter was excessive? If so, indicate the chapter and material that should be deleted.

5. We attempted to present a fair, even-handed treatment of the issues we believe are important in special education. Please list any chapters or sections of chapters where, in your opinion, we accomplished this and/or did not accomplish it.

6. Please indicate your reaction to the following selected areas of the book:

	Disliked very much			Liked very much	
a. Chapter outlines	1	2	3	4	5
b. Extensiveness of citations	1	2	3	4	5
c. Writing style	1	2	3	4	5
d. Choice of vocabulary	1	2	3	4	5
e. Overall level of content coverage	1	2	3	4	5
f. Legal and legislative review	1	2	3	4	5
g. The critical issue	1	2	3	4	5

7. What did you like most about the book?

8. What did you like least about the book?

9. Tell us about yourself (are you a graduate or undergraduate student, a professional; what is your major area; etc.).